THE POLITICS OF PUBLIC VENTURES

For Tom Wright
with high regard from
fellow artilleryman
Jack Beatty

Also Published by John Cabeen Beatty

D Day to VE Day, An Account of a Light Artillery Battery in Action

The Fourth Part of Gaul, a novel

Collected Poems 1937—2007

Comment on cover

The photograph on the cover was taken by Richard A. Shearer from the Portland Women's Forum site some eight hundred feet above the Columbia River at the western terminus of the Columbia River Gorge. In the foreground is the Vista House on Crown Point, elevation 733 feet above the river. Across the river in the left foreground is Cape Horn, itself the subject of two mammoth photographs, Nos. 17 and 18, taken in 1867 by Carleton Watkins.

When the cataclysmic Bretz floods created by the repeated glacial dam failures releasing Lake Missoula swept down the Columbia Gorge thirteen to fifteen thousand years ago, it has been estimated that the height of the water crested above the Vista House at Crown Point. *Cataclysms on The Columbia*, John Elliot Allen, Marjorie Burns and Sam C. Sargent, Timber Press, Portland, 1986, p. 166.

THE POLITICS
OF PUBLIC
VENTURES

AN OREGON MEMOIR

John Cabeen Beatty

To order additional copies of this book, contact:
Xlibris Corporation
1-888-795-4274
www.Xlibris.com
Orders@Xlibris.com
38084

CONTENTS

Aeneas warned them, sitting in the sun,
Old soldiers all, their backs against the wall,
The residue of Greek and Roman wars.
"You! Yes, none of you have dreams to spare.
They are but passing triumph over Time
Whose knotted cords are slowly strangling you.
Yet while you live, you dream in present tense
Composited of past experience
And ripened into life within your skulls.
The rest is darkness known but to the gods."
They nodded, relicts of their ancient wars,
Just as we also nod, the detritus
Of recent wars. We dream much as he said.

PREFACE

This memoir is a series of recollections: growing up, military service, raising a family, practicing law, serving as a judge and engaging in a variety of public activities with interesting men and women. The details of personal life will interest only family. However, my recollection of public and professional matters and the men and women with whom I have had the good fortune to work on schools, courts and government may provide useful background and a picture of how some important changes came to pass.

I think of tackling public problems as public ventures, and the art by which we try do this as politics, hence the title. Politics at its best enables us to create and manage a civil society to the extent we are able to do so. In writing about these matters I have undoubtedly overlooked some men and women who should be credited and failed to reflect fully the role played by others. In any event, all I can claim is that these are my recollections of life, and events and some of the remarkable men and women with whom I have worked in the Twentieth Century.

John Cabeen Beatty, Jr.
September 1, 2009

ACKNOWLEDGMENTS

William M. Frick, of Riverside, CT, a forward observer who served in both A and B Batteries of the 310th Field Artillery, reviewed the chapters dealing with the campaign in Northern France and Alsace. Robert Weiss, of Portland, OR, a forward observer in B Battery, 230th Field Artillery, reviewed the sections dealing with the campaigns in France and Germany.

Retired Chief Justice Edwin J. Peterson of the Oregon Supreme Court was good enough to review the sections dealing with the courts and the criminal justice system making a number of valuable suggestions.

Barnes H. Ellis, who chaired the Commission on the Judicial Branch, read the entire text making corrections and valuable suggestions.

Barbara Sepenuk volunteered to read and proofread the text making innumerable corrections and suggestions. I am solely responsible for any corrections that I failed to enter or introduced into my computer after the text left her accomplished hands.

In a different sense I am also indebted to the men and women whose names appear in the text as initiators, contributors and collaborators in the various adventures in law, public education and politics which I describe.

Finally, my thanks to my legal secretary and judicial assistant, Susan Rommel, and to the night law students at Lewis and

Clark's Northwestern College of Law who clerked for me during my service on the circuit court including Judge Anna J. Brown of the United States District Court for the District of Oregon. Their assistance and support made many of these legal, legislative and judicial ventures possible.

John Cabeen Beatty,

Daughters have I, they are three,
All rich in their variety,
And unlike Lear, I happily
Can keep my peace or loose my tongue
Quite unrestricted by these young,
And so with love I dedicate
This memoir of my earthly state
To these three daughters who deserve
Some recompense for their reserve.

Clarissa Jean Beatty
Barbara Shearer Meiers
Joan Shearer Baker

CHAPTER 1

The beginning:
Dunthorpe and Riverdale School

My father, John C. Beatty, was born and raised in Ravenna, Ohio. On graduating from high school, he received an unexpected appointment to West Point. He graduated from the academy in 1911 and was commissioned as a second lieutenant in the regular army. My mother, Jean Morrison Beatty, was the daughter of Dr. Albert Alexander Morrison, a native of Scotland who came to Portland from Brooklyn, New York in 1898 to became the rector of Trinity Church, a position he then held for thirty years. My grandmother, Caroline Conover Morrison, was a native of New Jersey.

Following graduation my father was posted to the 4th Field Artillery Regiment, then located at Vancouver Barracks, Washington. Shortly after his arrival he met my mother at a party in Portland. Following a prolonged courtship extending from 1912 to 1918, during which he served in the Philippines and other posts, they were married in June of the latter year. I was born on April 13, 1919 in Washington, D. C. where my father was stationed with the Ordinance Department at the close of World War I.

In 1920 my father was retired from the regular army for disability due to an injury to his ankle sustained in the Philippines in 1913. He brought his new family back to Portland where Jean had family and friends. He wanted to study law but could see no way to finance law school. He got a job as a salesman with the National City Company, an investment subsidiary wholly owned and controlled by the National City Bank. His job was to sell stock and bonds about which he knew nothing. With my mother's help he made lists of friends and acquaintances upon whom he could call, and then he made those calls. It was a difficult transition for him. He was not a natural salesman. But with grim determination he went to work.

Together with my Aunt Margaret and Uncle Tom Sharp, my parents rented a house owned by Helen Ladd Corbett on lower Military Road, four miles south of Portland. This large, white frame house had a broad covered porch which ran around the west and north side. The foundations of the porch and the house itself were screened by gray lattice. In one of my earliest impressions, when I was perhaps two years old, I recall sitting under an apple tree in the yard with Pauline, our German maid. Wearing a white starched apron, she was peeling long spirals of apple skin and feeding me slices of apple. The lawn was broad and sloped down to overgrown shrubbery and a house where Judge Gilbert and his family lived. The Gilberts raised ducks and gave us duck eggs from time to time.

I recall crawling under the legs of the mahogany dining room table which originally belonged to my Aunt Margaret Sharp. I remember a cat hiding under the porch and refusing to come out, perhaps frightened by our terrier Spot. The Peter Kerr girls, Ann and Jane, lived in what is now called the Bishop's Close at the end of Military Lane. They walked past our house daily on their way to and from Riverdale School. One day they carried to our door the body of Spot who had been struck by an automobile and killed. Faber Lewis, a boy three or four years older than I, lived in a large brick house across the street. Faber contracted infantile paralysis several years later and lost the use of his arm. I remember my mother speaking of this sadly.

My mother took me on daily walks through the Kerr gardens to a winding gravel path which ran through dark and mysterious places with ferns and trees down to Riverwood, a hundred or more feet below. The Kerrs had a small swimming pool and several fish ponds with gold fish. Another path ran more directly from our house down the hill to the Red Train stop in Riverwood, and from my mother's bedroom window we could look directly down the path. The winter I was two and a half, I remember my father coming home after dark. We heard the whistle of the Red Train down the hill from us, then the screech of brakes as it came to a stop. A few minutes later, my father would come whistling up the path. While we waited for him, if the stars were out, my mother would repeat "Twinkle, twinkle, little star" to me.

I only remember riding once on the Red Train, although I must have been taken on it more often than that. I had to urinate and my mother held me up to the small hand basin and insisted that I use it rather than the toilet. I did, but I thought this was an awful thing to do. Other than these episodes, my early impressions are of warmth emerging from darkness, arms about me, my mother reading or telling stories and nursery rhymes. She is a constant presence. My father comes and goes. His mustache tickles. His suits are wool and scratchy.

A local artist, Lucy Ramberg had previously done a lovely pastel portrait of my mother which hung in the Trinity Rectory where my grandparents then lived. When I was about two, she did another of my mother and myself. All I remember of the business is being taken to a dark building and put into an alcove raised above the floor. I hated whatever was going on and cried. Some sixty years later, Mrs. Ramberg's son, who was cataloguing his mother's work, called on me to arrange a view of the pastel now over our mantelpiece and the oil now in Jean Beatty's house.

*

One day my father came home with a 1921 Buick roadster, the family's first automobile. He called it "our car," and I considered that I was a part owner and felt enormous pride of ownership. I remember driving with my father into Portland to Union Station to meet Major Rucker, a friend who had served with him in the Philippines. The silver cup in which I drank my milk was a gift from Major Rucker, so I was told. I stood on the front seat of the Buick between the two of them as we drove home along the long stretch of Macadam Road which looked then very much as it does now, with the forested hill to the west and the fringe of tall firs to the east lining the bank of the Willamette River.

The first Christmas I remember was in 1922. There was a large Christmas tree in the living room and under it was a round circle of track with a small brown electric engine. My mother told me many years later that my father spent half the night trying to get it to run. Auntie Marg and Uncle Tom Sharp eventually left us and took an apartment in the Bell Court on Trinity Place. The Corbett house had a detached barn, originally designed for a carriage, in which the Buick was stabled. On the side nearest the house was a high brick walled rose garden which I longed to enter but which for some reason was always kept locked.

The Corbett house is gone. The property, several acres in extent, was divided after the Second World War, and three or four houses were built upon it. All I remember of the interior is a narrow back stairway, a large front hall, a broad main stairway to the second story with a landing and reversed second flight of stairs. Auntie Marg's room was on the west side, my mother and father's bedroom lay on the east side. I have no recollection of my own room.

My Aunt Dorothy and Uncle Donald Green lived in Garthwick, a recently developed gated community between Sellwood and Waverly Country Club, across the Willamette River. One winter day my mother took me in the Buick Roadster and drove down Macadam Road to the Sellwood Ferry which operated at the site of the present Sellwood Bridge. It was a frosty morning. The ferry was in the middle of the river, and my mother drove on to the sloping plank landing, the first car to await the ferry. The planks were covered with ice and the car began sliding toward the water. My mother opened the car door intending to throw me out before the car slid into the river. Fortunately, the tires finally caught and stopped the slide. Three quarters of a century later I found an Oregon Historical Society photograph of the ferry taken from the same angle as we had approached it on that frosty morning.

*

During our last year in the Corbett house, the state built a new section of highway 99 W, which crossed Military Road a short distance above the Corbett house and ran up to the top of the cliff overlooking the Willamette and bordering Dunthorpe. The new section bypassed the original route, now called Breyman Avenue, which curved and twisted sharply up the hill, then ran south past Riverdale School, then angled back to the cliff at the intersection with Greenwood Road. At the same time my mother and father were building a house on a one acre site at the southwest corner of the intersection of Greenwood Road and the Pacific Highway. We moved in before anything in the way of landscaping had been accomplished. The house was surrounded with mud and the flotsam and jetsam of construction. For a time we reached the front door by walking on planks.

Dunthorpe then was largely undeveloped. The roads had been platted and probably paved before the First War, but there were only five or six houses by 1922. At the top of Greenwood Road lived the Elliot Corbetts, the Tony Ladds, and the Harry Corbetts. Below the Harry Corbett property, on the west slope of the hill, was the farm of Old Mr. Tatfer, as we called him. South of our house and next door to us, the Anderson family built a house a year or two later, and a quarter mile south on Edgecliff road was the Conover family whose son Townsend was about my age and came to play with me. Mr. Conover had a model T Ford which he had to crank to start in the morning. We could hear it sputter and backfire when he got ignition.

Riverwood, Riverdale and Palatine Hill had been settled to some extent prior to World War I, but Dunthorpe was still covered with second growth fir already seventy or eighty years old. The big old growth had been logged in the 1870's and 1880's, some burned to provide charcoal for the iron smelter in Oswego. The woods were spotted with the remains of old charcoal pits. Our own property still had several old growth stumps six feet in diameter rising six to eight feet above ground with steps chopped into the trunks for buckboards on which men stood to handle the saw for the first cut. Generally, such stumps were split with dynamite, then burned, and the remains were finally dragged out by a team of horses.

Old Shopper, a husky old man with a walrus mustache, blue overalls, and a dirty broad brimmed hat, did much of the clearing work after we had moved in. Each morning he came with his team of horses up from Oswego using a wagon track through the Tryon Creek woods rather than the highway. I got my finger pinched poking a tall mole trap on the Isaac's property just to the west of us, and Mr. Shopper laughed unsympathetically, saying that would teach me not to fool with mole traps.

In those early years the neighborhood was a fascinating place for small boys. Basements were dug by horse drawn scoops. Rocks were blasted. Cement was mixed for the foundations, and then the carpenters went to work. We tagged around the workmen, hauling off pieces of scrap wood to use in building shacks. We watched the lathers and the shinglers who worked with their mouths full of nails, swiftly swinging the hammer with one hand as the other hand delivered a nail for the precise stroke. The smell of a house being built was a mixture of newly turned earth, drying concrete and plaster, fir boards, and cedar shingles. On week-ends we climbed through these houses until the doors were installed, and we were locked out. These were nearly all large houses with no uniform style but a generally pleasing aspect which is still evident to the extent the overgrown hedges permit observation. Nearly all were two stories high and designed with back stairs and quarters for at least one servant.

1. The Colonel with Jean and Jack. Who sits more easily on the lawn?

2. Jack and his Aunt Margaret Sharp walk the plank into the house on Greenwood Road.

3. The house on Greenwood Road is built, planting begun. The Buick Roadster stands partially obscured by the fir tree. Why Spot had to ride on the running board in an apple crate is obvious -- No back seat and no rear trunk! Jack's growth and the arrival of sister Caroline known as Pug doomed the little roadster.

The Tryon forest extended from Edgecliff and Iron Mountain Roads all the way down to Tryon Creek and up its south bank to the margin of old Oswego Village. The woods were traversed by Shopper's wagon road which came out near the Tryon Creek highway bridge at the outskirts of Oswego. The Tryon woods were also crossed by a number of trails. The timber, as I have said, consisted largely of fir but with occasional patches of cedar and a growth of alder along the creek. In several small meadows grew purple lupine, wild honeysuckle, camas, daisies, wild rose, and clumps of wild iris. The forest floor was covered with trillium, johnny-jump-up and violet. Tryon Creek was said to have no fish, but one day my Uncle Tom Sharp, who could catch fish anywhere, disproved this truth by catching a ten inch trout. The creek also had lots of crawfish, but my mother did not consider them suitable for family consumption.

As Dunthorpe grew, much of the timber was retained by those who built their homes, and the Tryon Creek woods remained inviolate until after World War II when they were threatened with logging and development. In the face of this threat, Borden and Lou Beck, to their everlasting credit, led a successful campaign to create Tryon Creek State Park, which now covers the greater part of the forested area.

*

The summer I was three, we spent a month in a cottage at Long Beach, Washington. We drove down the lower Columbia River Highway in the roadster with Spot in a fruit crate strapped to the running board. I cried when it rained en route because Spot in his crate was getting wet. At Astoria we drove on board the ferry, which crossed the Columbia estuary to Megler on the Washington side. From there we drove to Seaview, one of the settlements on the Long Beach peninsula. A narrow gage steam railroad also ran from Megler to Oysterville which lay on the Willapa Bay side of the peninsula.

One memorable day my father sent me to walk the railroad tracks to the store to buy a newspaper. Clutching the nickel in my hand, I trudged up the tracks, bought the paper and returned to our cottage triumphant. I should note that the train only ran twice a day at a fixed time so the tracks were as safe a route as could be found.

Another day, my father, wearing his gray and black West Point sweater built a log arch on the beach and photographed me and another boy on it. Once we walked south on the beach to the rocks below Cape Disappointment and I retain a picture of us there. It was common in those days to drive an automobile on the hard wet sand of the beach. We took the roadster down on the beach on one occasion and ran into soft sand. Someone, either my mother or father, murmured, "Quicksand!" and I sensed panic. Wheels spinning we made it back to hard sand.

The year I was four, I came down with whooping cough and did not recover quickly. I had trouble keeping food down except for bananas. My mother took me up to a small hotel or boarding house in Hood River for several weeks to experience the fresh air and sunshine which was then thought to be more beneficial than the climate of Portland. I remember my mother pointing out the fish wheels which operated at the apex of nets and scooped up salmon by the hundreds, so she said.

When I was five we spent the summer with the Hartwells at their cabin at Neakahnee. To get there we drove down the road to Tillamook, then took a corduroy or plank road for many miles across the flood plain to reach Neakahnee. Tory Hartwell was a year younger than I, but she was allowed to chew gum. I prevailed in my demand to chew gum also, Beemans I think it was. I promptly got my first wad of gum stuck in my throat. As I choked my mother picked me up by the heels and shook me. The gum came out, and I chewed no more gum that summer.

A children's author named Harper was staying at the Neakahnee Hotel, a gray shingled structure, a small version of the Gearhart Hotel as I remember it. I believe either my Aunt Margaret or Mrs. Hartwell steered Tory and me into Mr. Harper's hands. He read sections of his draft of "The Mushroom Boy" to determine our reaction. My reaction was essentially negative, though many children loved it. I was more interested in the stories my mother told of ships being driven ashore against Neakahnie Mountain, and of the legend of Spanish gold buried under some rock nearby. The Mushroom Boy was subsequently published, and Mr. Harper was good enough to mail an autographed copy to me.

My mother read to me a great deal in the years before I went to school. When I was three or four my parents bought a six volume set of books called "My Bookhouse" which contained illustrated stories and poems, graduated in complexity from preschool nursery rhymes to excerpts from the classics in volume VI. Many years later when I needed the model of a dragon to carve a figurehead for our boat, I retrieved the set from my daughter, and sure enough, there was a splendid illustration of a dragon being assaulted by Saint George on the front cover of one volume.

My sister Caroline, whom we have always called Pug, was born on August 15, 1923. Miss Blake, a tiny but formidable Scottish lady, was engaged to care for me while my mother was in the hospital. Miss Blake was a private nurse whose clients included the Corbetts and others in the neighborhood. She took no nonsense from small fry. I expected trouble from her and got it when I deliberately locked myself in the bathroom off the kitchen after being specifically instructed not to do this.

The day Pug was born Auntie Marg drove into the circular driveway of our house and shouted up to Miss Blake and me at an upstairs window, "It's a girl!!." Pug was the first girl born in the Morrison, Green, and Beatty families after five boys in succession, and there was great excitement.

The summer following we went to Gearhart, staying in the old frame hotel called Mrs. Schroeder's, which then stood in the meadows below the dunes. Our maid, Margie Berrith, came with us to look after Pug and myself. The beach when I was a youngster was not an exciting place. True, I could play in the sand and in the water, but the water was always freezing cold. The wind constantly blew sand in my eyes, and I got terribly sunburned, particularly my lips and ankles.

My father made a practice of telling Pug a bedtime story every night. After he had finished the story, he would tuck Pug in and say "good night." Invariably, a few minutes later Pug would call in a hopeful voice, "I want a drink of water," which she usually got until my father realized that this was purely a device to delay bedtime.

One summer day my mother left the house, taking Pug with her to a tea party. As she was driving up Palatine Hill Road, past the Henry Wagner house, the right hand door of the Buick came open and out went Pug. No seat belts or infant car seats in those days. The road had been freshly oiled, and when my frantic mother got the car stopped and picked her baby out of the ditch, Pug's first words were, "Bump baby, bump." I was playing on the back porch when my mother came racing home to call the doctor. She and the baby both had on white dresses and both were covered with black oil. Pug was undamaged save for scratches, but my mother was understandably shaken by the incident.

*

Before I started school my principal playmates were Townsend Conover, Ginny Sherwood, and on several occasions, Billy Wessinger. Ginny's father, Arthur Sherwood, was the brother of the playwright, Robert E. Sherwood. The Sherwood family moved back east before we started school. These play occasions were arranged by mothers because the houses were too far apart for four and five year olds to visit on their own. We were thrown into each other's company and left alone to make to make a go of it. My first contact with Billy Wessinger led to an argument about whose father could beat up the other's father. Neither Mr. Wessinger nor my father had any aggressive instincts, but we certainly did. Billy had a large collection of lead soldiers, imported from Germany, I believe, and these were of great interest to me.

On one occasion Rosina Corbett was brought down to play with me at a time I was required to wear what was called a "G string", a cloth wrapped around my bottom. The point of it was to expose me to the beneficial rays of the sun and fresh air.

I hated it and was fearfully embarrassed by it. I have no idea what Rosina thought. I don't even remember whether she was similarly clothed.

We started climbing trees at an early age, and I remember climbing a fir on the property next door and being unable to figure out a way to get down. My mother called my father at the office. He arrived home, stood at the foot of the tree and said in a fierce voice,

"You come down that tree this minute!"

Surprised and frightened out of my paralysis, I scrambled down. He marched me home saying,

"Don't climb a tree without first figuring out how you're going to get down."

*

Our groceries came from Oswego or from farms out in the Tualatin Valley south and west of Oswego. At first groceries arrived on an old flat bed truck with vegetables and fruits arranged on racks. The truck pulled into the driveway. My mother would go out, look the cargo over and purchase what she wished. Fancy groceries came from the Sealy Dresser store on Park Street in downtown Portland. Meat she always bought from the butcher in Oswego, and until my dying day I will hear my mother on the telephone insisting that meat must be "well hung."

Ice was delivered regularly by the iceman who carried chunks from his truck using his ice tongs and placing the ice in our icebox which was located in the laundry. When the iceman came in sight, we begged and were usually given scraps of ice to suck. I think it was not until the late twenties that we bought a refrigerator. By that time Rogers Brothers in Oswego provided most groceries and staples. Rogers had a delivery truck driven by Stanley, a lanky chap whose face was covered with freckles and moles. Stanley enjoyed company, and many days after school I rode with him as he pursued his delivery route through Dunthorpe.

4. Drama at Riverdale. From the left: Meta Ladd, Patricia Hampson, unknown, Stephan Babson and Jack Beatty in "Hansel and Gretel." Second Grade, March 16, 1927.

5. The Sellwood Ferry looking east in 1922. Site of the icy skid. Oregon Historical Society. OHI 12572 (John F. Caples).

Milk came first from the Riverview Dairy, and later from the Fulton Park Dairy which was located on open pasture, the present site of Wilson High School in Hillsdale. Hillsdale then consisted of the dairy and Lynch's food stand on Capitol Highway. Our family often went driving Sunday afternoons. If we came by Lynch's on our way home my father would buy white Bermuda onions, which were sliced, covered with oil and eaten for Sunday night supper. Sundays also meant Sunday school at the Trinity Parish House. The classes were taught by Mrs. Hartwell, Auntie Marg Sharp and several other ladies. Sunday School was never very interesting despite their earnest efforts. While we were at Sunday school my mother and father and other parents attended the eleven o'clock church service conducted by my grandfather. After the service we drove home to Sunday dinner which took place at one o'clock, usually with a roast chicken. Sunday supper was supposed to be a light meal, crackers and milk, or milk toast.

*

When I was six I was given my first bicycle. I thought I would never be able to ride it but managed to learn after a number of spills. There were no training wheels in those days. Traffic was light in those years and many of us rode our bikes to school. Those who did not, walked. We had no kindergarten so school started when we were six years old. Riverdale at that time had four closed in and two open air classrooms—roof only. Not surprisingly, in the Oregon climate open air classrooms were not a success and were used only in clement weather. So generally there were two grades to a classroom. Within a year of my starting school, the open air rooms were enclosed, and a north wing with two other classrooms was added. Riverdale was a small school. During my days as a student the school population hovered around 125 pupils, an average of 16 to a class.

Mrs. Hartwell not only taught Sunday School at Trinity but on occasion acted as impresario of dramatic productions at Riverdale. When I was in the second or third grade she had us doing an eighteenth century minuet. The boys had to wear cotton wigs and Mrs. Hartwell liberally applied library paste to our skulls around the edges to hold those wigs in place. That minuet is indelibly pasted into my memory.

I still remember the names and faces of all my grade school teachers, which is more than I can say for those I had in high school, college or law school. Miss Brown, a soft spoken and gentle lady with a large nose, taught the first grade. Mrs. Collette, an ample, businesslike woman taught the second grade. Miss Nelson had the third grade. Mrs. Herrenkohl taught the fourth grade. Mrs. Hollingworth taught the fifth grade and Mrs. McElveny (Miss New) the sixth. Miss Dean taught the seventh, and the principal, Miss Eva Campbell, taught the eighth grade. Mrs. Byron Beattie, the French wife of the printer, taught us French. All of them ran a tight ship.

Miss Campbell was a spare New England type and ran the school with an iron hand. She took no nonsense from the students, her teachers, parents, or the school board. She began as a teacher in 1917 and was appointed principal in 1928. Under her jurisdiction Riverdale became an excellent elementary school. Miss Campbell became difficult to deal with in her final years as principal and was finally retired by the board in 1953 over her objection. She and Mrs. Herrenkohl lived together in retirement, sharing an apartment in the Vista St. Claire. Miss Campbell was thought by some to have destroyed all the school records, including records of the school board, at the time of her retirement. At least none were found. When Helen Bledsoe wrote the centennial book, "Riverdale School 1888-1988," the story of Riverdale in the early days had to be pieced together from material supplied by parents and former students.

No provision was made for teacher retirement in those years, so a number of district parents and former pupils passed the hat to create a fund for Miss Campbell's support. As a Riverdale graduate and practicing lawyer, I was asked to make informal arrangements to handle the account. In this role I saw Miss Campbell and Mrs. Herrenkohl on a number of occasions. Those gimlet eyes still bored into me, but I really found her largely gentled by age.

Riverdale School was more like an extended family in those days. The eighth graders were gods, the first graders babies, and one's station in the pecking order was determined first by grade and then within grade in so far as the boys were concerned by some indefinable combination of physical and personal characteristics. We walked to school or rode our bikes. The boys all carried pocket knives, and in rainy weather played real estate. This game was conducted on bare patches of slick clay on which we drew large circles divided into pie shaped shares. The game was to flip your knife into another's share. If your blade stuck you acquired the slice next to your own property. The goal was to acquire property and to drive your adversaries out of the game by slicing up their share until it was too small to fit their shod foot within it. I never heard of anyone threatening another student with a knife.

From Riverdale school south, Breyman Avenue was built on fill over a swampy area which filled with water on either side of the road during the winter. A drainage ditch carried the bulk of the water to the east and over a rocky escarpment twenty feet above the Pacific Highway creating a modest waterfall. Before the drainage ditch was dug the area had been a large shallow lake on which, according to my mother, my grandfather and his friends shot duck in the early days of the century. The surface in my time was broken up with shrubs and small trees which had grown after the lake was largely drained. The waterfall was visible from the highway below it and always attracted my attention. When I was twelve or thirteen Pug and I dammed the drainage ditch above the waterfall, recreating a portion of lake behind it. Several days later the dam carried away causing a mud slide over the fall onto the Pacific Highway which in turn brought a highway crew to clear it. Prudently, Pug and I said nothing of our involvement.

In grammar school my principal playmates were Douglas Barnes, whose family lived on the northwest corner of Greenwood and Edgecliff Roads, Scot Redfield, who lived a bit farther up Greenwood, Lambert Snow, who lived down in Riverdale, Stephen Babson, who lived on Military Road and Gilbert Shepherd who lived in Glenmorrie, south of Oswego. In our younger years we played frequently on our property building elaborate systems of mud roads and villages on which we operated tiny lead automobiles and trucks. We engaged in imaginary occupations, selling gasoline, building bridges, charging tolls. By stages the games grew to involve tricycles and wagons, and the use of play money which we issued, banked, and invested in imaginary enterprises.

As we grew older we constructed "autos" with wagon wheels which we steered by means of a wheel attached to a broomstick around which we wound cords leading to a front axle pivoted at the center. I finally constructed a monster, a bus which held a half dozen kids, and on which we careened down Greenwood Road. Fortunately for us, its life was short because of the difficulty pushing it back up the hill.

By the time we were ten or twelve we seldom walked anywhere. The bicycle was our universal mode of transportation. "Cops and robbers" replaced "Still Water Still" and the game extended all through the Dunthorpe road net. The game was frequently complicated by dogs. Everyone had a dog, and everyone was followed by a dog. When disputes occurred and resulted in a fight, the dogs invariably joined in on behalf of their respective masters. The Babsons had a large bulldog named Bingo. The Bynons, who lived on Breyman Avenue, had a large German shepherd which liked to pull down passing cyclists by seizing their trouser legs. Dr. Frank Mount and his family had a German shepherd which sampled a piece of me on several occasions. The Henry Wessingers had a black German shepherd named Caesar who appeared threatening but was actually quite harmless. The Harry Corbetts had a German shepherd which was thought by everyone to be fierce, though I never had a run in with him nor heard of anyone who had.

My dog was Russler, a mixture of collie and shepherd. He originally belonged to a girl who lived in Ewawee on the river below us. She walked past our house on her way to Riverdale School, often accompanied by Russler. Russler gradually transferred his allegiance to the Beattys when his mistress graduated. Russler was a purely outdoor dog with a very thick coat. He preferred to sleep on the door mat in the front door vestibule, although he had a king size dog house in front of the kitchen. My mother fed him a mix of table scraps fortified by chunks of meat and other morsels which she cooked for him. Once a year she gave Russler a bath in the front yard using laundry soap and the hose. Occasionally in the dead of night Russ would bark, a long series of slow woofs. After fifteen or twenty minutes I would hear Mrs. John Banks, across the street to the north of us, throw up a window and call out in her clipped South African British voice: "Russla! Shut-up!" This rarely proved effective, but I think it helped Banksie relieve her irritation.

Mrs. Banks had her own dog problem. Whereas Russler and the other neighborhood dogs roamed the neighborhood, the Banks dogs, shaggy white terriers, were confined within a picket fence which entirely surrounded the several acres of their property. The Banks dogs longed to escape and seized every opportunity to do so. This meant that all deliveries to the Banks, milk, groceries, ice, cleaners and so forth, had to be carefully orchestrated to avoid releasing a dog or two. The system failed with some regularity. The dogs escaped to freedom, and Mrs. Banks panicked until they were safely corralled again.

*

In the mid 1920s my family belonged to Waverly Country Club. In that club's unheated swimming pool I was delivered into the iron hands of the swimming instructor, a woman qualified to train candidates for the Gestapo. The water was always icy cold, the instructor unforgiving, and within minutes I turned blue with cold. I learned to freeze but not to swim. Finally, my mother gave it up as a bad job. In the late 1920s the Lake Oswego Country Club was organized, and my father was one of the original members. The club had an enclosed swimming area on Oswego Lake which was much warmer than Bull Run water from the tap. There I did learn to swim, although never well. I did not float, and swimming was a struggle to keep my nose above the water. My mother regularly drove a car full of children down to the lake on summer afternoons and sat in a chair knitting while we splashed around the pool.

Glenmorrie, where Gilbert Shepherd lived, was a mile beyond Oswego. Gibby attended Riverdale, sometimes riding his bike to school, other times taking the Oregon City Bus. On several occasions I spent the night with the Shepherds, and it was always a bracing experience. Mr. Shepherd believed in boys taking cold showers before breakfast, a practice which my own father fortunately had no interest in following. Gilbert had a horse, a field full of fig trees and a very old single shot 22 caliber rifle which we used for target practice. One day as I was holding the gun and talking to Gibby in front of his garage, the gun discharged, the bullet missing his head by two or three inches and passing through the garage door. As I recall, it fired on safety without my finger near the trigger. The gun should not have been carried loaded in any event. It was a dangerous piece of equipment. We were both scared out of our wits and agreed to say nothing to anyone about the incident. I don't recall that we ever used that gun again.

When I was twelve my mother gave me her 22 cal. long rifle Winchester with an octagonal barrel, a gift from Thomas W. Lawson, and I used to march along Edgecliff Road with the gun over my shoulder on my way to Tryon woods to hunt birds and squirrels. I do not recall any specific admonitions about safety other than not to point the gun at anyone, but burned by the near accident with Gibby, I was very cautious.

Summers I rode my bike down the highway to Oswego Lake to fish for sunfish and bluegills. It was an easy coast down to Oswego, but a hard pull back. In those days geared bikes were unknown. One hot summer day, I brought home a bag full of fish and put several apparently expired bluegills in the Isaac's fish pond next door to see if they could be revived. The next morning when I went over to inspect them, I found the bluegills in fine shape and all the goldfish missing. My parents had to restock the pool for Mrs. Isaacs, who was quite upset.

One winter the Willamette froze from bank to bank, as did the Columbia, and the ice on Oswego Lake was a foot thick. One cold moonlit night, mother drove us down to the lake to skate. She wore her fancy round-toed figure skates, and she skated gracefully about, much to my envy. My ankles flipped first one way and then the other, and I had a dreadful time staying on my feet. In ordinary winters when it snowed, as it usually did, we went sledding down Greenwood Road. We enlisted one of the mothers to drive her automobile and tow us up the hill. By tying a rope to the rear bumper, which the boy or girl on the first sled held, and hooking toes onto the forward slat of the next sled behind, one car could pull a string of a dozen sleds up the hill. Traffic on the roads was light and cautious, and I recall no significant injuries sledding downhill save an occasional collision with trees when a sled veered off the road.

At Riverdale our gym classes mixed boys and girls because there were too few of either sex to warrant a separate class or, in the case of baseball, to make up teams. We had only two formal school sports, basketball and baseball, and to field a team of boys for either sport we had to use seventh as well as eighth graders. Riverdale played four or five other small county schools such as Multnomah, Capitol Hill, Lynch, Corbett and Troutdale. Gibby Shepherd, whose father had played professional baseball, was our pitcher, Jimmy Green our catcher, Lon Hoss played first base, I second base, Lambert Snow, shortstop, Donny Plympton third base. I don't remember who played in the outfield. I really wanted to be a pitcher so I constructed a plate and pitcher's mound at home and drafted Pug as a catcher. We spent hours, day after day, in pitching practice. I never became a successful pitcher, but Pug developed a splendid throwing arm. Pug was the athlete of the family, becoming a good ball player, skier, golfer and tennis player, but I claim credit for the excellence of her throwing arm.

Baseballs were expensive, and we treasured them. When the stitching wore out, we replaced the leather covers with black electrician's tape. Once Doug Barnes and I lost a ball in the tangled brush to the north of the Barnes yard. I had the brilliant idea of setting fire to the brush to burn away the leaves so we could find the ball. The fire promptly burned out of control, and the Oswego Fire Department had to be called to extinguish it. Mr. Barnes was a good deal more forgiving than I would have been and did not even mention the matter to my family.

Going to school meant getting into fights. Once the strangeness of school disappeared, the usual patterns of aggressiveness and timidity emerged. One boy in the class ahead of me, Norton Fautz, used to waylay me regularly on the way home from school. He was taller and a good deal heavier, and unless I could outwit him, he usually ended up on top of me on the grass or in the ditch. Most of my classmates were quite evenly matched and this state of affairs precluded bullying. For my part, I understood the unpredictable consequence of fights and avoided them in so far as this was consistent with honor and a hot temper.

One event in the seventh grade remains as a particular impression. The lunches, which we carried from home in lunch buckets or paper bags, we ate at our desks when it was rainy. One such day, Jimmy Green stuck his foot out and tripped me as I was carrying my empty sack and a half pint bottle of milk up the aisle. I recovered my footing, turned and threw the half empty milk bottle at him. I can't recall whether I hit him or not, but milk splattered across the room and it produced pandemonium. Both of us, scared out of our wits, were sent to Miss Campbell's office and punished for disturbing the peace. I was lectured on how serious it was to lose my temper and throw something which might have caused serious injury. My feelings of guilt and remorse were intense but tempered by the satisfaction that, by God, Jimmy would not try that again. My relations with Jimmy did not suffer from that episode, and his older brother George went out of his way to sponsor me for HY later at Lincoln High School.

In the eighth grade I had the lead part in the Christmas play, a big event at Riverdale in those days. A few days before the play we had our first basketball game of the season, and I played quite well. That night I developed acute abdominal pain and by morning felt badly. My mother took one look at me, suspected appendicitis, and called Dr. Frank Mount who stopped by a few minutes later on the way to his office in Oregon City. He quickly diagnosed acute appendicitis, called for an ambulance, and off I went, siren screaming, to St. Vincent Hospital. I was met by Dr. Tom Joyce, who operated immediately making a transverse slice across my stomach which left a large scar and some occasionally painful adhesions.

The anesthetic employed was ether, and the recovery process was unpleasant. I remember how sick at my stomach I was and how very thirsty. For medical reasons the nurses would not allow a drink of water. From time to time they washed out my mouth with a sponge. My mother was at my bedside as I gradually regained consciousness, and years later she remarked on how shocked she had been at my language coming out of the anesthetic. Dr. Joyce, she observed, was vastly amused. Old St. Vincent Hospital on the hillside above 23rd street was a Spartan brick structure. My room had a high ceiling, no decorations of any kind, and was furnished with a bed and a chair. Over the bed hung a crucifix. That was all. Nothing like the glorified hotels that pass for hospitals these days. I missed the play, the rest of the basketball season, and was kept in bed for a month after I got home from the hospital. There was no getting out of bed the next day in those times.

*

The 1925 Buick coach (which had replaced the 1921 Buick roadster) failed in numerous ways and was in turn replaced by a 1928 Buick sedan known in the family as Felix. Some weekends we drove over the new Interstate Bridge to Vancouver Barracks to watch a polo game. My father when stationed with the Fourth Field Artillery Regiment, horse drawn until the Second War, played polo at Vancouver Barracks and later in the Philippines.

My mother had learned to ride as a young woman and for a time had a horse named Glorious Gladys which she rode in horse shows and on roads and trails about Portland. Both parents thought I should learn to ride. I spent many a wretched Saturday morning at Nichols Riding Academy struggling to stay on a horse. Horses do not like me, and I do not like horses. Given the slightest opportunity they will turn and bite, buck, or run away with me. Once when I was leading a pony on which my daughter, Jean, age three was sitting, the pony turned and bit me without the slightest provocation. Horses are beautiful animals best cast in bronze. My parents finally gave up. Fortunately for them, Pug loved horses.

As we drove through Vancouver Barracks, my father would point out where he had been quartered and where General Grant had lived during his tour of duty before the Civil War. We also went to the Barracks Commissary where my father, as a retired officer, was entitled to purchase staples of various kinds and Virginia hams. The Army Air Corps had a landing strip, Pearson Field, adjacent to the parade ground, with several aircraft which we sometimes watched. Pearson Field was the common airport for Vancouver and Portland until the Swan Island Airport was completed in 1927, shortly before Lindbergh made his solo flight across the Atlantic. Our family marked the occasion by buying a canary, which was, of course, named Lindy. Lindy's cage hung in the dining room against the south windows, and there he sang for many years. Several months later, Lindbergh flew to Portland on his nationwide tour, and we drove out to Swan Island to watch him land in the Spirit of St. Louis.

The National City Company's offices, where my father worked, were originally in the Yeon Building. When the United States National Bank completed building its Greek temple on the corner of Broadway and Stark, the City Company offices were moved to the mezzanine floor of that Bank. By 1927 my father was the Northwest manager. The Rose Festival Grand Floral Parade always came up Broadway right below the mezzanine windows, and it was a great place to watch the parade. However, the most interesting thing about the office to me was the telegraph station located just outside my father's private office. The operator took the messages in Morse code which came from New York on a private line. He converted the code to letters and figures reporting stock transactions as well as other financial news.

I had a paper route off and on, at one time the Portland News, later the Portland Telegram, and finally the News Telegram when the two newspapers merged. The route ran down through Riverwood along the Willamette, and for a time Lambert Snow shared it with me. Several times we walked through the Red Train's Elk Rock tunnel, and once we found a cache of slot machine slugs which had been dumped over the cliff. They proved to be slugs of very high quality. Lambert used them successfully in the prize grabbing machine at the downtown bus terminal. I had visions of jail and remained a jealous but wary observer. In those days stern wheelers steamed up and down the Willamette carrying great rolls of newsprint from the paper mills at Oregon City. Gilbert Shepherd had a Philippine dug-out canoe with an outrigger which his older cousin, Wally, a seaman, had brought home on a freighter. Wearing no life jackets, we launched it in the Willamette and paddled around, riding the waves created by the passing steamers. We were soon swamped by the stern waves, but the outrigger prevented us from overturning. We managed to bail out the canoe and got safely back to shore. This adventure was also not reported at home.

One foggy morning our family got up early to see the Navy dirigible, USS Akron, which was scheduled to fly north along the Willamette river. As we waited the Akron suddenly loomed out of the fog at little more than eye level from our position on the terrace of our house and perhaps a half mile distant over the river. It was ghostly, enormous, silent, the size of the Queen Mary. I recall no sound of engines. The immensity of it was overwhelming. The Akron, the Macon, and the Shenandoah were filled with helium and supposed to be much safer than the hydrogen filled German airships of WW I. However, Akron and Macon were lost at sea, and Shenandoah broke apart above her landing site in Ohio. Only the Los Angeles, a dirigible built by the Germans after World War I as reparations for the United States, survived, its hydrogen replaced by helium. The Los Angeles made many voyages and was eventually decommissioned.

*

In October 1929 came the initial collapse of the stock boom of the late 1920s. The market and the economy continued to fall during the rest of President Hoover's administration. At dinner one night my father was unusually quiet. My mother, seated at the opposite end of the dining room table from him, asked,
"Is it all gone?"
I looked at my father, who replied quietly,
"Yes, it is all gone."

Our maid for many years, Margie Berrith, whom we called Miggs, had to go. The plans to enlarge the house were put away. As the Depression deepened, the National City Company cut its staff in Portland, and before long closed the Portland office. Throughout this period neither my mother nor my father ever discussed the extent of their difficulties with us or before us, but I was quite aware that money was tight and that hard times had hit the entire country. My father then opened his own stock and bond business, sharing an office with Lex Andrus. My father resigned from Waverly and the University Club. My mother resigned from the Garden Club. They stopped accepting invitations to dinner because they could no longer reciprocate. My mother did the housework and cleaning. My father did the gardening, and I took over cutting the lawn, a substantial task with a manual lawn mower.

When I reached my twelfth birthday, I became a boy scout and member of Troop 110. The troop met one night a week at Riverdale School. Scouting in those days was a paramilitary operation which offered considerable advantage in keeping a lot of free spirited boys under control. Most Riverdale boys became scouts at twelve and remained active members until they were fourteen or fifteen. Our first scoutmaster was Mr. Holford, who lived on Edgecliff Road. He was an architect and a gentle man who was never able to achieve control over his unruly troops. His place was taken over by Art Kaornahrens whose approach was quite different. Art was a young reserve officer and had no difficulty establishing law and order in Troop 110. The troop was very active during the four years I belonged. We had camping trips in the spring and fall, a role in the annual Scout Circus, and sent strong delegations to Camp Meriweather on the Oregon Coast during the summers.

My first year, when I was a tenderfoot, the troop had an overnight trip for fathers and sons to the Eagle Creek Scout Camp. My father came with me, as did Mr. Snow with Lambert. It was hard duty for them but they gamely played the camping role. Later that first summer, I signed up for four weeks at Camp Meriweather near Cape Lookout on the Oregon Coast. Meriweather was run on a quasi-military basis with reveille, retreat, mess call, lots of inspections, and whistle blowing, all of which I enjoyed. The camp was divided into four regular troop encampments, plus a sea scout "ship" built on the shores of a freshwater lake, and a Rover camp with stables and horses. The encampments consisted of half framed tent topped cabins for eight with four double bunks. The cabins were arranged around a central area with a cabin for the scoutmaster, usually a young adult with considerable scouting experience. We all ate in a central mess hall and there were shops for wood carving and leather work.

A second or third year boy who had demonstrated some aptitude for leadership was appointed as patrol leader for each cabin with the responsibility of supervising housecleaning and keeping his seven fellow campers under control and doing what they were supposed to do. The four regular troops ate at a central mess hall. All in all, it was an effective way of developing leadership and group responsibility at an early age. After a faltering start my first few days at camp, I thrived on this regimen, becoming a patrol leader my second year and receiving my third year the camp's highest award, a small bronze bar inscribed in Latin, "Vi et consilio." I worked my way up the scout ranks to Life but never became an Eagle scout because of my inability to swim well enough to pass the life saving test.

As I have said, my start at Meriweather was faltering. This was my first experience away from home. I was several days late in going to camp because of an infected leg. My family let me off at the gate at the end of the road to walk a mile or so through the pines and over the sand dunes into camp. I was assigned to the Lookout Troop, in which I knew none of the boys. We left within a day or two on a ten mile overnight hike to Pacific City. In my inexperience, I packed more stuff than I should have in my Trapper Nelson pack board, and I was soon exhausted, falling asleep at each rest stop. We finally got to Pacific City and I bunked down in a cow pie studded meadow with Lambert Snow. I was tired and homesick. I wept bitterly and was determined to go home at the end of the first two week period.

Two events changed my frame of mind. First, the mail was brought to us at Pacific City, and I received a letter from my father with a five dollar bill. This immediately raised my spirits. Next, Lambert had purchased some firecrackers, and was placing them one by one in cow pies, igniting them with great satisfaction. One cracker failed to go off. Lambert approached the cow pie, bent over to re light the fuse and bam! It went off in his face. This, I am sorry to say, provoked laughter all around and cheered me no end. I decided that life was endurable. But for the rest of my days I have never undertaken to carry a pack which weighed more than I was certain I could carry in comfort, and I have never lit a firecracker in a cow pie.

The Scout Circus was held each year in the Pacific Livestock Exposition Arena and was always well attended. The high point was the rapid construction of a log bridge by the pioneer troop. In my second year as a scout, a sleeping bag was offered as a prize for selling a certain number of tickets to the circus. I had no sleeping bag, having used my father's heavy old canvas bedroll from his army days, so I went after the prize, soliciting sales through downtown office buildings until I reached the magic number and won the bag. My father encouraged me, suggesting the buildings and offices to solicit. Not withstanding the prize, I disliked selling and always have. Dad thought it was good experience, perhaps because he had found selling bonds so difficult himself. I doubt I would have tackled the laundry job at Princeton if I had not learned that I could sell despite my dislike of the process.

*

Girls were a casual interest during most of grade school, but by the sixth grade we were beginning to take a closer look at them. Several times after school I walked down the trail to Radcliff Street with Patty Hampson. On other occasions I walked home from school with Rosina Corbett, Isabel Beckwith and Barby Besson. These were tentative gestures, harbingers of future interest. We had no television, no steamy web sites providing windows into the world of sex. Nothing was ever mentioned about sex in grade school. Not even mild explanatory material was available in the school library. I had been told pre puberty that babies grew inside their mothers, which was rather astonishing because there was no explanation of how they got there or how they came out. The mechanics of sexual reproduction were a total mystery until two of my friends, a year older and a grade wiser, enlightened me one day as we were walking home from school along Edgecliff Road. My immediate reaction was, "That's ridiculous!" A few months later nocturnal emissions followed by parental explanation confirmed my older colleagues' wisdom.

In the seventh grade we went to dancing school one night a week. The boys wore blue flannel jackets, white flannel trousers and white cotton gloves intended to protect the girls frocks from our sweaty little hands, or so we were told. Remember, in those days ladies always wore gloves when they were out and about. This dance schooling took place in the Masonic Temple ballroom The boys were generally on one side of the hall, the girls on the other. The girls, maturing earlier than the boys, were generally larger, some already developing what was delicately referred to by parents as a figure. Embracing them was sometimes awkward but pretty exciting business.

In 1933 the graduating class at Riverdale consisted of myself, Gilbert Shepherd, James Green, Donald Plympton, Henry Wagner, Lon Hoss, Lambert Snow, Rosina Corbett, Josephine Squires, Patricia Hampson, Marjorie Schippers, Jessica McClean, Tory Hartwell, Barbara Besson, Marion Olson and Isabel Beckwith. We had a class reunion in 1988 on the occasion of Riverdale's hundredth anniversary. Plympton, Corbett, Squires, Hartwell, Beckwith, Hampson, Snow, Beatty and spouses had dinner at Barbara Besson Martin's house on the Clackamus River. Some of us had not seen each other for more than half a century.

*

In the fall of 1933, I started high school. The Riverdale District had no high school. The school board made arrangements with School District No. 1, for us to go to Lincoln High School in Portland. Lincoln at that time was situated in the tan brick building now known as Lincoln Hall at Portland State University. The school was a melting pot, a mix of students from Portland Heights and Southwest Portland including the area south of Jefferson Street which was then largely residential. Most of the boys from Dunthorpe went to Lincoln. A few went to eastern prep schools, while a majority of the Dunthorpe girls were sent to Miss Catlin's School on Westover Terrace above the old St. Vincent Hospital. All Dunthorpe high schoolers, public and private, rode the old Dunthorpe bus which made morning and afternoon runs between Dunthorpe, Lincoln, and Miss Catlin's.

I remember that first day of high school, striding down Park Street past the Congregational Church toward the Greyhound bus terminal wearing new white corduroy trousers and new shoes with a steel plate in the heels which made a satisfying click on the sidewalk. I went out for freshman football in a burst of misguided ambition. I was then about five feet eight or nine and weighed about 125 pounds. The site of our efforts was Kamm field, a sawdust covered piece of real estate where the present Lincoln athletic field is now located. In my first scrimmage I was placed at tackle opposite Stanley Peters, a 200 pound behemoth. Peters knocked me this way and that, then flattened me. I saw no future for myself in football, and in a burst of good judgment, I turned in my suit that same evening.

*

By the time I was ten I had begun to read a good deal, what was available in the small Riverdale school library, then the full collection of the Oz books, Bomba the Jungle Boy, The Rover Boys, Hans Brinker, and then into Ivanhoe, Treasure Island, Robinson Crusoe, and some Kipling. By twelve I was reading Time Magazine and the Saturday Evening Post, and dipped into the set of Dumas and Victor Hugo. Each year I gave myself the Time Magazine test on the year's current events and then graded myself on the answers printed upside down at the end of the test issue. My family gave books, not only as Christmas and birthday presents, but also on other occasions when they came upon a book they thought would, or should interest me. H. G. Wells' *Outline of History* was one such. Out of this eclectic mixture of reading material I did develop a love of reading and a keen interest in history.

I also projected myself into the variety of possible roles to which my reading had exposed me. I suppose all adolescents who read a good deal probably do this. My father often spoke of his experiences at the military academy and of his later service at Vancouver Barracks and then in the Philippines. From childhood on, West Point and military service were my career goals. I knew from reading and from what my father told me that this meant more than passing entrance examinations; it meant competitive examinations for an appointment. Consequently, I had no doubt about what I was going to do in life and plenty of incentive to pay attention to my studies in high school.

Scholastically speaking, Lincoln was not much of a challenge in those days, though we did have several excellent teachers. I remember Mrs. Southworth who taught English, and Mrs. Peterson who taught Latin. One of the best was Mr. Walker, a lawyer who had given up the practice of law after a heart attack. Mr. Walker taught sociology. Leaving the practice of law to teach sociology in high school may seem like a strange choice today, but this was in Depression days, and lawyers, too, were going hungry. School teaching was a job that paid a regular salary, and students in those days were respectful of authority. Mr. Walker's real subject was human behavior, and he questioned us constantly trying to stimulate our thinking.

So far as I could see, only students who had a clear objective in mind worked very hard. The competition was limited and it was not difficult to make good grades. When my report cards came home with all "Es," my father concluded I was not working hard enough, which was true. He went in to see the principal who changed my number of courses from the regular four to five, and in consequence I was able to graduate in three years rather than four.

While in high school my physical exercise was largely obtained at Riverdale after school. The Lincoln Gym was located in the basement beneath the auditorium and was dark and smelly. By signing up for regular exercise in our neighborhood, we managed to get excused from gym. The boys riding home from Lincoln on the bus would usually stop at Riverdale School and play touch football, often with one or two girls to fill out a team. During the winter we played basketball in the Riverdale gym. These sessions were usually conducted by Henry E. Stevens, the physical education teacher at Riverdale, who was supposed to be paid extra for after school work but usually donated his time to this cause. Mr. Stevens was an amiable and conscientious fixture at Riverdale for many years. He knew my Aunt Margaret through the University of Oregon Extension Division where he took courses on various subjects and later became associate director. Basketball required only five boys to make up a team, and, coached by Mr. Stevens. we

regularly played other small neighborhood teams. Sometimes
Ned Babson, one of Stephen Babson's two older brothers, came
by in the afternoons to lead our games.

In high school, with most of the Dunthorpe girls going to
Miss Catlin's, we met other girls who generally lived on the
heights. In my class were Barbara Hervin, who later married
Herbert M. Schwab, my law partner and fellow judge, Margaret
Selling, who later married Dan Labby, and Nancy Holmes, who
later married my cousin Don Green. Virginia Rupp was a year
ahead of me. I saw her walking the halls with Rol Mersereau
and managed an introduction. By the start of my sophomore
year I began dating Ginny, and in a short time she was wearing
my "Hi Y" pin. Hi Y was an invitational, exclusively male
club composed largely of athletes, with its meeting place in
the downtown YMCA, which supposedly sponsored it. I was
sponsored by George Green, Jimmy's older brother. Why I was
asked to join was a mystery, but I wasn't about to question it.
The pledges had some weeks of hazing, which consisted of being
swatted with large wood paddles, no fun at all but endurable
for the honor of belonging.

Ginny and I dated the rest of our time at Lincoln. As the
yearbook put it, "Jack Beatty and Ginny Rupp leave together."
Ginny was a bright and pretty blonde with a sunny disposition
who had a good time doing whatever we did. She lived on
upper Montgomery Drive, and as soon as I got my driver's
license, which then was at 15, I drove the big, old 1928 family
Buick through the West Hills on the back roads from Dunthorpe
up Dosch Road to Patton, then down Patton to Montgomery
and Ginny's house. I don't recall ever having a quarrel with
her, which seems surprising because I was such a moody
youngster.

Dating in those days consisted of going to movies, football
games, basketball games and dancing. One of our favorite
spots for dancing was the Jantzen Beach amusement park,
which usually had a good band. At school we saw much of
one another, walking the halls hand in hand between periods,

eating lunch together. At Christmas time the girl's sororities, Jomas and Pirettes, held formal dances, and there were dances given by families of some of the girls. Ginny was a Joma. Going steady never struck my mother as a sensible arrangement. She urged variety, which is understandable when you consider the way the social life of youngsters had been organized a quarter century before. My mother, of course, was a prime example of playing the field. It took my father seven years to capture her. I think it was the automobile which produced earlier pairing in our generation.

Nonetheless, I spent a good deal of time alone, reading, constructing model airplanes, working in the yard. I built a small log cabin down in Tryon Creek woods after school, using a single bladed ax to cut the trees and a wagon to drag the logs to the site. I rebuilt the play house Dick Norton and I had constructed on the east end of our property, converting it into a chicken house for our bantam chickens. I saw a good deal less of Lambert Snow than I had while at Riverdale. Gilbert Shepherd went to Benson High School rather than Lincoln and consequently we lost touch with him. A new friend at Lincoln was Jim Goodsell, who worked on the Cardinal, the Lincoln newspaper. Jim was a boy who seemed to have interests similar to mine.

The summer I was fifteen the Boy Scouts scheduled a National Jamboree in Washington, DC. My father was struggling to make living expenses in the depths of the Depression, and I had no thought of going. Stephen Babson was going with a contingent from Portland. Mr. and Mrs. Walter Babson, quite out of the blue, generously funded the trip for me to go along with Steve. It was quite an experience for a boy who had never been farther from Oregon than Vancouver, Washington. Some twenty of us spent a week training at Reed College doing close order drill in squad formation marching around Reed, with a small drum and bugle band. I can still remember "Right by squads, squads right," a complex form of close order drill fortunately abandoned by the United States Army before we had to deal with World War II.

The Jamboree was called off just as we were about to entrain because of an infantile paralysis outbreak in Washington. The parents of our contingent decided to send us anyhow, so off we went, leaving Union Station in Portland for Seattle and Vancouver, BC. From there we took the Canadian Pacific Railway through the Rocky Mountains. The railroad provided us with several "Colonist Cars." These were old sleepers which had been used to bring Canadian colonists west when the CPR was first put through. The weather was hot. Our locomotive was coal fired. Our windows had to be wide open because of the heat, and the cinders came through the cars like black snow. None the less, we stuck our heads out those windows as we went through the mountains watching the locomotive curving ahead and sometimes snaking back above or below us on a switch back. We stopped at Lake Louise overnight, then went east and south, crossing the border into Minnesota to reach Chicago by way of the Chicago and Northwestern Railroad.

In Chicago we saw the Field Museum, the first museum of natural history for any of us. The way in which animals were pictured in three dimensional natural settings was the surprise. Moreover, one of our contingent was propositioned on the street by a young lady while he was wearing his scout uniform complete with short pants! From Chicago we went on to Niagara Falls, and from there to Albany, New York where we transferred to a Hudson River Day line steamer and sailed down the Hudson past West Point to New York City.

In New York we visited Rockerfeller Center, Grant's Tomb, the Statue of Liberty and other sights. Aunt Mary Miller, my father's sister, came into town from her home in Lambertville, New Jersey, and I spent the afternoon with her. From New York we went by train to Washington, saw the Capitol and visited Mount Vernon, which I thought was a more impressive memorial to the President than the Washington Monument. From Washington we headed home. All in all it was a great experience.

In the spring of 1936 I took the West Point competitive examinations for practice. They were held at Fort Lewis where I stayed with Colonel and Mrs. Fletcher Sharp in their quarters on the post. They were a striking couple, both very tall, and I remember them going out one evening, the colonel in full dress blues and Mrs. Sharp in a long evening dress. Six years later the colonel, then a brigadier general, commanded the last resistance in the Philippines. He survived four years in a Japanese prison, but died soon after the war. Fletcher Sharp was a cousin of Thomas Sharp, Auntie Marg's husband. Both were grandnephews of General Ulysses S. Grant. Albro Parsons, son of an army doctor, Major Parsons, lived next door to the Sharps, and we studied together for the examinations. I passed most subjects without distinction but failed in algebra and geometry.

That summer I spent a month and a half at Fort Lewis in Citizens Military Training Camp (CMTC). This was a program designed to train young men six weeks each summer for four years, leading to examinations and a commission as second lieutenant in the Army Reserve. It was a parallel program to the college Reserve Officers Training Course (ROTC). The program was well run. The noncommissioned officers were second and third year trainees. The officers were reserve officers called to active duty for the period of the camp. Albro Parsons was attending it also, and we were assigned to the same battery. We camped in tents in a dusty area north of the main fort. Our unit was a battery of 155 mm howitzers, old French Schneiders with solid rubber tires pulled by trucks. We also had some ancient French tanks which moved at a top speed of four miles per hour. Because the army could not afford live ammunition for the howitzers, 37mm gun barrels mounted on top of the 155 mm muzzles fired 37mm shells.

Our uniforms came from World War I surplus. We wore olive drab wool breeches, wool blouses with a choke collar, spiral wrap leggings and high top army shoes. The shoe leather was so rotten that I wore mine out in just six weeks. We also were issued blue jean pants and jackets for fatigue duty. It is difficult to imagine wearing wool clothing in August in Fort Lewis with the temperature in the 90s for guard mount or parade at 4:30

in the afternoon in the blazing sun. I managed the heat but not the boxing program.

The army promoted boxing in those days on the theory that boxing promoted aggressiveness. The ring was set on a hillside. The spectators sat on the uphill side, and there was a sharp drop off on the downhill side of five or six feet. I was selected as one of the protagonists for reasons unknown to me. When the second match came up, I was paired with a swarthy second year man with more than a little boxing experience. In thirty seconds he had me on the ropes and with a final punch lifted me clear of the ring. I landed on the hillside below. This honorably ended my boxing career in CMTC, and convinced me that boxing, like football, was not going to be my path to glory.

*

In the fall of 1936 my father scraped together enough money to send me back east to Stanton Preparatory Academy, a school located on the Hudson at Cornwall, New York, seven miles north of West Point. Stanton was exclusively dedicated to preparing students for West Point examinations. Nearly all the students were sons of regular army officers competing for the presidential appointments to the Academy. The head of the school, Colonel Edward Stanton, had been a classmate of my father at West Point.

At Stanton we lived and studied under conditions which simulated the academic conditions at West Point, and the instruction was hard, persistent, and thorough. Whatever the subject, we were expected to learn it thoroughly. There was none of the "Get your hand up first and answer a question you know" procedure I had used with great success in high school. We were tested every morning on the preceding day's assignment. At Stanton I learned for the first time the difference between general awareness and precise knowledge. Instructors emphasized dates, times, people, and places, as the way to put knowledge into an orderly structure.

My roommate was Donald V. Thompson, a business-like army brat from Texas. He graduated from West Point in 1941, elected the air corps and died in a plane crash a year later. I saw several home football games, and on other occasions walked the curvy highway around Storm King mountain to the Point to watch Sunday dress parade, a sight more dramatic than the changing of the guard at Buckingham Palace. Largely I kept to myself during my free time. On weekends, I climbed the hills above Cornwall. The forest was entirely deciduous, and during the winter one had a grand view of the mountains and the Hudson far below.

Christmas I went down to New York for several days, staying at the old Hotel Astor with Dave and Rol Mersereau, Bill Wessinger and Jimmy MacGregor. Dave and Jimmy were freshmen at Yale. Rol was at Amherst, Bill was at Cornell. The Astor Hotel was a traditional place for Army officers to stay in New York, and that was where the Stanton students were housed when taking West Point examinations.

Several weekends I took the bus to Poughkeepsie and ferried across the Hudson to Uncle Ned Beatty's farm near Wappinger's Falls. Uncle Ned and Aunt Helen had an apple orchard and a farmhouse built circa 1740. They stored quantities of apples and excellent applejack in the basement, which had thick stone walls and a dirt floor. The house was of simple Colonial design and very attractive. The second story was floored with wide pine boards, and you could see through the cracks into the rooms below. In the downstairs hall hung a framed portion of a union flag, the counterpart of the one which I had in my room at home. Both were taken from a large Union flag which the Beatty family women had sewn to hang out when their two surviving sons returned from the Civil War. The third, Captain H. Clay Beatty died in McReynold's charge on the Confederate flank at the second Battle of Bull Run. My mother had rescued the flag from the house at Bristol, Pennsylvania and had the two best portions cut and framed for Bob and me. I attributed the holes to bullets, but the truth is that flag had been attacked by moths.

Ned and Helen Beatty raised Macintosh apples, quite the best apples I had ever eaten, much better than the Hood River Delicious apples sold in Portland in those days. Macintoshes were crisp and juicy with a wonderful flavor. Uncle Ned bought the farm in 1914 just after World War I began. They had struggled through the agricultural depression of the 1920s and the great depression of the 1930s. Fortunately, the market for apples improved dramatically during World War II. I visited the farm in 1977 following my father's death. The area had become an industrial park in the midst of which Uncle Ned's farm stood, an agricultural oasis. Shortly after my visit, Uncle Ned sold the farm, moved to Texas and retired.

My cousin Bob Beatty was a husky chap, a year older than I. His sister, Eleanor, was two or three years younger. Both worked hard on the farm as youngsters, and I was impressed with how soft my own life had been in comparison with his.

In March of 1937 I again took the West Point entrance examinations, which were given in New York City. I easily passed the academic examination but ran into trouble with the physical examination. I had been having some discomfort with my eyes during the winter and cautiously memorized the eye chart as we stood in line for the examination. Then the examining doctor switched the chart when he came to me, and I could not read the letters on the 20/20 line.

I left Stanton following the examinations, taking the train for Detroit where I stayed with Aunt Jane Torrance for several days. Pat Hampson's brother, Alfred, Hunky in those days, was a student at the Hill School in the East. We had arranged to meet in Detroit and take delivery of a 1937 Buick sedan at the factory to drive home for my family, which had experienced a transitory glimpse of prosperity that year. Fortunately, Hunky had to retake an examination which delayed him and our scheduled departure, for I came down with a high fever for several days but recovered by the time he arrived. In Nebraska we slid off the road into a ditch during a snow storm. A farmer with a tractor came along and pulled us out.

Driving across the country then meant travel on winding two lane roads the entire way. There was little traffic save in one or two of the larger cities. For all practical purposes there was no interstate trucking. Most of the products which now move by truck were then carried by rail. We stayed in motels where three dollars meant luxury—a clean room, a shower, a towel and clean sheets. As we crossed the Oregon border, we cheered wildly.

Once at home, I found I had received a principal appointment to West Point from Senator McNary, a first alternate appointment from Senator Steiwer, and notice from the military academy that I had failed to pass the physical examination. A day or two later I was cutting the lawn by the east terrace when my father walked out and asked me if I really wanted him to try getting a waiver of the eye defect from the War Department. I thought about it for a moment, then told him, "No."

Why this response after all the effort I had put into getting into the academy, much less the effort and sacrifices my mother and father had made to assist me. I cannot understand it to this day, but I was comfortable with that decision. Perhaps it was simply relief at being home after a rather lonely year away. I am inclined to think my answer a few weeks later would have been, "Yes." Whether the defect could or would have been waived, I have no way of knowing,.

Why did my father put the question to me? I am sure he did so only after long discussion with my mother. I think they were having second thoughts about whether I was really suited for life in the peacetime army. Bear in mind that this was the summer of 1937. While Hitler was a disturbing figure in European politics, the prospect of any conflict which would involve the United States then seemed remote. In any event, without further discussion, they accepted that response, wrote off their effort in support of my quest for an appointment to West Point. We never revisited that decision in later years.

CHAPTER 2

Leavening the student body at Princeton

With West Point out of the question, I had to make other plans for college. I applied to Reed College in Portland where a number of my high school friends had enrolled. However, in the course of the summer, Joseph A. Minott, a close friend of my mother and father and a graduate of Princeton, suggested that I should apply to that university. Mr. Minott had read in the Princeton Alumni Weekly of a new program under which the university planned to admit twenty students from southern and western high schools based on their high school records and an aptitude test. This was an effort to broaden the student body geographically and socially. I applied under this program and in a remarkably short time was admitted to Princeton with a scholarship and loan which covered my tuition and part of my room and board.

So almost by accident, I found myself admitted to a university I had never thought of attending, and not knowing a single member of my class. The scholarship, student loan, student employment and $50 per month from my family would just cover the cost of the first year. I should add that $50 per month was a sum my parents could ill afford at that time.

The admissions office forwarded parents of incoming freshmen a recommended list of clothing and supplies. My mother sewed name tags on everything from underwear to sheets. For clothing she took me downtown to M & H. H. Sichel, then a fine men's clothing store on West Park Street, where I was fitted out with two jackets, several pairs of trousers, and a combination dinner jacket and tail coat. Mr. Sichel, a very large man with a commanding figure, suggested one jacket as "the latest style from Hollywood," and I remember my mother's crisp response, "Certainly not, Mr. Sichel!" In those days at Princeton, students wore coats, ties and slacks to class, dinner jackets or white tie and tails to formal parties.

That summer of 1937 I worked as a copy boy on the Oregon Journal in the old Journal tower on Broadway. I was paid $12 or $.27 an hour for a forty four hour week and thought it a handsome salary. With my first paycheck I bought a dark, slightly scratchy palm beach suit for $12.

Joan McKee was planning to go to Sarah Lawrence College in Bronxville, New York. Joan was the daughter of Paul B. and Dorothy Jewett McKee. Paul McKee was the President of Pacific Power and Light Company, a subsidiary of Electric Bond and Share Company. The McKees had come to Portland in the early 1930s from Brazil where Mr. McKee had been a power company executive. They lived first in the Percy Smith house on upper Greenwood road in Dunthorpe, then moved to the old Eugene Rockey house on Radcliff Street in Riverdale. Joan had a Chevrolet convertible with a rumble seat which her father had given her in return for a promise not to smoke until she was twenty-one. Joan was the only girl or boy I knew of our age who had an automobile. She was about to drive back east to enter Sarah Lawrence College in Bronxville, New York. Driving with her was her cousin from Massachusetts, Jack Jewitt, and Gracie, a delightful widow, a friend of the McKee's from their South American days. They invited me to make the trip with them.

The trip east was more of an adventure than my spring trip west with Al Hampson had been. The front and only seat of the Chevy was too narrow for three to sit comfortably so the three young members of the party rotated hourly driving and into the rumble seat. We took a wrong fork in the road in Wyoming and ended up spending the night in Greybull, an unprepossessing village. The only hotel had a bar below on the ground floor, a long straight flight of stairs up to the second floor rooms which had doors open for ventilation with the entrance partly obscured by towels stretched across the doorway.

I remember little of the scenery and places we stopped except for Greybull and a late night stop in upstate New York at a beautiful white colonial inn which was almost entirely empty. We reached the east coast just days after it was stricken by the 1937 hurricane. We drove across Massachusetts where we stayed at the Jewett family home overnight. Joan and I then drove south into New York City via the Bronx River Parkway, the first divided highway I had ever seen, or was to see, until I reached the autobahns of Germany seven years later.

Journey's end was Bronxville, a suburb of New York, where Bessie and Jack Scheetz, Joan's aunt and uncle, lived not far from Sarah Lawrence College. Jack Scheetz worked for United Airlines in an administrative capacity which still kept him in the air a good deal of the time. He had been a fighter pilot in the Army Air Force during World War I. Bessie was Dorothy McKee's sister and a lovely person. She and Jack took me in like a member of the family and for the next four years provided a home for me whenever I came into town from Princeton. After a day or two in Bronxville I took the train to New York, transferred from Grand Central to the Pennsylvania Station, and went on to Princeton Junction and the shuttle train which took me from the main line the three miles to Princeton.

*

In 1937 Princeton had some 2200 undergraduates, our entering class numbering about 600. The town had a small commercial section centering on Nassau street which fronted the campus. The University buildings were relatively compact, situated within a rectangle bounded by Nassau Street, University Place, Walker Road and Lake Carnegie. Nassau Hall, a brick and stone structure which faced Nassau Street, was built in the 1760s and ransacked by the British during the battle of Princeton in the Revolution. The science buildings were on the north side of Walker Road. The eating clubs for upper classmen lay along both sides of Prospect Street, which extended north from Walker Road. Freshmen and sophomores ate in the Commons, a large Gothic structure at the corner of Nassau Street and University Place. The earliest dormitories standing were built shortly after the Civil War; the most recent were collegiate Gothic structures built in the 1920s.

I was assigned a large room in the top of an old yellow painted wood three story frame building known and addressed as 36 University Place. This room was really quite handsome with dormers looking out in two directions through the treetops over the campus. Assigned to rooms in the same building were Chile Graham, Bob Wallace, and Ray Mount from Lawrenceville School, Dick Hager from Cantebury School, George Muehlick from Pomfret School, Larry Ackard from a Denver high school, Lou Prince from Milton Academy, and Chico Alley from Exeter Academy. Alley was a football player and left during sophomore year.

Some days after my arrival, Chile Graham and Bob Wallace bought a gallon of tokay wine and had a party in their large room on the second floor. I drank more than my share and had a horrible two day hangover. To this day, I have never knowingly touched a bottle of tokay. Chile Graham's family lived in Chile, as you might suspect. He and Wallace were the leading lights of 36 University Place.

Ninety percent of the freshman class came from private prep schools, less than ten percent from public high schools. I recently read with interest George Kennon's description of his experience entering Princeton in 1921 (Memoirs, 1925-1950) in which he described his loneliness as a freshman coming from the midwest in 1921 and his inability to approach boys from the east. It was certainly true that my own social life, like his sixteen years earlier, was limited by the fact that I entered with no cadre of friends, had very limited resources and substantial student employment obligations. Despite this, I found making friends easier at Princeton than it had been at high school.

During that first year I earned my board waiting on tables in Commons. We were paid twenty five cents for breakfast, thirty five for lunch, and fifty cents for dinner. These earnings were credited against our charge for board. Each table seated eight persons and each waiter was assigned a table for the meal. We carried the place settings and the food on large stainless trays on one hand over the shoulder from the kitchen down a broad flight of marble stairs into the Commons Hall to the table assigned. One day I tripped going down the stairs while carrying a tray with eight bowls of soup, a pitcher of milk and a pitcher of coffee. Down I went with the whole load. Milk and crockery in every direction. We were charged with all breakage, and everything on my tray was broken.

Once I was settled in, I found classes interesting and, not surprisingly, the professors a good deal more impressive than the teachers I had previously encountered in high school. I thought I was doing pretty well. Mid term examinations were a shock. I received a poor grade in history, a subject in which I had expected to excel. I promptly consulted my history professor, H. W. K. Fitzroy, a cherubic, bald headed man, who went out of his way to explain what I had failed to do. Professor Fitzroy took a friendly interest in my progress, and though I never had another course with him, we had dinner from time to time. I learned rather quickly that many of the students in my class had a good deal better grounding in the classics than I did, and that some were a lot smarter than I was. My job was to catch up and keep up with them as best I could.

I stayed close to my books and close to Princeton, having neither time nor money to spare. I kept in touch with Joan and spent Thanksgiving and Christmas 1937 with her at the Scheetz house in Bronxville. During spring vacation she drove down to Princeton and we had lunch at the Nassau Tavern. In those days no student was allowed to have an automobile at Princeton. Getting out of town for any purpose meant taking "the shuttle" to Princeton Junction on the main line of the Pennsylvania Railroad and catching a train to either New York or Philadelphia.

My first two years I signed up for ROTC. Princeton had an artillery unit with horse drawn French 75s, and we galloped around the riding hall pulling caissons and guns behind four horse teams. Despite my previously noted jaundiced view of horses, I found that when a horse was part of a team it was quite limited in what he or she could do to me, particularly if I rode the second team with a good rider mounted in front of me handling the first pair. My horse and its partner just had to follow.

The summer between freshman and sophomore year, my father got me a job with a U. S. Corps of Army Engineers flood control project near Independence, Oregon. Another boy from Portland, John Wood, and I were checkers. Our job was to weigh trucks loaded with rock before they dumped their load down the Willamette River bank to protect it from erosion. We recorded the weight of each load on tally sheets, and at the end of the day we added the totals and turned them into the Corps office in Salem. We had no adding machine. The figures were formidable, and neither of us were too careful with our addition.

One day the colonel in charge of the project called John and me into his office in Salem after work. He looked at us coldly for a moment, then said that he had checked our reports and found none of them accurate. We had until nine o'clock the following morning to redo all the reports we had made to date correctly. Otherwise we were fired. We worked all night, adding each set of reports three times until they agreed, turned them in at seven o'clock, and headed back out to the river.

This was a federal WPA project. Unemployment was in the double digits. The truck drivers earned $75 per month for an eight hour day, five day a week, and they were glad to get it. The Willamette River at this point wound through large hop fields which were alive with hop pickers, men, women and children, all at work in the hot sun. Some of the younger ladies dispensed their favors in the course of the day to their male counterparts, taking tickets in return which the ladies then turned in for cash at the hop office at the end of each day.

During that summer I lived in a boarding house on South East Commercial street in Salem with an interesting group of other boarders including a young public health nurse, a powder man who had lost most of his fingers from cap explosions, and another government worker. The nurse was an attractive young lady in her mid twenties who took me on as a juvenile to be educated, and we dated throughout the summer. Friday evenings, I caught the Greyhound bus home after work, spent the weekend at home, and bussed back to Salem Sunday evening. Our landlady fed us breakfast and dinner and provided sandwiches for lunch. Salem was hot, and the little house was stifling. There was no such thing as air conditioning, but we were used to the heat and managed nicely.

*

Sophomore year at Princeton I lived by myself in a single room on the second floor of Pyne Hall. I switched from waiting on tables at Commons to working the four to twelve shift in the Sandwich Shop three days a week. This arrangement gave me free meals at the shop. The juke box pounded out popular songs constantly, especially the one with the refrain "She kicked the bucket, buck, buck bucket." Some sharp-eared students claimed they could hear an "f" instead of a "b," and quarters flowed into that machine day after day. I still hear that refrain when I think of the Sandwich Shop. It was a better arrangement for me in terms of time, but not gracious living, and I was largely cut off from the friends I had made during freshman year in 36 University Place.

I also worked on the parking squad at football games and sold laundry contracts for the University Laundry, a privately owned business not connected with Princeton University. Three competing laundries: University, Blakely, and a third, the name of which I have forgotten, all provided substantially the same service. During the first few days in the fall when students were returning to school, the laundry candidates hawked term laundry contracts wherever students congregated, giving a pitch about the excellence of their service. As I have mentioned before, I disliked selling, but the four top sophomore salesmen became junior managers with a cut on all contracts sold by sophomores, and so I gritted my teeth and won one of those four spots. The top junior manager in sales then became the senior manager his senior year and received a cut on all contracts sold. This position I earned for my senior year.

During sophomore year I stayed at Princeton most weekends. Christmas vacation I spent at Princeton, but went up to Bronxville Christmas Eve and day with Bessie and Jack Scheetz. Joan had flown back to Portland for Christmas. In the spring of 1939, I went to Poughkeepsie for a weekend at Vassar with Augusta Davis, a Portland girl whom I had met on the Union Pacific train, City of Portland, coming east the previous fall.

That spring we also had Bicker Week, the annual occasion when the upper class eating clubs sent emissaries around to the sophomore living quarters to interview them and determine whether to invite them to join their club. Sophomores had the privilege of forming what were called "ironbound" groups which meant they would only join a club if all members of the group were accepted. John Sease, Chile Graham, Bob Wallace, George Muehlick and I formed an "iron-bound" and went to Dial Lodge where I was given a club managership paying most of my club expense including board. I must say that I enjoyed Dial Lodge. Being served by an experienced waiter with congenial company and comfortable surroundings was a delight after my first year of waiting on tables in Commons and my second year of serving up fast food to myself at the sandwich shop. The club also allowed members to invite faculty members to dine with them, and I took advantage of this opportunity.

Fraternities were prohibited at Princeton. Eating clubs were the functional equivalent of fraternities and were subject to criticism as exclusive and expensive, as indeed they had been in Woodrow Wilson's day as president of Princeton. Wilson attempted to abolish them but failed. It was certainly true that in my day there was a social hierarchy, Ivy being considered the most exclusive, and Tiger Inn the choice of major athletes, but the majority of the clubs appeared to be much the same in facilities and social composition. Most members of the class joined a club, and there was even an eating club for those who were not invited to join or refused to join one of the formal clubs. As far as I could see, the eating club system was closely regulated by the university and provided a workable breakdown of the undergraduate body into small social groups while avoiding most of the problems associated with the fraternity and sorority systems in other universities. Certainly there was none of the hazing business frequently seen in fraternities.

Early in the summer of 1939, Joan McKee, who had decided to transfer from Sarah Lawrence to Stanford, drove west in her Chevy, bringing with her two classmates, Clarissa Hager and Jane Phillips, who spent a week in Portland with the McKees. Evie Mills was having a dance at her family home on Palatine Hill, and Joan telephoned to ask me which girl I wanted to take to the dance, the blond or the redhead. Not knowing either, I picked the redhead, perhaps because my mother had always teased my father about some redhead he had squired about during the years she was fending off his courtship. I called for Clissa at the McKee house in Riverdale and drove her back to our house to introduce her to my mother and father before we went on to the party. Somehow we lost the cigarette lighter in the Buick that night. It was never replaced, and my mother would remind me of this delinquency from time to time for the rest of her very long life.

Clarissa Hager was born in Colorado Springs and raised in Princeton, to which her family had moved in 1921. At Princeton, the Hagers lived in a large colonial house on Library Place. Her father, Wilfred M. Hager, Princeton '95, had been a rancher and investment banker. Her mother, also named Clarissa, was a great granddaughter of Jay Cook, one of the early "Robber Barons." Clissa attended the Holmquist School in New Hope, Pennsylvania, before Sarah Lawrence. She was a striking looking young woman five feet eight inches in height with a full head of red gold hair, a glowing complexion, and a beautiful figure.

The weekend following the Mills party, we went on a house party at Ariel, the McKee's summer cabin on the lake above the Ariel dam on the Lewis River in southwest Washington. As I recall, those present were Joan McKee, Dave Mersereau, Martha MacLeay, Joe Beach, Cleone Faire, Clarissa Hager, Janey Phillips, Patrica Hampson, Jack Jewett, myself and Mr. and Mrs. McKee. The cabin was located on a meadow which sloped down to the lake. I had been a guest at Ariel on other occasions, but this was an unusually lively weekend with games, swimming, boating and evenings around the campfire. Paul McKee was an exuberant man who enjoyed young people, as did his quieter but equally warm wife, Dorothy. That weekend I monopolized Clarissa as far as I could and determined to pursue the acquaintance when I returned to college.

When I did get back to Princeton that fall, I was unable to reach Clissa by telephone, but wrote her at Sarah Lawrence. She replied, and a week later invited me to a dance at Sarah Lawrence. From there on our relationship quickly developed. By the end of the year we were dating regularly either at Princeton, Bronxville or New York City. Clissa was a combination of fun and business. While she played hard, she made it clear that she intended to be a scientist and that her studies were a primary concern. It seemed to me that she always had some experiment going which made it necessary for her to get back to Sarah Lawrence on time. She wore high heels on dates with me, and I can still hear the click click of those heels as she walked the flagstones paths of Princeton with me. I was immensely proud to be her escort.

During my junior and senior years I roomed with John Sease and Larry Ackard at 317 Foulke Hall, in an elegant suite in one of the newer collegiate Gothic dorms with a fine view over the campus. Even better, our door was just opposite the common bathroom and showers for that floor. Larry, a music major, had a piano in our common sitting room and provided a musical background for our studies. We each had a small adjoining bed room with our desk, chair, book case, and bed. John Sease was a chemistry major. His family lived in New Brunswick, New Jersey. His father, Dr. Virgil Sease, was a research chemist with DuPont, working at that time primarily on color photography. Some weekends when Clissa came down to Princeton we went over to the Sease house in New Brunswick, and Dr. Sease took color photographs of Clissa by the dozen because of her bright red hair and contrasting clothing. The Seases had a handsome Georgian brick house with a lovely garden tended by Mrs. Sease.

The spring of 1940 Clissa came down for house party weekend at Dial Lodge. Undergraduates were allowed to have automobiles at Princeton on that particular weekend, and John Sease had his family car. A group of us went off on a picnic. The boys were all drinking beer. Clissa was drinking coke so she was selected to drive. Driving an unfamiliar car, she managed to bump into a tree while parking off the road. Fortunately, no damage was done to the Sease bumper.

Clissa's much older sister, Janet Fisk and husband Arthur, had an apartment on East 52nd street in New York City where Clissa spent the night whenever she came into town. There was a small basement flower shop close by, and I regularly bought a single rose to pin to her coat. I had purchased a second-hand chesterfield overcoat with a shiny velvet collar from the janitor at Pyne Hall for twelve dollars and felt that I was resplendent. Janitors at Princeton frequently acquired items of clothing from impecunious students who needed ready cash. From the same source I acquired a silk top hat and later an opera hat which could be folded and carried in a suitcase.

One May weekend when Clissa came down to Princeton we went canoeing on Lake Carnegie, which bordered the campus below the athletic fields. We had a picnic along the bank in a wooded section. I captured a large turtle, and, while I was holding up my prize, he, or she, excreted vigorously on my trousers. After mopping up, we resumed paddling and were attacked by several angry ganders who resented our presence. It was a lovely afternoon notwithstanding these traumatic events, and subsequently both of us came down with poison ivy.

*

Athletics were an important but not predominant part of undergraduate life. The various university teams competed almost exclusively with other Ivy League eastern universities including Harvard, Yale, Dartmouth, Cornell, Columbia, Pennsylvania, NYU, Army, and Navy, all major academic institutions. Already such eastern teams were rarely competitive with large midwestern and southern universities. Princeton fielded varsity teams in nineteen different sports, plus clubs which pursued five additional intercollegiate sports. In addition, the university had an extensive intramural athletic program. Participation in athletics was encouraged but not required. Early in freshman year I had wandered into the gymnasium while exploring the campus and saw fencing going on in the gallery. It looked interesting, and I signed up.

I earned freshman numerals and continued fencing as an upper classman. The coach was an old Belgian, Monsieur Pirotte. He was then in his sixties, always had liquor on his breath, and could take the measure of any of us at any time. With a flick of his wrist he could send one's epee, foil, or saber spinning across the floor. I think of him as a very excitable, slightly shabby version of Agatha Christy's M. Poirot.

During my junior year the Princeton epee team, of which I was one of three members, won the intercollegiate championship. For this we received major letters, a six inch orange P on a heavy black sweater together with a small gold tiger embossed with a black "P' for a watch fob. Winning a major letter was a milestone, the apex of my athletic career. I wore that sweater rain or shine irrespective of temperature for the first month. Our trips to fencing meets at various eastern colleges were always great adventures. Following the Yale meet that year, I spent the weekend with Dave Mersereau. We had dinner at Dave's fraternity house and my raincoat was stolen. I had a cold, coatless trip back to Princeton.

In planning my schedule for the junior year in the spring of 1939, I dropped ROTC. I disliked the horses and was bored with the program. I also had plenty to do keeping up my studies and student employment. Dropping ROTC was hardly a prudent move. Hitler had taken over the German government in 1933

6. Two skiers: Bobby Kohler,   7. One soldier: Jack at CMTC
Ginny Rupp. Mt. Hodd, 1935   Fort Lewis, WA July 1935.

8. The Princeton fencing team in 1940. Standing: Sutton, Wood,
Brown, Lockart, Coach Pirotte. Seated: Trattler, Rimbault,
Zaugg (Capt.), Beatty. Dudley. Missing Flanagan, Green, Orteig.

obtaining from the Reichstag the power to rule by decree. He had promptly dismissed Jews from the public service, barred them from universities and from the professions. He reoccupied the Rhineland in 1936 in violation of the Versailles Treaty. He was rearming Germany, and in the fall of 1938 came the disastrous Munich Agreement by which he obtained the Sudetenland and subsequently swallowed the remaining portion of Czechoslovakia.

I was concerned about Hitler from the start and followed what was going on in Europe, but for some reason I did not make the logical connection between the possibility of war and being drafted into it. In September 1939 Hitler attacked Poland. Great Britain and France went to war in accordance with their previous guarantees to Poland. Poland was quickly crushed by the German Army assisted by the Russians. The two victors then divided that unfortunate country between them in accordance with their "Non Aggression Pact." On May 10, 1940, Germany launched its blitzkrieg into The Netherlands, Belgium, and France.

That was the end of my junior year, and as I was driving a new car west to Portland for another Portland purchaser, the British were evacuating the British Expeditionary Force and the First French Army from Dunkirk. The collapse of France followed. When I reached home, I found my father had in hand orders to return to active duty. He had been assigned as executive officer, the second in command, at Watervliet Arsenal, just north of Albany, N. Y. A few days later he left by train for the East. My mother, sister Pug, and the family furniture, were scheduled to sail from San Francisco by army transport through the Panama Canal and thence to Boston.

Our family finances were in even worse shape than I had imagined. The recession of 1937 within the Great Depression had finished off my father's small investment company. He had then gone to work as a salesman for E. A. Pierce & Co., but the investment business continued in the doldrums. By the spring of 1940 the mortgage payments were delinquent and a number of current accounts were unpaid. The roof leaked. The real estate market was flat, and the house could not be sold without substantial repairs.

My mother and I allocated some money to each of the bills in arrears along with a note saying that the balance would be sent as soon as possible. My mother and father had already decided to let the house go for the eight thousand dollar mortgage which was held by Douglas Nichols. Mr. Nichols had offered to let them defer payments until such time as they could resume them. My parents concluded renting the house was not feasible until repairs were made. They had no funds to make repairs, and they would be too far away to supervise them in any event.

This was a difficult decision The house and property cost approximately twelve thousand to build and was probably worth thirty to fifty thousand by the end of the war, and seven or eight hundred thousand by the 1990's. It was their sole remaining investment, a full acre completely landscaped with an unrestricted view of Mt. Hood. Nevertheless it was a sound decision to let it go. They could not have kept the house up and managed it from such a distance, and they could not have afforded to maintain it after the war. When my mother and sister left for San Francisco, I cleared up what remained to be done, turned over the keys to Mr. Nichols and then drove the family car east to Watervliet.

*

Watervliet Arsenal, established in 1807, was the oldest arsenal in the United States. It was situated several miles north of Albany, New York, opposite Troy, which lay on the east bank of the Hudson. In the extensive brick factory buildings the Ordinance Department of the Army built guns ranging from 75s and 105s for the artillery to sixteen inch guns for the Navy. The officers' quarters were spacious, high ceilinged, brick duplex structures in a park-like setting with huge old deciduous trees. With all the family furniture in place the interior seemed much like an expanded version of home and the residential area like a large park.

Powerfully impressed with our difficult financial situation, I had written Princeton earlier that summer to say that I would not be able to return for my senior year. Because of the move east I had not been able to work during the summer, and after adding up what I would receive from my laundry manager ship, loans and scholarship, I would still be at least five or six hundred dollars short. I received by return mail a letter from Dean Hermance saying that he was confident that something could be worked out and that by all means I was to return for my senior year and see him when I arrived. On the strength of that assurance, I took the train down to Princeton after spending two weeks at the Arsenal.

When I arrived at Princeton, I went directly to the Dean's office and reported in. His secretary sent me on to the Bursar's office where I found that my scholarship had been increased by a thousand dollars, considerably more than I needed to get by. I returned to the Dean's office and told him I had enough money as manager of the laundry with only half that much. He patted me on the back, saying,
"Take it and enjoy yourself this year. Have your girl down for some football games." And so I did.

*

During my freshman year I had began writing poetry, and I continued to do so throughout college. During my last two years the southern poet, Allen Tate, was Poet in Residence at Princeton. I saw a good deal of him although I was never able to schedule one of his classes. He reviewed some of my material and made suggestions on both style and substance. The process of writing and rewriting poems was good training for me. I had a number of poems published in the Nassau Lit, the Princeton literary magazine, and became an editor. During the war Tate included three of my poems in an anthology which he edited entitled *Princeton Verse Between Two Wars*.

My major, the last two years, was the School of Public and International Affairs, renamed post war The Woodrow Wilson School. This was then described as a combination of the politics, economics, and history departments. In my junior year we studied local government in northern New Jersey, an interesting introduction to seamy politics. Mayor Haig of Jersey City was then a national figure typifying the city boss and local corruption. We made field trips up to Bergen, the county seat, and interviewed local political figures.

While in college I had no clear idea of what I wanted to do post graduation. Graduate school never entered my mind. However, I had some thought of going into personnel work and selected labor relations in the shipbuilding industry as a topic for my senior thesis. In this study I planned to compare labor relations during the first War with the buildup we were experiencing in 1940-41. In the course of the study, I visited all the major shipyards on the East Coast, interviewing management and union leaders. Professor J. Douglas Brown, later chairman of the Department of Economics, was my thesis advisor. He was a quiet, thoughtful man who, as I recall, let me run with my project without undue interference. As I review it sixty-seven years later, the thesis is so tightly organized that I suspect I had more guidance than I now recall.

In September 1940, as the European war spread, Congress enacted a one year draft for military service. My number was one of the first pulled out of the fishbowl which was used for the first drawing. The law permitted deferment of students with one year to complete college, so I applied for and obtained deferment until graduation in June of 1941.

Christmas vacation, 1940, Clissa and I spent with my family at Watervliet. My sister was finishing her senior year at Emma Willard School and living at home. Albany was a social place and vacation was lively. We were invited to parties at the homes of new friends my mother and father had made. One friend of my father's, Henry Elliot, a former army officer, was a well-to-do manufacturer with a dozen children. These included a very attractive daughter, Dorothy, whom I squired to several dances after Clissa had returned to her mother's for the balance of vacation.

*

During my senior year, 1940-1941, the war in Europe was uppermost in our minds. France had fallen, The Battle of Britain had taken place. Rommel's Africa Corps threatened the British life line in the Mediterranean. Britain stood alone. Our senior class emblem, or logo, printed on the breast pocket of our white 1941 beer jackets, showed the world as Hitler's head, a bomb with a burning fuse sticking out of the side, and the Princeton tiger in a steel helmet, clutching a club, sitting on top. I was convinced we had to enter the war, but not all students favored intervention. There was a strong chapter of America First active on the campus. Both the Daily Princetonian and the Nassau Literary Magazine editorially supported intervention. Fred Freed and I wrote a column in the Lit called the Polit Board in which we advocated intervention. The Lit carried articles pro and con intervention, as did the Daily Princetonian. Two of Princeton's popular history professors, "Buzzer" Hall and "Beppo" Hall engaged in back-to-back debates on whether the United States should intervene, Buzzer favoring and Beppo opposing. The crowds filled the hall, standing room only.

I had entered Princeton a Republican reflecting the politics of my family, and I left a New Deal Democrat. This transition undoubtedly occurred as a result of reading in my major courses and discussion with the classmates with whom I associated. I became convinced that the federal government had a responsibility to see that the nation's economic activity was conducted in the nation's interest. Princeton had a strong tradition of "Princeton in the Nation's Service," and I am sure that this affected my thinking. While my economic views were undeveloped, I began to view government as an instrument by which the interests of all the people can be served, a Federalist as opposed to a Jeffersonian view of the American Constitution. Like many others, I have become convinced over the years that a market economy is the only workable industrial economy in the long run, but a market economy requires political limits and vigorous regulation to prevent abuse and monopoly, a position amply substantiated by the Great Depression and the market collapse of 2008.

When graduation week came that spring of 1941, the Seases invited Clissa and my mother and father to stay at their house in New Brunswick. The weather was sunny and hot. I was named class poet and read the class poem to the assembled multitude in front of Nassau Hall following the speech of our class valedictorian. My theme, "This generation has a meeting place with destiny," was lifted from a speech by FDR, who used the more felicitous word, "rendevous." Saving the world tends to be a recurrent theme in American life. In any event, we thought war was close at hand. ROTC graduates were ordered to active duty. Many of the rest of us had dates with our draft boards. The poem was not an artistic success, but it reflected the passion of the times, and I delivered it with all the force I could muster.

*

I have been back to Princeton on few occasions. Had we remained in the East, I would have gone to reunions and seen more of my classmates. Settled in Oregon, the distance and my occupation made this impractical. Nonetheless, my attachment to the university has been real. I learned much at Princeton, and I enjoyed every part of it. The beauty of the campus, the wealth of tradition, the intellectual stimulation in classes, and the quality of instruction were a constant pleasure. It was a great experience.

Following graduation Clissa spent a week with me at my family's quarters in Watervliet. We had exchanged class rings New Year's Eve, 1940, in a way which was novel if not traditionally romantic. We were having a beer at a restaurant in Times Square as we waited to see "Happy New Year" appear in the lights on the Flat Iron Building, I looked at her class ring, slipped it from her finger, and tried it on my third finger. For the life of me I could not get that ring off my finger that night. When I got back to school, I sent Clissa a Princeton seal ring in exchange. We knew that I would be in the service for at least one year and probably more. I had no prospect of a job beyond that. Clissa intended to begin graduate school at Columbia in the fall and pursue a career in science, whatever happened to me. The future was simply indeterminate. We were in love but not engaged.

8.5. Princeton Class of 1941 Logo, designed by Brooks Wall & Robert Leibowitz, stamped on our beer jackets. It marked three victories over Yale, saw the world as a bomb, the fuze lit, FDR in Hitler's hair and us off to war jauntily armed with a club and wearing a WW I tin helmet. That summed it up as well as any speech.

CHAPTER 3

Into the Air Corps and out to the Field Artillery

I reported to the Watervliet Draft Board for induction July 7, 1941. I was designated as the draftee in charge of the Watervliet contingent of ten or eleven young men. We boarded the train for New York City where we were transported to Fort Jay in New York Harbor. At Jay we were given physical examinations, and then sent on to a reception center at Fort Dix, New Jersey. At Dix we were assigned to provisional companies of 200, issued uniforms, given inoculations and started on a daily routine of close order drill in the morning and fatigue duty in the afternoon. For me, fatigue duty consisted of painting green an endless number of garbage cans. My platoon drill instructor was a lean, tough regular army corporal who was the closest thing to God we saw at Dix. Every few days orders were posted for one of the other companies, dispatching them to Army bases in various parts of the country. No orders were posted for us. It was rumored that we were lost. One weekend I got a pass and rode the bus to Princeton. I walked around the campus and had a beer in the Nassau Tavern. It was a world to which I no longer belonged.

On our first payday I was credited with $21 for the month, from which a charge for laundry was deducted. We had been issued both cotton summer and winter wool uniforms. The quality of that first issue of wool clothing was never matched in any later issue during the war. Finally, after six weeks, our company was put on a train and shipped south. Two days later we arrived at an army air force base, Cochran Field, Macon, Georgia. Cochran Field was then providing basic training for Royal Air Force cadets pursuant to an agreement made by President Roosevelt and Prime Minister Churchill. The field was actually located about ten miles north of Macon in rolling orchard country. The post newspaper always referred to it as "Cochran Field, which was only a peach orchard x months ago, commanded by Lieutenant Colonel D. D. Fitzgerald." It was a busy post. Aircraft landed and took off from morning to night. The roar of motors was constant. Platoons of RAF cadets wearing their blue uniforms made their slow arm swinging march from barracks to planes to study hall hour after hour.

We draftees were housed separately from other army personnel on the base who were organized into "School Squadrons." These squadrons maintained the aircraft. A headquarters squadron maintained the paper work and Lieutenant Colonel D.D. Fitzgerald. We draftees were called a "provisional squadron," and several elderly air force reserve officers were placed in charge of us. They gave us heavy doses of close order drill and extensive assignments of kitchen police more familiarly known as KP. Some days later we were assembled in a large hall and addressed by a captain who told us that we had been assigned to the Air Force by mistake. The Air Force did not accept draftees. However, we had been assigned to the 322nd school squadron, and they had no choice but to keep us. Presumably the paper work to rectify the mistake was beyond them. It was the captain's strong recommendation that if we wanted advancement, or anything other than kitchen police and odd jobs, we had better enlist for three years in the regular army.

The reaction was predictable. A handful enlisted. The rest said, "To hell with the Air Force. We'll do our year of service and that's that."

At the time Congress was considering legislation to extend the draft beyond October 1941 as well as the service of those already drafted into service. The outcome of the legislation was uncertain. The words "OHIO" appeared on walls and latrines, the acronym for "Over the hill in October." After five or six weeks of debate Congress passed the draft extension by one vote. The provisional squadron was dissolved and the draftees were distributed among the air force school squadrons. Because I had been to college, I was designated a clerk, attached to headquarters, and assigned for a short time as the assistant to the post chaplain, a job I ditched as quickly as possible. I was reassigned as assistant to the public relations officer, Captain Battle.

The captain was a big, amiable, reserve officer who allowed me a free run at writing stories about the post and its activities, as well as the use of a staff car and driver to go back and forth to Macon with news releases. His orders to me were, "Just make sure Colonel Fitzgerald's name is used as often as possible in every story." I did. Nearly every day I rode in style sitting in the back seat of a khaki sedan headed for Macon bearing stories for the local newspaper. The guards at the post gate, unable to distinguish through the window the difference between my garrison cap and that of an officer, saluted as I passed. I gravely returned their salutes and enjoyed the moment.

Captain Battle had an attractive young secretary who did the typing for me. This left me free to wander the post and follow the activities of the RAF cadets, the only exciting activity on the post aside from an occasional crash. They marched everywhere, singing as they did so. Their favorite was an Australian song which began with the words "There's a troopship a-leaving Bombay" and ended with the chorus, "There'll be no promotion this side of the ocean, so cheer up my lads, fuck 'em all." Each graduating class was flown back to Britain via Newfoundland and Greenland to the ongoing air battle in which many would lose their lives.

I had never lived in the South before, and I was appalled by the effective subjugation of Negro citizens. They huddled in the back of the bus, used separate facilities, and were treated essentially as non-human by the local community and by men in the service. I never saw a crack in the white facade. As time went on, my acute distress at their plight was worn down by constant association with prevailing attitudes which were beyond my power to alter under the circumstances. The armed forces were strictly segregated throughout WW II and remained so until President Truman integrated them by executive order in 1948.

Saturdays I usually went into town and had dinner at a steak house which also had good seafood. One evening I found a pearl in my oyster. Sundays I usually walked by myself in the countryside. Occasionally I went to the local Episcopal Church in an unsuccessful effort to establish some civilian contact. I was housed in a standard two story military barrack, 40 men to a floor. The radios blared out Western music from dawn to dusk. The favorite song, as I remember, was "You are my Sunshine."

I was recruited by the post intelligence officer to be one of his operatives charged with watching for any subversive activity or sabotage among the troops. I saw none beyond opposition to the extension of the draft. He later questioned me about a draftee who had become a friend of mine. He was an interesting chap who had gone to Spain and enlisted in the Abraham Lincoln Brigade of the Republican Army then fighting Franco's troops and the Germans and Italians assisting them. He had considerable combat experience and wisely got out of Spain before the Republican forces surrendered. I never found him ideological other than having a profound dislike of fascists and a willingness to fight them in anyone's army. I gave him a clean bill of health and suggested the army ought to take advantage of his experience and promote him.

In due course I was promoted to corporal, then to sergeant with accompanying increases in pay. As a sergeant, I ventured to write Clissa that perhaps we could now afford to get married. This met with a distinct lack of enthusiasm. Clissa was completing her MA in zoology at Columbia and planning to obtain a Ph.D. in physiology. She had no interest in exchanging those plans for the life of a camp follower. During college she had made clear her continuing interest in chemistry, and that she intended to pursue it. My response had never been negative, but I had no exposure to women working full time in a profession other than teaching school, and I thought of school teachers as different from wives and mothers with whom I was familiar. I suppose my Aunt Margaret Sharp fell into that category, but I thought of her as a special case. It is fair to say that I had no conception of a marriage in which both husband and wife were employed professionally or otherwise. I had, without knowing it, embarked on a long learning curve.

December 4, 1941 Cochran Field received a sabotage alert from higher headquarters. Orders required that all the planes be drawn into tight parks on the air field. Post personnel was formed into special guard units to protect the aircraft. This same alert apparently was given to Army units at home and overseas. On Sunday the 7th I took a long walk in the woods adjacent to the field. When I returned to barracks the middle of the afternoon, the radio was blaring news of the attack on Pearl Harbor. We sat on our bunks listening with astonishment. Within hours we were at war with Japan. Two days later Hitler recklessly declared war against the United States, thereby insuring our immediate involvement in the war in Europe. So, we were in the war, and OHIO vanished from latrine walls and draftee conversation.

*

Following the extension of the draft, I had decided that I had better obtain a transfer to another branch of the service so I could go to Officer Candidate School. My eyes were not up to Air Corps standards for flight cadet school, and I had no interest in becoming an Air Corps administrative officer. I discussed the problem by letter with my father. He found that the Fourth Motorized Division at Fort Benning, Georgia, was commanded by an old friend, Major General Fred C. Wallace. He learned from General Wallace that a transfer to the 42 Field Artillery Battalion of that division would be acceptable. General Wallace wrote me a note and invited me to come over to Fort Benning the first weekend in October, 1941 and talk to him about it. In a letter to my father the general said,

> I have already written to Jack to come over and talk it over next weekend. I have also given a resume of the regulations and if he wishes to transfer I will be delighted to approve it, of course. Here all he will have to do is to demonstrate the qualities that I know he has and obtain the recommendation of his BC. Having had some service I also do not believe he will have to wait the usual requirement of six months here, but will find out about that.

> If his CO should, and I don't believe he will, disapprove the transfer let me know and I'll try something else. I believe I will be able to help on that as I am sure that

> George Brett would never allow anyone to stand in a man's way to advancement. However I believe the application will be approved although we happen to be quite a little over strength right now. We are in the midst of assigning 465 who just arrived from Sill at noon.

> It was great to hear from you again and rest assured that I will do all I can. George joins me in very best to Jean and you, and I hope it will not be long before we have a glimpse of you again.

> Affectionately,

> Spec

General Wallace's note to me suggested that I come the first weekend in October. I obtained a pass and spent a pleasant weekend with him and Mrs. Wallace. When I returned to Cochran Field I applied for a transfer. Nothing happened. The first sergeant told me I was crazy. I had a good berth and would have an opportunity to be promoted to staff sergeant. The months passed. No transfer and no acknowledgment of my request. I inquired and was told that my request had been torn up without being forwarded. I resubmitted the request and was told that transfers out of the Air Corps were forbidden. I wrote my father and asked him to see what he could do.

My Aunt Margaret sent me a ring with three blue sapphires and two diamonds to use as an engagement ring. Thinking it was high time we formalized our engagement, I sent it off to Clissa in January, 1942, without prior warning. She wrote in reply expressing delight, and thereafter we both viewed ourselves as informally engaged. Clissa at this time was living in Bard Hall at Columbia and had embarked on studies leading to a Ph.D. in Physiology.

Meanwhile, my father had pursued an inquiry through the Chief of Field Artillery to determine why my request for transfer had not been forwarded. Air Force Headquarters in Alabama replied that the request had been lost in a fire. I submitted a third request. After further exchange of correspondence between various classmates of West Point, 1911, the request was approved, and Sergeant Beatty was transferred in grade of private to Battery A, 42nd Field Artillery, Fourth Motorized Division, at Fort Benning, Georgia. I packed my kit in a duffel bag, said good-bye with regret to Captain Battle's secretary, and left by bus for Fort Benning. At Benning I discovered that the Fourth Division had been moved to Camp Gordon at Augusta, Georgia, so I caught another bus and finally arrived at Gordon early in February 1942.

I was assigned to the battery survey section under an old regular army sergeant, Louis Reimer, who had come from the pre war 2nd Field Artillery regiment which had cadred the 42nd Field Artillery Battalion. Sergeant Reimer was chunky, weathered, gruff and hardworking. He used the old army style of third person speech in speaking with battery officers—"Would the captain wish the battery laid?" Sergeant Reimer's word was law to the men in his section, and he looked after us as his own as he soon demonstrated.

James Albert Quillian, a Georgian and graduate of Emery University, was another private in the instrument section and we quickly became friends. In a letter home dated February 23rd I wrote:

> "We are getting physical conditioning now—walls to climb, trenches to cross on logs, tank traps to go through, and long runs through the underbrush. Went to church at a very beautiful one—St. Paul's (Episcopal) in Augusta yesterday. A boy in the instrument section, Albert Quillian, took me there."

In March 1941 the Fourth Division Artillery had a quota of four candidates for Field Artillery School at Fort Sill, Oklahoma. Quillian and I applied along with a number of other enlisted men in other batteries and battalions. The first sergeant of A Battery took a dim view of such applications and assigned me to KP the afternoon I was to appear before the examining board. Fortunately for me, Sergeant Reimer discovered me in the kitchen when I was supposed to be at Division Headquarters.

"What the hell are you doing here?" he asked.

"The first sergeant ordered me to stay on KP." I told him.

"You get over to Division, I'll take care of the first sergeant. Get going."

I changed from fatigues into uniform as fast as I could and reported to Division Headquarters and the examining board.

On March 19 Quillian and I received orders to proceed to Fort Sill for duty as officer candidates reporting on April 7, 1942. Two years later Sergeant Reimer, then a master sergeant in a corps artillery unit, located our battalion in France and visited each of us, presumably to see whether his commissioned recruits were behaving themselves. In the old army way, he still spoke to me in the third person as he looked over my firing battery. After looking over the battery, he saluted and left, leaving me quite aware that we both knew I had been inspected and approved.

*

The Field Artillery School at Fort Sill, Oklahoma, like the Infantry School at Fort Benning, was an accomplishment of the small professional army during the lean years between the two world wars. Before World War I, American field artillery was relatively primitive in comparison with French artillery. During the first war, the United States Army grafted French artillery methods and organization into our system. We had, of course, been manufacturing 75 mm guns and 155mm howitzers for the French. Following World War I, the U. S. Army established a field artillery school at Fort Sill, Oklahoma and developed new weapons, new methods of organization. and new techniques of fire control. Most importantly, the artillery school and its infantry counterpart at Fort Benning, Georgia, developed and refined systems of training officer candidates in ninety day courses. With the defense buildup just prior to the outbreak of World War II, the Artillery School at Fort Sill began graduating weekly classes of second lieutenants capable of stepping into the position of a battery grade officer in any field artillery unit, ready for tactical training with troops

The curriculum was a shorthand version of teaching methods employed at the United States Military Academy at West Point. The officer candidates were divided alphabetically into sections in which we lived, ate and studied together. We rose at six in the morning, had reveille, breakfast, and were marching off to class by eight o'clock. We marched everywhere except to the latrine. Tactical officers supervised our behavior inside and outside of class. After dinner we studied until lights out. Faced with examinations the next day we crowded into the latrines and studied by their inadequate lighting into the early morning hours. The course was difficult, concentrated and exhausting, but it was well thought out, and every day was a progression. For all of us Officer Candidate School represented a way out of the enlisted ranks into the responsibilities and privileges of command.

The most exacting and most exciting part of the course was adjusting fire on the range. Despite hours of dry runs and verbal practice, the reality of locating a target through field glasses, then giving appropriate fire commands to an artillery battery hidden some distance to one's rear, was exhilarating. It is true that for the most part we fired 37 mm shells, but the suspense was just great as we waited to see whether we had figured our data and commands correctly. Finally, near the end of the course, we were allowed to adjust the fire of a battery of 105 mm howitzers, the standard light artillery piece of the new army. It was sensational when the shells went crump, and a cloud of dust and turf flew up close to the designated target.

The assistant instructors were drawn from graduates with the highest marks and ranged from good to excellent. The higher ranking instructors were more experienced officers. Their uniforms reflected the old horse artillery days—campaign hats, pink shirts, pink breeches, shiny riding boots, and Sam Brown belts. "Pink" in this context meant a light gray. The uniform coat was dark green. The blue dress uniform was not worn during the war.

Our last days at Sill were full of excitement. We went to the post exchange, where we were measured for our new uniforms. We purchased pink long trousers, not breeches, a dark green coat with brass buttons, an olive drab short overcoat and a garrison cap for dress wear, also cotton and wool shirts and trousers for service wear. Finally, we bought the shiny gold bars of a second lieutenant to pin to the shoulder straps of our dress coats and the collars of our service shirts. We speculated endlessly on where we might be assigned for duty. When the orders were finally published, Quillian and I were assigned to the 79th Infantry Division at Camp Pickett, Virginia. The 79th was in the process of being cadred by our previous unit, the Fourth Motorized Division.

CHAPTER 4

A green lieutenant in a new division

The graduates of Class 19 had ten days leave before reporting for duty to their new units. I took the train from Fort Sill, to Watervliet, and Clissa came up from New York to visit. We discussed getting married but did not fix a time. I was going to be tied up with a new job in a new division and she was busy with her studies at Columbia.

My father took me through the arsenal, showing me the various manufacturing divisions then turning out ordinance ranging from 105 howitzers to sixteen inch naval guns for the new battleships. They were then building the M3 or Grant tank, an awkward monster with a side-mounted 37 mm gun. I drove one for a few yards. I never saw one after that. The Grant tank was quickly replaced by the Sherman Tank, which was much faster and had a 75 mm gun. Part of this tour was made with Brigadier General Gillespie, the arsenal commander. My education in military niceties at Fort Sill had either not included, or I had not absorbed, the protocol for getting in and out of vehicles with superior officers. The junior officer is supposed to go first as General Gillespie explained to me when I said, "After you, sir," as we were getting into an automobile.

When leave was up, Clissa and I took the train down to New York, and I went on to Camp Pickett, Virginia. Pickett, named after the Confederate general who led the final rebel charge at

Gettysburg, was situated in a flat scrub timbered area, and was just being completed by a swarm of workmen. Quillian and I were assigned to B Battery of the 310th Field Artillery, to which we reported. Some days later, I was reassigned to Headquarters, 79th Division Artillery as aide to Brigadier General Augustus M. Gurney, the artillery commander. The division commander was Major General Ira T. Wyche, West Point 1911, a classmate of my father's. General Wyche probably suggested that General Gurney consider me for a vacancy Gurney had for an aide. I am certain my father did not suggest this, and it probably delayed my promotion to captain by a year. On the other hand, it did give me a year of experience at staff level that I would not otherwise have had. In any event I was not at all happy to leave a firing battery, and it was nearly a year before I was able to get back to one.

*

A division in World War I consisted of division headquarters commanded by a major general, two brigades, each commanded by a brigadier general with two infantry regiments per brigade and supporting artillery. These were called "square divisions." Shortly before World War II the division was reorganized to become "triangular," more flexible and reduced in size. The division was commanded by a major general, with a brigadier assistant division commander. The brigade was eliminated and the division had three regiments of infantry, each commanded by a colonel. Each regiment had three infantry battalions, a cannon company, an anti-tank company, and headquarters and service units. Each battalion had six rifle companies, a heavy weapons company, a headquarters company and a service company.

The division artillery was commanded by a brigadier general and consisted of division artillery headquarters, three battalions of light artillery (105 mm howitzers), and one battalion of medium artillery (155 mm howitzers). Each battalion of artillery had three batteries of four guns each, a service battery and a headquarters battery. In addition, the division had a reconnaissance troop with armored cars and light tanks, a quartermaster unit, a medical unit, and a battalion of combat engineers. In Europe anti-aircraft platoons were assigned to various division units as were tank detachments.

Technically a howitzer is a short barreled gun capable of high angle fire. Artillerymen ordinarily referred to their weapons as guns, irrespective of whether they were howitzers or guns. Some corps artillery units were equipped with long barreled 105 mm and 155 mm guns which had a greater range than the howitzers.

General Gurney was a quiet, introspective man who looked a bit like the Duke of Windsor. He never had a great deal to say and was certainly not demanding of my time. The division artillery executive officer, his second-in-command, was Colonel Lawrence H. Bixby, a rotund and competent officer who had earned his commission from the ranks in World War I. I was assigned to assist the division artillery operations officer or G 3, Major Robert H. Safford, a graduate of West Point in 1936. On maneuvers First Lieutenant Jim Simpson, General Gurney's other aide, and I assisted Colonel Bixby by running errands and carrying messages down to the battalion commanders and up to Division Headquarters.

Major Safford was a tall, lanky officer, serious and responsible. His father was a jeweler, and the major had learned to take apart and reassemble clocks and watches. In consequence he could take apart and reassemble all our small arms blindfolded. His wife, Edith, was an attractive and spunky young lady. Edith had, according to her husband, enlivened the wives of junior officers when the major was a second lieutenant. She and several other ladies were standing in line at the Post Exchange waiting to be served. An older woman bucked the line ahead of Edith saying, "I am Mrs. Colonel Jones."

Edith Safford stepped back in front of Mrs. Colonel Jones saying, "I am Mrs. Lieutenant Safford," and I was here first."

General Gurney seemed very old to me at the time. In fact he was several years younger than my father and General Wyche, who were then fifty three. General Gurney's face was seamed and his movements were slightly hesitant like those of an older man. Colonel Bixby was very much alive and you had the sense that he enjoyed shaping young officers and monitoring their performance. He encouraged, needled, and slapped us down according to his evaluation of our work. In his own words he wanted us "on the ragged edge of mutiny but not one step beyond." He wanted us to express our views on any subject without hesitation, and he wanted orders carried out without hesitation.

One of our two liaison officers with the infantry was Captain William Allen. He had been an aide to General Wyche and was still dating Betsey Wyche, the general's attractive daughter. I saw the Wyches on several occasions at social gatherings for Division Staff. Meanwhile Jim Quillian was occupied with his battery duties, and I saw him rarely during the time I was an aide.

The division adjutant general in the summer of 1942 was Colonel Lamar Tooze, a reserve officer lawyer from Portland, Oregon. He was an acquaintance of my mother and father and a friend of my aunt Margaret Sharp. Whenever our paths crossed, the colonel inquired after my family. Colonel Tooze was reassigned and left the division before we went overseas. After the war he commanded the 104th (reserve) division headquartered at Vancouver, Washington.

By and large my duties as aide to General Gurney were those of a messenger. Such messengers receive attention beyond their years and rank from those in the general's command because they bear the commander's orders. Colonel Bixby carefully instructed us to keep this in mind and not deceive ourselves with respect to our own importance nor presume on the authority we represented. During artillery maneuvers I was largely employed in fire direction under Major Safford.

*

From the time I entered the army Clissa wrote me at least three letters a week, and this continued after we became engaged until July 27, 1942 when she wrote breaking our engagement and returning the sapphire ring.

> July 27, 1942. Dear Jack, I am terribly sorry to do this but after thinking everything over for a long while, I have decided to break our engagement, I am afraid that I just don't love you quite enough. I am sending the ring and other articles of jewelry you gave me back. Please don't try and make me change my mind as I have absolutely decided.
>
> Clissa"

This was a bolt from the blue. I wrote of my disappointment, asserted my continuing love, and hoped she would change her mind. She responded firmly.

> August 4,1942. Dear Jack, I knew you would try to dissuade me, and darling I wish you wouldn't because I really don't feel that I should change my mind. As for after the war, I will be here when you get back. If, as you say, you have to leave sooner than you expected, it's no use now. I am sorry,
>
> Clissa"

Also included was another sheet:

> Dear Jack, I am awfully sorry the letter didn't arrive with the ring, I sent them together, Its my honest decision. Of course I will write to you and also would very much like to hear from you. And of course you can keep the ring. I could never wear it again after.
>
> Love, Clissa"

I had written my family of this development, and my mother replied promptly.

"August 3, 1942. Dear Brother, Your letter arrived this morning telling of Clissa breaking your engagement. I can only say my darling how sorry I am that you have been hurt, but try and realize how much better it is for you both that if she is not in love with you it should come now when it is not too late. Life at best is not smooth sailing it takes lots of devotion on the part of each to ride the storms. It isn't what happens to us but how we take what happens" that counts. I know that you will rise above all this and out of it will come growth and not bitter feelings. Somehow in life we do not know when these things come in the end they work out for our own good. I have always felt that way and have seen it come to pass to others . . . . in the meantime, my love, "Be of good cheer". Everything will reach its right perspective in due time.

Mummy

This was good advice. It reinforced my determination to stay with my relationship with Clissa and see what might happen. I did not have any sense of bitterness, just deep disappointment. All of this communication was by letter. Long distance telephoning in wartime was difficult and expensive at best, and nearly impossible from an army camp with few external telephone lines. Clissa continued to write, though not as frequently, but in an affectionate tone.

*

In late August the 79th Division was shipped to Camp Blanding, a one division post near Gainsville, Florida, to begin a training cycle. I wasn't feeling very cheerful, but I was busy. I took comfort in the fact that Clissa was still writing which suggested there was some possibility that she might change her mind in the future. Colonel Bixby, who took a paternal interest in his young lieutenants and was aware that our engagement had been broken, busied himself arranging dates for me with the daughter of an infantry colonel of his acquaintance. I dutifully took the young lady out but had no real interest in pursuing the matter. I wrote Clissa regularly, as I had in the past, telling the various things I was doing. The division was going through a basic training cycle at that time. The artillery batteries were learning how to handle and fire their 105 mm howitzers, and I was kept busy carrying messages and instructions to the artillery battalion commanders. It looked like a long war, and we were just getting started.

At Blanding division artillery headquarters was primarily concerned with supervising the training of the firing batteries in fire control. The firing range was a large square section in the middle of a scrub forest and had high wood towers at each corner. Firing batteries were positioned outside the square, and their forward observers fired into designated targets within it. Higher commanders as well as battery officers observed the fire from the towers. This was hardly firing under field conditions, but it was the best that could be done with the limited area and flat terrain.

Joan McKee wrote saying she would be in Jacksonville in September and asked if we could meet. With a two day pass in hand I caught the bus to Jacksonville and met her. We talked, had dinner and then went to a dance at the officer's club. We had just switched to winter uniforms and trying to interpret new uniform regulations I attached my gold bars at the wrong part of the shoulder straps on my blouse, a matter which was called to my attention by a captain on the dance floor. I told the captain this was a new regulation. He must have gotten a chuckle over the general's aide who had his bars misplaced. Joan had heard from Clissa that she had broken our engagement. I told Joan that I was still determined to pursue Clissa so long as any opportunity to do so remained. She no doubt relayed this to Clissa when she later saw her in New York.

*

At Camp Blanding, the married officers whose wives had followed them lived in rented quarters in the nearby town of Gainsville. The batchelers and those whose wives had remained home lived in bachelor officer quarters on the post. However, the three generals each had a small two bedroom cottage on the post at Blanding which they used when they spent the night on the post. One weekend in November my mother and father came down to visit General and Mrs. General Wyche at their house in Gainsville. My father spent one night with General Wyche and their classmate General John P. Lucus, the V corps commander, at General Wyche's cottage. Following retreat I was summoned to meet with them as they were having a drink. I remember their kindly efforts to include me in the conversation, but not a word of what was said.

Some ten days, after my mother and father had returned to Watervliet, General and Mrs. Wyche told me they would be pleased to have Clissa stay with them at Gainsville if she would like to come to Florida at Christmas. I promptly passed the invitation on to Clissa. Her response was immediate.

November 23, 1942. Darling, Of course I am mad to come but I can't possibly make it for Christmas. I have to be with Mother until the 31. Would that make it too late? If necessary I could leave mother alone for a night and leave on the 30, but I would rather not. I do hope it won't be too late. Will rush out and post this immediately so won't have time to add more.

All love, Clissa

PS Think vacation is until 11 so we would have several evenings and weekend together—the 2 and as many other evenings as the Wyches would have me."

November 25, 1942. Dearest Jack, Can't for the life of me quite figure out how long it will take you to get my letter and send one back. Just know its much too long. Have to be studying for exams all this week and next too in addition to classes. Don't know how I'll concentrate. Probably just won't. Janie and I met our neuroanatomy professor while we were out getting a coke last night and he sat and chatted for hours-12:00 then we had to come home and finish working. He is a most amazing old gentleman tho. Would rather teach than do anything else in life. Darling am haunting the mailbox.

With all love, Clissa"

The Wyches reported that over New Years would be fine, and I passed that information on to Clissa by telegram.

November 27, 1942. Dear Jack, It was so sweet of you to send a telegram. Am so excited darling. Am a little upset about trains tho. Knew they weren't giving out any more reservations but didn't want Pullman anyway as don't have the money. However my next door neighbor says her family won't even let her try to come home to Chicago at Christmas as half the time you can't even get on the coaches and on a long trip you may get stranded anywhere. However am going to investigate the matter via Grand Central before collapsing. Do you know anything on the subject? Of course your father and mother got their reservations before the 15 of November. I just can't believe that it won't work itself out. It must.

See you soon!

With all love, Clissa"

November 28, 1942 Dearest Jack, They are still running the Champion so am going down as soon as possible to make my reservation.

All love, C"

The invitation and arrangements had obviously been worked out by my mother and Mrs. Wyche during my family's earlier visit, but Clissa must have indicated to my mother she would be glad of the opportunity. The Wyches were wonderful hosts, and I also stayed with them on those days when I could be off duty. The Wyches went to bed early leaving Clissa and me in front of the fire in the living room to talk and plan our lives to the extent that planning was possible. It was a short idyll but a beautiful one. Engaged once more, we planned a wedding in June of 1943.

*

At Camp Blanding, along with constant firing exercises and working through the prescribed corps training cycles, we had the usual ceremonial garrison duties. Retreat parade took place every night. Uniforms and equipment had to be spic and span, and shoes had to be polished. On one memorable occasion a division review was held for Lt. General Ben Lear, the army commander in the southeastern United States. General Lear was a tall, spare man who still wore a campaign hat on all occasions. Generals, I had learned, were allowed considerable leeway in their dress. General Patton carried this privilege to an extreme. Lear had acquired the nick name "You Hoo" from the press for disciplining draftees who called, "You Hoo" to some girls on a golf course in the days before Pearl Harbor.

On the day of the parade and inspection the entire division in dress uniform was drawn up on the parade ground, all thirteen thousand men: three infantry regiments with fixed bayonets, four battalions of artillery, a reconnaissance troop, engineers, quartermaster troops, armored units. Centered in front and facing them were the division and division artillery staffs. My position was one step to the side and two to the rear of General Gurney.

General Lear arrived in a staff car to our front, dismounted, exchanged some formalities with General Wyche. Then accompanied by General Wyche, General Lear in his campaign hat set off to inspect the ranks. He strode to the right flank of the division to begin the formal inspection. Here he was joined by a bitch in heat and a nondescript gaggle of dogs in attendance upon her. She followed General Lear all the way. We stood, rigid at attention in silent laughter, tears streaming down our cheeks. As the general passed though the ranks of the infantry, we could see the tips of the bayonets swaying as the mad humor of the scene became apparent in turn to each battalion and each regiment. It was a great day for the troops and worth every minute spent polishing boots and standing in the sun. I regret that I never asked General Wyche after the war how he felt on that occasion.

The latter part of January, Colonel Bixby called me into his office. He understood I was going to be married. I replied that I was. He asked when. I told him June. He looked at me for a moment and then said,

"If you expect to get married before the end of the war, you had better take leave before the middle of February and do it"'

We had already seen signs of a coming move and it was widely thought to be to England. Colonel Bixby left me with the clear impression that it would be overseas. I telephoned Clissa with this information. She said she was facing examinations critical to her Ph.D., but she could come down to Florida for five days on February 7th and then return to New York for her examinations. With the assistance of Mrs. Wyche, we scheduled the wedding for February 8, 1943 in the Presbyterian Church at Gainsville. The division was on alert at the time so the wedding party was limited to General and Mrs. Wyche, Colonel and Mrs. Bixby. and Major Safford, the best man. Mrs. Wyche had instructed the minister to omit "obey" in the service and was chagrined that he forgot to delete it. Neither Clissa nor I recalled hearing it. We had dinner at the Wyche's house and then spent the night at a Gainsville hotel where the Wyches had a bottle of champagne and flowers sent to our room. In the morning we caught a bus for Saint Augustine.

9. Cochran Field, Macon, Ga. September 1941. Basic training for RAF cadets who marched to class singing "There'll be no promotion this side of the ocean," and a brief life on the other side for many.

10. Wedding Bells. Feb. 8, 1943. Jack and Clarissa, Gainesville Florida.

11. Maj. Robert H. Safford, best man, caught at ease on Tennessee maneuvers.

Saint Augustine, the oldest city in the United States, was founded in 1565 by Pedro Menendez de Aviles. It was captured and burned by Sir Francis Drake in 1586, and possession passed back and forth between the British and the Spanish until 1821 when Florida was purchased by the United States from Spain. The population of St. Augustine in 1943 was approximately 12,000. The town was quiet. The streets were tree lined with many old houses including one which was claimed to be the oldest house in the United States. We stayed in a small hotel, white painted, two stories high. We saw the sights in a horse drawn carriage. We rented bicycles and cycled to points of interest, including one long ride to an alligator farm with the wind at our back. It was a very long pull back to town against the wind. We talked and planned. Part of the time Clissa studied for her exams. She came down with a cold the last day and I stood on the platform watching her train pull out for New York as she waved and sneezed.

*

The division left Camp Blanding within a month but not for overseas. We headed for Tennessee and maneuvers in the vicinity of Bell Buckle and Shelbyville. The countryside was mountainous. The roads were narrow, few of them paved. The fields were bordered with irregular stone walls. Many of the houses were scarcely more than shacks. It was a beautiful area, and the population was obviously dirt poor. A good part of the time it rained. In the evenings before chow, Colonel Bixby invited Simpson and me to crawl into his pup tent for a snort of scotch whiskey and discussion of the state of the artillery.

I received a letter from Allen Tate which mentioned that he and Mrs. Tate were living at Monteagle, Tennessee. I reached Allen by telephone, and he invited me to visit them the following weekend. The Tates had rented a house in a chatauqua park situated on the level top of Mount Eagle. The park had a formidable entrance gate, then a lengthy gravel drive forming a rectangle. Along the outer edge of the drive large shingled houses were set back among huge deciduous trees. Several assembly buildings were located in the center of the rectangle. As I remember, some of the trees were newly in leaf, but there was no sign of any other inhabitants than the Tates. Allen took me on a walk through the park to a place on its perimeter where standing on a granite ledge we looked out upon range after range of mountains to the west. It was a delightful weekend and a great change from sleeping in pup tents and eating out of a mess kit.

One of the curious aspects of my position as an aide was that I remember little of what I did. My duties were so varied, often so trivial, that each day blended into the next without any distinguishing features. On maneuvers I was again employed as a messenger from division artillery to the battalions and, occasionally, to division headquarters. I assisted Major Safford at S 3 when division artillery fire control was required, though these exercises were all dry runs because no firing range was available in this area. The exercises were designed to train commanders to move their troops in a coordinated way and to give those units experience in field conditions. Division Artillery Headquarters was responsible for how the four artillery battalions and their batteries performed. After each exercise the conversation at headquarters compared the qualities of the four battalion commanders and their subordinate units. Here also Major Safford had his thirtieth birthday which we celebrated with scotch whiskey at $1.30 a bottle. Simpson, my fellow aide, was reassigned to a firing battery, and I was increasingly anxious to be returned to one.

We completed maneuvers, reassembled at Camp Forrest, Tennessee, and then received orders to move the division to the Desert Training Center at Yuma, Arizona. Reasonably enough, we thought this meant we were destined for North Africa. Major Safford was transferred to the command of the 310th Field Artillery Battalion, relieving Colonel Bennett, and I was transferred to A Battery of the 310th as reconnaissance officer. A Battery was commanded by Captain John A. Hinkle, a big, beefy Virginian. Lieutenant Beaune was the battery executive officer. This grated a bit because I thought Beaune, who had been in my section in OCS, was something of a blowhard. However, within a few weeks Beaune was transferred to B Battery as executive under Jim Quillian who became B battery commander, and I became executive officer at A Battery. Captain William F. Thomas commanded C. Battery, Captain Charles Dorrier commanded Headquarters Battery, and First Lieutenant William Kopp had Service Battery.

According to the Field Artillery Guide and the table of organization, the battery commander, a captain, supervised the entire battery which consisted of four gun sections, a wire section, a fire direction center, a reconnaissance section, and a maintenance section. The executive officer, a first lieutenant, commanded the four gun sections. The reconnaissance officer, a first lieutenant, commanded the reconnaissance, survey and wire sections and a fourth officer, a second lieutenant, commanded the maintenance section and acted as an assistant to the executive officer. The total authorized strength of a firing battery was four officers and 110 enlisted men.

At Fort Sill and while training in the states, the executive officer (exec) stood about twenty yards behind the four gun sections with his instrument corporal, telephone operator and driver assisting him. He received fire missions from the division artillery fire direction center, the battery commander or the reconnaissance officer by wire or radio, and shouted his fire commands to the gun sergeants in front of him. When given a particular target, the executive consulted his firing tables contained in a paperback size manual and calculated the commands he should give to the guns. These calculations included direction to the target, the elevation and powder charge necessary to put the shell on the target with fine adjustments to account for differences in elevation between gun and target, and adjustment required by air temperature and wind conditions.

Following Tennessee maneuvers the army provided us with slide rules to speed up the process of calculation. When I was a school boy, my father tried to interest me in using a slide rule for mathematical calculations. I was never comfortable with a slide rule and never gave it a fair trial, preferring to work things out on paper. Now I found the slide rule essential to handling fire missions with speed. One difficulty was that the issue slide rule was relatively small and difficult to read, so I constructed a slide rule three times larger. It proved useful under stateside conditions, but too awkward to handle in combat.

We began to modify the text book approach prescribed as we became more experienced, using discretion as to the time and place. When we went into combat the modifications increased dramatically. As soon as the firing battery occupied a position, the guns were positioned where they could best be camouflaged and fire in the direction required. Battalion then surveyed in our position, if they had not already done so in advance. Where possible, we dug the guns into the ground so that only the muzzle was exposed. All personnel dug slit trenches. The ammunition likewise was dug in to protect it against counter battery fire. Camouflage nets were spread over guns and trucks.

The reconnaissance officer and the assistant exec became forward observers, spending most of their time with the first battalion of the 313th Infantry regiment, which with the 310th Field Artillery made up a combat team. We laid wire from each gun to the battery fire direction center, the executive's position. Giving fire commands by telephone rather than by shouting was obviously more accurate. Under combat conditions nearly all fire missions came from forward observers with the infantry by wire or radio to the battalion fire direction center operated by the Battalion S 3. Battalion fire direction in turn sent such fire missions to whichever battery was available and best situated to handle them.

The actual transmission of fire commands was frequently carried out by enlisted personnel at both battalion and battery when the officers were otherwise occupied. Seldom did a battery commander establish a command post from which he conducted the fire of the battery, although this was the usual practice in the States. In general the battery commander did whatever was needed to keep his unit up to the mark. He relieved the battery executive on occasion, looked to the ammunition supply, foraged for critical parts, and reconnoitered new battery positions with the battalion commander.

John H. Hinkle was in his early thirties, a reserve officer called to active duty. He knew his job and had a commanding presence. I had great respect for him, worked hard at my new job, and received all the support I needed from him. I found the firing battery reasonably well-trained and the howitzer chiefs of section competent, responsible NCOs. My task was to make the most of an adaquate firing battery, to make it the best in the battalion. Lieutenant Louis Pascal, the reconnaissance officer, was a thoughtful, hardworking chap, as was Lieutenant William. C. Delbridge, supposedly the assistant executive and actually our second forward observer.

One of the principal functions of the battery officers during the training cycles through which the division passed was teaching the enlisted men subjects ranging from war aims to anti-tank defense. In one of my early classes I reprimanded a soldier who was not taking notes on the subject although I had suggested that the men do so. After the class Sergeant Tillison Simpson, chief of the first section, came up to me.

"Sir, Private X can't read or write. Don't worry about him. We'll take care of him."

This I had not known. The incident impressed me with the importance of learning as much as I could about each man in the battery. I was also impressed with the way Sergeant Simpson quietly set me straight.

*

We arrived in Yuma, Arizona, the middle of August, 1943, and when we set foot in that desert, I found it hard to believe that human beings could survive in the heat, much less work in it. We were issued salt tablets and canvas water bags with orders to carry them slung over our shoulder at all times. We were required to take a siesta from noon to 3:00 PM each day for the first two weeks, which we did in our 110 degree tents.

However, the nights were cool, and in a matter of days, we became acclimated. Thereafter we maneuvered constantly, dragging our equipment through the hot sand. While we were in the desert, Jim Quillian was transferred from command of B Battery to liaison officer with the 1st Battalion, 313th Infantry, Captain William F. Thomas took over command of B Battery and Lieutenant William Kopp took command of C Battery.

The hot weather continued. One night I was in my sleeping bag dozing off in the twilight about 11 o'clock when I felt a tickle under my chin. I opened my eyes and was nose to nose with a big fuzzy tarantula. I let out a yelp, split the sleeping bag in half and was out of it before the poor beast knew what had happened. We maneuvered as batteries and practiced patrolling against enemy infantry. I led a patrol on a tortured path up a cleft in a cliff and kept on going because I could not figure out any way to back down.

On weekends we sometimes went to Yuma, Arizona, or Brawley, California, the closest towns. They weren't much, just hot, scruffy little settlements in the desert. A few of the officers and NCOs had their wives follow them and rented a room in a house or a motel unit in these towns. On one occasion I had dinner with Jim and Eloise Quillian. Another weekend I visited Philip and Betty Warner. Phil was class of 39 at Princeton and assigned to Headquarters Battery, Division Artillery which he later commanded. It was a constant struggle for married officers and NCOs to get enough gasoline to be able to see their wives on weekends, and they resorted to complicated carpooling arrangements to save on fuel.

CHAPTER 5

Final training and overseas

We left the desert in late autumn, moving by train to Camp Phillips, a post near Salinas, Kansas. All troop movement of any great distance was by train during the war. Trucks, guns and tanks were loaded on flat cars. The troops rode in coaches which were always completely filled. The coaches had no air conditioning in summer and little heat by winter. A baggage car was set up as a kitchen and mess car. The cooks filled a couple of big pots with some mixed food. The troops filed past, as the cooks ladled food into their mess kits. The men then squatted or stood in the lurching train to eat, after which they dipped their mess kits into a GI can of what was once boiling water to clean their kits. By the end of the chow line the water was a greasy soup. It is a wonder that we did not all become ill.

When we detrained at Salinas we were picked up by trucks for a short drive to Camp Phillips. En route we were astonished by flights of huge bombers roaring low overhead. These were B 29s, then going into production for service in the Pacific, but not yet in combat or even mentioned in the press. Camp Phillips was bleak and cold with snow already on the ground. We were here for winter maneuvers, and winter had arrived. We were issued winter clothing, white pup tents and a variety of specialized equipment for operating in extreme cold. This was quite a change from the desert.

The first morning, as we took A battery out to the range to fire, the temperature was close to zero. I received a fire mission and called out the fire commands:

"Battery adjust, shell HE, Charge V, fuse quick, Base deflection right 175, On No. 1 open two, SI 300, No. 1 one round, Elevation 353, Fire!"

At the command "Fire," the No. 1 cannoneer pulled the lanyard. The propelling charge exploded. The tube slid back in full recoil and stayed there. Then slowly, very slowly, the tube crept back into firing position. It was fifteen minutes before we could fire another round. The problem lay in the oil with which the hydraulic recoil system was filled. It had virtually solidified in the low temperature. We had to replace it with low temperature oil which someone had forgotten to issue to us. This was a small sample of the kind of difficulty which beset the German Army when Hitler invaded Russia without making provision for the Russian winter.

The pup tents to which I referred were made of a nylon material, white on one side, khaki on the other, and came with a nylon floor. Great camouflage and very waterproof, but when you buttoned them up for a cold night on the snow, your breath condensed, and by morning the floor of the tent was soaked with water. Our footwear was also inadequate, consisting of leather high shoes to which a six inch flap of leather with a buckle was attached, making what was called a combat boot. Fortunately for me, my father was able to get me a pair of heavy black boots with felt inner soles which were being manufactured and sent as lend lease to the Soviet army. They were well designed for cold weather.

Christmas, 1943, Clissa came out by train to Salinas during her vacation, and we rented a room in Salinas. She studied during the day while I was on duty. I took a bus after retreat, arriving in town about 6 PM for a drink and dinner in a small restaurant. I got up at 5 AM to catch a bus to for camp in time for reveille at 6:45 AM. We opened our Christmas presents at

Phil and Betty Warner's rented room on Christmas Eve and attended a party on the post Christmas Day. There was little other entertainment. It was a good thing Clissa had plenty of studying to do. Life was difficult for wives who followed their husbands from camp to camp.

*

In January, 1944, it became clear we were finally headed overseas. The artillery commander, General Gurney, was replaced by General Wahl, and Colonel Bixby was replaced by another colonel. While winter training continued, detailed preparations were underway. Enlisted men were issued new clothing. Officers checked their clothing and equipment. We all had another round of physical examinations. There were thirty two officers in our battalion and while all were basically healthy, not all met the rigorous standards prescribed by regulation. Our battalion surgeon was in charge of the examination and carefully instructed everyone who was basically healthy on how to pass minor sticking points such as pulse rates, hemorrhoids, stiff backs and fallen arches. No one wanted to be left behind.

In February we received the ten days leave authorized prior to going overseas. I managed to get a Pullman reservation all the way to New York. Someone citing his leave experience convinced me I could get a priority and fly out of Wichita thus saving two days each way. I succumbed to the vision of seven or eight hours in a plane as opposed to two days on the train. I caught a ride from Salinus to Wichita and as we drove into that city on a cold and cloudy afternoon it began to snow. At the airport all flights were canceled. I left my name and telephone number at the airline desk and went to a hotel downtown in a black depression, my Pullman reservation gone, my flight canceled.

Sometime after midnight the telephone rang. A sepulchral voice said: "Your flight leaves in one hour." I caught a taxi and raced out to the airport. It was snowing heavily. Just before dawn the DC 3 took off. Every other passenger was a newly graduated bomber pilot on the first leg of a flight to Britain.

It was still snowing, dark as pitch. Once we were airborne, the aircraft bucked and shook so violently that nearly all of us became sick. I longed for the plane to crash and put me out of my misery. We were supposed to land at Chicago, but Chicago was socked in. No other airport to the East was open. Finally, hours later we landed back at Oklahoma City with no prospect of any other plane and no sign the weather would clear. I spent the night sleeping on the marble floor of the cavernous railroad station with hundreds of other stranded soldiers. Later the next day, I caught an eastbound train with no seat, much less a berth, and alternated standing and sitting on my dufflebag between two coaches all the way to New York.

Clissa and I stayed for two days in the apartment which she shared with two other girls who had tactfully disappeared, then we went up to Watervliet for three days with the family. We all knew it was the last leave before embarkation. When my time was up I took the train back to Kansas where last minute preparations were under way. A number of enlisted men in the battalion were transferred out for physical deficiencies. We were assured that we would receive healthy replacements at the port.

In March we moved by train to Camp Miles Standish and the Boston Port of Embarkation. There we were sealed off—no leaves, no passes, no visitors and, toward the end of our stay, no telephone calls. On March 30th I wrote my mother and father:

> "Couldn't tell you much over the phone and can't tell you anything more now. Quillian and Kopp are both waiting for babies due today. Right now Colonel Safford and three quarters of the officers in the battalion are in the room here discussing babies, deliveries, labor pains, and how long or rather how much late they can be. Will you send me a copy of The Federalist. Don't insure it, of course."

The fact that the division was embarking was as secret as the date of embarkation. In March of 1944 German submarines were still sinking allied shipping and still attacking convoys of troopships, heavily guarded though they were. We were given another series of shots, including yellow fever, which convinced some of our contingent that we were headed for the tropics. I shared a room with John Hinkle and ran a high fever for several days following the shots. I remember John sitting on the edge of my bunk and pushing me down on the bed as I tried to get to my feet to conduct some imaginary mission. For a few hours I was wildly delirious.

Our guns, battery equipment and vehicles had been turned in at Camp Phillips; all we took with us were our personal effects and side arms. Our promised replacements arrived looking as though they had been hauled in by an eighteenth century press gang. The men we had lost for physical disability had minor defects and were well trained. These men had only been through basic training and had all kinds of physical and mental defects. One man was blind in one eye. Another was almost totally deaf. A third, a rotund little man, was crazy as a march hare. But we had them, and we had to sail with them.

The officers of A Battery at this time were: Captain John A. Hinkle, battery commander; myself, battery executive; First Lieutenant William C. Delbridge, assistant executive; First Lieutenant Louis R. Pascal, reconnaissance officer.

We sailed with a substantial part of our division on the SS Strathmore, a 23,000 ton British liner chartered from the Peninsula and Oriental Steamship Company. The Strathmore and two sister ships were built in the 1930s for the far eastern run. C. Northcote Parkinson's wonderful imaginary biography of Horatio Hornblower described Admiral Hornblower as a founding director of the P & O Company. The Strathmore was a beautiful ship. The officers were all British; the crew all Lascars, diminutive, dark skinned chaps, very agile and hardworking. The dining room staff were all British. The officers were berthed in passenger cabins. The enlisted men were berthed on what were referred to as the troop decks, quarters built for the transportation of troops on the ship's prewar runs through the Suez canal to India, Singapore and Hong Kong. The dining room was immense, two decks in height. The waiters wore black tie, and each dinner had a soup course, a fish course, a meat course entree' and desert. We loved it.

The enlisted men did not think their arrangements were very amusing. The troop decks had a ceiling of no more than six feet. They were divided into bays holding about one hundred men who were supposed to sleep in hammocks. In the center of each bay were large brass cauldrons. These were filled with food at meal time, and the ration was then dipped out of them and poured into mess kits. Many of the men, unused to hammocks, just slept on the metal deck.

Daylight hours we were allowed on deck. The convoy stretched as far as the eye could see in any direction. From time to time destroyers and destroyer escorts raced through the convoy on mysterious missions. Once we saw them dropping depth charges. We saw no ship in our convoy sunk.

Every day battery officers conducted classes for the enlisted men, teaching them to identify German and Allied aircraft and tanks by the use of flash card kits. One of our Boston replacements was a cocky little fellow, loud, noisy and unpleasant, and convinced he knew more about everything than the NCOs. He got into the nurse's quarters and chased one of them down a corridor according to a complaint addressed to me. I assigned him to Sergeant Simpson, our senior gun sergeant, thinking that if anyone could put the fear of God in him, Simpson could.

*

Early in April after eight days at sea we sailed up the Clyde. Bill Frick, then a sergeant with Headquarters Battery, recalls that the Battleship HMS Duke of York passed us sailing out to sea with her band playing on her afterdeck. I must have been occupied with some duty at the time for I have no recollection of seeing or hearing about it. When A Battery disembarked, it was dark, and we boarded a troop train with sealed blinds covering the windows. We traveled some hours, and eventually detrained at a railhead near a town called Wiggan twenty five miles east of Liverpool. The entire division of some sixteen thousand troops was billeted on the grounds of the estate of the Earl of Garswood, surrounded by a brick wall eight feet high. The estate was adjacent to a village called Ashton in Makersfield. We were quartered in rows of pyramidal tents, and the scene reminded me of Brady photographs of the Army of the Potomac in winter quarters. It was cold and it rained day after day. All we did for nearly a month was huddle in tents trying to keep warm and dry.

The ground water level appeared to be at ground level. The paths were awash. The latrines were ghastly, consisting of wooden planks with holes in them under which were tall metal buckets. These buckets were supposed to be emptied each day by contractors who came through the camp with horse drawn vehicles known as honey wagons. The contents were no doubt returned to the fields in an organic cycle. Some days the honey wagons didn't show up, and desperate men ran along the planks looking into the holes searching for one not full to the brim.

When I was off duty and the rain let up, I walked through the countryside to get some feel for the locality. In that area the houses were nearly all hidden behind tall walls and heavy planting. You rarely got a look at a house. I walked into Wiggan several times. On one occasion an Englishman invited me and a companion to come to the Conservative Club for a drink. He stood us each to a stiff drink of scotch, a rare commodity, and related a cornucopia of off-color stories. At battery level we had no maps, no equipment, and no information as to what we were going to do. It was a very uncomfortable month. Finally Hinkle and I bought a three speed English bicycle and for several days we were able to extend the perimeter of our exploration.

The weather improved and we resumed intensive training, although we had no space for maneuver and no range on which to fire. The training program now concentrated on an obstacle course through which we crawled, avoiding barbed wire while machine guns fired overhead. We were given practice in identifying and disarming booby traps and mines. We practiced trying to do this while blindfolded so that we could do it in the dark. Small explosives were attached to them and went off whenever the trainee blundered. Few of us ever succeeded in disarming one, and I think all booby trap training accomplished was to give us the sense that every tree, bush and rock would be trapped, and that we had little prospect of surviving.

Near the first of May our equipment, all brand new, arrived by ship, and I went to the Liverpool docks with a party of drivers and gun crews to pick up our trucks and guns and uncrate the remainder of our equipment. Once this was done, we prepared to move south to Wales to calibrate the guns. Calibration meant test firing to establish corrections for each artillery piece so that it could be fired the same distance as each of the other pieces in the battery when using the same numbered powder bag, powder lot and projectile. Leaving Wiggan meant leaving the bike. There was no room to transport it. Captain Hinkle bought my half interest saying he would ship the bike home.

The Division Artillery traveled south from Wiggan on a route laid out by division headquarters with soldiers standing as route markers at every crossroads. As I have said before, we had no maps at battery level, and the British had removed every road sign on the island in 1940 when preparing to meet a German invasion. Had the Germans invaded England the lack of road signs would have been a problem, but they would have had detailed 1/20,000 maps to guide them as we did in France and Germany. From what I saw on a trip Clissa and I made through England in 1971, our route was probably from Liverpool through Cheshire, Shropshire and Hereford, then west into Wales to the town of Merthyr Tydfil.

Wales was green, rocky, hilly and barren. I presume the hills were forested at one time, but cutting followed by sheep herding simply destroyed the capacity of the forest to regenerate. The little towns and villages were nestled in the folds of hills scarred by the slag piles of worked out coal mines. What level ground existed was spotted with subsidence hollows above collapsed mine shafts. We camped in a flat area and set to work on the process of calibration, firing into another hollow three or four thousand yards away with observers on the hills carefully noting the location of each shell burst and reporting by telephone to the fire direction center.

I have referred to telephone lines before and more detail may be useful. Field telephone lines consisted of two twisted wires unreeled or laid by the wire crews to run from point to point where communication was needed: battery to battalion fire direction and battery to forward observers with the infantry. The telephones had a leather case and a crank to ring the operator or switchboard at the other end of the line. In combat wire was the preferred method of communication. The forward observers tried to have wire where possible to link them to battalion fire direction, but often used their portable radios when they were moving, when the wire was shot out, or could not be laid. In rapidly moving situations, radio was the principal communications link.

The 610 portable radio was a vacuum tube set slightly smaller than the size of a five galleon gas can and weighing approximately twenty pounds. The radio was carried by the forward observer's radio operator and required frequent attention from the battery communications sergeant. Wire was laid as rapidly as possible when the battery moved into a new position, and it was picked up, actually reeled up, by the wire crew the moment the battery moved from one position to another. A competent wire crew was essential.

When we finished calibrating the guns, we resumed battery training in the field. In one memorable exercise, Colonel Safford instructed us to manhandle a howitzer to the top of a steep hill just in case we had to do it in combat. We managed to do this with immense effort, but doubted that we would ever be called upon to do it in France. In fact, we had to do so on several occasions, although ordinarily in a difficult position we were able to winch the guns into or out of a position using the gun truck winches.

Training in Wales was interrupted by orders to return to Ashton where we packed and loaded our equipment on the trucks and drew a full load of ammunition. We knew then that the invasion was imminent. The only questions were when and where. The latter part of May, the 79th moved south from Wiggan to the Channel coast. The artillery camped in the fields near the junction of four sunken lanes called Raleigh's Crossroads. This crossroads was situated on the high point of a ridge which eventually runs down to an arm of the sea, but the six foot hedgerows then lining the roads made any extended view impossible. At the crossing stood a combination pub and inn, and a 1940 concrete pillbox sited so naturally between the roots of a huge tree that a passer by would seldom notice it. Our battery bivouacked in the highest portion of the field, the guns and trucks dispersed over several acres and concealed beneath new camouflage nets. The radio announced that Rome had fallen to Allied troops.

The morning of June 6 was gray and cold. All night great flights of aircraft had roared over us headed south, and shortly after daybreak, Private Robert E. Ryan heard on the radio that the invasion was on and shouted the news to the battery. After the excitement subsided, life in the bivouac went on much as before. A wet landing was expected as Landing Ships Tank, (LSTs), grounded in depths of two or three feet of water. All equipment had to be waterproofed for such depths. The drivers took their vehicles down to the ocean to "wade" them with their exhaust lines and air intakes extended above the water level anticipated. The first results were not encouraging. The jeep successfully made seven voyages, but many of the trucks stalled and had to be winched back to dry land. Our weasel, a so called amphibious jeep, took a heavy wave which drowned the motor and had to be paddled ashore. With this experience to inspire them, the drivers worked steadily to improve their waterproofing.

Each section loaded and reloaded its equipment in an attempt to get everything packed tightly and efficiently, but no matter how many times they were reloaded, the trucks were always overloaded and looked like gypsy wagons. At the end of work each day, there was recreation: warm beer in the Raleigh Crossroads pub, ball games in the meadow between batteries, poker and crap games. By the time the battalion left England, Sergeant George Smith had most of the loose money in the battery.

Neither officers nor enlisted men had any clear idea of what combat would be like. Back in Ashton, General George Patton had delivered one of his fire and brimstone speeches to the officers and NCOs saying, "The Third Army was going to fight, not dig its way to Berlin!"

By the time we reached the German border we thought we had dug our way there and were lucky to have done so. All of us were mine conscious. We expected to find a teller mine under every clump of grass, an S mine under every stone. We expected fortifications and pill boxes everywhere, but no one anticipated the crazy quilt of hedgerows which so greatly affected fighting in Normandy. Hedge rows were completely overlooked in the invasion planning, as military historians have noted.

Some of us thought it would be a long, difficult fight. Others thought it would be a quick fight ending with a victory parade into Paris. I had a healthy respect for the German Army derived from what I had read. I thought we were in for a tough fight. My chief concern was doing my own job properly whatever we encountered. My comprehension of combat was necessarily theoretical until the experience itself. With experience came capacity to differentiate risk and handle it emotionally. What was more significant was that, despite individual apprehension, we believed we would prevail. The sense of being a part of an irresistible tide was pervasive, induced, perhaps, by our awareness of the magnitude of the forces the United States had assembled in England. There were, however, surprises in store for us.

June 10 we learned that the 313th Infantry, our combat team partner, had left their encampment. Jim Quillian, now a captain and liaison officer with the 313th, haunted the Rail

Transportation office in Taunton, the point from which our orders would come. Lieutenant Beaune returned from a bomb disposal course and lectured each battery on unexploded bombs. According to Beaune, who was inclined to exaggerate, France would be covered with unexploded bombs which would explode whenever an artillery piece was fired in their vicinity. In point of fact our cannoneers concluded this was bunk after they had fired over several unexploded 500 pound bombs.

March order came at four A.M. the morning of June 15. A cold rain drizzled down as we drank hot coffee outside the mess truck. The mess section was to be left behind until cross channel transportation became available for "non essential" vehicles. Then our column of trucks pulled out of the field onto the road and moved slowly eastward. We passed through a forest where thousands of vehicles and stacks of supplies were hidden under the trees. We reached the concentration area at noon, pulled up bumper to bumper along the right hand side of the road, and spread camouflage nets over the vehicles. 30th Division trucks were similarly parked along the left hand side of the road. Meanwhile, a constant stream of ambulances heading the opposite direction passed between us bearing casualties from France, a sobering sight. Ordinance inspectors moved from truck to truck checking the waterproofing.

In late afternoon, the battalion personnel, with the exception of drivers, were instructed to take their personal equipment and march up a hill to a series of tents and prefab huts concealed in the woods. We were fed a good dinner and settled in for the evening. We exchanged our English money for invasion francs, and received emergency rations of chocolate and cigarettes. A movie was shown: "My Kingdom for a Cook." Everyone remembered the title; no one remembered the film. That was our last hot meal until September.

Late in the evening Colonel Safford called a meeting of battalion personnel and reported the plans for us. He concluded saying the battalion was not scheduled to embark until the following afternoon. As we were dismissed, a public address system called battalion commanders to Concentration Headquarters. Some men went to takes showers, others to bed. At 11:30 PM whistles blew and the cry went through the camp: "March order! We're pulling out!"

It was a wild hour. It was pitch dark. To add to the confusion, we had to pull gas-proof fatigues over our regular uniforms, put on our field harness and an inflatable life belt over the fatigues and roll up our bedding into a U-roll pack. Sergeant Tully and Private Organ accidentally inflated their life belts in the process. All six hundred of us stumbled down hill to the main road and the parked truck columns. There was a frantic search for the right truck, no lights, of course. The exec truck was mine, and Corporal Rosalis, my driver, was behind the wheel. The order, "Turn 'em over," was passed down the line. Officers went from truck to truck to be sure everyone was accounted for. Then our column moved out for the port, showing only blackout lights, two tiny white x s in front and two tiny red x s in the rear.

The column moved slowly down the road. There was little conversation. A dozen search lights caught a plane high above us. A machine gun chattered tracers into the sky. Then, with the plane apparently identified, the search lights blinked out, one by one. I had a feeling that the Luftwafe was searching for the 310th Field Artillery. The column reached the coast and drove onto a broad, flat beach and stopped. On either side of us were other columns, indistinct in the darkness. Someone passed the word to me that men could get a hot meal somewhere in the vicinity. I suppressed the information fearing if they left their trucks and we had to move, we'd never get them back. Red Cross girls passed up and down the column with hot coffee and doughnuts. Every few minutes the column moved, the men scrambled back on the trucks, we moved a few yards, then stopped.

At last the column moved off the beach onto a road which ran into the small port of Weymouth and down to a cobblestone quay against which were tied two landing ships tank (LST), their bow ramps resting on the quay. We learned that all vehicles had to be backed up the steep ramp into the ship so they could be driven off when we hit the beach. Makes good sense, but no one had told us, and we had not considered the possibility because none of us had ever seen an LST. I suppose we assumed the LST was like a ferry. The problem was the extraordinary difficulty of backing heavy guns and heavily loaded ammunition trailers up a steep ramp. The ship's crew had no helpful ideas. The gun sergeants solved the problem by backing in the prime movers, then winching the guns on the ramp and finally turning the guns around on board. Guns, gun trucks and other two and a half ton GMCs were carried on the main deck, the lighter vehicles, three quarter ton trucks and jeeps, were taken by elevator to the upper deck.

The battalion completed loading by 3:00 A.M., June 14 with Headquarters, A and B Batteries on LST 400, and C and Service Batteries on the adjacent LST. Each truck and gun was chained to rings welded to the decks to insure that none broke loose in rough water. Our two ships and others nearby, packed like ferry boats, remained moored to the quays until ten o'clock in the morning when the cry "cast off" rang out. LST 400 took in tow a section of Mulberry floating dock, and the flotilla of LSTs put to sea bearing the 310th Field Artillery to Normandy.

CHAPTER 6

Normandy and the battle for Cherbourg

Our convoy moved within sight of the English shore for several hours, then turned south toward France and into rain and thick fog. A hospital ship loomed in front of us. Our LST captain threw his engines into reverse narrowly avoiding collision. Over the LST's communication system Corporal Cantrell heard our ship's captain say the hospital ship would have sliced us in two. Some men were seasick, others played cards, tried to sleep, or wrote letters home. I wrote the family a short note:

> "I am aboard ship and headed for France. When you get this letter you will know I've arrived safely. I will probably not be able to write often for a good while, but don't worry when you do not hear from me. I will be quite busy and there may be some difficulty with getting mail out. Important as it is, supplies are more important. The channel is a rough damn stretch of water. I'm not seasick, but 9/10 are. We have everything we need and are all set to go. Think I shall take a snooze now and store up a few hours of sleep."

By afternoon we stood off Omaha Beach where the 1st and 29th Divisions had made their difficult assault six days before. Our LST dropped anchor behind some ships sunk as a breakwater and cast off to a tug the section of Mulberry floating dock we had towed from England. We spent the night at anchor off the beach surrounded by a number of vessels. Toward shore along the beach lay half sunken craft of all kinds. That night a lone German plane flew over the anchorage, the target of every antiaircraft gun in the vicinity. The plane escaped, but a barrage balloon protecting the fleet was not so lucky and came down in flames.

In the morning of June 17, our LST weighed anchor and ran west parallel to the shore until we reached Utah Beach where the 4th Division had made its D Day landing. There were ships around us as far as the eye could see. The LST headed for shore and grounded. It was necessary to wait until the tide fell sufficiently for us to off-load. Amphibious two and a half ton trucks (Ducks), ran back and forth with messages from the beach to anchored ships. Vehicles moved up and down the beach. To the northwest of us the battleship Texas and the cruiser Augusta shelled the Cherbourg Peninsula with tremendous broadsides. The tide fell. When the order came to unload, the water was only inches deep, and all our waterproofing proved unnecessary.

It was getting dark as we began unloading. I was down on the lower deck with the guns and because my exec truck was on the second deck I climbed into the 2nd gun section's truck, and off we went. Military police guided us up the beach and into a de-waterproofing area. The battalion was hopelessly mixed up. Many vehicles had not arrived from the beach. Officers ran back and forth looking for lost trucks. The division assistant G 4 shouted at me, "What's the 310th doing here, you're supposed to be in another area." The division assistant G 3 shouted back, "Leave him alone, for God's sake! You don't know where they go!"

I was sweating under multiple layers of clothing and harness carrying all our gear. The confusion of landing, the mixed up vehicles, the presence of unknown hazard, and the pervasive rumble of artillery fire created a remarkable sense of disequilibrium. We waited for instructions and sorting out.

Moments later a call came for the 310th to "pull out," which we did, each truck following the truck ahead, anxious not to lose sight of its dim blackout lights in the darkness. After a time, we were flagged down by Captain Fred Thomas of B Battery and turned into a field where the battalion trucks and guns were being distributed around the periphery up against the hedgerows. In the center of the field were two smashed gliders. As we entered the field, a German plane flying low strafed the road hitting several vehicles from other batteries. Later in the night our lighter vehicles, jeeps and three quarter ton trucks including the exec truck from the upper deck of the LST rejoined us, and thus reassembled we felt more secure.

The night was cool, but with morning the sun came out. We climbed out of our bedrolls, shed the rest of our impregnated gas protective clothing, stowed it in the trucks, and looked around. Our field, and all the other fields, were surrounded by hedgerows four to six feet tall and six to eight feet thick. Out of the top of the hedgerows shrubs and brush grew ten to twenty feet tall with an occasional tree. French farmers later explained that the Germans had forbidden trimming the hedgerows in order to create more obstructions for gliders. Ordinarily a ditch several feet deep lay on either side of the hedgerows and one entrance was cut into each field just wide enough for a farm wagon to pass. Many of the fields were studded with wood poles strung with wire. The poles were called Rommel's Asparagus and were designed to destroy gliders and their crews. These fields looked like an Oregon hop yard without the hops, and many were filled with wrecked gliders, some impaled on the poles. One glider was lodged in the roof of a stone barn.

Despite heavy losses the 82nd Airborne troops who survived the landings had rapidly formed into loose units and fought along and through the hedgerows. All the hedgerows had small beaten paths along the crest of the earthen mound and concealed by the foliage. These paths were littered with ration boxes, ammunition cases, bloody shoes and leggings. The tree trunks were scarred, their branches clipped, the ground covered with leaves stripped by the fire fights that had followed the landing.

Up ahead of us we heard the low rumble of artillery. The Battalion Command Post (CP) was set up in a field nearby. We gradually learned the general position of our section of the front. Utah Beach lay just east of the Cherbourg peninsula, and we were now behind three divisions which had been assigned to cut the peninsula at its base and then capture the port. These divisions were the 9th on the left, the 90th in the center, and the 4th on the right. The 82nd Airborne troops faced south across the peninsula covering our rear.

Colonel Safford's CP and Headquarters battery were set up in an adjacent field. General Wahl's aide, Lieutenant Stivers stopped by the CP, after contacting the 90th Division. He painted a grim picture of the 90th's situation: no observation, intense machine gun fire, repeated counter attacks. He spoke of colonels falling like flies and regiments with fifty percent casualties after two days fighting. His account was exaggerated, but in fact the 90th Division had suffered fairly severe casualties and was badly shaken.

Late in the afternoon the battalion moved up to a rendevoux area near Sebeville, just south of St. Mere Eglise, and A Battery pulled into a large field adjacent to a destroyed farmhouse and scattered the vehicles against the hedgerows. Some twenty cows now five or six days dead lay sprawled about with their bellies bloated and legs extended. The smell was indescribable. The body of a dead German sat in a foxhole with a mess kit in his lap. The mess kit was said to be booby trapped. We found more bodies. An intense fire fight had taken place between the paratroopers of the 82nd and the German infantry who had dug neat, deep emplacements at the intersections of the hedgerows so they could cover four fields without exposing themselves to hostile fire. Artillery and mortar fire had little effect on these positions unless they scored a direct hit. German entrenchment was always constructed thoroughly and neatly.

On June 18 the 79th Division was ordered to relieve the 90th, and the latter was withdrawn for refitting and reorganization. Meanwhile the 9th Division on our left punched through German defenses to the western side of the peninsula, so the way was cleared for the drive on Cherbourg, the port we thought we had to have to sustain the invasion. Captain Hinkle took a work party forward to prepare a battery position, and just before dark the battery moved up to a gun position along a sunken road. The gun crews spent the better part of the night digging their howitzers into the bank. No fire missions came from battalion during the night or in the morning, and there was considerable grumbling among the men about waiting three years and coming three thousand miles just to have the war fizzle out like this. Then at 0925 the morning of June 19, we received a fire mission and fired a battery five rounds.

*

After several moves, A battery went into position June 19th in an apple orchard with the gun tubes pointed over and through a hedgerow. Twenty four hours in that position was a swift education for us all. Within moments of laying the guns, the battery was given a mission by Captain Quillian with the 2nd Battalion, 313th Infantry. When firing ceased, we set to work digging slit trenches and foxholes. There were plenty of German fox holes around, but the men distrusted them, fearing booby traps. Four 88 shells crashed into the battery position. We dropped into our slit trenches. My heart was pounding. I pulled my steel helmet down over my ears and waited. The GP telephone rang again. My operator said,

"Fire mission!" They couldn't be serious, I thought. We were under fire. My feet were anchored to the bottom of that trench. Then out I scrambled out, shouting,

"Fire Mission! battery adjust! . . ." the gun crews came out of their holes. The mission was under way. The guns roared with the first battery volley. There was a blinding flash at number 4, and the crew fell back, their gun wreathed in smoke.

"No. 4 is out!" called Sergeant Miller.

"Medic!" called someone else.

Captain Hinkle took over as executive. The first sergeant and I moved quickly to No. 4, finding Sergeant Miller wounded in the leg, Corporal Smushko in the forehead, Private Ruddock in the arm and Private Norton also injured. The first sergeant and Lieutenant Pascal organized a new crew from drivers and spare cannoneers, and within ten minutes we had No. 4 back in action, and the wounded were on their way to the battalion aid station.

Some men argued that the shell No. 4 had just fired must have struck a twig in the hedgerow and exploded within a foot or two of leaving the muzzle. However, the fuse in shell HE, which is what we were firing, does not arm until substantially farther from the muzzle than any possible brush in that hedgerow. I concluded that unless the fuse was defective, the burst was from the 88 which was shelling us. The thick hedgerow shielded the gun crew from much of the blast. In any event, Major McNeely, battalion S 3, reported the injuries as accidental according to the 310th Unit Journal.

Later in the day, battalion fire direction telephoned, "Enemy tanks in front of your position." We leveled the muzzles, cleared brush from the top of the hedgerow, and laid out armor piercing shells to deal with the tanks. I deployed bazooka teams to cover our flanks. The gun sections threw off their camouflage nets lest they interfere with direct fire. I thought of my lectures on the Strathamore in which I had tried to indoctrinate the men with the old tradition that artillerymen never leave their guns.

I also thought of those flash card exercises on the Strathamore trying to distinguish between German and American tanks. I heard the distinctive clatter of tanks to the front of us. Then a column of tanks came into view through the brush and long grass. They were moving on a road several hundred yards in front of us. I stared at them through my field glasses. They were ours.

Lieutenant Delbridge was our forward observer with the 3rd Battalion of the 313th Infantry that afternoon. Lieutenant Colonel Porter, the battalion commander, used Delbridge's radio calling Colonel Sterling Wood, the 313th regimental commander, saying, "Sterling, for God's sake, get us tanks and reinforcements!"

Chaltrow, Delbridge's radio operator, sent four or five fire missions direct to us by radio and reported that they had broken up the counterattack. Colonel Wood was a hard-bitten regular who always carried a walking stick. Radio operators always referred to him as "The Stick." By nightfall we learned that things were going better after all. I completed reorganizing the gun sections, putting Sergeant Jerry Tully in command of the 4th section.

In the course of that afternoon, we had reports from our forward observers that some of our fire was falling short and causing casualties to our own infantry. Lieutenant Pascal rechecked our own survey, and reported it was accurate. However, later that evening we learned that the battalion survey section had run in a new orienting line and place mark for A battery during the afternoon but failed to tell us they had done so. We had continued to use the orienting line we had surveyed when we arrived in the position, while battalion fire direction had begun sending us fire commands based on their own survey. Thereafter the battalion survey section made sure the batteries were told of any new survey.

By the time battalion discovered the discrepancy. it was dark. The S 3 section telephoned me directions on how to find the new place mark, a stake they had driven into the ground somewhere in front of the guns. Before I began my search, I passed the word to our sentries on both flanks that I would be out in front of the battery position. I then worked my way several hundred feet in front of the guns, sweeping the ground with a masked flashlight looking for that elusive stake. Private Ledford heard me scuffling around out there and cut loose with three rounds from his 50 cal. machine gun in my direction, tracers and all. I shouted, "Ledford! God damn it! Cease fire! It's Lieutenant Beatty!" A few minutes later, as I was returning to the gun position, Ledford fired three more shots from his carbine. I told the first sergeant to take Ledford off guard duty for good and then turned in.

The morning of June 20th, Captain Hinkle left with Colonel Safford's BC party to reconnoiter new gun positions. A short time later we received orders from battalion to move out. Led by Major McNeely, the battalion S-3, and Major Beadel, the battalion executive, we turned north on a road flagged by battalion route markers at every intersection. Our column passed infantry command posts, a reconnaissance troop vehicle park, turned down a winding road through some barbed wire and past an abandoned German camp. We passed through an infantry battalion on the march, single file on each side of the road, then passed infantry scouts. We climbed up a steep grade into a deserted village named Brix according to our map, and stopped in the village square to get our bearings. Inhabitants began pouring out of cellars. Tricolors broke out on flag poles. Women and old men clustered about the trucks with bottles of cider, wine and calvados.

Then I received a call on the radio from Captain Hinkle. Omitting the call signs, it went something like this:
Question: "Where are you, over?"
Answer: "On the road, over."
Question: "Are you on a black top road, over?"
Answer: "Yes, over".
Reply: "For God's sake stop where you are! Out".

A few minutes later, Captain Hinkle came racing up the hill into Brix in his command car, turned our column around and we retraced our route, passing once again that infantry battalion on the march. They certainly looked puzzled. It seemed that a battalion officer had marked the route to the wrong village, one considerably in advance of the front line. These errors committed in the maze of hedgerows were a painful caution to all of us.

For the next five days the battery made short moves forward to support the advancing infantry In one position, just north of the village of Hou de Long, a tremendous explosion occurred some thirty yards in front of the guns, showering them and my position with clods of earth. The concussion was so great that all four guns had to be relaid. We waited for the next round, speculating whether it would be longer or shorter. My own thought was that if we were going to be shelled like this we would never survive. No second shell came. We concluded that it was a twelve or fourteen inch naval shell, from one of the battleships firing at the Cherbourg forts. We speculated that someone aboard ship had made a hundred mil error in elevation.

We moved to another gun position a few hundred yards from Hou de Haut in front of a half completed V 1 launching site. Had the invasion been delayed several months, these missiles might have been a major factor in the German defense. A Niebelwerfer, a multiple short range rocket launcher, repeatedly fired rockets into a field to the rear of the battery, and one cratered the road into our truck park.

The 1st Battalion, 313th Infantry, was assembled nearby the battery position, and Lieutenant Pascal, our forward observer with that unit, returned to the battery to pick up rations. We were living on 10-in-one rations, a box containing two packages of food for three meals for five men, or, for that matter, 10 day's food for one man. These rations could be cooked or eaten cold. That was the last we saw of Lieutenant Pascal, who was seriously wounded by mortar fire that afternoon and evacuated. Private Atlee Taylor, his driver, returned to the battery with Pascal's bloody dispatch case.

From midnight on the battalion area was shelled intensively for three hours. This was our first experience with sustained incoming fire, and we spent the night sleeping in fox holes. The shells hit all about us but none in the actual gun position. One blew up an infantry ammunition dump up the road. With daylight we found that despite all the fireworks we were undamaged and ready to get on with the day's work after hot coffee.

All day the 22nd, the battery fired heavily as the infantry began the assault on the last ring of defenses on the hills around Cherbourg. The Air Force planned a close-in bombing mission. The infantry pulled back and marked the front for the bombers. Despite these precautions the bombs hit some of our troops. P

39 and P51 fighters roared over us at tree top height strafing, a terrifying experience on any occasion, especially the first time. I reported this by telephone to battalion which replied these were German planes with American markings and to fire on them. When the next flight roared over us we opened fire with our machine guns. Battalion then called saying,

"Don't shoot, the planes are American."

Finally, a flight of P-38s came over strafing, and we knew they were American—the Germans had no twin fuselage fighters. In fairness to the pilots it was undoubtedly very difficult to distinguish between friend and foe in that tangle of hedgerows, or to identify the markers we laid out on the ground.

A flight of P-47s circled high overhead. My driver, Corporal Felix Rosales, was digging a slit trench and stopped to watch. One plane circled lower, and Rosales called out, "Look at the bomb he's dropping!" The bomb struck a few yards away and exploded, cutting our wire to battalion and covering the battery switchboard with dirt. Sergeant Schaefer, chief of the wire section, called me to complain that the bomb had cut our line to battalion.

I snapped, "Fix the damned line, Sergeant!"

Moments later the P-47s dropped three one hundred pound bombs in Hau de Haut. After that experience, whenever close air support was called in by the infantry, we made for our slit trenches.

Late in the afternoon the battery came under increasing enemy fire and, with battalion's approval, I decided to shift to an alternate position. The first sergeant and I found a position four hundred yards west on a reverse slope. We moved two guns at a time so that two guns were always ready to fire on call from the infantry. While locating the site and making the move, I left Abernathy, the instrument corporal, in charge of the remaining guns. Abernathy, a bright and self reliant school teacher, was quite capable of handling a fire mission in an emergency. While looking for that new position, I ran into sixteen infantrymen

looking for their command post. They reported they were all
that was left of their company of 150 men. More likely they had
become separated from the others in the course of a fire fight.

The evening of June 23rd I reconnoitered a new position for
the battery in order to support the infantry which had reached
the outskirts of the city, and the following morning the battery
moved forward to a position near a crossroads just beyond the
German antitank ditch. Captain Dorrier had a fire mission for
us almost immediately, German guns on the shoreline. I gave
the guns an elevation command which was 100 mils in error.
Sergeant George Smith overheard the error on the telephone and
immediately interrupted the fire commands so I could correct
the error before the battery fired. A 100 mil error in elevation or
deflection was probably the most frequent mistake made in the
conduct of fire. In most instances it was caught by the executive
who could see one gun out of alignment or by a chief of section
who noticed a 100 mil deviation.

All day long German 75s and 88s shelled the crossroads and
adjacent fields around our position. An astonishing percentage
of these were duds, shells that struck but did not burst. We
thought of them as the work of friends in the German munitions
factories. We also discovered that so long as you are dug in and
have slit trenches handy you can take quite a bit of fire without
damage. Sniper fire occurred sporadically, but was usually
inaccurate. That same evening Lieutenant Delbridge and his
forward crew were hit. Corporals Bushman and Chaltrow were
killed and Private Taylor was seriously wounded by a 170mm
shell which struck a tree close by. Delbridge had his throat
grazed by a shell fragment.

June 26th was a relatively quiet day on our front, but 4th
Division on our right and 9th Division on our left had heavy
fighting. Each of those divisions had a broader front than the
79th and were behind our flanks. Our infantry now entered
the city in force, and prisoners were streaming back on the
road past the gun position. We were astonished at the numbers
of non-German prisoners. Two of the divisions defending

Cherbourg were static or reserve divisions and contained a mix of Germans, Poles, Russians, Czechs, French and others. Sergeant Gierascimowicz gave a Polish PW a piece of his mind for serving in the Wermacht. Of course, we had no knowledge then of the circumstances under which these men had been drafted into German service.

The next morning I took the 4th section down into the city and positioned their gun in a garden behind a house, a position from which they could fire up into gun casements cut into the face of the high cliffs behind the city of Cherbourg from which the Germans continued to fire, knocking out a nearby jeep a few minutes before. We placed the gun behind an iron gate. The crew opened the gate just long enough to fire, closing it after each round. Using a mix of armor piercing and white phosphorous shells, the crew silenced the casements.

General Wahl, the artillery commander, came by in a jeep and stopped to watch. Corporal Censoni had borrowed a 313th soldier's German field glasses to watch the effect of our fire. The general borrowed the glasses from Censoni, tried them, then wanted to purchase them from the 313th owner. The owner declined the sale, saying money was of no use to him. The general finally closed the transaction by autographing a 500 F invasion franc note and promising to return the glasses after the war.

*

With the silencing of the forts, Cherbourg fell on June 28th. The deep water harbor, the prize for which the battle had been fought, was a wreck. The Germans had blown up all the port machinery and sunk innumerable ships and hulks. It took months of labor to restore it for use as a port. A Battery left its final Cherbourg firing position and moved to a bivouac in a field near Fierville where the men cleaned up and caught up on sleep. We reorganized the firing battery to reflect our experience so far, eliminating the machine gun section and using those men to enlarge the ammunition section. The battery had fired far more ammunition than we had anticipated. We created two complete forward observer sections using the reconnaissance officer and the assistant executive as forward observers.

Lieutenant Charles Dillahay joined us to replace Lieutenant Pascal. I put together a gun position (GP) group to assist me as executive to operate battery fire direction using the scout corporal, Julius Abernathy, the artillery mechanic, Sergeant Kimple, my driver, Felix Rosales, my radio operator, Corporal Chaia, 1st Sergeant Osborne, and the mail clerk, Bernard Jude. I trained these men as a team to perform the duties assigned to each other and to me as the battery executive so that we always had men on hand to carry out a fire mission if I was absent from the battery or otherwise engaged.

These first two weeks settled the battery down. We had learned to distinguish between the sounds of incoming Niebelwerfers, mortars, and 105s. When a shell exploded without a sound of passage through the air, we knew it was a high velocity 88. We had learned to tell the direction from which fire comes and to recognize the pattern of fire characteristics in which American and German artillery differed. Our forward observer crews and wire section had acquired some of the skills of infantrymen in dealing with enemy small arms, machine gun and mortar fire.

The weather was beautiful and remained sunny and warm through July and August. I had brought an air mattress in my bed roll and used it only once. Blowing it up was a waste of time and effort. By the time I got to sleep the ground was soft enough. The lack of bathing was unpleasant for the first few days, but thereafter one adjusted to it. We had enough water to shave and wash our face and hands. From time to time a creek or well supplied water to wash socks and underclothing. For drinking water we relied entirely on water points provided by division, never local water. Army secured water was distributed in five gallon bidons. There was very little illness from any source until fall and winter, and then it was primarily the infantry which suffered from cold and trench foot.

Despite some satisfaction with how things had gone so far, my feeling was that if the Cherbourg campaign was a foretaste of what was to come, a hedgerow battle all the way across France would be deadly business. Those of us on the ground had no idea how far the hedgerow country extended. The infantry had already suffered heavy casualties. Our forward observer crews had sustained fifty percent casualties, two dead and two wounded out of eight officers and men, a rather impressive figure for two weeks of action, and we had lost five wounded in the gun sections.

Up to this point we clearly outnumbered the Germans in artillery, and our fire was far more intense than theirs. What we did not realize was that each German infantry company had fifteen machine guns while our infantry company had only two. Consequently our infantry was a good deal more dependent upon artillery support than the enemy. Moreover, many of the troops defending Cherbourg were second line troops, Russians, Poles, and Czechs, with a cadre of German officers and NCOs to stiffen them. Meeting veteran German divisions would be a different story. So far we had almost complete control of the air, but we did not think this imbalance would continue, and we expected to be hit hard by the enemy before our bridgehead was much enlarged. We also anticipated the kind of counter battery fire we were inflicting on the enemy's artillery.

The days seemed very long. The army was on Double British Summer Time, and at that latitude it did not get dark until nearly 11:00 PM. Five hours later dawn brightened in the east. The crackle of small arms continued until darkness and commenced with daylight. Only during the hours of darkness did infantry fighting and the call for artillery cease. In effect we had been working an eighteen hour day, and accumulated fatigue was a significant factor early in the Cherbourg campaign. However, one soon learned to catch sleep at any opportunity.

*

On June 30th the 79th Division relieved the 82nd Airborne which had been covering our rear as we attacked Cherbourg. We now faced south and went into a gun position just south of

Fierville which we dug in thoroughly because it was exposed to high ground held by the enemy. The front was quiet for several days. Captain Hinkle came to the gun position saying,

"Jack, you're off duty. Get some sleep. I'll take over the firing battery." He handed me a half bottle of calvados and sent me on my way.

I walked up the hillside behind the guns, stretched out on the grass beside a stone wall, took a couple of stiff drinks and was soon fast asleep. The next thing I knew it was dark and the first sergeant with a flashlight was shaking me.

"Lieutenant, battalion's sent us a high burst adjustment."

"Tell the captain," I said, sleepily. "I'm off duty. He's the exec."

"The captain's gone. We don't know where he is." I scrambled to my feet and made my way down to the guns.

A high burst adjustment in daylight was difficult enough. I had never done one at night. It worked out all right. But I had a clear picture in my mind of what the colonel's reaction would have been if A battery had reported no officer present to conduct fire. Fortunately, I had told Sergeant Osborne where he could find me. When the captain returned to the battery in the morning, I told him we had done a high burst adjustment. He just asked how it had gone. Apparently he had forgotten that he had relieved me. I thought it prudent not to remind him.

The infantry attacked south the afternoon of July 4th and made good progress. The battery displaced forward in the afternoon to a position in front of the village of Baudreville on a narrow road confined by thick hedgerows on either side. As we moved the battery forward, we found the road jammed with the 3rd Battalion of the 313th Infantry, their vehicles and those of other artillery units. Using the antiaircraft platoon's M51 half-track as a bulldozer we broke through a hedgerow and got the guns off the road and into a firing position.

No sooner were the guns laid than the battery received a fire mission. The infantry was attacking high ground around Montgardon against heavy resistance and had to fight off a number of counter attacks. Eventually we fired more from this position than from any previous position. In this position we also received precalculated barrage fires which enabled the forward observers to simply call "Fire barrage 17" instead of sending back detailed fire commands to respond to counterattacks. The gun sections pre-set a pile of ammunition stacked and chalk marked 17 with the correct fuse and powder charge, and the section chiefs recorded the settings for elevation and deflection for barrage 17. Thus the battery was ready to fire in a matter of seconds. In some instances, the guns were loaded and kept on a particular barrage setting so that nothing remained to be done but pull the lanyard when a forward observer called for the barrage.

At Montgardon it was difficult to keep the wire functioning because of the intensive fire, and the battalion S 3 told Captain Hinkle to keep the wire in if it took half the battery to do it. We took men from the ammunition section and gun sections to supplement Sergeant Schaefer's wire crew. Gradually the infantry cleared the entire north bank of the Ay River and the battery moved to a position south of La Haye de Puits on a ridge which overlooked the entire Ay Valley.

One of our replacements, the nurse chaser, caused so much trouble with the observer crew to which he had been assigned that the lieutenant brought him back to me saying that if he had to keep him any longer, he was going to shoot him. I gave him to one of the gun sergeants with instructions to keep him busy and quiet. The man alternately wailed and smart-mouthed the gun crew, and a day later the sergeant told me the crew would kill him if I didn't get rid of him. I took the man back and put him to digging slit trenches at the battery fire direction center. He refused to do what he was told and created so much turmoil I found myself with my 45 in hand telling him to shut up and get to work. I was frantic trying to conduct fire with this idiot on my hands. Fortunately, I was able to put him on a truck headed to the rear for water. I told the driver to tell battalion to get rid of him any way they could. We later heard he had been discharged with a section 8 and returned to the States. Subsequently two

11.5 General Dwight D. Eisenhower confers with 12th Army Group commander General Omar Bradley and 79th Division Commander Major General Ira T. Wyche in Normandy shortly after the American landings on Utah and Omaha Beaches. (Ira Thomas Wyche Papers (#210), Special Collections Department, J.Y. Joyner Library, East Carolina University, Greenville, N.C., U.S.A.

battalion officers reported letters from home saying that he had visited their families posing as a decorated veteran discharged for wounds.

On our east flank a major drive against the German lines began July 28, and early in the morning of July 29 hundreds of B 17s and B 26s in formations passed over us to bomb the German lines. As we watched, German 88s erupted and the white puffs of their exploding shells appeared within the formations. Stricken planes trailing smoke spiraled downward, but the others continued on in their formations. This air bombardment coupled with our infantry attack finally resulted in a breakthrough on our front, and the 2nd and 4th Armored Divisions passed though the infantry and down the road to Coutance.

We followed the infantry across the Ay River, a small muddy stream meandering through mud flats which were heavily mined. From our new position we began registering the guns, and while we were doing so Colonel Safford stopped by and spoke to me for a few minutes. He then drove on down the road to Lessay and ran over two teller mines. His command car was blown apart, and the colonel and four enlisted men with him were seriously wounded. His driver subsequently died. The colonel was evacuated to England, and Major Beadel, the battalion executive, took over command.

Colonel Safford kept as tight rein on the battalion as he had on those of us who had worked under him at Division artillery. In the year he had commanded the battalion, he had brought it to a remarkable level of efficiency. We had become accustomed to his long rapid strides as he came through the battery positions checking on what we were doing and how we were doing it. Serious, energetic and extremely competent, he created absolute confidence in his leadership. Everyone felt his loss. We assumed we had lost him for good.

CHAPTER 7

Turning the German flank

When the 2nd and 4th armored divisions reached Avranches at the base of the Cherbourg penninsula, they turned west into Brittany. The 79th, following the armor, moved through Pont Orson to a position four or five miles from Mont St. Michel, planning to drive west across Brittany to invest and capture the port of Brest. However, August 1 the Third Army was activated with General George Patton in command, and on August 2 Patton was ordered by General Bradley to turn General Wade Haslip's XV Corps consisting of the 79th Infantry, 90th Light and 5th Armored Divisions, to the southeast behind the German Seventh Army's open flank. The envelopment of the German Seventh Army was now underway.

During the long run across France the 79th Division ordinarily marched as combat teams, each infantry regiment with its supporting light artillery battalion, tanks and tank destroyers (TDs). Sometimes our three combat teams moved on parallel roads, sometimes in a single column. On one hair-raising occasion Combat Team 3 (313 Infantry and the 310th Field Artillery) shared a road with the 90th Division which was driving east to the north of us, each taking half the road. Whenever our infantry ran into resistance, one or more of the batteries plunged off the road into a likely meadow with a clear field of fire and prepared to take fire missions from the forward observers moving with the infantry column.

One feature of the campaigns in France and Germany that amazed me was the fact that both countries were mapped at a scale of 1/20,000 or 1/25,000 with every house, hedgerow and improved road laid out. We could locate our gun positions within a few feet by inspecting the map and taking a careful glance at the terrain around us.

*

For me the most unhappy incident in the entire campaign occurred one evening near Laval. The battery had pulled into firing position beside the road shortly before dusk. Captain Hinkle, who had been absent from the battery for several days, drove into the battery position and attempted to give me a fire mission. He had been drinking. He identified no specific target and was not communicating with our forward observers or with battalion fire direction. I tried to talk him out of it, concerned that we might fire into our own infantry whose exact location I did not know. We already had that one instance of friendly fire during the Cherbourg battle.

The captain became infuriated and demanded that I fire the mission whatever it was. I refused to do so. He threatened to have me court-martialed. I still refused, distraught and humiliated, saying that he had no basis for ordering artillery fire. He then relieved me from command, put me under arrest and ordered me confined to my pup tent behind the firing battery until morning when he would deal with me. I complied. From my pup tent I could hear him yelling down at the guns. The gun sections did not fire, and a few minutes later the captain drove out of the battery position.

In the morning he returned, fully sober, acting as though nothing had occurred the night before. When I questioned him on my status, he dismissed the matter out of hand, told me to forget it. He neither apologized nor referred to that night thereafter. I said nothing further and resumed my duties, but I was outraged at his treatment of me within earshot of my command. This incident destroyed my confidence in him. I was determined to request transfer out of the battery at the first opportunity, but Major Beadel, the acting battalion commander, was a friend of Hinkle, and I thought it best to defer the request until a more favorable opportunity.

*

As we left Normandy the country became more open in character. The fields were larger with fewer hedgerows. The villages were more open with wider streets. Houses in Normandy were largely of stone, but as we moved east the houses in larger villages were often brick or plaster and more modern in design.

Some days later our column reached Vallon sur Gee and halted on the west edge of town. A fire fight broke out down a lane off to our right where a couple of tanks cornered some seventy five Germans in a barn. Burp gun fire swept the road, and the battery personnel dismounted the trucks and took cover in the ditch, a procedure we normally followed when a halted column was taken under fire. General Wyche came down the road in his jeep, the red two star flag flying from the short staff on the fender. He spotted me standing in the ditch and stopped. I saluted and climbed up to the side of his jeep and told him the situation. He wanted to know why I didn't form the battery into patrols and go after the cornered Germans. Before I could explain the difficulty I would cause if I left the trucks and guns blocking the road to go hunting Germans, the column ahead began moving. My dilemma was solved. We climbed back into our respective vehicles. The general waved good bye. The tankers were left to deal with the Germans.

On another occasion, General Wyche came by in his jeep while the column was halted and the road was being shelled. He saw me, stopped, inquired about my mother and father and carried on a five minute conversation while everyone else was prudently taking cover. He closed the conversation saying, "Remember me to them when you write, Jack," and told his driver to move on. As his jeep took off, I dropped back into the ditch. General Wyche was an artilleryman and kept a close eye on his artillery battalions as well as his infantry regiments. So far as I know in his travels up to the infantry he always came in a jeep with his driver and no other escort.

The drive east from Coutance to the Seine River took the 79th past a large body of German troops facing the British 1st Army which had a section of front east of the two American Normandy landings. One day we pulled off a secondary road on which we were moving in column into a field with a high hedgerow to our north. Hearing artillery and small arms fire to the north, we took our glasses and peered through the hedgerow to find the 30th Division marching on a parallel road to the north and somewhat behind us. Their artillery was firing on road junctions adjacent to our position.

For several days the principal threat was German tanks attempting to break out of the Fallaise pocket. When we went into position off the road, we faced the guns north prepared for tank attack. At one point a German tank force was spotted in a wood two thousand yards to the north. The air force dispatched P47s which bombed them into submission, relieving us of the necessity to intervene.

We thought the 79th was headed for Paris until we received word that the French 2nd Armored Division had been designated to enter Paris. In fact General Eisenhauer's plan was to bypass Paris for the time being, and the 79th was intended to establish a bridgehead over the Seine at Mantes-Gasscourt. The French 2nd Armored under General Leclerc was released at the insistence of General DeGaulle to strike for Paris along with the 4th Infantry Division to prevent demolition of the city by Hitler's order and avoid takeover of the capitol by communist elements of the FFI. So while Paris was being secured upstream, the batteries of the 310th went into position on the hills overlooking Mantes, and the 313th Infantry effected a crossing of the Seine using a narrow dam until a pontoon bridge was constructed by our engineers.

The Germans threw a large number of planes at the bridge in an effort to cut off our infantry in the bridgehead over the Seine. For the first time we heard the swoosh of rockets fired from German aircraft. We had a grand view of their attack on our bridgehead and a shot at their planes as they came up over us from their bombing runs. Our own antiaircraft section, using their quad .50 machine guns and 40 mm gun, shot down three planes in two days. The battery was in more danger from anti-aircraft fire than from the German planes because the anti-aircraft gunners at either end of the pontoon bridge followed the planes in their sights and kept firing as they flew over and behind the hill on which we were situated.

On the 23rd of August the battery crossed the river on the pontoon bridge and went into position on the edge of an air strip to support our infantry dug in on the far side of the strip. We used a fifty foot wooden control tower as an observation post. The feeling of exposure as we climbed that rickety structure was intense. The local French told us that the Germans used the structure to observe the effect of bombs dropped on sheep. I felt like a sheep standing on the top platform which swayed back and forth, particularly after one of our trucks ran into and broke one of the guy wires. Captain Hinkle and I fired several daylight missions against German infantry crossing a hillside in front of the 313th. They were wearing long gray overcoats as they scuttled across over the fields under fire. I thought it a strange time of year to be wearing overcoats, but I suppose they knew it would be a long time before they could replace any lost clothing or equipment.

In this position the Germans mounted a series of counter attacks, and the battery fired almost constantly, day and night. In addition we had behind us corps artillery batteries which sent a stream of shells over us, some falling uncomfortably short. One of the units behind us was a black battalion, and we heard the cannoneers singing as they served their guns. One of their chants was, "Hitler count yo men." Three days later the fight was over, and the Germans withdrew, leaving their dead and wounded. The 2nd Armored Division (American) passed through us, and the 79th was transferred from Third Army under General George F. Patton to First Army under General William H. Simpson.

September 1 we received orders to head for the Belgian frontier as rapidly as possible. With the exception of a pause of some hours while engineers completed a bridge over the Somme, we made a run of 189 miles from the Seine through the battlefields of World War I to Tournay in Belgium. At that point, on September 3, we literally ran out of gas. The service units could not haul fuel by truck from the Normandy beachhead in sufficient quantities to sustain the speed of the advance. For five days the division was immobilized enjoying sunshine, Belgian girls and rest. Then fuel trucks arrived from Normandy, and once again we were mobile.

*

On September 8, 1944, the 79th was detached from First Army, returned to the Third Army, and ordered to the south flank of Third Army along with the French 2nd Armored Division. The latter, returned from its Paris mission, together with the 79th constituted the XV Corps under General Wade Haslip. This move required us to drive back into France, and then cut south across the main supply routes of all the Third Amy divisions. We drove day and night, trucks nose to tail in blackout, sometimes halting in traffic jams, occasionally lost, sometimes moving at speeds up to forty miles an hour to catch up to the vehicle ahead. We passed through Reims in midmorning, bought cases of champagne from the crowds which lined the streets and halted a few miles east of the city to refuel. Our water was low, and I brushed my teeth with champagne for the first and last time that morning.

Our fueling point was a World War I battlefield which had been left untouched for twenty five years, a stretch of land with blasted trees, slumping trenches and pockmarked with giant shell holes. The harshness of the destruction was overlaid by the growth of grass and brush and erosion of the soil, all of which gave the landscape an unreal softness.

September 10 we reached Joinville on the upper reaches of the Marne River, having traveled 281 miles in two days. Seventh Army, which had landed in the south of France on August 14, was pushing north toward us but was still several hundred miles away. Many retreating German units lay between the two armies. The morning of September 11 we marked our maps and prepared to move east. Division had posted tanks and armored personnel carriers at every crossing from which a road led south to guard against a sudden attack from that flank. The 315th Infantry was detached to clear a strong unit of Germans from Neuf Chateau, two or three miles south of our column. The 314th Infantry pushed on ahead to seize a bridgehead over the Moselle River, and the 313th Infantry was positioned to drive the Germans out of Mirecourt, another village a mile or so south of the road on which we were traveling. At one point another battery was firing directly over our heads at some target to our right as we drove east.

The evening of September 11, A Battery reached the village of Chef Haut where I laid the guns to support the 313th which was attacking in an easterly direction. In the next three or four days we repeatedly shifted our gun position because the infantry front faced east, then south, and finally west to assist the 315th. In the course of this engagement the 79th captured a German division of six thousand men. When the engagement was over the battery went into position on a hillside overlooking the crossing of the Moselle at Charmes. Here we received A rations instead of 10 in 1 rations, and we reopened our kitchen truck establishing a battery mess. Division set up quartermaster showers, and the battery was able to send men back for their first shower since landing in France.

Colonel Safford, recovered from his wounds, returned to duty and resumed command of the 310th to nearly everyone's relief. We had abandoned the practice of always digging in our positions as we made the rapid run across France. When the colonel first visited A Battery on his return it was raining and the ground was a quagmire. He took one look at our position and told me in no uncertain terms the battery was to dig in the moment it took up a new gun position. I was embarrassed, to say the least. As he left the dirt began flying, and we followed that order without exception until the end of the war.

I requested in writing transfer to a forward observer position in one of the other batteries. Major Beadel came by the battery and asked why I wanted a transfer. I described my confrontation with Captain Hinkle. The major asked no questions. He simply listened to what I had to say. Some days later Colonel Safford stopped by the battery. He made no reference to my conversation with Major Beadel but said, "Sit tight. I want you to stay where you are for the time being." I was satisfied that something would be worked out.

Meanwhile, on September 14 Jim Quillian, 310th liaison with the 313th Infantry, was wounded and evacuated, leaving a vacancy which converted Sergeant Bill Frick of Headquarters Battery into a temporary forward observer and subsequently led to his battlefield commission.

September 19 and 20 the battery moved forward through several positions to reach the flood plain of the river Meurthe just west of Luneville. The 315th infantry regiment, having cleared Luneville, and the 313th and 314th having cleared the Foret de Mondon, all three regiments massed along the south bank of the Vezouse River facing the Foret de Parroy. That forest extended six miles east to west and over four miles north to south. It was largely flat but thickly wooded with heavy brush undergrowth and crisscrossed with fire lanes, World War I trenches, new timber roofed dugouts, and barbed wire. The forest was a key to the defense of the Saverne Gap, the principal route through the Vosges Mountains into Alsace.

The original plan was to have the air force strike German positions, after which one regiment of the 79th would attack the forest from the west while a task force of the 2nd French Armored swept around the east side to entrap the 15th Panzer Grenadier Division. Unfortunately, heavy rain descended. The air strikes were postponed for three days, then attempted in poor flying conditions with meager results. Battalion Headquarters moved to Chanteheux, and on September 29, the battalion surgeon delivered a 7 lb. baby boy to a French woman next door to the command post.

The planned French 2nd Armored envelopment of the Foret de Parroy was abandoned because the ground was too mushy for the tanks, and the 79th began a drive to clear the forest with two infantry regiments. Heavy fighting took place as the infantry fought through dense brush and scrub forest for nearly three weeks. It rained constantly and the river rose to flood stage, requiring A Battery to relocate our third and fourth gun sections. At night we were assigned defensive barrages to fire in the immediate front of our infantry in case of counterattack by the Germans.

On October 12 the battery moved to our final Foret de Parroy position where we remained. October 21 a strong counter attack began during the night. The struggle continued until well into the day and the enemy was only thrown back after desperate fighting by the infantry. The battery fired barrage after barrage at the maximum rate of fire for two hours. The tubes of the howitzers became so hot that they could not be touched, and the paint peeled off the tubes in long ugly strips. The fifth section, responsible for carrying ammunition to the guns could not keep up with the rate of fire even with the assistance of all other hands at the battery position. Some 313th infantrymen from their service company had trucks parked nearby and came over to lend a hand hauling ammunition. When the cease fire came the last ammunition truck was being unloaded in the gun position.

*

On October 26 the infantry of the 79th Division was relieved by the 44th Division which had just arrived from the States. One battery of 105s from the 44th went into position behind us, and Colonel Safford told me to show them the ropes, so to speak. They were miserable, baffled by the rain and mud. They had never operated in such conditions. We tried to teach them the important tricks we had learned, such as winching the trucks and guns through the mud and how to keep the powder dry. But the skill of keeping one's self minimally comfortable had to be learned by experience.

The question uppermost in our minds was whether the 79th artillery was going to be relieved by the 44th artillery. The doctrine we were taught in school was that artillery was never in reserve, but shortly after this we too were relieved and sent into a rest area a few miles to the rear in the little village of Blainville sur L'Eau.

Blainville was a small village with a main street and number of side and lateral streets. The kitchen and fifth section with the motor park were located in a vacant factory beside the Meurthe River, a stream slightly larger than the Tualatin River back in Oregon, perhaps thirty to forty feet wide. The rest of the battery was billeted with French families under arrangements made by an advance party. We rolled into the village covered with mud and whiskers, and these families took us in as special guests, doing everything they could to make our short stay as pleasant as possible.

I was assigned to a room in the Zirnhelt family home, a two story common wall house in the middle of a long block. The family consisted of Monsieur and Madame Zirnhelt, their daughter, Marie Therese, a pretty girl of sixteen, and Grandmere Zirnhelt. Their joy with the end of German occupation outweighed the problem of living in an active war zone and having an American officer billeted in their living quarters. The house fronted directly on the street. The rooms were small. The parlor, which was opened in my honor, was rarely used. The kitchen had a sink, drain board, stove, and a large kitchen table. They had electricity, one bulb to a room at that time, as I recall, and I wrote letters at that kitchen table with Grandmere looking on. She always inquired to whom I was writing, and when I told her my wife or my parents, she invariably said, "Bon, bon," and instructed me to present her regards to them. As I look back through the years I cannot see Grandmere clearly, but I feel her presence. Small, black dress, iron gray hair, composed, inquisitive. She was quite a person.

Monsieur Zirnhelt had a governmental position, post office, or railway, as I recall. He was a veteran of the first World War, tall and spare, a man of dignity occupying a responsible position in his community. In France November 9, 1944 was La Fete de la Medale Militare. M. Zirnhelt, was a holder of that military honor, one which lay between our Silver Star and Distinguished Service Cross, and was awarded to noncommissioned officers. He took me to the town hall where the veterans of World War I gathered to drink a toast to their fallen comrades and another to Les Etats Unis using a superb wine which they had buried in 1940 before the German occupation. Then we all marched through the town in a miniature parade. One night the battalion held a dance for the enlisted men in the auditorium of the local school. The girls came from Blainville and surrounding villages well chaperoned by four or five family members per girl. Everyone had a good time under those watchful eyes.

During our stay in Blainville, I was assigned to sit as the junior officer on a general court-martial to try a number of infantrymen who drifted to the rear in the course of the long battle in the Foret de Parroy. They were charged with desertion in the face of the enemy. They were a sad group of fairly simple soldiers who struck me as bewildered, separated from their units and, pounded into a state of insensibility, they had drifted to the rear where they had been picked up by the military police.

The court consisted of a lieutenant, myself, a captain, several majors and a colonel. After we had heard the evidence and determined guilt, we considered the sentence. As the junior officer, I was required to state my recommendation for sentence first. Obviously, desertion was a serious offense, but I saw little justification to impose a death sentence, or a sentence of twenty years for these cases. But when I ventured ten years, the others would glare at me and bark out fifteen, twenty or more years. I don't recall ever having my recommendation followed by the other members of the court who were infantrymen. I believe these long sentences were nearly all commuted at higher levels.

In our army, at least the part of it in which I served, men generally did their duty because of personal responsibility, pride in their unit, loyalty to their comrades and no doubt with an underlying sense of loyalty to their country. The pains and penalties of the Articles of War underlay order and discipline, but they were not the source of individual motivation or high morale. Nevertheless, if one could simply walk to the rear with impunity when the going got tough, an army would soon disintegrate.

*

The evening of November 11, 1944 we moved forward after dark to an assembly area behind the French Second Armored Division and from there moved into a position near Vauxainville. Over the hill was a French 2nd Armored Division battery equipped with M 7 105 howitzers. We shared with the French a barn on the hillside below our guns, using it as a mess hall. The weather was miserable, a cold wet snow was falling and the fields were soft mud. Getting the guns into position was difficult and required winching the guns, doubling up trucks, and other expedients. The plan of attack was for the Second Armored and the 79th to break though the German defenses, go through the Vosges Mountains and break into the Alsatian plain. The initial infantry attack successfully cracked open the outer German line. November 20 the battery moved out to the road in the afternoon to follow the infantry. We were still on the road after dark and passed through a village on a street along which every building was on fire.

Sergeant Edward Kozak, now chief of the second gun section, had been after me to let him spend some time with a forward observer crew. Kozak was a fine soldier and a first rate chief of section. The forward observer crews had no vacancy for a person of his grade, but I finally let him go up with Lieutenant Lee's crew one morning to sample working with the infantry.

Within the hour word came that Kozak was dead, and Corporal McBride and Lieutenant Lee had been wounded and evacuated. Sergeant Earnest Compton won the Bronze Star carrying a wounded infantryman to safety through heavy enemy shell fire. A sound argument can be made for rotating men in the forward parties, but letting Kozak go up with the observer party just for the experience was, I think, a mistake on my part. He was a fine chief of gun section, and not easy to replace.

We began climbing into the Vosges mountains toward the heavily prepared defenses of the Saverne pass. Fortunately for us, the French Second Armored Division sent Task Force Massu by way of a narrow winding road through the Wolfsberg Pass to the south, and another task force through La Petite Pierre Pass to the north. These two task forces, and a third which followed them, hit the Germans defending Saverne from the rear, a feat which saved us from the necessity of assaulting a well fortified position with many emplaced 88 mm guns stocked with ammunition. A fourth 2nd Armored task force carrying 1st battalion 313th Infantry to reinforce their armored infantry raced across the Alsatian plain to attack Strasbourg.

Meanwhile the 310th Field Artillery, following the remainder of the 313th Infantry, moved through Phalsbourg and Saverne. One notable event was the capture of several railroad cars with giant cheddar cheeses strapped down on them. They looked to be five or six feet in diameter and a foot thick. Each battery received a large slice of the captured cheese to supplement its rations.

The division had now reached the Alsatian plain with its right flank anchored on Strasbourg and its left flank extending Northwest along the old Maginot line. The resistance was sporadic. There were still German units in the Vosges Mountains to our right rear struggling to slip by us and cross the Rhine into Germany. Other German units lay to our front, and our left flank was entirely exposed. The infantry dug in along a line facing northeast toward the German frontier as it joined the Rhine with the purpose of holding the ground while waiting for other divisions to move up on that vulnerable left flank. When they did not materialize, both infantry and artillery sent work parties to the rear to prepare withdrawal positions should that become necessary.

On December 2, 1944, as a result of a strategic conference between Generals Eisenhower and Bradley, Devers and Patch, Seventh Army abandoned the possibility of crossing the Rhine and was redirected north to assist the Third Army. This resulted in reassignment of divisions to XV Corps under General Haislip to the west of the crest of the Vosges while VI Corps under General Brooks was assigned from the Vosges crest east with the 45th, 103rd and 79th Divisions in line with the latter's right flank on the Rhine. In addition VI Corps had the 14th Armored in reserve. Unaware of these decisions of the high command, we moved forward from day to day, following our infantry. On December 14th we went into position at Neewiller just north of Seltz.

At night one member of the fire direction crew was always on guard. He sat at the table in the rear of the exec truck with a Coleman lantern burning, the telephones, firing chart, and plotting materials at hand. The guard also had the duty of keeping the pot bellied stove glowing in the rectangular tent attached to the rear of the truck. The floor of the tent was earth, sodden or frozen, depending on the weather, and as we pulled into each new position, we covered the tent floor with six inches of straw. I generally unrolled my bed roll on the straw several feet from the stove. Here I was at hand in case battalion phoned in a fire mission during the night. Inevitably some straw got too close to the stove and ignited. The guard woke me. I scrambled out of my bed roll in a hurry, and we spent some anxious minutes stamping out embers in the straw. In Alsace with snow and freezing weather, we put the fire direction center in a house or barn if one was handy. The cannoneers, however, had to sleep by their guns under tarps.

December 17, 1944 we crossed the Lauter River and reached Lauterberg, a village on the German frontier. The infantry just ahead of us ran up against the Sigfried Line which was constructed through the forest several miles back from the frontier on the German side. The German resistance was heavy with the first large masses of German artillery fire we had encountered. Our gun position was in a depression, and fortunately for us most of the enemy fire burst either in front of the guns or some distance to the rear. We could not dig in the guns in this position because it would have required too high an angle of fire. We solved the problem by filling ammunition boxes with dirt and constructed parapets around the guns. Much of the enemy shell fire was from dual purpose 88s used for both antiaircraft and ground fire, but it was seldom massed in the coordinated way we employed artillery.

CHAPTER 8

"North Wind," the German counter attack in Alsace

By December 18 the three 79th infantry regiments were still struggling to break through the Sigfried line when the attack was called off. Von Rundstedt's surprise counterattack through the Ardennes Forest far to the north of us had begun three days before, and the Third Army was rapidly shifting divisions away from our left flank where we had few enough forces for the task. On December 23rd we undertook our first withdrawal since reaching France. During the night the ground had frozen. The weather was cloudy and cold. A Battery recrossed the Lauter River and pulled back through Lauterberg. As the battery cleared the village, the Germans dropped a tremendous barrage on the road behind us. We returned to our former position at Neeweiler where we could cover the infantry who now dug in along the south bank of the Lauter river.

Christmas day A battery was detached from the 310th and assigned to support the division recon troop which was covering the Rhine bank from Lauterberg south to Selz. We moved the battery to a position in a frozen hollow on the east edge of the village of Eberbach well back from the river so we could cover a broad front of the Rhine. We found in our gun position two German 88s which had been abandoned in good condition. Corps Artillery removed one but left the other for us to play with. The battery ammunition section located some 88 ammunition in an abandoned German munitions dump, and the gun crews practiced firing the 88 across the Rhine into Germany. The 88 had a considerably longer range than our 105s.

We set up a fire direction center in a house where we were protected from the weather and could plot the various points on which we might be asked to fire in the event of German attempts to re-cross the Rhine. I had the wire section lay two separate telephone lines to the Recon Troop command post so our communications would be secure. We then ran a third line to two corps artillery batteries behind us, one with 8 inch howitzers and the other with 240 mm guns. Their mission was to support the infantry dug in along the south bank of the Lauter River to the north. They agreed to take fire missions from us in defense of the Recon troop strung out along the Rhine when they were not firing in support of our infantry to the north. Thinly stretched, the recon troop faced a string of German pillboxes lining the other side of the Rhine and the possibility of Germans crossing by boat at any point. Six inches of snow now covered the frozen ground with more on the way. We waited while the Battle of the Bulge raged in the north.

The winter of 1944-1945 was the coldest in Western Europe for many years. Across the entire front, Belgium to the Swiss border, the ground was frozen, the snow cover a foot deep. Our trucks with wheels chained slithered along the rutted ice packed roads. The German attack through the Ardennes Forest to the north of us was the same point of penetration the Germans had employed in 1940. Allied generals had considered the Ardennes a quiet sector unsuitable for attack, and it was thinly held by an untested division. The German attack was a complete surprise and threatened the Allied line of communications and what was now its principal port, Antwerp.

The Stars and Stripes, our only detailed source of information, reported regularly on the action in the north, and we followed the news with close attention. We knew the attack was serious but thought of it as a final German effort to forestall defeat. With our guns sited in the Eberbach position we set up an observation post in the roof of the church at Munchhousen, a village on the bank of the Rhine. From this post we could see the series of German pill boxes along the Rhine. One night a German patrol crossed the river and blew up two of the Recon Troop's light tanks. Several times the battery fired barrages at German patrols attempting to cross the river.

On New Year's Day, 1945, we received orders to prepare for parachutists and gas attack. Colonel Safford transferred Captain Hinkle to battalion staff as liaison officer with the 1st battalion 313th Infantry, replacing Captain Quillian who became assistant S 3 at battalion fire direction. I took over as A battery commander. Lieutenant Delbridge, became battery executive. Lieutenant Dillehay became reconnaissance officer, and Lieutenant William M. Frick, with a recent battlefield commission, was transferred from B Battery to A to became our forward observer.

I was delighted to get Frick. He had acquired a reputation among battalion officers as an unusually able sergeant who ought to be commissioned. Several days later, Frick and I positioned ourselves in the church roof in Mothern and adjusted the big 240s on several German pill boxes across the Rhine. We thought we observed some direct hits but saw no discernible physical damage other than blackened roofs. However, the impact of 240 shells on any pill box must have rattled the skulls of the occupants.

Third Army had shifted divisions north to attack the southern flank of the German penetration in the Bulge, and perforce Seventh Army had to take over part of Third Army's front. As a result the Seventh Army now was stretched from Saarbrucken on the west side of the Vosges across the mountains to Lauterbourg on the Rhine, then south along the Rhine to Strasbourg with only six infantry divisions to cover 126 miles of front. This meant over two miles per infantry battalion assuming all battalions were in line, though normally each regiment would hold one battalion in reserve. This was very thin coverage indeed. Two armored divisions, the 12th and 14th, constituted a reserve. South of Seventh Army, First French Army in the High Vosges faced a tenacious German army which the French had been unable to clear from the left bank of the Rhine south of Strasbourg to the Swiss border.

When the German offensive in the Ardennes was finally brought to a halt, the enemy shifted troops south to Alsace for an offensive code named Northwind by which Hitler hoped to break through the weakened Seventh Army lines. In discussing Northwind as the battle developed, it will help to bear in mind the two rearranged Seventh Army corps in order to picture the central position in which the 79th Division and the 310th Field Artillery Battalion found themselves. However, at battery level, my knowledge and that of the other battery commanders was pretty well limited to what we could see and hear, and what Colonel Safford told us.

The XV Corps now consisted of the 103rd, 44th, and 100th Divisions west of the High Vosges. The VI Corps now consisted of the 45th, 79th, and 36th Divisions plus Task Forces Linden, Herren, and Harris composed of the infantry regiments of the new 42nd, 70th and 63rd Divisions respectively. These new divisions, just brought up from Marseilles, were not ready to be committed as operational divisions. The VI Corps front now extended from the high Vosges along the German frontier to Lauterbourg on the Rhine, then south to Gambshein near Strasbourg, as shown on the map.

The Northwind attack broke New Years Eve west of the Vosges against the XV Corps. This attack was contained after hard fighting by January 4. The attack then shifted to the Bitche sector to our left, and the Germans drove a ten mile salient into the corps boundary between the 100th and the 45th Divisions. We knew a major battle was going on to the west from the sound of artillery fire. This thrust threatened the entire Seventh Army line of communications through the Saverne Pass, but was finally contained by those divisions with the aid of one regiment from the new 63rd Division and the 141st regiment of the 36th Division. The process of plugging holes with different units less than division size had begun.

At battery level we had virtually no information on this redistribution of units. Anticipating the possibility of further withdrawal, Colonel Safford ordered working parties from each battery back to the Maginot line to prepare gun positions. General Wyche was temporarily assigned to VI Corps and General Wahl replaced him as 79th division commander. Mindful of his artillery, General Wahl came by several times to see how A Battery was doing on its mission of supporting the Recon Troop. Once the general thought he had found one of our .50 caliber machine guns unguarded. Just as he laid hands on the gun Corporal O'Rourke, armed with a carbine, challenged him from a doorway a few feet away. The general left without comment.

On January 2, 1945 German advances in the Bitche sector made what was now a salient held by the 79th untenable. Seventh Army ordered withdrawal in stages, first to the Maginot Line, second to the Moder River line north of Hagenau, and third to the Vosges Mountains. The latter stage would have meant abandoning the Alsatian Plain and Strasbourg. I received orders just before noon January 2nd to prepare to move. We spent the afternoon packing gear as inconspicuously as possible. We had no way of telling whether the Eberbach population was pro allied, pro German, or mixed in this historic cockpit, and we could trust no one.

The 88 had no carriage available so we had to destroy it. My plan was to jam one round of high explosive down its muzzle and then fire another round through the breech. I cleared the area, attached a long lanyard and fired the piece myself. The lanyard was obviously not long enough. The doubled explosion sent fragments of the tube whistling by me, and I was lucky to escape alive. However, the destruction was a success. The 88 looked like a half pealed banana.

A Battery was the last battery scheduled to withdraw. I reminded the infantry guards not to blow the bridges over the small river south of Eberbach until we had crossed them. After dark the kitchen, ammunition and wire sections moved out.

The guns remained in firing position until 0430 the morning of January 3, so we could provide fire for the last infantry units if needed. Then the gun trucks pulled out of Eberbach as quietly as possible. As dawn broke, with deep snow on the ground and everything frozen tight, we reached our new position, a barren field between the villages of Niederbetchdorf and Kulendorf.

Shortly after the battery went into firing position Colonel Safford called for battery commanders, and we went on reconnaissance to locate our next withdrawal position on the Moder River line near Hagenau. The plan, as the colonel explained it, was to make this second withdrawal after dark that night. We picked out our respective battery positions and then returned to battalion headquarters, only to find that the withdrawal order had been suspended. The decision at Seventh Army was to fight it out on the ground we now held.

*

We waited. General Wahl had temporarily taken over command of the division during General Wyche's absence a few days before the withdrawal from Lauterberg. Brigadier General John Sheridan Wynn, Jr., replaced General Wahl temporarily as artillery commander. General Wynn inspected A Battery a few days after he assumed command. He asked the wire section how often they sharpened their wire pliers. Their response was that they did not sharpen wire pliers. The general then lectured them on the necessity of sharpening wire pliers. Sergeant Schaefer, who had laid wire across France, listened respectfully, but when he later reported to me, he shook his head over a general who didn't know about wire pliers.

Captain Philip Warner commanded Headquarters Battery, Division Artillery. I ran into him some weeks later and inquired about General Wynn. Warner told me he had gotten into big trouble with General Wynn for questioning orders that he provide the staff officer's mess with better rations than the rest of headquarters battery. The general,

Phil said, was very put out. The night the division withdrew from Lauterberg, the general had personally posted him at a road junction where he was directed to stay until he was relieved. As the last infantry pulled out one of the regimental commanders stopped his jeep and questioned Warner, who was standing by the two lane snow covered road. On each side of the road a column of infantry slogged along single file. Warner explained.

"Well, you'd better come along with us," said the colonel.

Warner replied that he could not. General Wynn had told him to stay there until he was relieved.

"I'll take care of the general," said the colonel. "You get going."

Shortly after that General Wyche returned to division, and General Wahl came back to Division Artillery. We heard a rumor later that General Wynn had been reassigned to the Pacific as commandant of Manila, but no one could vouch for it. The register of graduates of the Military Academy lists his highest command in the service as Commanding General, 79th Division Artillery, a position he held for a very few days.

*

The field in which A and B Batteries were situated was so barren and exposed that Fred Thomas and I went up to Kuhlendorf to see if we could find better cover for the guns and shelter for the men. With Colonel Safford's permission, we moved both batteries up to Kuhlendorf. I took the east side of town for A Battery, and Thomas took the west side for B. 3rd battalion 313th infantry was dug in along the Maginot line to our left front. The 242nd infantry regiment of the 42nd Division was to our right front. The roads were crowded with French refugees who had gotten wind of the retreat and were trying to keep ahead of the Germans and behind our lines. The French had received us as liberators and knew what to expect from the Germans if they were still around on their return. They moved on foot and on bicycles. They pushed small carts loaded with their possessions, and they walked for miles on the icy roads

until they reached a railhead where the army provided trains
to carry them back into Lorraine.

General Wyche now had a hodgepodge of units to manage
from the Vosges to the Rhine: 242 Infantry, 222nd Infantry, 315th
Infantry, 313th Infantry, 232nd Infantry, then down the Rhine:
314th Infantry, CCB 14th Armored Division, more elements of
232nd Infantry, and elements of 3rd Algerian Division, plus
miscellaneous tank, tank destroyer, engineer and cavalry units.
At A battery we spent the 5th, 6th and 7th of January digging
deep pits for the guns and deep covered foxholes for the
cannoneers. There were several concrete pill boxes, outworks
of the Maginot line, in our gun position, but it did not seem
practical to attempt to use them. Vision from inside them was
limited and a pill box was an obvious target. We located the
battery command post and fire direction center on the second
floor of a house on the edge of town behind the guns. Sergeant
Prather, our motor mechanic, took his maintenance truck to the
supply depot at Hagenau, which was handing out gasoline to
anyone who would take it. The stores would all have to be blown
up in the event of further retreat. He filled the truck with five
gallon cans and brought them back to the battery as a reserve
fuel supply.

The battle about to begin was vividly described by Colonel
Hans von Luck of the 21st Panzer Division in his book, *Panzer
Commander.*
> "In these two villages of Hatten and Rittershoffen
> there now developed one of the hardest and most costly
> battles that had ever raged on the western front."

Early the morning of January 7th the Germans attacked 3rd
Battalion, 313th Infantry, with infantry and tanks. A Battery
expended all but 13 rounds of ammunition before Service Battery
trucks could get a resupply to us. The attacks continued through
the 8th and then broke off without successful penetration of
3rd Battalion's defense. On the 9th the enemy attacked the
242nd Infantry regiment. This was the 242nd's first experience
in combat. On the 10th the enemy broke through the 242nd's

defenses with infantry, tanks and flame throwers. The 2nd battalion, 315th Infantry, was rushed to the village of Hatten to stop the breakthrough and managed to secure a foothold although it was nearly surrounded as the 242nd fell back. The enemy held most of Hatten and moved tanks and infantry down the road toward Rittershoffen which was occupied by the headquarters company of the 315th infantry and a few tank destroyers.

In the course of a few minutes it appeared that the enemy would be able to overrun both Rittershoffen and Kuhlendorf. One of A Battery's guns had gone back to ordinance for repair, and consequently we had only three guns in battery. We pulled the three guns from their pits and placed them in the open fields to the east of Kuhlendorf to cover the road to Rittershoffen and the other approaches to the town. The fight was too close for indirect fire, and it was impossible to determine who was holding what part of Hatten. I put bazookas out on our flanks and the fifty caliber machine gun in a pillbox covering the Kuhlendorf—Hatten Road. The anti-aircraft quad 50 covered the open fields where we could expect infantry. One man in each of the abandoned gun pits had a grenade and instructions to destroy our supply of M 1 "Proximity" fuses if our position was overrun. We then dug additional slit trenches and waited for developments, listening to the crackle of the fire fight in front of us.

The division air observers in their light plane flew overhead watching for German tanks. They spotted two headed into the eastern side of Kuhlendorf and adjusted fire of our three guns driving the tanks back and knocking out a half track. The air observers also obliged by giving us a running account of the battle as they saw it from their vantage point. Then the 3rd battalion 315th, passed through our position headed for Hatten to reinforce the 2nd battalion. No infantry ever looked better to us than those tired veterans shuffling along, single file on each side of the frozen road. By evening they had a foothold in the southwest corner of Rittershoffen, and we could move the guns back into the gun pits.

By this time the 79th's infantry was scattered along the front as General Wyche fed troops into the line where needed to reinforce defenders and plug the holes opened by new attacks. This meant that combat teams were broken up, and the artillery batteries were engaged in supporting different battalions wherever the need was greatest. Lieutenant Dillehay and his crew were with the 3rd battalion 313th as forward observers in Rittershoffen. During the night the enemy attacked once more, and the remaining 42nd division troops withdrew, leaving the 79th infantry to hold the position alone. That same night Sergeant Schaefer's wire crew ran a telephone line up the Kuhlendorf—Rittershoffen road to keep communications open with the infantry and our forward observer.

Lieutenant Dillehay returned in the morning to what had been his observation post in a small church. He opened the back door and saw a church full of Germans with rifles at port arms running between the pews. He quietly shut the door and escaped unnoticed. Our other observer, Lieutenant Frick, and his crew were holed up in a pillbox near Oberrodern on the left shoulder of the German penetration. They spent eleven days in this position and when they finally emerged they were black with soot and powder from the shells that had struck the pillbox.

Enemy jet planes appeared over us for the first time. One bomb took the roof off the house in which I and the fire direction crew had been sleeping. Another bomb destroyed two of our trucks and one sheep. Our anti-aircraft had great difficulty shooting at jets because of their speed. Our 40 mm and quad .50 fire was nearly always far behind the target, but they finally brought one jet down. The American P47s could not touch them, the jets were so much faster. Fortunately they had a very limited fuel capacity which sharply reduced their effectiveness. Had the Germans brought them into service sooner they would have made life a good deal more difficult for us.

All during the night of January 10th and the early morning of the 11th the enemy shelled the front line villages and the fields around them with a greater volume of continuous fire than we had ever experienced. From thirty to sixty rounds per minute fell for hours on end. About nine o'clock in the morning heavy fire began falling in Kuhlendorf, two more trucks were hit, many buildings struck, and rounds fell throughout the gun position, cutting the telephone lines to the guns and destroying the latrine with a direct hit. Only the fact that we were dug in so thoroughly kept us from sustaining casualties. We were protected from everything but a direct hit.

The infantry in Rittershoffen was taking a fearful beating and might not be able to hold out much longer. I reconnoitered a new position in a creek bottom north of Schwabwieler where there was a small amount of flash defilade. I thought that unless we moved out of Kuhlendorf we might never get our guns out because our trucks would be destroyed. Unlike the guns and personnel, trucks could not be dug in. Just before noon, January 11, battalion headquarters released A battery and allowed us to withdraw to the more protected position. With the help of one truck from B Battery and several Service Battery trucks we managed to extricate the guns from Kuhlendorf.

The fighting in Rittershoffen raged from house to house. The Germans used tanks and infantry in repeated attempts to flush our infantry from buildings and basements. Our infantry in turn had the help of tanks from the 14th armored Division to counteract the enemy in the streets. Captain Hinkle won the silver star for his work directing tank fire in the village, reportedly sitting on top of one of our tanks as he did so.

Our wire section ran a new telephone line from battalion headquarters in Niederbetchdorf to Rittershoffen, laying it entirely cross country through the fields rather than along the road which was being shelled so heavily that the wire was cut as fast as it was laid. The new line ran up a slight valley or depression between the Kuhlendorf—Rittershoffen road and the Neiderbetchdorf—Rittershoffen road. This depression which offered some protection from direct enemy fire, ended

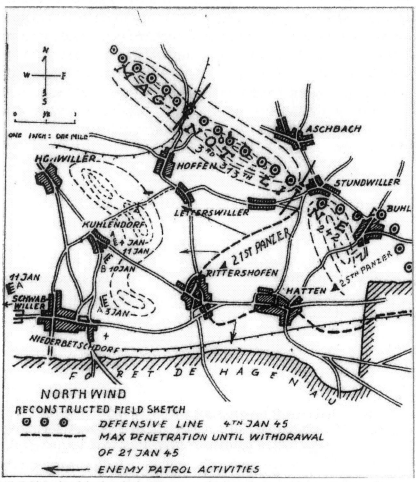

11.7 Sketch of the battle for Hatten and Rittershofen, Alsace, France, January 7 to 21, 1945. Elements of the 21st and 25th Panzer Divisions were contained in bitter street fighting.

about eight hundred yards from a small orchard which marked the western edge of Rittershoffen. That barren snow covered plateau was exposed to enemy artillery, machine gun, mortar and small arms fire.

That telephone line was the sole secure link between the infantry in Rittershoffen and the outside world from January 11th to the 21st. The line was cut by enemy fire an average of thirty times each day, and often would be cut by shell fire both in front and back of the wire crew as they spliced a break. The wire crew worked day and night no matter how bad the weather and heavy the fire. The only time the wire was out over night occurred when armored troops laid a mine field across the plateau using British mines and then were unable to tell us the location of the mines. Colonel Safford decided to use radio until daylight when the wire crew could see the ground and spot the mines.

Having looked the terrain over myself, I thought keeping the wire in was asking too much of the wire crew. I told the colonel with some emotion that if he insisted the wire be kept in, I would take the wire crew myself. The colonel replied quietly but firmly, "Yes, the wire is essential," and "No, you will not take the wire crew yourself. You take care of your battery." With all of his concerns Colonel Safford never lost his composure, his concept of what had to be done, or his understanding of our emotional pressures.

The battalions of 79th infantry fought off the German attacks until January 21st when a decision was made to withdraw to the Moder River line north of Hagenau. By this time the Germans had crossed the Rhine in force taking Gambesheim and threatened Strasbourg behind our right flank. On our left they had driven within a few miles of the Saverne Pass. The stretched and scattered troops of the VI Corps were in danger of being overwhelmed by the forces the Germans had massed to recover Alsace and take the pressure off the American and British counter attacks in the north following the Bulge. The mechanics of withdrawal had to be carefully planned to extricate our two battalions from Hatten and Rittershoffen where they were separated from the enemy by only a street or a house.

Late in the night of January 21st A Battery pulled out of position and into the long column of the retreating 79th Division. This time Fred Thomas and B Battery remained to cover the last of the infantry. A driving snowstorm limited visibility, and the roads were covered with ice. Along the route military police wrapped in blankets over their overcoats warned of treacherous spots in the road and indicated turns at road junctions. Our orders were to destroy any vehicle or gun which slipped off the road. The column could not be halted, and no wreckers or repair trucks could be sent back to tow vehicles disabled or ditched. The last infantry pulled out of position just before daylight, and A Battery moved into a position we had previously prepared in a frozen creek bottom below Neidershofflesheim, a village behind Hagenau. The enemy did not discover the withdrawal until daylight.

The Moder line proved defensible, and the Germans abandoned their offensive on January 25, although we prepared defensive positions still further to the rear in case further retreat was necessary. The infantry was exhausted after three weeks of intense fighting and heavy casualties. Unlike the practice in earlier conflicts, in World War II American divisions were generally kept in the line of battle and replacements were fed into them as losses occurred rather than taking units out of the line to refit. This was more efficient in some ways but led to exhaustion of the survivors. The practice would not have been possible had we encountered the trench warfare of World War I.

The battle in Alsace was almost wholly defensive from Christmas forward and conducted in our locality primarily by elements of three divisions: the 79th, the 42nd. and the 14th Armored. The 79th had the advantage of six months of previous combat under varied conditions. The 42nd Division was thrown into a defensive battle in its first combat experience. Reinforcements were simply not available because of the previous shift of Third Amy units north to deal with the German offensive in the Ardennes. The 310th Field Artillery was awarded a Presidential Unit Citation for its conduct in the Hatten Rittershoffen Battle, and the 79th Division was awarded the Crois de Guerre by the French Government.

CHAPTER 9

Crossing the Rhine, Occupation
and home

On February 6, 1945, the 79th division was relieved by the
101st Airborne Division, put on the road, and headed
back through the Vosges Mountains via the Saverne Gap. Little
had changed since our drive east three months earlier. The
trenches, ditches, stacked German ammunition and concrete
obstacles looked the same, untouched as yet by the grass and
leaves of spring. Only the rusting 88 mm German guns and the
burned out Sherman tanks showed the passage of time. The road
we followed had been our main supply route and the surface
was pitted and rutted, almost totally ruined, by the thousands
of wheeled and tracked vehicles it had carried the past several
months. We continued on west and reached the Moselle river
near Pont-a-Mousson where the Third Army under Patten had
fought over the approaches to the Fortress Metz. The area was
completely destroyed, the villages abandoned, not even a cat
or dog remained.

The battalion was instructed to secure billets in Thiacourt,
a small village half way between Nancy and Metz where the
damage was not so extensive. Some of the land around Thiacourt
had not been touched since the battles of the autumn of 1918,
and the ground was covered with a network of trenches and
splattered with giant shell holes. Above the village was a
cemetery in which five thousand American soldiers who died

in World War I are buried. During the occupation the German authorities allowed the French to tend the cemetery, and they had kept it in beautiful condition, although the Germans would not permit the American flag to fly over it.

We spent ten days in Thiacourt, days devoted largely to repairing our equipment which was badly in need of attention after the winter battles. Division authorized three day passes, and a number of men in the battery took the opportunity to go back to Blainville and visit the French families with whom they had been billeted in November. Colonel Safford and General Wahl inspected the battery equipment and material, and pronounced it good. The general also told me that the recommendation for my promotion had gone forward several weeks before.

*

The 79th was now transferred from the 7th to the 9th Army, and on February 17th A Battery left Thiacourt, joined the battalion column, and headed north some hundred miles to Rosmer, a village west of Liege in Belgium. The division had been selected, although we did not know it at the time, to make the Rhine crossing when German resistance on the left bank of the Rhine was cleared. The Roer River was presently the front line, and the river was in flood. Until the waters subsided, the sector was quiet. We reconnoitered new battery positions west of Heinsberg where we could support a crossing of the Roer.

Four days later I moved the battery into a field just south of Heinsberg and put our observation post in a partly demolished schoolhouse on a hill top overlooking the Roer. Here we waited while other units to the south of us cut the German forces remaining west of the Rhine into pockets and gradually reduced them. Then, after several displacements and a short crossing over the Roer, we were withdrawn back into Holland and billeted in Waubach, a recently liberated village three miles from Heerlan on the Dutch side of the German border.

Waubach was a great place for soldiers who had just spent the winter in Alsace. There was no training schedule because we were planning for the Rhine crossing and sending work parties daily up to the area just west of the Rhine. The population welcomed us with enthusiasm. There were movies every night and dances for the troops in Heerlan. A Battery's guns were inspected by 9th Army ordinance officers who congratulated my chiefs of section, saying that their condition was superior to those of any other artillery unit they had inspected.

I was billeted with the Kramer family in a large, almost empty house situated in a park-like property on the edge of Heerlan. They had two attractive young daughters, Simone and Didi. Mr. Kremer owned coal mines in Alsace as well as in Belgium, and the family was fluent in French, German, Dutch and English. They explained that most of their furniture had been scattered around in different houses in the area to prevent the Germans from looting it.

On March 14 Captains Thomas, Kopp and I reconnoitered gun positions near Budberg, southwest of Wessel, from which we could support the Rhine crossing. Our batteries spent the following days digging in these projected positions and camouflaging them. Lieutenant Eric C. Phillips, joined us as a replacement for Lieutenant Lee who had been evacuated with wounds. Phillips took over Lee's forward observer crew. Phillips had a difficult time at first, coming as a green second lieutenant into a unit which had been together for two and a half years. He was, however, a bright and energetic officer who learned quickly.

The Germans were still pounding Antwerp with flying bombs to keep us from clearing the port which was essential to shorten our supply line still dependent on Cherbourg. Our location was under the flight path of the bombs called V 1s. These were slow flying jet powered cylinders with stubby wings, and they went chugging overhead their exhaust burning brightly as they were generally fired at night. One clear night I was absently watching them when something went wrong with the guidance system of one rocket which suddenly turned in wide circle and headed back into Germany, striking the ground with a tremendous explosion.

While in that location, I happened to be in the battery fire direction center when the telephone rang. I picked up the phone and answered it, "Able GP," meaning the A battery gun position. It was a sergeant at battalion headquarters who thought I was the telephone operator.

"We have a supply of liquor we've found," he said. "Send a jeep over, and we'll give you a few gallons."

"This is Lieutenant Beatty," I replied, "and we don't need any of your liquor, thank you." I wasn't about to have gallons of hard liquor distributed at this point. Several hours later we got an urgent call from battalion telling us to round up that liquor. It was not drinkable alcohol, but liquid fuel for V1 rockets, and several men from other units had already been evacuated to the hospital.

On March 16, 1945, I wrote my mother and father:

> "Got a letter from Clissa yesterday, and she passed her exams OK. Great Day. She is now a doctor. Also my promotion came through. It bounced in the 7th Army, but went through OK here, it seems, and very rapidly. I've been a 1st lieutenant a long time."

While the gun sections were digging in the new position, forward observers and the infantry rehearsed river crossing in assault boats on the Maas river. When the new gun positions were completed and ready for occupancy, the drivers and chiefs of gun section were shown how to load guns and trucks on assault boats. This was an extra precaution. It was anticipated the engineers would have a pontoon bridge in place by the time the artillery crossed the river.

On March 20th Sergeant Charles Griffith, A Battery's very capable chief of the battery survey section, was commissioned a second lieutenant and transferred to C Battery. That same night the 310th firing batteries moved up to their Rhine positions under cover of darkness, a fifty mile run in blackout. The next three days we spent preparing for the intensive fire which would occur in support of the crossing. The trails of the guns were backstopped with horizontal logs to prevent displacement under repeated fire. Each gun section dug an extra ammunition pit to take part of the 500 rounds per gun we were allocated. Sergeant Baygents and his Fifth section planned their ammunition resupply.

March 22nd General Wyche came by my observation post to look the battery over and congratulated me on my promotion. He said he had written my mother and father as soon as he saw the orders cross his desk. I noted in my letter home that the general "Looks wonderful—ten years younger than he did in Alsace." This was not surprising considering the stress of command in that chaotic battle.

I took Lieutenant Phillips and a crew down to the dike which ran along the west side of the Rhine, and told him to tunnel into the back side of the dike and then poke a small hole up to the surface through which they could insert the head of a BC scope to observe and conduct fire. He and his crew worked all night completing the tunnel, and just as they finished it the whole thing collapsed. The soil was too sandy. Phillips reported back to me, covered with mud. I gave up the project and relocated the battery OP to a house six hundred yards back of the dike. Lieutenants Frick and Dillehay with their forward observer crews joined their assigned battalions in the infantry assembly arca to go over plans for the assault.

The day before the crossing, I manned the observation post and watched the Air Corps work over enemy positions across the river using P47s and medium bombers. I heard a tremendous roar behind me. Looking to the rear, I saw the woods in which A Battery was located almost completely covered with smoke. I thought my battery was gone. I took off in my command car to see what, if anything, was left. I found the battery intact, but it had been a close call. Ten 500 pound bombs struck the battery position, all missing the guns and the thousands of rounds of ammunition dug in. Many more bombs were dropped in the vicinity and a 311th battery to our left had several men killed. Our men were still laughing at Sergeant Gierascimowicz who was having his hair cut when the first bomb fell. He ran for a slit trench with his white sheet flying behind him.

*

The artillery plan for the crossing was more elaborate than any we had heretofore experienced. I think the high command was still smarting from failure to detect the Bulge attack and the Market Garden air drop disaster and wanted to be sure it did not have a failed river crossing on its hands. In our sector the 79th and 30th Divisions were to make the assault. Behind their own eight artillery battalions, Corps had massed forty-six more battalions of light, medium, and heavy artillery. Artillery fires were planned so that every possible point of enemy resistance would be smothered. Each 79th firing battery had two forward observers with the assault battalions, and the fire direction centers of each battalion were linked through Division artillery to the supporting corps artillery.

The schedule of fires came down to the battery the evening of March 23. The preparation was to commence at 2:00 AM March 24 with the assault boats to move out at 3:00 AM. Everyone but the guards turned in early to get some sleep. We had no problem waking up. The British, who were making a crossing to the north of us, began their fire at midnight, and the sky was filled with the flash and rumble of guns in the distance. Precisely at 2:00 AM Lieutenant Delbridge gave the order to fire to our guns, and as he did so, the other 860 guns opened fire. Most corps artillery was located to the rear of us and their shells came whistling over head. The sky was constantly alight with the explosion of propelling charges and an occasional premature air burst of some of the shells.

At 3:00 AM our fire was shifted from the area along the river to targets farther inland. The infantry climbed into their assault boats and pushed across the river. They had far better luck than anticipated. The Germans along the shore line were so stunned that they were helpless, and the infantry lost fewer men making the crossing than they had lost practicing crossing on the Maas River. As soon as the east bank was secure the engineers set to work on a pontoon bridge. Unfortunately, upstream the U. S. Navy let a sea mule get away from them. It floated down stream crashing into the nearly completed pontoon bridge, tearing it apart. The Germans now had the bridge site under artillery fire and scored repeated hits with 170 mm guns.

Shortly after noon I took the third gun section under Sergeant Gierascimowicz down to the river, loaded it on a barge, and made the crossing about six hundred yards downstream from the bridge, watching the shelling of the bridge site as we crossed. We hauled the gun into the new battery position and registered it. Later in the afternoon the remainder of the battery crossed by barge and assembled in the new position which was on the outskirts of a town called Dinslaken, a few hundred yards east of the bridge site where the engineers were still struggling to complete the bridge. Shells intended for the bridge sailed over our heads and the Germans made repeated attempts that night to bomb the site using aircraft. The bridge was protected by a large number of anti aircraft guns, and the amount of flac they put into the air was awe-inspiring. 50 caliber slugs, tracers and 40 mm shells ripped over us and occasionally through us as the gunners followed the aircraft which were coming in and departing from the bridge at low altitudes.

*

With the end of March the fighting was substantially over. The division moved slowly through the Ruhr cities clearing pockets of resistance in Hamborn, Bottrop, Gelsen, Watten, Bochum, Witten and Dortmund. On March 31 I wrote home:

"Am now in a battery position with the exec's post
in a power station and the rest of the battery (except
guns) in an apartment house. Law! Fort Sill was never

like this. Germany seems to be disintegrating under our feet. It is a strange war indeed. I do believe that whatever or who ever runs Germany is viewing this with sadistic pleasure. It is a very peculiar business, to say the least. The fight is gone out of most of them, but there is no one to officially give up. No grand cataclysmic climax, no thunder of the last guard. A shot here, a strong point there, and everything slips into the quiet of a graveyard. Ruins everywhere and people waiting in the cellars, for what they do not know. What a war!"

President Roosevelt's death on April 13, 1945 had a real impact on the troops. Most of the enlisted men were apolitical, drafted before they were of voting age. But they had a sense of loss that is difficult to describe. FDR had been the president for much of their lives, and he bore the public responsibility for the successful conduct of the war. Now he was gone, and we had an unknown senator in his place to make the peace.

On April 14, 1945 A battery fired its last round in combat from a position in the town of Witten, making a total of something over 35,000 rounds fired since Cherbourg. On April 17 we moved to the town of Bergkamen, charged to keep order in a ten square mile area containing wrecked mines, an oil refinery and a huge forced labor camp with displaced persons of many nationalities. The inmates were half starved. We rounded up German rations for them but had trouble with inmates foraging in the surrounding area. While standing on the running board of my command car chasing escaping offenders with my 45 in hand, I accidentally discharged it, putting a hole through the running board and just missing the toe of my right boot.

May 7 we were shifted east to the town of Werl and assigned the job of guarding a civil prison. Werl was situated on a road to Berlin, and considerable military traffic moved through it. There had been an acute shortage of cigarettes for several weeks, reportedly caused by black marketers hijacking supply trucks on the long run from Cherbourg. A steady number of supply trucks were turning the corner by the battery command post when one took the corner too fast and overturned, spilling cigarettes cartons on the road. The battery turned out en masse to help reload the cigarettes into a following truck retaining some cartons as compensation for the service.

The evening of V-E day, May 8, 1945, a British jeep with two British officers stopped for directions at the CP about dinner time. I invited them to have a drink and eat dinner with us. Both officers were members of Parliament, one Labor and one Conservative. They were good friends and had served for years together, but their politics were distinctly different. On one thing they agreed. The Americans and the British should keep right on heading east and take on the Russians. I thought they were out of their minds and said so. They rejoined that we were going to have nothing but trouble with the Ruskies and had better get on with it.

They were better informed than we were on the promises which Stalin had already broken concerning the countries of Eastern Europe, particularly Poland, but it would have been unthinkable for the British and Americans to turn on the Russians at this point no matter how difficult and obstreperous they were. The British were broke and exhausted, and we had not the slightest desire to march in the footsteps of Napoleon and Hitler into that military quagmire.

Following V-E Day we remained for some days at the crossroads waiting for further orders. General Wyche was transferred from the Division and was replaced by Brigadier General Watson from the 29th Division.

*

Ninth Army called for a 79th Division artillery battery to fire a salute on Memorial Day at the new American cemetery at Margratten in The Netherlands. The 310th Field Artillery and the 3rd Battalion, 313th Infantry, had just been awarded the Presidential Unit Citation for the Northwind battle in Alsace, and the 310th was asked to send a battery. Colonel Safford picked A Battery, and it was quite an honor. I had the guns painted a dark green, the tires blackened with stove polish, and, as a final, if unorthodox touch, I had the gun wheels painted red, the traditional artillery color. Division ordinance gave our gun trucks a new coat of green paint and the 3rd Battalion, 313th Infantry, who had just received their presidential unit citation bars, loaned them to us. While we were polishing up our gear, I learned that I had received the Bronze Star.

We left the morning of May 28th, Delbridge, Dillehay and I in my command car, followed by the four guns sections, and set out across Germany for Holland. I had written in advance to Simone Kremer who had invited me to visit if I could after the war. The gun sections were billeted in a Maastricht rest center, and we three officers in General Simpson's staff house. The morning of the 29th we cleaned the trucks and guns and took them out to the cemetery, a new one with fourteen thousand graves, stark white crosses on raw clay mounds. The grass had not yet grown. When we returned early the morning of May 30th, some 20,000 Dutch came to the cemetery with flowers. The bare earth on every one of those fourteen thousand graves was banked with flowers as a tribute to our dead.

General Simpson made a speech. The chaplains said prayers. We stood at attention beside our red wheeled guns for forty five minutes. Then we fired the salute. The ceremony called for a twenty one gun salute at 1100 hours with blank rounds fired at two second intervals. We had drilled the gun sections prior to departure to insure precision. Unfortunately, part way through the salute the fourth section fired simultaneously with the third. The first section picked up the count without hesitation, but we had a twenty gun salute. I had warned poor Delbridge to be careful that did not happen, and I was furious, but I doubt most persons there were aware of the actual count, and I heard no subsequent criticism. After the ceremony we took the guns back to the rest center and were issued passes until the morning of June 1. About half the men visited friends in Waubach overnight. I went to Waubach to stay with the Kremers.

The Kremers had reassembled their furniture from various hiding places, and the house looked beautiful. Mr. Kremer explained how they had been required to continue operating the coal mines but reduced the output as far as possible during the German occupation. The two girls had some horses which looked more like plow horses to me, but we saddled them and went riding. The evening of the 31st they had a dinner party for me and several old friends. One was a Belgian soldier named Sammy who had a wonderful voice and sang for us. Another was a Dutch woman who had spent a year and a half in a German concentration camp near Stettin as a political prisoner for helping Jews escape. The camp had been overrun by the Russian army which turned the prisoners loose. She and two other girls walked 150 kilometers to the Elbe River, traveling by night and hiding from Russian soldiers during day. At the Elbe the Americans put them on a truck and sent them home. She was in her mid twenties and looked forty.

The two Kremer girls were planning their post war careers. Simone intended to go to Paris and study music. We exchanged Christmas cards for many years. Simone did go to Paris and became a concert pianist. In 1989 I had a letter from Didi saying that Simone had died of cancer.

I reassembled our small convoy the morning of June 1st, and we retraced our path to Werl. By the time we returned, Colonel Safford had received orders to have those lovely red howitzer wheels repainted olive drab. Our trucks and guns had been identified by some higher commander who had read 310 F.A. stenciled in white on the bumpers. Other than telling me to put someone to work with a paint brush, the colonel did not seem overly concerned.

*

We resumed moving, this time south and east through Germany. At the battery level we had no information as to where we were going. We simply followed route markers and instructions from battalion headquarters. We had no newspapers other than the Stars and Stripes and hence little information on the maneuvering which was taking place between the allied powers concerning the final line of demarcation between the armies. We drove as part of a long column of trucks, guns, tanks and motorized infantry, and we passed equally long lines of thousands of civilians on foot, trudging along both sides of the road. Some pushed baby carriages piled with household goods. Some pulled wagons themselves. These were the captured workers whom the Germans had used so effectively to man their factories and work their farms.

The autobahns were magnificent, but every bridged overpass was blown, and we had to drive down a steep bulldozed dirt grade and ascend the other side of the bridge in a similar manner. Our journey ended at Eger, Czechoslovakia, renamed Cheb by the Czechs, a prosperous town of ten thousand inhabitants in the mountainous Sudeten border region. Battalion Headquarters was located in the center of the town, and the batteries were scattered around the outskirts, A Battery was billeted across a deep gully on the south side of town.

Lieutenant Frick and I took a room in a house near the battery command post. That evening, after we had the battery settled, we took off our boots and stretched out on the bed falling asleep almost at once. We were awakened shortly afterward by a racket which we identified by flashlight as a large cuckoo clock mounted on the wall. As we discovered, it sounded each quarter hour with a little quail popping out of the left hand side above the face, and sounded the hour by a cuckcoo popping out of the right hand side. I inspected the clock carefully in the morning.

It was a lovely piece of work with carved leaves, a rabbit on one side of the case and a pheasant on the other side together with a carved musket and a powder horn below. Before we left Cheb, I asked the German lady who owned the house whether she was interested in selling the clock.

"What have you got I can carry?" she replied. She explained that she and all the German speaking inhabitants, the Sudeten

Deutch, were being "repatriated" to what was left of Germany. She would not be able to take the clock with her. She also said that money would be of no use to her for it would all be confiscated. So I finally bought the clock for a package of twenty Hershey bars which Clissa had sent me and threw in a hundred marks for good measure. Sergeant Kimple, our battery mechanic, crated the clock using all my dirty clothing as packing. Then I mailed the clock back to the United States, doubting I would ever see it again, at least in one piece. Remarkably enough, the clock was properly delivered to Clissa and the only damage was to one ear of the carved rabbit.

The 310th at this point was simply occupying territory without any administrative responsibilities. The infantry was manning border posts facing the Russian army standing a few miles to the east. One evening I was invited with other battalion officers to a party with Russian officers inside the Russian lines. We arrived and found not only Russian officers but also Czech girls whom they had recruited from the local population. I recall speaking to one quite attractive girl, who came from Prague. She was clearly frightened of the Russians and said so. The Czechs had lived through occupation by the German army, and now they faced occupation by the Russian army.

The battalion received instructions concerning re-deployment of troops. The system gave points for length of service, wounds, battle stars and decorations. Those few with the highest number of points were to be sent back to the United States and discharged. The remainder were to remain with their present units. As the first orders came through transferring personnel, we held a final grand party at battalion headquarters for all the officers in the battalion, most of whom had been together for three and a half years. It was a great success with drinking, singing and farewells for those lucky ones who were leaving. I managed to get lost walking home and was rescued by my driver, Corporal Rosales, and First Sergeant Osborne in the gully adjacent to the battery. They told me the next morning that in my befuddled state I claimed to be looking for my maps in order to find my way home.

Early in July, several days after the party, A Battery moved up into a mountain resort village. I was billeted in the lap of luxury in a hideous square residence of the mayor with carpets so thick they were like grass. Battalion headquarters said we were expected to stay in this village for a long time, and the news was welcomed by everyone. The local girls had seen no soldiers of any kind during the war, and soldiers and girls were mutually enthusiastic.

*

Three days after settling into our mountain resort, we received new orders and the division moved in a long convoy back to a training area in eastern France to begin a cycle of basic training preparatory to deployment to the Far East for the invasion of Japan.

The requirement that we go through a basic training cycle made good sense from the army's point of view, but it produced near mutinous behavior from the troops. After fighting a long campaign during which each gun section, wire section and survey section had worked out shortcut procedures to solve problems in a distinctive way, they were expected to return to the formal prescribed methods taught according to the book at Fort Sill as though they were new recruits. Colonel Safford handled the situation with a masterly touch. He didn't raise an eyebrow when the battery column swung smartly down the encampment street in front of battalion headquarters singing to the tune of the Battle Hymn of the Republic:

> "When the war is over we will all enlist again,
> When the war is over we will all enlist again,
> When the war is over we will all enlist again—
> We will in a pig's ass hole!"

It was not clear to us at battalion level whether the division would be shipped to the States and then to the Pacific or sent directly through the Panama Canal. Jim Quillian, who had been wounded twice, had been returned the States on leave. He wrote me from Atlanta describing the delights of family life and expected to rejoin us in the States. I thought it more likely we would go through the States for final training and wrote Clissa to see what arrangements she could make to spend some time with me while we were stateside. I knew that would be a complicated matter for her.

However, on August 6, 1945, we learned the atomic bomb had been dropped on Hiroshima, Japan. I thought it meant the end of the Japanese war, and of course it did. We knew next to nothing about what an atom bomb was, but no one questioned that it was a watershed in warfare. In particular it meant that we would not have to hit the beaches in Japan, a prospect to which no one looked forward with pleasure. I don't recall any great jubilation, just immense relief. We were sobered by the implications of the bomb.

*

With the war over, the army turned its attention to the problem of administering the occupation of Germany, by now divided into four zones; French, British, American and Russian. The 79th Division was ordered to head east once more, this time into southern Germany. A Battery was assigned to a mountain village named Gleisenau some ten miles from Bamberg. The battery was billeted several miles up a small valley in a castle called Schloss Gleisenau. Between the village and the castle was an abandoned prisoner of war camp which had contained British and Australian prisoners.

This was an agricultural region with fields extending up to hills crowned with carefully tended forests. These forests were crossed by narrow lanes which did double duty as fire lanes and access for selective logging. The life of the community went on with little interruption from us. When I drove through the countryside, which I was presumed to be keeping under control, the farm workers in the fields stood up and tipped their hats. I suspect their ancestors did the same to Napoleon's captains and those of Marlborough a hundred years before Napoleon.

The castle was five stories tall counting the basement, which was partly above ground. The walls were three to five feet thick. It had a grand staircase of stone and all the floors were stone. The interior walls were hollow with ample space to walk within them, and each room had a great porcelain stove with a stove pipe which ran back through the interior wall and then up through the wall space. The furniture was sparse. I am quite sure that the good furniture had been hidden somewhere for safe keeping. I would guess that the castle was built in the fifteenth or sixteenth century. It had been modernized to the extent that running water, flush toilets, and bathtubs had been installed, as well as electricity, but it was a pretty formidable place for anyone to choose as a home in the twentieth century. Of course for us, it was the lap of luxury. We set up the battery kitchen in the cavernous castle kitchen and dined like feudal lords on army rations.

My bedroom was a small alcove off a large room on the second floor which we set up as the battery office and message center. When we had arrived in Gleisenau, we relieved a unit of the First Division. As we were moving in I noticed a good looking German woman, perhaps twenty-five or thirty years of age, standing about. I asked the first sergeant what she was doing there. He told me that Sergeant Schaefer, who was fluent in German, had questioned her. She told him she had been the interpreter for the company commander of the First Division, the Big Red 1, which had preceded us in occupation of that site. I had Sergeant Osborne tell the lady that we had our own interpreter and would not need her services. It developed on further inquiry that she had been my predecessor's bed fellow as well as his interpreter and was putting in a bid for that position with me. I declined the honor, but she did speak good English and was determined to help, so we put her to work as the interpreter at the prison camp headquarters building.

Some days later with almost no warning, two thousand SS troops were shipped into the abandoned prison camp and placed in our charge along with the responsibility of guarding and feeding them using largely the resources of our valley. I explained to the battery that as occupying troops and guardians of the camp we had to change our ways and look like spit and polish soldiers if we were going to be able to control two thousand prisoners and the civilian population with one under strength battery. They got the message, and for the next three months A Battery looked like the prewar regular army. Every shoe was shined, every brass buckle gleamed. Every piece of equipment sparkled. I borrowed some M1s from the infantry, and had the guard at the prison headquarters and at the castle stand at parade rest with fixed bayonets.

The first few nights at the prison camp the prisoners milled around in the dark between the barracks and in the confusion three escaped under the fence. We then put a guard with a 50 caliber machine gun in each of the four wood towers at the corners of the camp. Thereafter, at lights out they fired a cross burst of tracers over the camp. All prisoners were ordered to remain in barracks after lights out and warned that anyone moving outside barracks would be shot. The first night after this order was issued, a prisoner went out into the forbidden area. The sentry in front of the camp headquarters spotted him, leveled his rifle, and shot him dead.

The sergeant of the guard reported to me by telephone that the sentry who had fired the shot was very upset. I saw the soldier the next morning and told him that he was following orders. It was my responsibility, not his. I explained that this action would prevent the much greater loss of life that would occur if we were unable to maintain firm control of the prisoners. The battery was under strength. We had only 90 men, and we could not possibly control two thousand trained SS troops if they sensed any weakness on our part.

12. Parade of the holders of the Medale Militaire from W. W. I Blainville, Lorraine, France. M. Zirnhelt is to Jack's left. The parade ended at the city hall where the major led a toast to Les Etats Unis. Nov. 9, 1944.

13. Schloss Gleisenau, some ten miles east of Bamberg. Hq. of A Battery while guarding the SS PW prison camp down the road. The homemade flag flies triumphantly.

As a practical matter, there was no way in which we could do more than maintain security over such numbers. I went over the records and experience of the officers and had the highest ranking officer, a major, brought in for interview. His records indicated he had been in an SS infantry division, not in any special SS unit assigned to camps. His background appeared unexceptional. I designated him as PW Camp Commander, and gave him a desk in the camp office. The German woman interpreter was installed to facilitate communication between the officer of the guard and the German major. Major and interpreter got along famously, or so I was told.

Thereafter all orders to the prisoners were issued through him with the clear understanding that he would be responsible for carrying them out. This proved successful from our point of view. Our relations were cordial. We both understood that this was a temporary arrangement until decisions were made about prisoners of war. We had several crises when food ran short, but the local population of Gleisenau, when called upon, produced food to meet the shortage.

Life at Gleisenau settled into a pleasant garrison routine. Reveille, breakfast, cleaning equipment and drill in the morning. Lunch at noon, then a baseball game, and free time until retreat formation. Then dinner. All personnel except the cooks were rotated on guard duty at the camp. The Gleisenau tavern became a rendezvous for the enlisted men in the evening.

*

In the course of the campaign the army periodically distributed paperback books to the troops as a sort of combined intellectual and entertainment ration. One such booklet fell into my hands: "Island Victory," by Colonel S. L. A. Marshall. This was an account of the Iwo Jima island assault based on debriefing the troops following that costly battle. I was impressed by Colonel Marshall's methodology and decided I would try it in a simplified form in writing a history of the campaign for our battery.

I had saved a nearly complete set of maps issued to us including those which showed the location of the firing battery in each position we occupied. I gathered all battery personnel not on guard duty each afternoon for several weeks to discuss the campaign while it was fresh in our minds. Knowing the account would be printed and mailed to their home addresses, the men entered into the process enthusiastically. I put questions. They answered, arguing contested points vigorously and exciting each other's recollection until we reached agreement.

I took notes on these discussions and then worked the material into a story of the campaign as we experienced it at battery level. I typed it out with two fingers on a battered Underwood someone had liberated along the way. Sergeant John Schaefer, who remained in the army of occupation, followed up on printing, binding and distribution of the book titled D Day to VE Day.

Several months later we received orders to ship our prisoners to a railhead some miles away. Division agreed to provide the trucks, but A Battery had to do the scheduling and provide the security. The prospect of trying to move two thousand prisoners in two and a half ton trucks with a handful of guards was daunting. I could visualize what might happen if they all just stopped cooperating and left the trucks. A few would be killed, most would escape, and we would have SS prisoners scattered all over southern Germany at my expense. We managed to work out a logistical plan which kept the trucks covered with sufficient firepower to discourage any thought of escape and kept the trucks moving to the railhead without stoppages which might create unmanageable opportunities for escape.

*

During the spring of 1945 both my father and Clissa wrote asking me what my post-war plans were. My father pointed out the advantages of the GI Bill which would provide a year of schooling for each year of service plus a $75 monthly living allowance. Both suggested I might be interested in law school.

I had never previously considered law school, but this sounded like opportunity. I wrote Dean Christian Gauss at Princeton asking if he would send the necessary academic records to Harvard and Columbia. The Dean must have done well by me for I was admitted to both universities. I finally chose Columbia because Clissa had a job teaching at Columbia and had found us an apartment on 176th Street in New York.

In late November of 1945 the division left Germany and moved to Marseilles where we turned in our equipment and shook down the troops to be sure no unauthorized equipment went with them. I had acquired a German P38 pistol which I did not particularly like and traded it for a Luger which I did want. By this time I was the only original A Battery officer left, and only a handful of the enlisted personnel were original A Battery men. Our roster was filled out with artillerymen from other units. We boarded a five thousand ton Liberty Ship which had been converted into a troop carrier, and off we sailed into the Mediterranean, past Gibraltar, and into the Atlantic. A Liberty ship was built like a box car with a single screw and a maximum speed of six knots. We ran into the tail of a hurricane and pitched and rolled in the heavy seas. We were sleeping in three tiered bunks in a small compartment with no ventilation. I took my blankets and went out on deck to sleep. As the ship went over the swells the propeller would come out of the water and run wild until it sank below the surface once again. We were driven far south of our planned route and the weather was humid as well as stormy.

The food was awful, largely because the ship's cooks were indifferent. The cooks among the soldiers were outraged to see the rations so misused. A potential uprising was quelled when the army cooks took over the galley and the responsibility of feeding the passengers. The meals were greatly improved. We finally landed in New York on December 20, 1945 and were trucked to a separation center at Fort Dix. I telephoned Clissa to tell her I had landed and would be sent on terminal leave whenever the separation center finished processing me, probably before Christmas.

The processing involved signing off on a number of documents relating to the unit I had on board. I settled my accounts with the army, declined interest in a commission in the regular army, and much to my surprise, was released December 21, 1945, a day earlier than expected, on terminal leave until March 2, 1946. I caught a train into New York, took a subway uptown, and finally located the apartment building at 617 West 176th Street. By then it was 9 PM. I climbed up the stairs to the fourth floor and knocked on the door. The apartment was full of Clissa's classmates and colleagues from the Medical School celebrating my expected arrival the next day. There were introductions, congratulations, handshakes and hasty departures. The war was really over.

*

Justice Oliver Wendell Holmes in his moving address, "Memorial Day," referred to his service in the Civil War, saying, "In our youth our hearts were touched by fire." We were, all of us, touched to some degree. Touching, in the sense of exposure to danger, is relative. Holmes was wounded three times, the only original officer of his regiment to survive the war. My exposure to hazard was minor compared to that of our forward observers, and not comparable to that of those who served in the infantry rifle companies. To put this in perspective, on D Day A Battery had four officers and one hundred and two enlisted men. Our casualties were five killed, four officers and fifteen men wounded, twenty-one percent of our original strength. All the deaths and a majority of the wounds were incurred in forward observation with the infantry. Some rifle companies had casualty rates exceeding one hundred percent of their original strength.

The impact of World War II on our generation is more properly evaluated in terms of the effect of that experience upon our subsequent lives. In my own case the effect of that four and a half years was profound. The leveling rigor of service in the ranks and the later responsibility of small unit command were certainly educational. Perhaps most significant was the sense that we had shared in a great national enterprise, one which ended, as we were convinced it had to end, in victory.

That collective sense we carried with us even as we went our several ways in civil life. I think it was shared by my classmates in law school, nearly all of whom had served from three to five years in one of the service branches. The value of our service was tangibly reciprocated by the federal government's great public investment, the GI Bill of Rights, which paid for our post war education at levels which most of us could never have obtained. It was a prudent investment intended address the fear of widespread unemployment as the the armed forces were demobilized. The investment gave a tremendous boost to our national graduate and post graduate educational system and fueled an economic boom.

CHAPTER 10

New York and Columbia Law School

Our New York apartment was nominally on the fourth floor of an old brick apartment house at 619 West 176th Street. In reality it was a five floor walk up because we had to climb a full flight of steps to reach the first floor. The basement apartments which were only two or three steps down from the street were really the first floor. This arrangement apparently satisfied the city code which required an elevator in buildings with more than four floors. A few blocks to the west lay the Henry Hudson Parkway, and beyond it a grassy park sloping down to the Hudson River. Columbia University was located at 116th Street, Columbia Medical School at 168th Street.

The apartment had a long, narrow entrance hall, kitchen, living room, bath and bedroom. It lacked the fire place which I had suggested as essential in letters from Europe. Clissa, having struggled to find any apartment at all, thought this requirement off the wall. By the time I reached New York the apartment seemed grand enough without a fireplace, and Clissa had done a great job furnishing it. Subsequently we papered the walls with old fashioned wall paper under the guidance of Mr. Foy who lived on the floor above us. The rent was rent controlled at $35.00 per month. This was later raised to $40.00 after we complained about the refrigerator and received a new one. We had given the landlord an opportunity to hike the rent 14%. However, the fridge was worth it.

Under the GI Bill I was entitled to one year of education for each year of service, a total of four years and seven months. The bill provided tuition, cost of books and a living expense allowance of $75.00 per month later raised to $90.00 per month. Clissa received a salary of $166.00 per month as an instructor in the Department of Physiology at the Medical School. She had saved nearly all of the allotment I had sent home during the war, and also had $14,000.00 in US. Savings bonds which she had inherited from her father. The existence of the bonds she kept to herself until she was satisfied our marriage was going to stick.

One of our early problems was to find civilian clothing for me. I had grown an inch and put on weight during my years in the army. I could wear none of my pre-war clothing, and civilian clothing was difficult to find. Led by Clissa, I made the rounds of Macy's, B. Altman's, Gimbel's, and other department stores to find three or four white shirts, two pairs of slacks, a gray herringbone jacket, and a heavy dark gray overcoat suitable for Arctic weather. The overcoat was great for New York winters but thereafter hung in the closet, bagged and saturated with moth balls, insurance against return of the ice age. But these searches and purchases lay in the future. On December 24 we took the train up to Albany for a Christmas reunion with my mother and father and Pug.

Following the end of hostilities, my father was retired once again from active service. He and my mother had moved from their quarters at Watervliet Arsenal to a house belonging to a friend, Mrs. Henry Sage, a widow who lived on a large estate in Watervliet. The family's house was a rambling brick structure converted from servant quarters. My father was now employed by the New York State Department of Commerce as Director of the Bureau of Small Industry. Pug and Tony Morse were living in a small house in Schenectady where Tony, discharged from the Navy some months earlier, was employed as an engineer by General Electric. One afternoon Clissa and I borrowed the family car and drove to Schenectady to have dinner with them. Another day my father took me across the Hudson to his tailor in Troy who measured me for two suits, one blue and one gray, at a cost of $90 each. The price staggered me, but the suits were beautifully cut and lasted for many years.

When we returned to New York, I went down to Columbia and registered at the Law School which was located in Kent Hall on 116th street, a narrow, brick building opposite the domed center of the campus. The law school was operating year round so that students could graduate in two calendar years with no summer vacation rather than in the usual three calendar years. Thus my class began in February 1946 and was known as the class of February 1948, the date when we would graduate. A second class started in June 1946, and a third in September 1946.

Our daily routine was quickly established. Clissa walked down to the medical school at 168th Street. I walked to the 176th Street subway station and rode the subway down to the University at 116th street. Most New York blocks are four or five hundred foot behemoths unlike the smaller 200 foot ones in Portland. We reversed direction at the end of the day, Clissa walking home and I riding the subway. Once a week Clissa cashed a check for $20.00 and bought groceries on her way home. There were no super markets, but a series of small shops—groceries, meat, fish, hardware, dry goods, cleaners, laundry and so forth. She knew the proprietors, and they knew her. It was very much like a small town within a large city.

Once a month we took the train to Westport, Connecticut, where Clissa's mother was living in a comfortable small house with a nurse companion. I had not met Mrs. Hager before, though Clissa referred from time to time to the problems she and her sister had taking care of her. She seemed to have become a semi-invalid following the death of Clissa's father, Wilfred M. Hager, in 1936. Mrs. Hager was a small, frail woman in her seventies, pleasant but quite withdrawn. Several times we stayed overnight, but the spare bedroom had only a cot sized bed, and a cot was a very tight squeeze for the two of us. The beach was a block or two away, and in good weather we swam in the warm Atlantic surf.

We acquired a small gray cat named George. George was a fine cat with one serious behavioral defect. She preferred to defecate on enamel in preference to the cat box. The only deterrence we were able to devise was to fill the wash basin and the bath tub with a couple of inches of water when we left George alone in the apartment. Then she would use her cat box. When we left New York we gave George to Monica Reynolds, a graduate student at the medical school, who lived on the ground floor. Monica became a professor at the University of Pennsylvania School of Veterinary Medicine, but I never learned how long George lasted in her apartment. On weekends, when the weather was good we walked in the park with George on a leash.

Of Clissa's friends we saw principally Marjorie and Howard Zucker and Vivian and Danny Kline. Vivian was Mardy's sister. Mardy and Danny were fellow physiologists at P & S with Clissa. Howard Zucker was a physician specializing in psychiatry. We visited Franny and Peter Goldmark several times. Franny Trainer Goldmark was a classmate from Sarah Lawrence. Peter was an electrical engineer and worked on the early development of television. The Goldmarks invited us to watch the Army-Navy football game in the fall of 1946 on a set in their downtown apartment. This was the first television I had ever seen. The game was being played in the rain on Soldier's Field in Philadelphia, and the camera must have been located on the highest and most remote seat in the stadium. Franny later divorced Peter and married Richard Salant, a CBS executive, later president of CBS News. We also saw Mary Prue and Louis Engel. Mary Prue had been a Sarah Lawrence classmate. Louis was an executive with Merrill Lynch and subsequently wrote a best seller on the stock market.

Clissa's sister, Janet Fisk and her husband Arthur lived nearby in Connecticut. Arthur Fisk was a Yale graduate and lawyer, house counsel for the Johns Manville Corporation. He was a tall, well built, handsome man. We spent several weekends with them. On our first visit Arthur explained to me how he outwitted the employee's union as well as the government in several matters which offended my liberal sensibilities, but fortunately I managed to keep my opinions to myself. Janet Fisk was tall and slender, with delicate features. She was sixteen years older than Clissa, and the two of them were quite unlike in appearance. During the years following the death of their father and the illness of Mrs. Hager, Janet kept a helpful eye on Clissa for which she was deeply grateful.

Bob Safford came through New York and had dinner with us in the apartment. After two substantial martinis he went to work on the cuckoo clock which had arrived safely wrapped in my dirty clothes but needed setting up. He got the clock running, but it stopped some hours after he departed, and I had to carry it to a German clock maker in Yorktown, a German neighborhood in the city. The clock maker promptly offered me $250 cash for it, probably $1500 in today's money. I turned him down.

*

My class in law school consisted of 145 men and 5 women. Most of the men had served in one of the armed services for four to five years, the consequence of the government policy of demobilizing based on number of points given for length of service and decorations. More than half my classmates were married; many had a child. They were an active and mature group only momentarily awed by the senior professors who taught the first year courses and were accustomed to submissive entering students. The lectures were excellent, the professorial interrogation was rigorous. The students responded with equal vigor, and our really good students (law review types) devoted themselves to matching wits with their interrogators. It was fun and it was exciting.

For me the most interesting first year course was Development of Legal Institutions conducted by Professor Julius Goebel, a fascinating character who used a mimeographed text book he had created from extracts of old documents and early authorities to show the development of English law. Professor Richard R.B. Powell taught real property in a brisk pedantic manner which clarified a very confusing field for the beginner. During the summer of 1946 we had visiting professors among whom was Professor McDougal from Yale, a legal iconoclast who set himself out to demolish our conventional beliefs and the more conventional teaching of our regular Columbia professors. McDougal stirred up a firestorm of discussion.

I worked hard at my studies. As I recall I was generally in the upper quarter of the class but my grades were not sufficiently high to make the law review. I had no reason to quarrel with this ranking. The men who made law review were better students than I was, and I don't think I could have handled the time requirements of that extracurricular activity. As it was, I resumed writing poetry—perhaps as a psychological counter balance to the law.

By the end of the first year my close friends were made: Rick Watson, Harold Solomon, Brooks Beck and John Bangs. Rick was a tall, slender, engaging blond chap who had been a naval aviator in the Pacific and had received the silver star for flying a PBY into Tokyo Bay to rescue a downed flier. Brooks was a tall, dark, sardonic Bostonian, married to Emily (Wendy) Morrison, daughter of Samuel Eliot Morrison, the writer and naval historian. Brooks was a naval officer who had served on destroyers in the Pacific. His chief claim to fame, or so he said, was bringing his ship into harbor at Newport News, Virgina at twenty knots, an escapade which resulted in considerable official attention. Harold Solomon was a dark, plump New Yorker full of ideas and energy. John Bangs, bright and soft spoken, came from the Midwest and before military service had gone to the University of Iowa with William C. Martin, later one of my law partners in Portland. Rick became an admiralty lawyer. Brooks Beck became a partner in an old Boston firm. Harold became Dean of the University of Southern California Law School, and John Bangs became house counsel with W.R. Grace and Company. John and Betty had their first baby about the same time John Beatty was born.

I made a trip east in the early 1960s and had lunch with Brooks in Boston. Harold Solomon, then practicing law in

New York, took me to spend the weekend with his family at their house in Connecticut on Long Island Sound where the Solomons were holding a family reunion. It was an enormous old mansion with spacious grounds and the gathering of his large and talented Jewish family welcomed me warmly. Three out of four of these close friends at law school died at an early age, Rick Watson, his wife and one child died in a fire in their house on Long Island, Harold Solomen and Brooks Beck died from heart attacks in their early forties.

A number of the liberals in our class were active in the Columbia chapter of The American Veterans Committee or AVC, a newly formed veteran's organization distinctly more liberal than either the American Legion or the Veterans of Foreign Wars, the two established veterans groups. In the AVC I learned about left wing politics. Some Columbia College AVC members had an agenda of their own and a bag of tricks to accomplish it. The law school members, including my classmate Bill Kuntsler, then not the radical he later became, found ourselves resisting proposals by the leftists who insisted that we take a variety of political positions on matters which had nothing to do with veterans or politics as we saw it. One such resolution was to picket Governor Dewey in protest against some action he had taken in New York state government. The radicals' favorite technique was to prolong the meetings far into the night until their opponents, usually law students, had sensibly headed for home and bed. Then they would spring some outlandish resolution or attack some foreign policy decision of the federal government. We learned to adjourn meetings while we still had a working majority.

One evening Clissa smelled smoke. I did not. She insisted it was coming from our bedroom window. Finally, I stuck my head out the window, and indeed smoke was pouring out of the window in the apartment above us. I ran upstairs and beat on the door to no avail. I tried the handle. It was unlocked. I ran in and met a disheveled woman in a nightgown. She said her mattress was burning. I ran into the bedroom and found her mattress ablaze. I managed to wrestle it through the window over her protest, and it dropped safely to the open court below. Sirens wailed, an engine and the police arrived. The firemen put out the fire. The police bodily carried off the lady still protesting about her mattress, and peace descended on west 176th street. Later that day the police returned the lady still wearing her nightgown.

*

During our second academic year Professor Wechsler taught the course in Constitutional law. Herbert Wechsler had clerked for Mr. Justice Stone on the United States Supreme Court in 1933 and had been the chief technical advisor to the American judges at the Nuremberg Trials. He was a great teacher and a delightful person. I had the opportunity to work for him on an appeal to the United States Supreme Court which he was handling. *Gayes v. New York* was a criminal case involving a writ of error corum nobis, a legal remedy long abolished in the State of Oregon. I reviewed the trial court record and labored on a draft of the brief. Professor Wechsler received it with his usual courteous interest in student work. When I later read the brief as it left his hands it bore no visible relation to my draft. His polished sentences marched logically, dramatically and convincingly page after page. He set the standard to which I aspired as a young lawyer. When the *Gayes* case was decided adversely by the Supreme Court in a five-four decision, Professor Wechsler thoughtfully had the briefs and opinions of the Court bound and sent to me with the following inscription:

"For Jack Beatty with appreciation for his aid and the hope that he will never lose another case.

Herbert Wechsler, May 1948."

On several occasions Herb and his wife invited Clissa and me for dinner and wide ranging talk at their apartment near Columbia. His king size old fashions were memorable. For me he provided greater personal contact than I had with any other Columbia faculty member. His interests extended from the technicalities of law throughout the field of national politics.

Herbert Wechsler was recognized in 1993 as one of the greatest teachers in the history of Columbia Law School in a series of articles in the Columbia Law Review which set forth his accomplishments. I had not seen him for many years but stayed in touch by letter and through messages carried by Ernie Bonyhadi who graduated from Columbia in 1951 and remained active in Columbia Law School affairs. Herb died on April 26, 2000 at the age of 91 and was eulogized by Justice Ruth Bader Ginsberg among others as the greatest academic figure in the history of Columbia Law School.

During our second year I was elected class president and in that role I became involved in a number of controversies. One arose in connection with moot courts. At that time the moot courts were strictly private associations. I was invited to join Kent, the oldest and supposedly most prestigious. I declined the invitation because Kent did not accept Jewish members, an exclusionary policy which several Kent members, including Rick Watson, were attempting to change. While this effort was going on, a number of Jewish students proposed formation of an exclusively Jewish moot court. I wrote a letter to the organizers pointing out that we hoped to eliminate exclusivity in Kent and that their action would scuttle the whole effort. Kent did change its policy, and the concept of a Jewish moot court was abandoned. As a footnote to this controversy, I was never invited to become a member of the local chapter of the national legal fraternity, Phi Delta Phi, and one of my friends told me I was "blackballed" because of the moot court affair. As a practical matter neither moot courts nor fraternities played any great part in student life during those postwar years.

During the break between my first and second term in 1946, Clissa and I took a week's vacation in the Pocanos Mountains of New Jersey, staying at a lakeside resort. The lodge had a number of small sailing skiffs for its guests, and this was my first exposure to life on the water. Clissa had previous experience sailing with family on her Uncle Pa Barney's large sailing yacht, but my seagoing experience was limited to Gilbert Shepherd's outrigger canoe on the Willamette.

That fall Clissa concluded she should have a baby before my graduation and the move we might have to make at that time. She suspected she was pregnant in March, 1947 and took the frog test. I returned to the apartment from law school early the day the frog test report came in the mail. I telephoned Clissa at work but could not reach her in the lab so I imprudently gave her associate, Mardy Zucker, the message. The entire physiology lab had the news before Clissa, and she was a bit miffed.

Clissa worked on through her pregnancy but felt poorly a good deal of the time, and her blood pressure reached undesirable heights. During the early break in the summer of 1947 we flew out to Portland to explore the job possibilities for each of us. The flight was on DC 3s both ways and very rough. In Portland we stayed with my Aunt Margaret in the Stelwin Apartments. My grandmother Morrison at that time lived in "The Village," a group of brick cottage apartments constructed between Vista Avenue and 20th place. Granny Morrison gave us a crab lunch in her apartment. Clissa loved cracked crab, but Granny plied both of us with food, and her efforts nearly finished Clissa off with her queasy stomach.

During my last term at Columbia, Professor Wechsler suggested that I apply for a job on the staff of Oregon's Republican Senator Wayne Morse. He offered to see what he could do to arrange it. I was flattered by his offer, but concluded that at my advanced age I had better get busy practicing law. I thought that a temporary position in Washington would complicate the problem of getting jobs for both of us.

At the instance of my father, I had talked to a partner at the New York law firm of Sherman, Sterling and Wright. He had served with my father during the recent war and was friendly but painted a dismal picture of life for young lawyers in the firm. He warned me that two out of three associates failed to make the grade after four or five years with the firm. The net impression I received was that a man was fortunate to be allowed to serve the firm but was unlikely to succeed unless he put his entire heart and soul into the firm's work, values and political views. I had the naive belief that I was potentially a valuable commodity and was startled by his general denigration of prospective associates. In fact I was apprehensive at the thought of practicing law in New York. I thought I would be lost in a huge law firm.

I thought that if Clissa could get a position at the University of Oregon Medical School and I could land a paying job in a law firm, Portland was the choice to make. If I found a job that didn't work out, I could always find another job in Portland. The situation was different for Clissa. She was leaving her friends, her family, and a part of the country with which she was familiar and where she would have no difficulty changing jobs. For her, moving to Oregon meant living in a community where the number of scientific positions in her field were limited at that time to one employer, and where her professional contacts would be far more limited.

*

In the fall of 1947 we purchased our first automobile, a 1947 Oldsmobile, one of the first off the post war assembly lines. It was beautiful to behold and unreliable to operate, but we loved it. Our first excursion was a trip out to see the Zuckers at their Long Island beach house. We were driving happily along a largely deserted parkway when I remarked to Clissa what astonishingly good gas mileage we were getting. Minutes later we ran out of gas with the gauge still showing half a tank. That was only the first of many problems.

John Cabeen Beatty, III was born Thanksgiving Day, November 27, 1947 at Harkness Pavilion in the Columbia Medical Center. Clissa, as a staff member, had a delightful private room in contrast to most hospital rooms in that period, and she was ideally situated for visits from her friends in the medical school. I came by after law school and had dinner with her during her week in the hospital.

When we took John home from the hospital, Clissa arranged with Mrs. Foy, another lady who lived on the floor above us, not the mattress lady, to care for him during the day. Mrs. Foy had several children of her own of school age and proved a good choice. John was long, thin and a bit roughed up by forceps when he was born. My first sight of him was through a window beyond which which several babies were lined up. An Irish family was examining the baby next to John. One of the women turned and pointed at John saying, "My God, look at that!" It was an unnerving experience for a new father. However, John plumped up quickly and became an extraordinarily happy and handsome baby. My sister Pug and Tony had their first child, Anthony Morse Jr., the spring before Johnny was born.

Six weeks after John was born we drove up the Hudson River to Watervliet in the new Olds through the worst snow storm in years. We carried blankets, food and milk. I still marvel at our confidence. New York City had eighteen inches of snow, and the snow was even heavier up the Hudson River. My mother and father, now Granny and Gramps Beatty with two grandchildren, had moved into another house which Mrs. Sage had refurbished on the south section of the estate. The long drive into the house was barely passable when we reached Watervliet. During the night more snow fell and the next morning I shoveled for hours attempting to keep the drive open so I could get the car out to get more baby food and milk.

That fall Harold Solomon and I organized, he chairing, and I vice chairing a "National Law Student Conference on Legal Education," a bold enterprise for students in those days—or any day, for that matter. Strangely enough it went off very well. We had delegates from law schools all across the country and put on what we thought at the time was an interesting program with many stimulating ideas, all of which are now wholly beyond my recollection. Nor can I now recall how we funded the affair. But it was a new world, and we thought we were going to make changes in it starting with legal education.

The conference culminated in a banquet at Columbia. During the planning stage Professor Wechsler suggested that we approach Judge Jerome N. Frank of the Second Circuit Court of Appeals as a speaker. Harold and I went down to the federal courthouse to invite the judge. We explained the conference and the program for the evening and asked that he speak from twenty to thirty minutes, pointing out that he would be followed by the conference vice chairman (myself) and a faculty member summing up the conference findings and conclusions. The judge graciously accepted. We had a full house at the dinner, and the food and drink were good. I sat beside Judge Frank with others at the head table. As we finished desert and prepared to start the proceedings the Judge pulled a thick yellowed manuscript from his brief case. My heart sank. When he rose to speak he held the manuscript in hand, and page by page he went on for more than an hour.

When he finally sat down I thanked him, abandoned my prepared summary of the conference to the obvious relief of the audience, and turned the podium over to our faculty speaker who shortened his remarks to five minutes. By this time the males at the head table were more interested in a dash to the men's room than in anything any speaker had to offer. It was a lesson well learned. The rest of my life whenever I have chaired a meeting I have kept a firm grip on the time and never hesitated to tell a speaker, "Time's up."

*

As the result of our trip to Portland, Clissa was offered a position as a fellow in the biochemistry department of the University of Oregon Medical School at $300 per month. Somewhat later, after an interview with Paul L. Boley, a partner in Hart, Spencer, McCulloch and Rockwood, I was offered a position as an associate at $250 per month. My class graduated in February 1948, but Clissa had a teaching contract to fulfill until the latter part of May, so I took several courses during the spring term and studied for the Oregon Bar examination. No copies of prior examinations were available. The Board of Bar Examiners released no information other than that we were expected to be familiar with a long list of areas of the law, and that the questions and written answers would take place on two successive days. I did discover that every student from the University of Oregon Law School had passed the examination for a number of years and that two—thirds of the applicants from law schools in other states had failed. With four months to study I selected a horn book (text) on each subject required by the Oregon Bar, outlined it and then annotated the Oregon decisions reported for the previous twenty years in the Oregon Reports into my outline. It was laborious, but it forced me to learn the basic outline of the many fields of law on which we were to be questioned. When I finished that review, I had Oregon Supreme Court decisions coming out of my ears.

CHAPTER 11

Portland, the practice of law and politics

In May 1948 we had a final visit with my family in
Watervliet, then packed our meager worldly goods for
shipment to Portland, delivered our cat, George, to Monica
Reynolds, closed the apartment and spent the last night in
New York with Mardy and Howard Zucker in their apartment
at 333 Central Park West. In the morning we said good-by to
the Zuckers who left for work, leaving their children, Andrew
and Ellen, with their housekeeper. I carried our overnight bags
down to the fully packed Olds and went back up to the Zucker
apartment for Clissa and the baby. Alas, I had locked the keys
in the car. After a number of desperate telephone calls I found
a locksmith who opened the car door, and several hours late we
started off on our journey west.

With the exception of a few miles on the newly constructed
Pennsylvania Turnpike, the entire route was two lane blacktop
practically unchanged from the prewar road net. Fortunately
the traffic was relatively light, and on most sections we were
able to move along at 60 miles per hour except when passing
through cities, towns and villages. Motels were not fancy but
reasonably comfortable.

Johnny was then six months old. He traveled in a bureau
drawer laid on top of suitcases on the back seat of the two door
Olds. In this position the passenger in the front seat could feed
and change him while we were under way. We carried bottled

water, canned milk, and cans of baby food. A supply of diapers came with cardboard packages in which to mail the dirty ones back to the diaper service after they had been rinsed out in each motel. Johnny traveled like an experienced trooper. The only difficulty we experienced with him occurred the evening we reached the east entrance to Yellowstone Park. It was cold and snowing lightly. We stopped at an office to make arrangements for a cabin inside the park entrance. Then, as we pulled up in front of the cabin, Johnny threw up all over himself and the bureau drawer in which he was riding. The cabin was ice cold. I got a fire going, and between us we cleaned Johnny and the bureau drawer. By morning he was fine and back on his feed.

As we crossed the country we read of flooding along the Columbia River and the destruction of Vanport, a city of 30,000 located between Interstate Avenue and the Spokane, Portland and Seattle railroad embankment. A dike failed, and Vanport was underwater in minutes. When we reached The Dalles, state police diverted us from the Columbia River Highway to US 97 and then US 26 over the south shoulder of Mt. Hood. The Columbia River Highway, US 30, was closed to all traffic. The flood waters were 34 feet above mean low water at Portland, the highest they had been since the great flood of 1893. There were only two dams on the Columbia in 1948—Grande Coolee and Bonneville. These two were insufficient to control the heavy spring runoff that year. Later construction of two more dams on the upper Columbia and four on the Snake River, together with centralized control of the dam system by the Bonneville Power Authority, have limited the spring run-off most years to little more than fifteen feet above mean low water.

We drove into Portland and stopped in front of my Aunt Margaret Sharp's office, which was then located in the Education Center Building at Second and Washington Streets. She had arranged for us to rent the George Fortune house on the corner of SW 16th and Elm streets for three months during the summer. Mr. Fortune was an Englishman, the representative of the Balfour Guthrie importing firm. He and his family were spending the summer in England. This gave us plenty of time to look for a house. Because Clissa would be working at the medical school, and I would be working downtown, we needed a housekeeper and a house on Portland Heights with access to the Council Crest trolley. No private residential housing had been constructed during the war and the housing market was still very tight. We looked at a half dozen houses in the Southwest area, no more than three in the Council Crest area. Auntie Marg had previously written to us of a new house on Elizabeth Street priced at $28,000. This I had rejected out of hand as far too expensive to even consider.

A few days after our arrival, Dr. William Yeomans at the medical school told Clissa of a medical student just graduated who was moving to California and had a house on Dosch road for sale. We looked at it. The house, built in 1929, was empty, the woodwork a bit battered, the yard overgrown. The garage was below the house on Dosch Road with a double flight of some forty steps up to the house. However the structure was well built and arranged with two bedrooms downstairs and two upstairs so that we could put a housekeeper in the bedroom next to the kitchen. The price was $10,500 with a $6,000 mortgage at 4 % interest. My uncle, Donald W. Green, had a friend familiar with construction who checked the house for soundness. We decided to buy it. With the assistance of Tom Stoel in the Hart Spencer office we concluded the purchase just two weeks after our arrival in Portland.

Clissa engaged a middle-aged widow, Ada Manse, who had been flooded out of her home in Vanport, to be our housekeeper. Mrs. Manse was a square lady, hard working and responsible. She loved Johnny and he took to her at once. Mrs. Manse's own household furnishings were a total loss. She had been buying a refrigerator on time from Montgomery Ward. Most companies forgave the balance due on such losses, for few of the inhabitants had insurance covering their possessions for flood. However, Montgomery Ward insisted on payment in full. Their local office told me it was company policy and could not be changed.

Sewell Avery was the president of Montgomery Ward. I remembered Mr. Avery from a photograph I had seen in the

Stars and Stripes while I was overseas. Avery had refused to follow some wartime regulation of the federal government and the photo showed him being carried out of his office by soldiers. I wrote him a letter urging that he reconsider the policy citing Mrs. Manse's situation. I received no response from him, but the manager of the Portland store telephoned several weeks later to say that under the circumstances the debt would be forgiven. Mrs. Manse stayed with us for more than six years until her death early one morning from a heart attack.

We had the lease of the Fortune house until September and made use of our spare time during the summer working on the house. The woodwork was all vertical grain fir which had been varnished twenty years before, with no attention thereafter. I was determined to brighten the house. Instead of cleaning and re varnishing all that beautiful vertical grain, old growth fir, I covered every bit of it with white enamel. Much of it I stripped ten years later and re varnished the bare wood.

The Oregon bar examinations, three days of essay questions given once a year, were set for the first week in July. The office gave Bill Wyse and me the rest of June to prepare for the examinations, and I took advantage of the opportunity, though I was already over prepared. Bill and I roomed together in the old Senator Hotel in Salem. The weather was fearfully hot, and the Senator was not air conditioned. The examination was conducted in the State Capitol. Those who could type were allowed to do so. Most of us scribbled. I used the full time allotted for each group of questions, but I found it a bit demoralizing to see other candidates rise after an hour or so, turn in their papers and saunter out. Each evening we compared notes on how we had answered particular questions.

One question involved a writ of error coram nobis, the precise procedural writ upon which Professor Wechsler's case, *Gayes v. New York*, had been appealed. I wrote furiously citing case after case. No one present could possibly have known more about coram nobis than I did. That night I realized to my dismay that I had forgotten to cite the Gayes case itself! The results of the examinations were not announced until the first week in September, so we lived through the summer in a state of shaky confidence. I thought I had done reasonably well, but the consequences of failure appeared so overwhelming that I could not put the possibility out of my mind.

When my name appeared in the Oregonian among those who had passed, I felt more relief than triumph. The bar admission ceremony was held in the capitol at Salem. Justice George Rossman, a lanky, avuncular man, whose opinions were notoriously lengthy, gave the admission address to the new lawyers. The burden of his remarks was that there was no such thing as an unimportant case. It was sound admonishment to do our best in every matter entrusted to us, irrespective of the amount involved.

Some years later a Columbia classmate practicing in the midwest asked me to handle the appeal in a case his client had lost in the Wasco County Circuit Court. It was an action to recover the purchase price of a small press which the client had sold to a small company in The Dalles, Oregon. *Brandt v. Brandjen Kluge.* The amount involved in the case was only six or seven hundred dollars. The trial court record left a lot to be desired, and I told my classmate that reversing the trial judge looked like a very long shot indeed. "No matter," he said. "Our client wants to pursue it as a matter of principle." So I took the case, briefed it and prepared for argument.

How could I present a six hundred dollar matter to a busy supreme court with a heavy docket of "important" cases? I remembered Judge Rossman's talk. So I began my oral argument before the seven justices in the mahogany and marble courtroom as follows:

> "May it please the Court. When I was admitted to the bar some years ago Mr. Justice Rossman admonished us that there was no such thing as an unimportant case. The case at bar involves no more than a few hundred dollars, but it raises an important principle."

As I look back on that argument, I am willing to bet that the moment the court withdrew, the chief justice must have said, "That's your case, George," and roared with laughter. When the opinion came down many months later, we won. The opinion written by Mr. Justice Rossman was twenty pages long, supported by innumerable citations and difficult to follow, but I loved it!

In 1986 Chief Justice Edwin Peterson asked me to give the admission address to new members of the bar. The chief's introduction was more than generous. I began my address quoting the advice Mr. Justice Rossman had given my class of newly admitted lawyers thirty eight years before and told them how it had served me well. The story got a chuckle from the young lawyers, but I don't think they thought it as grand a story as I did, and, of course, they did not know the late Justice Rossman.

*

With the bar exam behind me I began work at the office. Bill Wyse and I were each assigned a table in the firm library. At that time Hart Spencer had the fourteenth floor of the Yeon Building with the exception of the short north wing. George Fraser, who by now had an office of his own, came into the library frequently, quoting an ancient legal text called "Cowen on Cattle" as authority for some outrageous theory he advanced. We called the library The Peons' Patio. When the firm took over the north wing of the fourteenth floor and installed us together with George in those offices, the wing was designated as the Peons' Patio.

George Fraser came to the firm from Harvard in 1947 and had settled into trial work under Hugh Biggs. Bill Wyse was doing corporate work for several partners. I indicated no interest in trial practice and was assigned to miscellaneous work largely for Paul Boley and Tom Stoel. Our working hours were officially from nine to five Mondays through Friday and nine to two-thirty on Saturday. I found it difficult to get through my assignments in these hours and during the first several years, more often than not, I came back to the office after dinner and worked until ten or eleven o'clock. I had trouble developing a precise and organized response to specific questions. I certainly could not match the marvelous capacity of Bill Wyse to define a legal problem and work his way to a logical conclusion. I gradually drifted into trial work for George and Hugh Biggs and found that I liked it.

My first venture into the trial field involved working with Manley Strayer on an appeal of a case Manley had tried and lost, Finn vs. SP&S, a truck train collision at a crossing in Northwest Portland not far from the Blitz Weinhard Brewery. We lost the appeal. It was one of the last of the crossing cases which had peppered the Oregon Reports for a hundred years.

My first and only criminal trial as a lawyer was a *pro bono* defense of a criminal case in federal court. My client was charged with forging bonds belonging to his uncle. He earnestly maintained he was innocent. His uncle had told him to sign his signature to the bonds. I had him take a polygraph. The results were equivocal. I tried without success to convince the deputy United States attorney to dismiss the case or at least allow the jury to see the polygraph. He declined. We went to trial before newly appointed United States District Judge Gus J. Solomon.

I offered the polygraph. The U. S. Attorney objected. The judge sustained the objection. The case went to the jury about four o'clock. The judge invited me back into chambers, gave me a drink and told me not to worry. "He's guilty as hell and they'll convict him." The jury did. Ruth Peterson's brother, Henry Dixon, a psychiatrist, later assured me that properly given polygraphs were quite reliable except for psychopaths and trial lawyers. I subsequently found this to be true, as far as run-of-the-mill criminals are concerned. I have had no statistically significant experience with polygraphing trial lawyers.

My first circuit court trial involved an automobile accident case in Oregon City. The firm represented the defendant. Hugh

Biggs sent me off to try the case with Glenn Jack sitting in as local counsel. George Hibbard represented the plaintiff. When George made his argument to the jury he demonstrated how the accident happened using small cars on the blackboard. Glenn and I split our argument with Glenn concluding. His argument went something like this:

> "You know George worked in my office for several years before he went out on his own. He's a fine boy, but I taught him everything he knows, and here is why he's mistaken the way he runs those little cars together."

Glenn proceeded to move the little cars around on the board in accordance with his theory. Jack was the leading lawyer in Clackamas County, then largely rural. He knew some of the jurors by name. I think all of them knew of his reputation. We got a defense verdict. Most of the trials I recall are the ones I lost. From time to time I read of famous lawyers who claim to have never lost a case. I suspect they either have very selective memories, or they have settled every case that wasn't a sure winner.

The first insurance defense trial I handled by myself was the case of *Denton V. Arnstein*. Our insured, Mr. Arnstein, was a small, round, abrasive jeweler driving a Cadillac which had rear ended a pregnant Mrs. Denton driving an old Hudson. In deposition Mr. Arnstein testified that Mrs. Denton had stopped in front of him in the middle of an intersection on Northeast Grand Avenue. "So I gives her the horn." Mrs. Denton moved on. Then she suddenly stopped in front of him again, and he could not avoid striking her rear bumper. The policy limit was $10,000 and Mrs. Denton was suing for the limits plus $10,000 punitive damages for deliberately bumping her. The plaintiff's lawyer wanted our $10,000 limit to settle, so we went to trial.

In the course of the trial, Mrs. Denton's lawyer produced a believable independent witness who testified that Mrs. Denton was having motor trouble. The driver of the Cadillac blasted her with his horn and then rammed her.

We argued the case. Judge Alfred P. Dobson instructed the jury, and then asked the jurors if they had any questions. Juror number 11, Mrs. Banz, spoke up.

"Why don't insurance companies settle cases like these, your honor?"

The courtroom was silent. I sat frozen at the counsel table. The dread word "insurance" had been spoken. In this moment of silence, I heard muffled laughter behind me. I turned around. Glenn Jack, who had just come into the back of the courtroom, was convulsed with laughter. Finally, Judge Dobsen shook his finger at the juror, saying,

"Now, Mrs. Banz, you shouldn't ask questions like that."

I moved for a mistrial. The motion was denied. The jury returned a verdict for the plaintiff in the full amount of her prayer. We appealed and lost. I suspect the transcript provided laughter in the conference room when the Supreme Court considered the case.

*

Omar Spencer, the second lawyer in the firm name, lived with Mrs. Spencer on a Sauvie Island farm which Mrs. Spencer's family had settled under a Donation Land Claim. Mr. Spencer commuted to the office via the Sauvie Island ferry. Mr. Spencer was tall, slightly stooped, and had short cropped white hair. He was a reservoir of anecdotes concerning the early days of the firm and early days on Sauvie Island. In 1956 Mr. Spencer wrote a fascinating account of his birth and childhood on his family's homestead in the upper Nehalem Valley where he was born in 1881. Unfortunately, his full account of those early years has never been published.

Hart Spencer in 1949 had no retirement plan or provision for retirement of its partners. Mr. Spencer told me to look though the literature and draft a plan for the firm. I have no idea what became of the lengthy memorandum I prepared or whether it contributed in any way to the plan which was ultimately adopted after I left, but it was an interesting exercise for me.

Hart Spencer was a great firm for young associates. We were treated well and given sympathetic assistance by partners and older associates. But the general atmosphere created by the senior partners seemed pretty conservative to me even though Hugh Biggs, Manley Strayer and Tom Stoel were registered Democrats. Oregon voters were predominately Republican in registration. The Oregon State Bar was overwhelmingly Republican. Firm clients were largely Republican and conservative. All major state office holders were Republican. My interest in politics, particularly Democratic politics made some partners restive, David Lloyd Davies, anyhow, and Mr. Davies was the managing partner at that time.

The morning after the 1948 General Election when it became clear that President Truman had defeated Thomas E. Dewey, the Republican candidate, Mr. Davies, a heavy set man with a large round face and a felt hat set squarely on his head, strode into the elevator in which I was standing, a frown on his face. I could not suppress a wide grin as I said good morning to him.

By the end of my second year at the firm Mr. Davies told me,
"You know, Jack, you are going to have to decide whether you are going to practice law or be in politics."

I took this to be a warning and a fair warning. If I wanted to engage in political activity I would have to move on. Bill Wyse urged me to stay, saying that we could change that atmosphere. I thought that pretty unlikely. However, Bill's prediction proved to be correct. The firm grew rapidly and younger members of the firm led by Bill did eventually change the atmosphere. This may have been facilitated by the subsequent shift in political party strength in Oregon which made Democrats more respectable than they had been for many years. Two decades later a young partner, Hardy Meyers, was elected to the State House of Representatives as a Democrat, chaired the House Judiciary Committee for two terms, served as a very distinguished Speaker of the House for two terms, followed by three terms as Attorney General. However, in the early 1950's few people foresaw the shift in political climate that was about to take place. I certainly did not. So I began looking around for another association.

While still in law school I had contemplated running for public office someday. The United States Senate looked like an inviting goal. In our first years in Portland I thought that the legislature might be the place to start. Clissa said firmly this might be a fine idea but not until the children were both in school and considerably older. She was right then, and by the time the children reached that stage, I had other fish to fry. As a practical matter it is difficult for a lawyer with an active trial practice to serve in the legislature unless he, or she, has partners able and willing to pick up the load during the six to eight months of the biennial sessions. Moreover, while I enjoyed political activity and always considered it a critical component of civic life, I could never live the frenetic life a full time politician has to lead to be successful. But that was more obvious to me later than it was then.

*

In the fall of 1948 Clissa and I attended a Democratic Party dinner which was addressed by President Truman in the closing days of his campaign for reelection. In the course of the dinner we ran into Jim and Jane Goodsell. I had known Jim at Lincoln where we became good friends. His father was a minister, rather strict, I understood. Jim had some difficulty getting approval to spend the night with me at our house in Dunthorpe. He graduated a year behind me and went to Columbia University. We kept in touch. He had married Jane Neuberger, the sister of Richard L. Neuberger, then an Oregon State Senator and prolific writer. Dick's wife, Maureen, was a state representative. Jim was the editor of the Oregon Labor Press, a weekly newspaper published by the Oregon AF of L.

Through the Goodsells, we met Dan and Rusty Goldy. Dan was the director of the Oregon office of the Bureau of Land Management, Department of the Interior, which managed the O & C lands owned by the federal government, a checkerboard of timbered sections along the route of the failed Oregon and California Railroad. Through the Goodsells and the Goldys I quickly became involved in local Democratic Party politics. In the 1950s and 1960s party organizations were far more active in state politics than in later decades in which candidates for local and state office campaigned largely on an individual basis.

*

The summer of 1949 Clissa and I with John spent a week vacation at Gearhart with Jim and Jane Goodsell whose daughter Ann was our two year old's age. We stayed in what had been Mrs. Schroder's hotel in the flats in Gearhart and which had been moved recently to the crest of the dunes and renamed The Ocean House. The hotel was largely empty, and it rained the entire time we were there. Jim and I tried flying kites, They came apart in the rain. We reconstructed them using wax paper which survived the downpour. We became so interested in kites that we continued flying them when we got back to Portland. We bought a surplus army weather kite, a huge box affair, and flew it on Council Crest until it crashed, nearly braining me. That ended my love affair with kites, though Jim continued to experiment for several months longer.

One wet day of that vacation, Jim and I went salmon fishing on a Bumble Bee trawler with his friend Bob Holmes, a state senator who lived in Astoria. It rained the entire day and we caught nothing, but Bob kept us entertained with talk of politics. He was an engaging person, a very decent man, though not a political heavyweight. Politics in Clatsop county and Astoria, the county seat, centered on the fishing industry in those days, and Bumble Bee was the principal packing company.

The chairman of the Multnomah County Democratic Central Committee was Nicholas Granet, whom younger party members viewed as representing old style ward politics. Granet's own precinct then included Council Crest where he lived, and the precinct took in a good part of Dosch Road, including our house. The county chairman was elected by a majority of the precinct committeemen in the county. I was encouraged by some committee insurrectionists to run against Nick Granet for precinct committeeman in order to oust him as chairman. I campaigned throughout the precinct, calling at doors and leaving literature. When the votes were counted, I had defeated Granet by a substantial margin, and he lost his chairmanship along with his membership on the central committee. The committee then elected Bill Way, president of the Boilermakers Union, as chairman. Several years later Way was replaced by Ken Rinke, a shrewd political hand who later became a full-time lobbyist in Salem and a friendly political associate. I remained an active member of the county central committee for the next six years.

In 1948 State Senator Dorothy Lee ran for Mayor of Portland on a reform ticket in the primary election and defeated the incumbent Mayor Riley, largely on the basis of a City Club report highly critical of law enforcement. My aunt Margaret supported her in this effort. When the new mayor appointed a committee to investigate alternatives to the commission form of city government, at my aunt's suggestion, Mayor Lee appointed me to the committee. Mrs. I.E. Hervin, Barbara Hervin Schwab's mother, was another member, as was city attorney Virgil Langtry, later a circuit judge and then a judge on the Court of Appeals. Subcommittees were assigned to study the existing commission form, the strong mayor form and the city manager form. I was assigned to the city manager subcommittee. That committee was my introduction to Portland's city government.

We went through the literature and the experience of cities which had adopted a manager system and concluded it had worked well for cities our size or smaller. The full committee accepted our report and recommended that Portland change to a city manager. The chief defect of the commission form was its combination of legislative and executive powers in five largely independent commissioners. The council manager form separated the legislative function with a part-time elected mayor and council and centered the executive function in a professional manager appointed by the council.

The first step was to convince the city council to put the measure on the ballot. We had two votes on the five person council but failed to persuade a third. Two years later we tried again under the impression that we had three council votes committed to us. We found that we did not. Finally, in 1957, I persuaded Hugh Barzee, a lawyer and former president of the City Club, to join me and co-chair a committee to put the measure on the ballot by initiative petition and then campaign for its adoption. My secretary, Mary Erskine, acted as secretary and manager of the campaign. We thought it was a propitious time because the Rose City Transit company had just outraged the public with its mishandling of the city bus system. We got the measure on the ballot.

Charles Taft, son of former President William Howard Taft and brother of Senator Robert Taft, came to Portland to speak in support of our campaign. During the final days of the campaign I debated City Commissioner William Bowes on a half hour television program moderated by Tom McCall, then KGW's news commentator. Tom, a Republican, had run against Edith Green for the House of Representatives in 1954 and lost. Bill Bowes got so worked up toward the end of the debate that he turned red in the face and became inarticulate. Tom thought Bowes was having a heart attack.

"Bill! Bill!" Tom cried, "My God, Jack! he's having a heart attack!" Bill revived moments later, hale and hearty.

A week or so before the election one of our local polling outfits tried to sell me a poll he had just taken for a client on another subject. He had included a question on the council manager proposal thinking I might be willing to buy it. I thanked him for the offer but told him we were out of money. He said,

"Oh hell, Jack, I'll give it to you." He told me we were ahead by a fairly good margin, though I don't recall the exact figure.

When the ballots were counted we lost by six thousand votes, primarily due, I think, to an effective last minute effort of a very healthy Bill Bowes who marshalled city employees against the plan by telling them their jobs were at stake. He was aided by the fact that the Rose City bus scandal was off the front pages and interest had largely subsided by the election. We ran the campaign on a shoe string. Fifteen or twenty thousand dollars of radio and TV advertising might have countered Bowes and put us over the top.

On two subsequent occasions an effort was made to replace the commission form with a strong mayor form of government. I supported both campaigns but took no part in leading them. My conclusion remains that the commission form of city government is the worst of the three common forms, but Portland more often than not has had mayors and council members with sufficient energy and ability to make the system function despite its inherent inefficiency. Put another way, Portland's city government has never been bad enough since the Baker administration to persuade Portlanders to break with their traditional city commission structure. Portland then and today remains the only major city in the United States with the commission form of city government.

*

Leonard Nicoloric, a partner of C. Gerard Davidson, had asked me to come over to their office and discuss joining their firm. "Jebbie" Davidson had been a political appointee in the Department of the Interior as an assistant secretary under President Truman and was active in Democratic politics. My conversation with Nicoloric left me ambivalent. Their practice was an interesting mix of law and politics, and Nicoloric said they had enough business to be able to take me on, but I was not quite happy with the description of life in their firm or the mix of business as Nicoloric described it. He said they enjoyed life but worked hard, usually not getting home until seven or seven thirty in the evening. He made some comment to the effect that their wives were well trained and expected this. That schedule concerned me. While I frequently worked in the evenings at Hart Spencer, I nearly always got home by five thirty for dinner though I often went back down to work after dinner. Someone suggested that I talk to Gus Solomon, a Portland lawyer who was a Democrat and knew Davidson, so I went to Mr. Solomon for advice. This was before President Truman appointed him to the federal bench. Mr. Solomon discussed the pros and cons of my leaving Hart Spencer for Nicoloric and Davidson and confirmed my sense that this would not be a wise move for me.

Subsequently Soloman was nominated by President Truman to fill a new position on the United States District Court for the District of Oregon. There was considerable opposition to his appointment because of his advocacy of liberal causes. David Lloyd Davies, a conservative Republican, who had been a classmate and friend of Solomon at Stanford, testified strongly in his support at the Senate Judiciary Committee hearings on his confirmation. Judge Soloman followed my subsequent career with a friendly interest. On one occasion in the courtroom during a recess he suggested that I buy a suit to replace my summer uniform which a tailor had stripped of shoulder straps and brass buttons. I thought it was a good substitute for a new suit, but the judge obviously did not.

CHAPTER 12

The Dusenbery office, Korea and the trial of William Culp

Not long after we arrived in Oregon, I met Herbert M. Schwab, a lawyer who had married my Lincoln High School classmate, Barbara Hervin, following the death of her first husband. Herb was practicing law with the firm of Dusenbery, Martin and Schwab with offices in the Spaulding Building. We found each other's company enjoyable and our interests compatible. Herb had a unique background. He graduated from Lincoln High School at the age of sixteen and went to work as an office boy. He obtained his law degree going to Northwest College of Law, then a privately owned night law school. Herb had also earned a commission in the naval reserve and managed to exchange that for a commission as 2nd lieutenant of infantry. In 1941 he was called to active duty and ended up a full colonel and Adjutant General of the Tenth Air Force in the China, Burma, India Theater. In 1950 Herb was elected to the Board of School District No. 1, Portland. He had a first rate mind and a ruminative, conversational approach to any matter which engaged his attention. One of his many resources was an endless fund of stories. He suggested in 1951 that I think about joining him in the Dusenbery office.

That move was attractive to me. The question was whether there would be enough trial business to carry me. I thought I needed $5,000 a year to balance the family budget. Herb thought he had enough insurance defense work to keep me busy, and said that figure was possible. We both had discussions with Jim Goodsell and Bill Way, the president of the boilermakers union. I knew Way through the county Democratic central committee. Way indicated some union legal business might be forthcoming, a prospect which never materialized. With several other prospective clients, the game seemed to be worth the candle, so in the summer of 1951 I took a deep breath and walked into Mr. Davies' office and told him I would be leaving September 1st. Mr. Davies could not have been nicer and wished me luck. Davies subsequently referred the new director of the Oregon Historical Society, Thomas H, Vaughan, to me for help in buying their first house in Portland, a referral which led to our lifelong friendship with the Vaughans.

The Dusenbery office at that time consisted of Vern Dusenbery and Herb Schwab as general partners. Vern was a quiet gentleman in his early sixties who had practiced law in Montana. During the depression his practice in Montana evaporated. Vern packed his family and his worldly goods and drove to Seattle, then to Portland, looking for some place to scratch out a living. He found an office arrangement with Virgil Crum and started practice along with Carey Martin, a migrant lawyer from Iowa where he had been mayor of the town of Atlantic.

Vern Dusenbery was a careful draftsman, a very capable lawyer and, above all, a man of principle. He was one of the first lawyers to represent Americans of Japanese descent displaced during the war and worked hard on their behalf to eliminate discriminatory legislation after the war. Sidney Teiser, a courtly graduate of the University of Virginia, had an office arrangement with the firm, but spent the greater part of his time in Chicago developing a method of microfilming legal authorities for the American Bar Association. The development of computers overtook the project, which was eventually abandoned. Carey Martin also had a separate office relationship with the firm. He represented primarily Northern Life Insurance Company which wrote an unusual kind of employer's liability insurance for logging and lumber companies, which rejected the Workman's Compensation Act, a policy which produced a good deal of litigation. William C. Martin, Carey Martin's nephew, was a graduate of the University of Illinois Law School and a very competent general practitioner.

For the next six years I worked primarily with Herb Schwab as we developed an insurance defense practice. From time to time, when one of Carey Martin's Employer's Liability Act cases went to trial, Carey had me try them. One of Herb's original insurance clients was Preferred Insurance Exchange, a privately owned corporation with its head office in Seattle. Preferred was rapidly expanding, selling automobile coverage to high risk drivers. This, not unexpectedly, produced a large number of accident claims and plenty of litigation throughout Oregon. Several times a year Herb and I drove up to Seattle with a suitcase full of Preferred files to go over with the claims manager and to maintain relations with management.

When I first knew Herb, he drove a Hudson, one of the ugliest passenger vehicles ever manufactured in the United States. Later he replaced the Hudson with a large second hand Chrysler with power steering, which he drove to Seattle on its initial voyage. We needed fuel as we started for home. Herb turned into a gas station, and as he did so, the engine died. Power steering and power brakes died with the engine. Without power the Chrysler steered like a tank. We were headed straight for the gas pumps. Herb barely managed to turn the wheel and stop the car before we took out the pumps.

We began representing the Morrell P. Totten Company, which had a Portland office but was headquartered in Seattle. Morrell P. Totten, the owner, was a polished and urbane man, physically the shape of the Buddha. Totten had developed extensive personal contacts with the Underwriters at Lloyds of London. These contacts he cultivated in frequent trips to London. In consequence he received a good deal of Lloyds business, some directly, and some through the law firm of Mendes and Mount, the large New York law firm which supervised much of Lloyds insurance litigation in the United States. Totten had both automobile and employers liability coverage, the latter largely logging and mill risks. In addition, Herb handled insurance defense work for Ohio Casualty, and I began handling defense work for United Pacific Insurance Company and several California based insurance companies.

In those days plaintiffs' litigation in Portland was concentrated in three local firms, Green, Landy and Peterson, Anderson and Franklin, and Vergeer and Samuels. The Green office subsequently split with Nels Peterson and Frank Pozzi, creating a new firm, Peterson and Pozzi. Every month or so Herb and I would call Nels Peterson, Frank Pozzi or Wes Franklin, and take a briefcase full of files over to Mannings coffee shop on Fourth and Alder, where we would sit in a booth and go over the cases to see which ones we could settle. We settled most of them in this manner. Litigation was far cheaper in those days. In the usual accident case we exchanged depositions of the drivers, ran down any independent witnesses, got a medical examination if any permanent injury was claimed, and then we were ready for settlement or trial. The attorneys fees for defending a case settled before trial ordinarily ran to no more than three or four hundred dollars.

The Employers Liability Act cases, which involved injury to loggers and mill workers, were more complicated, and the stakes were higher. For a short while I had the dubious honor of having the largest verdict in the history of Oregon against me. I represented the insurance carrier for a gypo mill sued by an employee who lost his arm in an edging machine. Dan Dimick in Roseberg represented the plaintiff. The case was tried in Roseberg before Judge Wimberly, an irascible, opinionated Douglas County circuit judge. We engaged Robert Davis, the part time Douglas County district attorney, as local counsel. Bob was the best defense lawyer in the county, though at that moment he was under a social cloud. He had ordered a raid on the Roseburg golf club for maintaining illegal slot machines, and consequently he was *persona non grata* with his fellow members of the club.

Our lawsuit was a case of obvious liability, and we tried to settle it. We made a substantial offer which Dimick recommended to his client. The client refused. We finally offered the policy limit. The plaintiff, now the county dog catcher, refused to settle. He said he wanted a jury to decide what he was entitled to have. We pled contributory negligence, but the evidence was grim. Dimick called a grey-headed old engineer as an expert witness and asked him what kind of an edger it was. The witness replied that he could not say. There was no name on the machine and it had been manufactured long before his time. The plaintiff testified that he had to kick the machine each time he used it in order to get it started, and had to reach between the blades each time to remove the lumber. The plaintiff was right handed, and his left hand was the one he lost. Bob Davis thought this would be important in holding down the damages.

The jury returned a verdict of some $64,000 late in the day, the largest verdict to that date in the State of Oregon. After the verdict Davis and I, stunned, picked up our papers, walked down one flight of stairs, meeting at the landing the foreman of the jury, Sid Likens, client and friend of Davis descending the other flight. Davis glared at Likens said accusingly, "Sixty-four thousand dollars, and he's right handed!"

Likens angrily snapped back, "Left hand, right hand, who gives a shit!"

Bob and I had a drink in the hotel bar. He went home to his wife. I ate dinner by myself and started the long six hour drive back to Portland on a curvy two lane highway lit for miles by the glowing wigwam burners of the gypo mills which lined US 99 from Roseburg to Eugene.

A few months later Herb tried a case for Ohio Casualty in Pendleton defending an Employers Liability Act claim for serious injuries suffered by an electrician employed by the Wasco County PUD. The jury returned a verdict for some $80,000, wiping out my record. These cases were difficult to defend. Generally the critical question was what they were worth, and the evaluation process was necessarily a crude mechanism. Most cases were settled, and those we tried were lost in the sense that the plaintiffs usually won a jury verdict. If the verdict was less than the amount we had offered in settlement, we considered the case a victory. Because most cases were tried in the county where the injury occurred, most trials took place in the timber counties. Generally speaking, local counsel and the local judge were fair enough to lawyers from the big city. In a few instances they made life difficult—Judge Dall King in the Coos—Curry judicial district for one.

*

In 1956 Vern Dusenbery retired as a partner, and Herb reorganized the firm with William C. Martin, himself and myself as the partners sharing equally in profits and losses. Vern and Carey Martin continued as associated counsel, sharing office space but handling their own clients without reference to the firm. The system of having partners share equally continued for many years until after I left the firm to go on the bench. In 1957 Alex L. Parks, a neighbor of mine, left the firm of White, Southerland and Parks to join us. Alex was an admiralty lawyer and a talented writer. He brought several admiralty clients to the office, including Inland Navigation Company and the Columbia River Pilots. Inland was an interesting corporate client. The stock was divided equally between two owners who had fallen out. Their acrimonious relationship produced a good deal of legal business.

One memorable Rose Festival week, six Canadian destroyers were scheduled to arrive in Portland at a particular hour. The squadron was late in reaching Astoria, where they took on a river pilot. The river was in flood, as it usually was in the latter part of May. The squadron commander ordered twenty knots. The pilot objected saying that he could not run the river at that speed. The commander said he was going to get to Portland on schedule. The pilot refused to con the ship. The commander took over and conned the flotilla all the way to Portland. The wake created havoc all the way up the river, wrecking small craft and damaging shore structures. Many claims for damage were filed, and the State Department intervened to avoid an international incident. The pilot, having refused the order, was cleared of responsibility.

In 1958 Kenneth Kramer, a Portland lawyer and friend of mine, mentioned to me that David P. Templeton, a Harvard law graduate who was house counsel for General Electric at Richland, Washington, was interested in moving to Portland. Ken recommended him highly. We subsequently asked Dave to join the firm. He was a quiet, soft spoken, scholarly lawyer and his arrival substantially strengthened the firm.

Vern Dusenbery was the conscience of the office; Herb Schwab was the energy center. Herb had a unique capacity for interesting people in his views and activities. This was true of lawyers, clients and people in general. Herb was formidable in a jury trial because of the force of his personality and the subterranean growl of his voice. Witnesses wanted to agree with him. He contributed the most to the partnership, yet he consistently adhered to the principle that the senior partners should share equally. He also settled the policy that we should freely engage in public activities without any firm limitation on the productive time involved. We worked hard at practicing law and acquiring business, but never counted comparative hours or clients. This made for a wonderful climate in which to practice, provided one's objective was not primarily focussed on making money. This arrangement survived Herb's departure and continued for the next eleven years while I was in the office and for several years thereafter. I thought it was a great way to practice law, but obviously it could only be done in a small firm in which all the partners had a similar view of the practice.

*

In 1952 John was five years old. Clissa had sustained a significant increase in blood pressure with his pregnancy, and the Hager family had a history of hypertension. This made another pregnancy medically risky for her, so Clissa suggested that we adopt a baby. We applied to the Boys and Girls Aid

Society. The agency social worker who interviewed us seemed dubious because Clissa was working full time despite the fact that our arrangements for a full time housekeeper had worked out well with Johnny. After many months of waiting for some encouraging sign we concluded the Society was a lost cause and turned to private adoption. Herb Schwab suggested we talk to Lena Kennon, a physician who lived down the road at the intersection of Hamilton Street and Dosch. Lena's husband, Harry, was a musician and head of the local musician's union. As it happened, Lena had a patient, a young college student, who was having a baby and intended to give it up for adoption. Herb handled the arrangements. So on May 27, 1953 Clarissa Jean Beatty, named for Clarissa and my mother, Jean Morrison Beatty, was born. Three days later Clissa, John and I drove down to Good Samaritan Hospital and brought Jeannie home in Clissa's second hand Austin.

Initially Jeannie slept in a crib I constructed in the hall at the head of the stairs outside our bedroom. I had carefully measured the dimensions of the hall and then constructed the crib in the basement. We carried it upstairs and discovered we could not get it over the banisters. I returned to the basement, made changes and tried again. This time I found that I had failed to account for the floor molding. Back to the basement. The third attempt succeeded. Later that year our friend John Storrs, the architect who had added the dining room in 1950, added a room upstairs for the baby and a second bath for us.

Mrs. Manse, wholly devoted to John, was not sure she approved of the new arrival until we brought Jeannie home. Then she was delighted and took good care of both children until her death a year later. Mrs. Manse was followed by several housekeepers, particularly Flossie Cabble and Aleta Vinson, both of whom did a wonderful job for us until Jean reached high school age. Flossie's husband, Banks Cabble, was a railroad conductor. Flossy worked for us for a number of years and then took a commercial job with Owens Corning. When John developed an allergy to cats, this put an end to our dynasty of

Siamese cats, and we gave the last, a large male named Duke, to Flossie. Duke lived on with Flossy for many years.

*

When the Army reserve system was reorganized in 1947, I joined a reserve unit in New York which met intermittently in downtown Manhattan. After we moved to Oregon, I was assigned to the 387th Field Artillery Battalion of the 104th Infantry Division with headquarters at Vancouver, Washington. The division was then commanded by Portland lawyer Lamar Tooze, the former adjutant-general of the 79th Division. As a reserve division, the 104th was a skeleton organization, a cadre to be filled out with draftees should it be ordered to active duty. Other officers in the battalion were Major Arno Denecke, who had married Selma Jane Rockey, and Captain William F. Dirker, who had married Molly Herring. Molly was a niece of Jimmy MacGregor, who had gone to Yale with Dave Mersereau. Arno Denecke had graduated in Class 13 from the Field Artillery School at Fort Sill, six weeks ahead of my class.

The 387th was commanded by Lieutenant Colonel Calvin Emeis, a Portland contractor. We met Monday nights each week for training sessions at Vancouver Barracks and spent two weeks each summer in camp at Fort Lewis, Washington. Camp the summer of 1949 was uneventful. However, in the spring of 1950 Clissa and I discussed whether I should continue in the reserve. I was already credited with ten years service toward retirement. However, the summer camp obviously was going to soak up vacation time even though employers were encouraged not to count summer camp as vacation, It was no vacation for Clissa when I was off at camp. I applied for and was transferred to the inactive reserve. Some weeks later Clissa raised the subject again. "Why don't you go to camp? You enjoy it. Go ahead. We'll get more vacation time eventually."

I put in a request to transfer back into the 387th. Days later the Korean War broke out. All transfers were frozen. We had no idea whether I was back in the 387th and probably destined for Korea, or in the inactive reserve. Several weeks later I learned that I was, indeed, back in the 387th and ordered to summer camp at Fort Lewis fully expecting to be called to active duty and headed for Korea when our two weeks were up.

Fort Lewis was a beehive of activity as we arrived. The 2nd Division was encamped in the North Fort preparing for shipment to Korea. Another regular division was in the main Fort. Our Division, the 104th, was training in the summer camp area. McCord Air Base, just north of Fort Lewis, was roaring day and night with bombers taking off to cross the Pacific and transports flying special personnel to Japan and Korea. Eric Phillips, who had been a replacement lieutenant in my battery of the 310th Field Artillery in WW II, had stayed in the regular army and was now a captain commanding a battery in the 2nd Division artillery. We had dinner together just before the 2nd shipped out, taking officers from the inactive reserve called to active duty as replacements. Some months later when General McArthur pushed his troops up toward the Yalu River, the 2nd division was ambushed by the Chinese army. Eric was captured and spent three years in a Chinese prison camp. I saw him shortly after his return. He was emaciated but otherwise in reasonably good shape.

As camp ended that summer, we were still expecting orders for active duty. Clissa drove up to Fort Lewis to meet me. She put Johnny, then two and a half, in the back seat. In the front seat she carried a supply of toys, and every few miles she tossed another toy into the back to keep him occupied. We spent a night in a motel near Black Lake and then drove on up to Vancouver, B. C. Canadian Customs politely impounded my 45 automatic at Blaine, Washington, and we then caught a ferry for Victoria where we spent a three day vacation.

The 104th was never ordered to active duty. It was retained as a potential cadre in case more divisions were required. In 1951 I went once more to summer camp. By 1952 I was in the Dusenbery office. Herb Schwab had accumulated thirteen years of service and was a full colonel. We concluded that if both of us were called to active duty our practice would be gone, and Herb had better hold on to his more valuable commission. So I resigned my commission in the reserve.

*

While President Truman won his first full term election in 1948, he still had to contend with an acerbic group of new Republican senators and representatives who had been elected in 1946. These included Richard Nixon and Joseph McCarthy. President Truman had appointed General George C. Marshall, the wartime chief of staff, Secretary of State in January, 1947. The general resigned following a serious kidney operation in December, 1948, but during his tenure in that post he had proposed and set in motion the American plan for the revival of a prostrate Europe subsequently known as the Marshall Plan. With the outbreak of the Korean War in 1950, President Truman called General Marshall back to active duty once more, this time as Secretary of Defense.

Now the general who had been hailed as the architect of victory was attacked by Senator Jenner of Indiana as "a living lie" and "eager to play a front role for traitors." When General Douglas McArthur was removed from his command in the Far East for disobeying orders, he returned to the United States hailed as a hero and made a speech to Congress in which he attacked General Marshall, saying that his mission to China in 1946 was "the greatest political mistake we have made in a hundred years." Marshall refused to be drawn into a public quarrel with McArthur.

Following President Eisenhower's election as president in 1952, Senator McCarthy charged that Marshall was a traitor, had tricked us into World War II, and had lost us China and Korea. Everyone expected President Eisenhower to defend General Marshall against these scurrilous attacks. He failed to do so for political reasons, and this failure was a significant blot on his career.

I wrote General Marshall as a former officer who had served under his command, deploring these attacks. Five days later I received his response thanking me, which does show how deeply he felt. It is difficult for those who did not experience it to conceive the intensity with which some politicians fanned the fires of suspicion and divisiveness over communists and communism.

Richard Nixon won election as a senator accusing his opponent, Helen Gahagen Douglas of being a "fellow traveler." Senator Joseph McCarthy pilloried many able career diplomats in the state department and finally took on the United States Army with charges of treasonable conduct. This led to the Senate Army McCarthy hearings. The cross examination of the senator by counsel for the Army was relentless and effective. I followed the hearings closely and was delighted when McCarthy was censured by the Senate for his misconduct. This effectively ended his political career, but the effects of this disgraceful period in our national life lingered on.

*

A year after the armistice was signed, I experienced directly the legal and human consequences of that atmosphere. Mr. Dusenbery asked me to step into his office. He introduced me to William Culp, a tall, thin young man and asked him to tell me his story. Culp, a navy veteran of WWII, enlisted in a reserve unit and was serving as a sergeant in an infantry unit in Korea. Captured by the Chinese, he was held in a prisoner of war camp until the exchange of prisoners following the armistice. On his return to the states and stationed at Madigan General Hospital, he was notified by the War Department that he had been accused of improper conduct as a prisoner of war. No details as to time and place were set forth, nor was he told who had made the charges. His choice was to accept the charges, in which case he would receive a dishonorable discharge and forfeit all benefits, including his pension for wounds, or he could request a hearing before a board of officers in Fort Lewis, Washington. The board would appoint an officer to represent him, or he could appear by his own counsel. I was not familiar with this administrative procedure, but it appeared to be seriously lacking in due process.

The sergeant had with him the papers which had been served on him. That was all. He was also penniless. I questioned him at some length. Following capture of his unit, the Chinese had separated the officers from the enlisted men, putting the latter in a separate camp. The sergeant was the highest ranking noncommissioned officer in his camp unit and was held responsible for the internal camp administration. He was the interface between the prisoners and their captors. He adjusted quarrels, presented grievances and transmitted instructions. There was nothing unusual about this procedure. I had established a similar prison administration when I operated the SS prisoner of war camp at Gleisenau, Germany in the fall of 1945.

The camp conditions he described were Spartan. The food was poor, the cold intense. The prisoners endured Chinese indoctrination classes, and the general procedure, while not conforming to the Geneva Convention, was not surprising under the circumstances. The sergeant's story made sense and, if believed, fully exonerated him. The question was, who made the charges, and what were his or their motives? The sergeant's fellow prisoners had long since been dispersed. He had the names and addresses of only three men who had been in the prison camp with him, one in Salt Lake City, Utah, one in Oregon City and a third I was never able to locate.

I agreed to represent the sergeant and requested a hearing on his behalf. I asked that army counsel be appointed to assist and advised the board that I would appear as private counsel. At the same time I moved for disclosure of the witnesses to the alleged improper behavior and for specification of the improper behavior charged. I received a reply that War Department regulations prohibited divulging that information. Fortunately, I was able to locate the Utah and Oregon City men by telephone. The former, John McCoy, was cooperative but said he was a Mormon and doing his year of missionary work. He would need to be excused by the church. Accordingly, I wrote the church authorities explaining the situation. They agreed to let McCoy come to Fort Lewis for the hearing. I offered to pay his way, but McCoy said he could manage it. So Sergeant Culp, our two witnesses, and I drove to Fort Lewis and entered the one story temporary building for what was to be in effect a court-martial.

The board consisted of three officers, a lieutenant colonel as president and two majors seated at one end of the room. A lieutenant referred to as "the recorder" acted as the trial judge advocate or prosecutor. Lieutenant Colonel Rudmann was appointed to assist me as defense counsel. He described the procedure to me and sat with me but allowed me to handle the defense as I wished.

The president convened the proceeding, I moved for disclosure of the charges and the names of the witnesses, arguing that it was impossible to prepare an adequate defense to unknown charges made by unknown persons. The president denied the motion saying that under the regulations such disclosure was not permitted. He then warned me the board had been unable to obtain a regular reporter, and the lady typist who was doing the reporting asked that we speak slowly and carefully. Since I expected to litigate the case through the federal courts, I was careful to comply.

The recorder then read the general charges that the sergeant had been disloyal by aiding the Chinese, sympathizing with the communists, reading propaganda to the prisoners and other similar charges. The recorder then said that the supporting evidence was before the board and concluded,
"The government rests."

That was the government's case. The president advised that I should proceed with the defense.

I moved again for disclosure of the precise charges, the names of the accusers and disclosure of the evidence given to the board. The motion was denied.

I then called the sergeant to the stand. I told him to keep one eye on the court reporter and the other on the president of the board as I questioned him. I had him relate his entire military career, the circumstances of his capture, the nature of his wounds and the details of his two years as a prisoner. I tried to cover every conceivable aspect which might be twisted by some malcontent into these charges. There was no cross examination.

I next called my Oregon City witness, Charles Brooks, who backed up Culp's testimony but added little. The board then recessed for dinner.

When the board reconvened, I called John McCoy, the man from Utah, the Mormon doing his year as a missionary. He was a well dressed, good looking young man. I gave him the same warning about speaking slowly and keeping one eye on the court reporter and the other on the president of the board.

"I regret I cannot do that, sir," McCoy said firmly.

I was startled. What on earth was he talking about? Was my witness going to turn on me? The courtroom was deadly quiet.

"Why not?" (I had to ask the question.)

"I lost one eye in Korea, sir."

I was stunned for a moment. He'd said nothing of a wound! McCoy was a great witness. He described the frigid Manchurian winter living in prison huts, the problem of maintaining discipline, and the harassment they underwent from the Chinese. He fully supported Sergeant Culp.

There was no cross examination. The hour was late. I told the Board I would be brief in argument. The president replied that he wanted me to take as much time as I needed in argument. The recorder made no argument other than to say that the board had the materials before it and had heard the evidence the defendant had offered.

In making my argument I pulled out all the stops. I pointed out that I came from a military family. My father was a graduate of West Point. I had served four and a half years during World War II. I had served in combat as a battery commander. I had sat on general courts-martial during the war, and I had run a camp containing several thousand prisoners of war.

This procedure, I said, was unconscionable. I recognized that the board was bound to follow the procedure, but it was inexcusable to place that burden on them as honorable men. We had no way of knowing what lay in the files before them. We could not speak directly to any charge or question the motivation of any hidden witness. The evidence we had produced showed that the sergeant had conducted himself in the best traditions of the service. I thanked the board for their consideration and rested. The president of the board adjourned the hearing, saying we would be advised of their decision in the morning.

Colonel Rudmann agreed to take the verdict for me and telephone the result in the morning. I headed back to Portland on that long windy two lane road. It was long after midnight when I got back to Portland.

Later that morning Colonel Rudmann telephoned to say that the board had cleared the sergeant of all charges and had commended him for his conduct.

I think I felt more concerned about that hearing than almost any other legal proceeding I have undertaken. The consequences of losing were so unjust, and the procedure so grotesquely unfair, it is hard to conceive how responsible officials could have devised or accepted such regulations irrespective of the pressure from McCarthy, Jenner and other such legislators. The result was fortunate for our firm. Had we lost, we would have had to challenge the procedure through the federal courts, and it would have cost us a fortune.

The president of the Board was scrupulously fair in his handling of the proceedings, determined to follow his instructions to the letter and to give me every opportunity to make my case against the procedure. The fact that a lieutenant colonel was assigned as defense counsel and a lieutenant was assigned as the recorder qua trial judge advocate tells us something.

The transcript, which I later secured, does not look to me now, more than a half century later, like the product of a troubled typist desperately unfamiliar with court reporting. It looks quite professional. The answers of the witnesses are consistent with my general recollection, but expressed in better usage than I recall. Only my argument looks awkwardly natural—like an opinion of mine spoken but not read from the bench, uncorrected, just as spoken. This suggests that the typed transcript was cleaned up with the exception of my argument. Curiously, there is no mention of the preliminary instruction I gave to John McCoy about eyes nor any mention of his reply. Perhaps that is because the stenographer thought it was an instruction and neither question nor an answer. In any event, the court or board handled the case as fairly as they could within the regulations they were obligated to follow. But what would have happened to Sergeant Culp had he appeared before a different board without counsel to round up his witnesses, or inclined to point out the injustice of the procedure?

CHAPTER 13

Explorations, Meadow Lake, the City Club, and boating

In 1949 we had traded in the Olds with its electrical problems for a Studebaker sedan, a fine looking vehicle. Unfortunately, the Studebaker also had a defect that could never be remedied. The front wheels could not be kept in alignment, and we wore through a set of front tires every five thousand miles. In 1951 we traded in the Studebaker for a Nash Rambler station wagon, a small but sturdy vehicle which served us well for many years. The summer of 1952 Howard and Mardy Zucker came west to vacation with us. Four adults, one Beatty child and two Zucker children plus baggage got into the Rambler, traveled to Eastern Oregon and Paulina Lake, then back across the Cascades to Portland. We left Andrew, Ellen and John with Mrs. Manse for several days and drove up to Spirit Lake below Mount St. Helens and stayed at the lodge overnight. The weather was fair, the lake beautiful, and the old growth timber magnificent—all this was destroyed by the 1980 eruption!

My father retired from his New York state job in 1954 as he reached sixty-five. He and my mother moved back to Portland, taking an apartment with Margaret Sharp in the red brick village apartments near the north end of Vista Avenue. On occasion John took the bus down to their apartment after school, if for some reason there was no one at home. In 1955 we took a cottage at Neskowin for a month and Morses, and Beattys, junior and senior gathered

233

at the beach. Jeannie rode her first horse, one from the Nescowin livery stables. As I led the amiable animal with Jeannie perched on the saddle, it nuzzled into my shoulder and bit me, confirming my mistrust of the horse as a means of transportation.

*

The summer of 1956 we bought a silver 1956 Chevrolet station wagon, a great car. Clissa, I and the children drove it east to Yellowstone. I took the children fishing in the Yellowstone river just west of the park. John hooked a trout almost at once. I suggested that he give the rod to Jeannie to reel in saying, "There'll be lots more fish, John." Unfortunately, that was the last rise we had, and John has never forgotten the injustice. We then drove down past the Grand Tetons and over a twelve thousand foot pass into Estes Park, Colorado where we met the Zuckers and Amos and Lynn Landers. We spent two weeks, hiking, sunning, and lying about. Estes Park was a mountain town in a sloping glacial valley.

*

In 1949 Clissa and I had met a young orthopedic physician, William Earl Snell, at a party in Lake Oswego. One thing led to another, and I mentioned that I was having some back pain. He proceeded to probe around my back and announced that I had something called Marie Strumple's disease, and this accounted for my back problems. He also said the vertebrae were partly fused, and if I did any more skiing I was out of my mind. Bill and Tedi Snell became good friends. Bill was an active hunter and fisherman. He organized my first duck hunting expedition on Sauvie Island following a late night party at his house. The participants were Bill, Arno Denecke, Bill's brother in law, Dan Fry and several of Bill's fellow physicians from the medical school. The blinds were on a small lake adjacent to Sturgeon Lake. We went out at five o'clock in the morning.

The temperature was well below freezing, and the lake was covered with several inches of ice. Bill distributed us into individual blinds. Arno was in a blind not far from me. I had my Uncle Tom Sharp's Daley Diamond shotgun with damascus steel barrels in which I had to shoot black powder shells to avoid rupturing the barrel with modern ammunition. As the sky gradually lightened, birds began whirring overhead. Eventually they became visible. I saw one high above me, aimed and fired. The black powder created a magnificent yellow flash and a cloud of black smoke. The duck, a splendid mallard drake, dropped like a stone, hitting the brush on the front of the blind. I reached out and pulled it in. I was the talk of the expedition. Moments later I brought down a widgen. I basked for several weeks in the role of a great hunter. Sadly, it was pure luck. I never repeated that success.

One Saturday when Jean was a baby, the Snells and Beattys arranged with Mrs. Manse to take care of Kitty Snell and Jean for the afternoon while we took the Snell twins and John fishing at a stocked trout pond in a small valley off US. 30 below St. Helens. The children caught fish, and it was a great success. The Snells lived in a house on Skyline Boulevard at that time. They suggested we have a picnic supper in their yard. We were half way through supper when Clissa shrieked "We've forgotten the babies!" Indeed we had.

Bill and I drove back to our house to apologize to Mrs. Manse and retrieve the babies. After supper I made up a story for the children about a king without an army who created that necessary element of royalty by pulling teeth out of a dragon and planting them to grow into soldiers, a theme stolen from the myth about sowing dragon's teeth. I memorialized the occasion by doing a watercolor of tooth extraction from a dragon and gave it to the Snell children for Christmas. When the last Snell child went off to college, the Snells returned the water color as a Christmas gift. Trask has the picture now.

*

In 1956 Bill Snell became a member of the Meadow Lake Club, and then proposed me as a member. The lake was located in a meadow on the divide in the Coast Range. The springs which fed the lake constitute the headwaters of the Nestucka River which flows west into the Pacific. In the early 1880s some enterprising fellow built a rock crib dam at the western end of the meadow where the stream fell off into a steep canyon and established a shingle mill cutting the cedar interspersed in the old growth fir timber. The dam created a shallow, winding lake perhaps a quarter mile wide and a mile long. The cedar was cut out in a decade or so, and the mill was abandoned. In 1904 a group of sportsmen led by H. L. Corbett in Portland bought the sections of land surrounding the lake and created a fishing lodge using the farmhouse at the east end of the lake. Mrs. Helen Ladd Corbett, mother of Henry, Elliott and Hamilton Corbett, was issued membership #1. In 1924 the farmhouse lodge burned and a new clubhouse was rebuilt.

My mother recalled weekend parties in the days before the first World War to which she and other young ladies from Portland were invited. She described how they took the electric train to Carlton where they were met by carriages and driven up to the lake. By the 1950's the timber in the club-owned sections had become extremely valuable. The surviving members of the Club were in their seventies and eighties. They sold the timber to Willamette Valley Lumber Company and leased back the lake with a substantial fringe of old growth timber left about it as protection. They then divided the proceeds of the sale and opened the club to young new members at a modest initiation fee, thus renewing the club for another generation.

The lodge was a log structure and consisted of a large sitting or living room, a dinning room with a long wood table and bench seats, a kitchen and quarters for a live-in couple who acted as caretakers and cooks. A wing contained perhaps sixteen Spartan cubicles as sleeping rooms for members. On the edge of the lake was a boathouse containing several dozen rowboats and racks for outboard motors. The boats were owned by the club. The motors were owned by those members who wanted them, however size was limited to five horsepower.

It was a lovely setting with huge old growth firs rising in the hills on either side of the lake. The lake was originally stocked with German brown trout which thrived naturally from then on. The club stocked rainbow each year but the water proved too warm for rainbow to reproduce successfully. The road up to the lake was gravel but reasonably good, and the drive from Portland took about an hour and a half. One could telephone the lodge in the afternoon, make arrangements for a steak dinner, drive up after work, fish for an hour or two, have dinner and drive home.

In December of 1964 we had early snow followed by a thaw and extremely heavy rain in western Oregon. Both the Columbia and Willamette rose above flood stage, the Willamette to within a foot of the surface of the Hawthorne Bridge. The parking lot of the Portland Yacht Club was under water. The Meadow Lake dam collapsed, draining the lake. The waters washed out sections of a road recently constructed by the Bureau of Land Management below the dam. German brown trout were scattered down the valley of the Nestucka, and substantial flood damage was done to farms all the way to the sea. That was the end of the Meadow Lake Club. Reconstructing the dam would have been prohibitively expensive. Willamette as landowner faced claims in the millions.

Some months later Mendes and Mount in New York, who represented Lloyds of London, Willamette Valley's insurer, sent their file on Meadow Lake to me to supervise a proposed settlement of the claims by the federal government. Lloyds had already settled with private landowners down the Nestucca valley. The investigation file was thorough. It described through the eyes of observers how the dam had failed. A geologic report on the terrain revealed that the dam had been built adjacent to an ancient slide dated by the position of a large, leaning fir to around 1840. The new road below the dam had cut across the toe of the slide, and the evidence indicated that the combination of road cut and heavy rain had activated the slide which carried away the dam. Lloyds had treated the case as one of absolute liability under the famous English case of *Fletcher v.*

Rylands. I thought Willamette had an arguable defense against the government. Nevertheless, Mendes went through with the settlement, and they were probably correct. Nothing substantial had been done to maintain the dam for many years. It looked like a jerry built structure, and a jury might well have ignored the causal argument.

*

In 1950 I had joined the City Club, spurred to do so by my Aunt Margaret who described it as an important club which I should join. The membership at that time consisted of some six hundred, largely business and professional men. The luncheon meetings held each Friday noon at the Benson Hotel featured guest speakers on subjects ranging from local to international affairs. The club also undertook research and investigation by committees of its members. Research reports were usually well done, timely and, in one recent instance, political dynamite. In 1948 a report critical of the Portland police cost long time Mayor George L. Baker his job and resulted in the election of State Senator Dorothy Lee as mayor to clean up the Police Department.

My first research committee assignment was to examine a state ballot measure proposing a constitutional amendment to allow para mutual gambling. Tom McCall and I dissented from the committee's majority which favored the measure. We relied heavily on facts and arguments taken from a recent United States Senate Committee report on gambling chaired by Senator Estes Kefauver of Tennessee. The club considered the report at a meeting in the old Benson Hotel banquet hall, with several of the wives, including Clarissa, observing the debate from a small gallery. In those days women were not permitted to attend the luncheon meetings. Tom and I lost the debate. The ballot measure, which cleverly guaranteed a share of the proceeds to support county fairs in every county, was approved by the club and subsequently adopted by the voters.

My second assignment was a research committee charged to look into the question of fluoridating Portland's water supply.

The chairman, Dr. Frank Queen, moved from Portland early in the study, and I was appointed to replace him as chairman. We worked for more than a year, read the literature, and interviewed many witnesses. Clissa reviewed my drafts and educated me on the meaning of statistical significance. The report was comprehensive and was adopted by the club by a heavy majority. In the year following publication the club received requests for thousands of reprints from all over the country and from overseas. None the less, half a century later Portland still does not fluoridate its water.

In 1956 I was elected secretary of the City Club and the following year to a three year term on the board of governors. The board met weekly for lunch at the Aero Club where it planned the programs, reviewed committee reports and discussed the state of the city, state and nation. These luncheon meetings of the board were the most lively, free wheeling intellectual discussions I had ever experienced.

In 1960 William W. Wessinger, elected to the board after my term had expired, called to say that the board wanted to nominate me for president for the year 1961-1962. Would I accept? I was, of course, pleased to do so. One of the duties of the president was to introduce the weekly speaker. Vern Dusenbery congratulated me on my election and reminded me that members came to hear the speaker, not the president. Bearing this admonition in mind, I kept my introductions short, but being a fan of Walt Kelley's comic strip "Pogo" I did my best to work one of Pogo's pithy comments from that comic strip into each introduction.

*

By 1957 Clissa and I had reached a point at which we had to decide whether to enlarge our house on Dosch Road or move. The location was a good one for us despite the forty steps up to the house and a garage built for a Model T Ford. Clissa was five minutes from the medical school. I was ten minutes from my office downtown. The Council Crest bus, which had replaced the Council Crest trolley in 1950, ran to the intersection at

Greenhills, so our housekeeper had public transportation. We finally decided to stay, enlarge the living room by pushing the west wall out and change the entrance to the house.

John Storrs, whose practice was now flourishing, flatly refused to design a third addition to our house. We should build a new house designed by him. So I hired a contractor to do the work. It went well, the enlarged living room was successful as was the new entrance. Unfortunately, the value of a supervising architect became evident when the first heavy rains came in the fall. The roof over the living room leaked badly where the shallow slope tied into the deeper slope of the original pitched roof. The contractor had left town. We re-roofed the addition and re-tiled the interior ceiling at our expense. Several years later I noticed that the ceiling molding of the addition no longer appeared straight. The addition had settled several inches. I discovered that the contractor had rested the addition on concrete blocks with no firm support beneath them. I tried jacking the addition up using three house jacks, then gave up and hired a contractor to pour footings, which solved the problem. So much for building without an architect!

Much of the work in the garden involved moving earth and building rock walls. Gradually I eliminated the patches of lawn and planted shrubbery and trees. On the south side of the house I created a terrace by building a retaining wall and filling the slope behind it with earth obtained from leveling a portion of the rear yard. We graveled that flat area, then later black topped it. I put in a sprinkling system front and back which worked well for several years then failed when the water pressure dropped substantially because of building in the forested area on the west side of lower Dosch Road.

Dr. Joseph and Ranee Trainer and their two children, Brian and Lynn, lived on Gaston Street, a short L shaped street that extended west, then south from Fairmont. A path ran from our house across the Schreiber property to Gaston Street. Another path ran across the Donald Sterling cutting yard, a 25 foot square piece of property between our property and that of the Talboys

whose house faced Talbot Road. Mr. Sterling was the editor of
the Oregon Journal and one of the pallbearers at my grandfather
Morrison's funeral. Mrs. Sterling was a friend of my mother's.
Their son, Donald Jr., graduated from Princeton in 1948, later
became editor of the Journal and assistant to the publisher of
the Oregonian when the two papers merged. Don's sister, Sis,
married Ned Hayes, son of Mr. and Mrs. Edmund Hayes who
lived above Riverdale School on Military Road.

Dr. Joseph Trainer was the student health physician at the
Medical School and a remarkable fellow. Trained as an electrical
engineer before he went to medical school, Joe Trainer dealt with
mechanical and electrical matters with the same imaginative
competence that he applied to a full range of medical problems, as
well as every other household difficulty in the neighborhood. His
basement was a warehouse of fittings, tools and spare parts for most
things made or used by man. The Trainer's two children, Bryan and
Lynn, were the same ages as ours and played together. Dorothy
and Alex Parks lived in a small house on the corner of Gaston and
Fairmont with their children, Penny, Douglas, and Chris. Penny
later married Phil Knight, the founder and CEO of Nike.

Mr. Schreiber, the retired brew master of the Blitz Weinhard
brewery, built the house south of us in the eighteen nineties.
He was a tall stooped man with a white handlebar mustache.
He always wore a broad brimmed slouch hat and looked like
Mr. MacGregor in the Peter Rabbit book of my childhood. Mr.
Schreiber died during the 1950s, but his widow, Marie, lived on
in the house for some years. Mrs. Schreiber's sister, Mrs. Freeman,
known as Freemy, lived in an even smaller house just south of the
Schreiber house. Mrs Freeman baby sat for the neighborhood.

When we arrived in 1948, the interior of Brentwood Drive,
the circle immediately north of Talbot Road, was dominated by
Burt Brown Barker's elegant small replica of a French chalet. Mr.
Barker, a great friend of my Aunt Margaret, made his fortune
in Chicago as a young lawyer. He then left the practice of law,
came to Oregon and established a connection with the University
of Oregon faculty. On the east side of his property he built a

house for his daughter who married the French Consul, Alfred Herman. The Hermans were divorced, and the house passed into the hands of Bill and Cornelia Hayes Stevens. Later two more houses were built on the property, one by Mr. Barker's grandson, Alfred Barker Herman and his wife Helen.

Mr. Barker was a historian by avocation and wrote a book on Dr. John McLoughlin as well as a number of articles about him. Every day Mr. Barker took the Council Crest trolley, and later the bus which replaced it, to work in the morning and home in the evening. I often rode the trolley with him in the late forties. He was an interesting old gentleman with bushy white hair, a white mustache and eyes that sparkled.

Frances and Arch Diack lived next to the Parks, their house facing Fairmont and backing on Gaston Avenue. Their dog, Willy, irrepressible, dug holes year after year in the Parks' garden. Arch Diack was a physician, conservationist and inventor. He and his brother Sam had cabins and substantial old growth fir acreage on the Sandy River where every Christmas they invited their friends and neighbors from Portland to come, cut a Christmas tree, plant two replacements and then have drinks for the adults and cider for the children. In their wills Arch and Sam Diack left their beautiful and extensive Sandy River property to the Nature Conservancy.

Mary Alice Rockey Sneed lived in a small house at the turn of Gaston Street. When the Parks moved to a house on Council Crest, their house was taken by Robert and Lois Miller and their five boys. Bob was a radiologist, and Lois, a former nurse, was active in Republican Party circles and involved in numerous public matters. I think it is fair to say that in those days we suffered no lack of children or creative minds in our neighborhood.

*

A summer camping expedition in the fifties with the Snells to Big Lake in Deschutes County convinced me that Clissa was not going to be happy with camping for recreation. As a practical matter, I had enough sleeping on the ground during the war to last me a lifetime, so we were on the lookout for an alternative. In 1955 Joe and Ranee Trainer acquired an eighteen foot inboard cruiser which they moored at the head of the Multnomah Channel of the Willamette River. One weekend they took us for a run on the river and I was smitten. A boat looked like the answer to our outdoor interest. Clissa had sailed on large sailboats belonging to her "Uncle Pa" Barney of Smith Barney fame in the East. My experience was minimal.

We had joined the Racquet Club and both children learned to swim in the Racquet Club pool, a prerequisite to serious boating. We purchased books on boats and read magazines. Finally, in the fall of 1957 we bought a new 23 foot Owens outboard cruiser and a 50 horsepower Johnson outboard motor. The Johnson was new on the market, an outboard motor developed for small landing craft during the war. The Owens started our family on forty years of adventures on the waters of the Pacific Northwest.

We acquired the Owens through the Oregon City Marina during the winter of 56-57 and stored it in a large warehouse across the road from the marina, which was located on the east bank of the Willamette several miles above the Falls. Clissa and I both took the basic piloting course of the United States Power Squadron, and I took the subsequent navigation course. Early in the spring of 1957 the motor was attached to the hull, and we launched the Clarissa Jean. Her maiden voyage was intended to be down the Willamette, through the locks at Oregon City, on through Portland to the Columbia, then up through North Portland Harbor to the Jantzen Beach Moorage. For this trip we acquired an extra five gallon can of gasoline. Alas, as we approached the locks the steering connection between wheel and outboard motor failed, and we had to work our way back to the marina for repairs. The following weekend we started off once more, and this time successfully negotiated the locks and accomplished the voyage.

Jantzen Beach Moorage lay on Hayden Island just upstream of the bridge over North Portland Harbor, the body of water which separates Hayden Island from the Oregon mainland. Just south of I-5 on Hayden Island was Jantzen Beach still the amusement park of our youth somewhat gone to seed. The moorage consisted of three or four small floats and a fuel dock. Upstream several hundred yards were the remains of the pilings of the old streetcar trestle which terminated at the ferry dock where the south approach to the interstate bridges now stands. This was the streetcar line my father rode in 1911 and 1912 when he was stationed in Vancouver Barracks with the 4th Field Artillery Regiment and courting my mother. He crossed the river on the ferry, took the streetcar to downtown Portland, changed to a 23rd street car and rode up Washington and Burnside streets to Trinity Place.

That first summer we took our vacation on the Columbia in the boat. Clissa and I slept in the v berths in the cabin. The children each had a folding canvas cot set up in the cockpit. Off we went loaded with groceries, thirty gallons of water and three cans of gas. I managed to run over a submerged wing dam above Government Island and dented the propeller. We changed the propeller and ventured on. Some days later we had to abandon our anchor which became tangled in submerged brush in the mouth of the Lewis River. But these were light skirmishes.

We ran back upstream between Government Island and McNary Island and decided to spend the night in a shallow protected area of the river. Lacking an anchor, I thought a forty pound can of spare fuel would at least hold us in quiet water. I attached a line and tossed the can overboard. It bobbed on the surface, its contents being lighter than water. Clissa howled with laughter. My dignity suffered, but I was learning. The beaches were clean, the weather was sunny, the children had a wonderful time playing in the water. We kept them wearing ski belts for floatation as a safety measure for many years.

It soon became obvious that the 50 horse Johnson was a very thirsty engine. Carrying multiple five gallon cans of gasoline was a nuisance and a hazard. I had Sells Marine Service at the Portland Yacht Club build a flat 35 gallon permanent tank in the shallow bilge with an outboard intake and semi-fixed hose connection to the motor. This extended our range considerably. Three years later we turned in the Johnson for two Scot 60 hp three cylinder engines. I then extended the length of the boat by three feet, enclosing the motor well. This worked well in theory except that I failed to allow for the amount of air those thirsty Scots needed and had to convert a considerable portion of the cover to louvers for adequate air intake.

Carey Martin at the office had a similar Owens outboard cruiser and a trailer which his family had taken north to the San Juans. In 1959 we arranged to take both boats north. The Harold Berenson family used our boat for two weeks cruising with the Martins. Then we cruised with the Trainers using the Martin boat. We made this exchange again in 1960. Both years we ventured through the American San Juans and over into the Canadian Gulf Islands. There were very few boats on the water in those days and we were able to take clams and oysters around Stuart Island in the American San Juans and in the De Courcy Islands of the Canadian San Juans.

In 1961 Dr. Trainer bought Dr. Bill Todd's old 18 foot outboard with a rusty Mercury motor, and we again went north with our respective children. It rained steadily. Joe's Mercury had all sorts of problems. We finally took motel rooms at Friday Harbor to dry out, then abandoned the trip and returned to the Columbia. The sun came out and we ran the boats up river to Miller Island above the Dalles Dam, then back down with the Trainer's old Mercury outboard protesting all the way.

In 1962 Joe Trainer heard that the City of Portland was auctioning the former harbor patrol boat, F.W. Mulkey, a 60 foot tug the city had retired from service. His mouth watered. Joe was the only bidder at the reserve figure, $2,000. The GMC diesel motor alone was worth the price, according to Joe. The Trainers spent the next four or five years on the Mulkey during summer weekends, often taking large parties out for the day and occasional overnight trips. One memorable weekend we went with them up to Reed Island above Washougal. In those days

there was sufficient water between Reed and the Washington
shore to get the boats into a quiet anchorage behind the island.
Joe ran the bow of the Mulkey on shore as he was wont to do,
and we tied the Clarissa Jean to his starboard quarter. During
the night the Corps of Engineers reduced the water coming over
Bonneville Dam and the water level dropped three feet. Morning
found the Mulky aground and at a fairly sharp incline. Because
our boat was tied to the Mulkey's stern we were still afloat, but
barely. Joe removed his batteries and plugged all openings into
the engine. Then we took the Trainers home in our boat leaving
the Mulkey largely high and dry.

Monday when the flow over the dam resumed, the water
came up over the Mulkey's stern and filled her bilge. Monday
noon we flew up in Harry White's float plane to look her over.
The stern half of the boat lay under water. Monday afternoon
Harry White, proprietor of a marine shop, with Joe and a couple
of friends, towed a small barge with a motor and pump up to
Reed Island. I followed them with the Clarissa Jean. With the
barge in place, deck openings closed, and the hose thrust down
into the Mulkey's bilge, Harry started his pump, which spewed
out a good four inch stream of water. Gradually the stern began
to rise, and after an hour of steady pumping the Mulkey was
afloat. with a few small fish stranded behind her bulwarks.

Joe wrestled his batteries back into place and hooked up the
Jimmy diesel. He threw on the switch and pressed the starter.
The motor roared into action. By now it was pitch dark and
raining. The Mulkey backed off Reed Island and started down
river with the Clarissa Jean tied alongside. At the helm of the
Mulkey was an acquaintance of Joe Trainer, who claimed to
know the river like the back of his hand. Joe went below to the
galley to scramble eggs and bacon for everyone. The Mulkey
came out of the Reed Island lagoon into the river and headed
toward the Washington shore. I ventured a comment to Joe's
acquaintance about the reef which I knew lay ahead. He told
me not to worry and kept on his course through the darkness.
I left the pilot house in a hurry, cast off the Clarissa Jean, and
headed sharply to port and back into the channel. Moments

later the Mulkey suddenly swung sharply to port and followed after me.

The Mulkey had many weekend cruises with Joe Trainer's friends and neighbors aboard, but she was a beast to maintain, a Jonah to moor, and impossible to insure or sell. Joe found her a lot more difficult to get rid of than she had been to buy.

CHAPTER 14

Reapportionment, The Neubergers and Mrs. Green,

The Oregon Constitution required that the legislature reapportion its two houses among the counties using the major fraction method following each decennial census. The legislature failed to enact a general reapportionment after the 1910 census. By 1950, because of demographic changes, the eighteen counties of Eastern Oregon with 16 % of the state population elected almost 27 % of both houses of the legislature. Their senators and representatives could outvote Multnomah County, which had 33% of the state's population. Lane county was even more under-represented than Multnomah. The existing apportionment enabled the more conservative parts of the state to control the legislature.

Following defeat of State Senator Richard Neuberger's bill to reapportion and the narrow defeat of an initiative measure which would have guaranteed rural counties a disproportionate share of legislative seats, reapportionment was at a standstill. State and federal courts at that time considered reapportionment a political process which they were not empowered to require.

Clay Myers, president of the Young Republicans, telephoned to ask if I as a Young Democrat would like to meet and discuss the possibility of a joint effort at reapportionment. I agreed to do so. Clay would bring Shirley Field, also a Republican, a young lawyer and member of the League of Women Voters whose convention had called for an enforceable reapportionment. We met after work in a small off-street room near the old Spaulding Building and discussed the situation. Clay was prepared to support an initiative that carried out the existing major fraction apportionment and some method of enforcing the process in a bipartisan approach, provided we agreed to support legislation creating districts for counties with multiple representatives. Districts made sense to me. Having our present thirteen Multnomah County representatives run at large made it virtually impossible for voters to make an intelligent selection from a field of twenty or thirty candidates. Clay, of course, would hope to pick up several Republican seats in Multnomah County. We expected to elect better Democratic candidates.

I handled drafting with the assistance of Phil Levin, a Democrat, and Field. The result was an initiative petition for a constitutional amendment which created a temporary apportionment until 1960, and jurisdiction in the Supreme Court on petition of any qualified elector to review any subsequent apportionment made by the legislature or by the Secretary of State, who was required to make an apportionment if the legislature failed to do so. The enforcement provisions were the heart of the measure. We each agreed to press our respective parties to support the proposal, and to form a "Nonpartisan Committee for Constitutional Reapportionment."

With the support of our three organizations and that of the AF of L and the CIO we collected thousands of signatures. However, as the deadline for filing approached, we needed a good many more. Under state law at that time the signatures presented to the Secretary of State had to be verified by county clerks before the filing deadline, and the county clerks were only required to verify a minimum number per day without a charge for each signature. It looked as though we were going to be short of signatures on the one hand, and short of cash to pay for verification if we did get enough signatures. I assured Emily Logan, state president of the League of Women Voters, that I would raise enough money to pay for verification if the League went all out to get the signatures. With Jim Goodsell's help, I then assured George Brown of the CIO and Jim Marr of the AF of L that if they put up the verification money, the League would get the signatures. It all worked out. The League produced sufficient signatures and the unions produced the money to verify them. Just before the filing deadline we took our final bundle of signatures to the capitol.

The reapportionment amendment passed in the November 1952 general election by nearly a two to one vote. Significantly it passed in all but one county west of the Cascades and failed in all but two counties east of the mountains.

In March of 1953 Dave Baum, a representative from Union County, whose district had been combined with Wallawa County under the temporary reapportionment, filed a suit for declaratory judgment against the Secretary of State, challenging the constitutionality of the Act. Shortly after the complaint was filed, I received information from a lobbyist friend in Salem that sometime after the election the chief justice had been overheard to comment in a capitol lavatory that someone ought to challenge the constitutionality of the reapportionment amendment.

To say I was concerned puts it mildly. It was inconceivable to me as a young lawyer that a judge would commit such an indiscretion and dismaying to think that the chief justice had already concluded the amendment was unconstitutional. The allegations of the Baum complaint looked specious to me, but I feared he might have come upon some defect we had overlooked. I was also acutely sensitive to how this challenge would look to the League of Women Voters ladies who had worked so hard, and to the unions which had contributed the money to count the signatures.

I drove to Salem to see who in the attorney general's office was going to handle the defense. The new Democratic attorney general, Robert Y. Thornton, handed me off to E. G. Foxley, the longtime deputy attorney general, saying he would handle the case. Mr. Foxley insisted the defense should be based on the contention that the suit was "not ripe for decision" under the declaratory judgment act. I thought that was a technical defense highly unlikely to impress the supreme court, particularly if the chief justice already thought the amendment was unconstitutional. I suggested the case had to be defended on the merits. Foxley flatly disagreed. He had been deputy attorney general for many years and was clearly not interested in my suggestions. I left his office convinced that he would present a wholly inadequate defense on the merits, and this proved to be the case.

14. Over the top!. Lawyers Stanley Darling and Jack Beatty escort Emily Logan State President of the League of Women Voters and her reapportionment leaders up the Capitol steps to file petitions which put the measure on the ballot.

15. Clissa, Jack and John at Gearhart, Summer 1949.

I concluded we had to intervene if a defense was to be made on the merits. Moreover, because a member of the court apparently had given Baum encouragement to file, we needed some heavyweight lawyers on the defense team. I discussed the problem with Tom Stoel of Hart, Spencer, McCulloch and Rockwood. Tom agreed to go on the brief and suggested that we enlist Stan Darling of Eugene and Nicholas Jaureguy of Cake, Jaureguy and Tooze of Portland. Both men agreed to join us on the brief. We selected Richard Deich of Portland and Olga Freeman of Eugene as interveners. Dick Deich was a liberal Republican representative from Multnomah County and Olga Freeman was a former state president of the League of Women Voters. I prepared the brief for our interveners, submitting the draft to my senior colleagues. Their deft use of language significantly sharpened the bite of the substantive sections of our brief.

At the trial court level, Judge Rex Kimmell of Marion County found the amendment valid in all respects and entered judgment for the defendant. The plaintiff promptly appealed. George T. Cochran of La Grande, A. S. Grant of Baker, John F, Steelhammer of Salem, state senator Anthony Yturry of Ontario, and John F. Kilkenny of Pendleton were on the brief for Baum as the appellant. These were the political heavyweights of the Eastern Oregon Bar. Douglas Spencer, an attorney of Eugene, appeared on behalf of Walter Dodd of Eugene who wanted to intervene separately from our group.

The case was argued before the Supreme Court March 24, 1954. George Cochran and A.S. Grant argued the cause for appellant Baum. Foxley was allotted the bulk of the defense time to argue. I was allotted ten minutes to argue for interveners Deich and Freeman as was Douglas R. Spencer of Eugene for intervener Dodd. Cochran argued that the amendment violated the principle of separation of powers and the federal constitution, which guaranteed each state a republican form of government. Foxley doggedly argued that the case was not ripe for decision. Twice Chief Justice Latourette interrupted him, suggesting he move on to the merits. Finally, the chief said, "Mr. Foxley, the fact that you are here indicates that we want to hear the case on its merits."

I remember nothing of my argument. It was, of course, a summary of our brief on the merits, The questions from the bench indicated the judges had read the briefs thoroughly. One judge asked Mr Cochran whether he questioned the right of the people to amend the constitution, provided they followed the requirements of the constitution. Cochran agreed they had this right which, to my mind, disposed of the case.

The Supreme Court announced a decision in less than two weeks. The opinion by Chief Justice Latourette demolished appellant's position point by point and concluded that the amendment was indeed valid. The opinion concluded that plaintiff had brought the suit in good faith and the court did not feel that costs should be taxed against him. I suppose one would have to agree that under the circumstances the suit was brought in good faith considering the wash room comment, but the fact was that none of the contentions raised by plaintiffs' counsel raised a substantial question of constitutional law not previously settled by either the United States Supreme Court or the Oregon Supreme Court.

Representative Baum went on to become commanding general of the Oregon National Guard. His son, Ray Baum, became a prominent lawyer in La Grande, and carried on the family tradition of public service, serving as representative from the combined Union and Wallowa district, his father's reapportioned seat, and as majority leader of the house in 1995. John Kilkenny was appointed by President Nixon to the United States District Court and then to the Court of Appeals for the Ninth Circuit, where he served for many years.

Ten years later the United States Supreme Court in the case of *Baker v. Carr*, 369 U.S. 186 (1962), overruled its previous holdings that legislative apportionment was a political, not a judicial question, and held that a state could be compelled under the federal constitution to fairly apportion its legislative bodies. The "major fraction" formula in the Oregon Constitution which our initiative amendment enforced was subsequently held invalid as failing to provide sufficient equality between districts, but our enforcement provisions remain in effect today.

The 1953 Session of the legislature submitted a constitutional amendment authorizing division of the counties into electoral districts, which was adopted in 1954. In the 1955 session I spent a good deal of time before the committees on elections using large cardboard posters to suggest acceptable ways of combining census tracts to form five new electoral districts for Multnomah County representatives.

*

Between 1948 and 1956 the Democratic Party of Oregon underwent a substantial reorganization. In 1948 Monroe Sweetland, a liberal Democrat, ran against Mike Dicicco, a conservative Democrat, for the position of Democratic National Committeeman and defeated him. In 1952 Ken Rinke, an experienced practical politician, was elected Chairman of the Multnomah County Central Committee to succeed Bill Way, and Howard Morgan, a Reed College graduate in economics, was elected state chairman of the Democratic Party. Howard was married to Rosina Corbett, a classmate of mine at Riverdale and the daughter of Henry L. Corbett, former Republican state senator and president of the senate. Morgan, handsome, bright, energetic, and sardonic, brought many young active recruits into the party organization. Morgan appointed me counsel to the Democratic Party of Oregon. C. Girard Davidson, a former assistant secretary in the Interior Department under the Truman Administration, replaced Monroe Sweetland as Democratic National Committeeman.

In 1953 Dick Neuberger, contemplating a run against Oregon's Republican United States Senator Guy Cordon, asked me to manage his campaign. I declined by letter Nov. 2, 1953, explaining that other obligations prevented me from doing so. Monroe Sweetland and Edith Green, a former school teacher, were considering a run against Congressman Homer D. Angell for the latter's congressional seat in the Third District. According to A. Robert Smith, Neuberger dissuaded Sweetland from the House race, concerned that Monroe's previous record as a "Norman Thomas socialist" would endanger the ticket. In any event, Neuberger made the race for the Senate and Edith Green ran for Homer Angell's seat in the House.

Edith Green handily defeated her Democratic primary opponent, and in the general election ran against Tom McCall who had defeated Congressman Angell in the Republican primary. Tom was a radio commentator and a former administrative assistant to Republican Governor Douglas McKay. The evening of election day. November, 1954, Clissa and I, Jane and Jim Goodsell, and several other couples had dinner at Herb and Barbara Schwab's home in Eastmoreland. At that time voting machines were not permitted in Oregon, and each ballot had to be counted by hand. Exit polls were not permitted at that time, so the first returns came from those precincts in which the voters were inclined to vote early, the so-called white collar precincts. Partial returns were reported, but complete returns from each precinct awaited the full count of late voters.

Early in the evening it became apparent that Edith Green had won the seat in the Third Congressional District. Dick Neuberger's race against Senator Guy Cordon, while close, appeared lost when the party broke up around eleven PM. The next morning Jim Goodsell telephoned me at 7:00 AM in great excitement to report that the margin had narrowed to a thousand votes and appeared to be closing with the final counting of "the lunch bucket vote." By noon Neuberger had pulled ahead and was declared the winner.

One of Edith Green's most effective campaign strategies was to scatter lawn signs about the city of Portland. This was the first widespread use of lawn signs in Oregon. The signs, as one might expect, were green. I had first met Edith in 1952 when she was considering a run for the position of Secretary of State against Earl Newbry. She came into our office to consult Vern Dusenbery as a senior Democrat. Vern called me into his office to meet her. Edith was quiet, well spoken, and quite in command of herself. Her appetite for hard work and her steely determination were attributes, we later recognized.

Following his 1954 election, Dick Neuberger asked if I would go to Washington as his administrative assistant. I appreciated the invitation and his confidence in me, but declined. It was not a practical step for a lawyer building a law practice, Clissa was settled at the Medical School, and I was not convinced that the role of a staff person would lead anywhere. Following the election I handled legal well as political matters for Edith Green and had written a will for Dick Neuberger. I continued to act as Edith's personal attorney until I went on the bench in 1970.

As counsel to the state Democratic Party I recruited some fifty young Democratic lawyers around the state into a legal department for the party. One of our projects was to review Oregon Statutes dealing with elections in the light of some changes made by the 1955 Legislature and our experience in the 1956 general election. We had joined with representatives of the Republican State Party including Mrs. Fred Young, the Republican State Chairman, in drafting legislation to amend election procedure and to draft a tight corrupt practices act cooperatively with a legislative interim committee chaired by State Senator Mark Hatfield. This was my first contact with Senator Hatfield. I was impressed by his willingness to work across party lines for a common public objective. When the proposed legislation was ready, we had to obtain the approval of our respective state central committees for the legislation in general and for the specific amendments. The twenty four lawyers serving on the Election Laws Committee of the Legal Department of the Democratic Party of Oregon are listed in Appendix C.

The Democratic State Central Committee meeting that year was scheduled for Coos Bay. I drove our new Chevrolet station wagon, taking as passengers three fellow lawyers: Sidney Lezak, Ernie Bonyhadi and Paul Meyer. Sid came from Chicago Law

School, Ernie from Columbia and Paul from Yale. All three were Jewish and great story tellers. They began telling jokes, one after another, as we left Portland. Just beyond McMinville I had a flat tire. I got out of the car to change it. My friends stood on the roadside, hands in their pockets, continuing their stories, each one followed by roars of laughter while I got the spare wheel mounted. We climbed back in the car and drove off. A mile down the road I realized that, distracted by their stories, I had left my flat wheel by the side of the road. I turned around, drove back and retrieved it. The stories continued without a pause. As we neared Coos Bay they finally closed the competition with a round of stories in Yiddish. It was an unforgettable trip.

The Democratic State Central Committee approved the legislation, and the Republican State Central Committee did likewise. Senator Hatfield was elected Secretary of State in the 1956 general election and said he was relying on our bipartisan group to push the election law reforms through the 1957 session of the legislature, which we did.

*

That 1956 election was hard fought. The Democrats had substantially increased their registration. Democratic lawyers around the state kept an eye on local election boards to see that matters were properly handled. Then suddenly, a few days before the election, the Multnomah County Republican Party organization charged the Democrats with improperly registering Democrats, naming four individuals as fraudulently registered. The Oregonian and Journal carried the story with black headlines. I suspected the charges were phony from the outset because one of their examples was Dr. Lena Kennon, a physician, who had delivered our daughter, Jean. Lena, I found, was temporarily in Washington DC on a professional assignment. We tracked down the other three cases as rapidly as possible. Each person was properly registered and all four authorized legal action on their behalf. We then filed suit for libel against the Republican officials, creating more black headline spread across the front pages of the Oregonian and Journal.

Democrats won the election. The charges had been refuted, so following the election, with the consent of the four victims, we dismissed the case.

*

In 1952 Senator Wayne Morse had changed his registration from Republican to Independent. From that time on there was constant speculation whether he would change registration once again and become a Democrat. Dick Neuberger blew hot and cold considering this possibility during the 1954 campaign. He was uncertain whether this would help or hinder his candidacy. It was clear post election that without the support Morse had given him, Neuberger could not have won. I was unaware at that time of Neuberger's complicated relationship with the senator at the University of Oregon in the mid 1930s, which is described in detail by Mason Drukman in his biography of Morse published in 1997 by the Oregon Historical Press. Morse was dean of the University of Oregon Law School at the time Neuberger matriculated as a freshman and when he abandoned law school and left the university. In any event, Morse finally made the jump February 17, 1955 and was reelected as a Democrat in 1956. From then on, the relationship between Oregon's two senators was a huge complication in the Democratic Party of Oregon.

Paul L. Paterson, Republican, was elected governor in 1954, and died January 31, 1956. He was succeeded by Elmo Smith, a Republican, who was defeated by Robert D. Holmes, a Democrat, of Astoria in the 1956 election. Howard Morgan masterminded the successful Holmes campaign. As governor, Holmes appointed Morgan Public Utility Commissioner, a post for which he was well qualified. The demands of that position may have limited the amount of attention Morgan could give to the governor in office. In any event, Bob Holmes had two years to make his mark as governor, and his performance was lackluster. Mark Hatfield, now Secretary of State, used those two years to solidify his political connections and prepare to challenge Holmes in 1958. When the time came, Hatfield won decisively.

*

Following the 1958 election the governor-elect told me he was going to ask the legislature for three additional circuit judges for Multnomah County, and at least one would be a Democrat. Was I interested? I declined with thanks. I was not ready to give up dabbling in politics. Subsequently, the governor called to ask whether I was interested in an appointment as Public Utility Commissioner. I declined interest in part because I felt technically unqualified and, perhaps more importantly, because I felt acceptance of that highly sensitive position in a Republican administration would create problems if I were to run for office as a Democrat in the future. Herb Schwab then decided that he would like an appointment to the circuit court, but it was too late. The governor had filled the new positions with Alan Davis, Arno Denecke and John Murchison, all Republicans. However, when Judge Martin Hawkins died later that year, Governor Hatfield promptly appointed Herb to fill the vacancy.

This left a serious hole in the Dusenbery office. Herb made every effort to effect transfer of his business clients to Bill Martin and his insurance clients to me, and he was remarkably successful in doing this. However, his personality and abilities as a trial lawyer were irreplaceable. We were fortunate that David Templeton, a Harvard Law graduate with several years experience at General Electric, had joined the firm just before Herb left, and he helped to fill the gap.

At the time Herb, Arno and the others were appointed to the circuit court, the salary was $13,500 per year. The Oregon State Bar undertook a major effort to increase judicial salaries in the 1961 session of the legislature. Tom Tongue, a partner in Hicks, Davis, Tongue and Dale in Portland, was asked by the bar to organize support around the state and did so very effectively. I was asked by the bar to handle the legislative lobbying. A major problem was to persuade Ways and Means, which had to approve any appropriation, that substantial increases were essential. I took the income tax returns from Schwab, Denecke and Davis to demonstrate that all three judges were earning more than twice the salary of a circuit judge the year before their appointment. The bill, having passed the House and cleared Ways and Means, went to the Senate and was referred to Senate Judiciary. There it sat. I could not get a date for hearing by the committee which was chaired by Senator Tom Mahoney of Multnomah County. I finally collared Ken Rinke, who had moved on from the chairmanship of the Multnomah County Democratic Central Committee to become a lobbyist, and asked Rinke for advice.

"Go see Tom Mahoney. Tell him you need his help and would really appreciate it," said Ken. "You gotta ask him."

Tom Mahoney was an old time politician, smart, articulate and considered rather unscrupulous. I braced myself and asked to see him. The senator was pleasant. Said he'd be glad to help, as though he had nothing to do with sitting on the bill. It was promptly set for hearing. We had to compromise on the salary level, but the bill as enacted provided $16,500 for circuit judges, a 22% increase, and a comparable increase for the Supreme Court. However, with the approval of the judges' legislative committee, I had to agree that the retirement pay previously fixed at 50% of final salary be separated from the judicial salaries and remain at the previous dollar figure. At that time the cost of living had been stable for more than ten years and showed no sign of changing. This did not appear to be as much of a concession as it subsequently proved to be.

The 1961 session of the legislature also began moving to full funding of the Public Employees Retirement System and the Judicial Retirement System. Ways and Means inaugurated the practice of requiring an actuarial report of the effect of proposed salary increases upon the retirement funds, and insisted upon appropriation of funds to retirement reserves to cover any salary increase. State Senator Alfred H. Corbett played a leading role in establishing this policy which, sound as it was, made any increase in judicial retirement to catch up with the increase in salary difficult. At that time Alf had an office with our firm next to mine in the Spaulding Building. He also designated me as his legislative replacement pursuant to a state statute designed to deal with a cold war catastrophe.

*

Meanwhile, it had not taken long for the two Oregon Democratic United States Senators to have a falling out. Both were talented egotists. Wayne Morse was essentially a political lone wolf. Senior in office, he considered himself chairman of the Oregon Democratic delegation. Dick Neuberger was a tall, rambling quick study and a fluent writer. He was chosen as editor of the University of Oregon student newspaper in his sophomore year. He had a very substantial record of publication in newspapers and national magazines. In addition to his own formidable talents, Dick had Maureen, his wife.

Maureen Brown Neuberger, a Lincoln High School teacher, became a political figure in her own right following their marriage. Elected a state representative, she introduced a bill to repeal the law which required margarine to be white, and she demonstrated how ridiculous the prohibition was by mixing the coloring into the margarine at her desk on the floor of the House. She and Dick were a political team in every sense of the word.

Dick Neuberger went to Washington with great excitement and an understandable sense of self importance. In one of his first gambits he criticized President Eisenhower for removing the squirrels who were interfering with the presidential putting green. The publicity he invoked was not what he expected, nor what he liked. He quickly adapted himself to the new environment and made friends of the elder senators of both parties, whom Wayne Morse by this time had throughly offended. When the two Oregon senators fell out, the sparks flew.

Dick Neuberger was not a person to shun a conflict, and he was a good deal more clever than Morse in handling their exchange of bitter correspondence over disagreements which most people would consider trifling. Underlying this angry exchange lay a complicated relationship between Morse, then Dean of the Law School, and Neuberger, a junior who abandoned his studies and left the University in 1933.

On one occasion Senator Morse asked me to drive up to the Dalles with him on some political errand, and I made a cautious attempt to negotiate peace in the senatorial ranks with no success whatever. The senator was obviously not interested. I backed off, and we had a pleasant trip.

In 1958 Dick Neuberger developed testicular cancer. He was operated upon and the affected testicle was removed. He returned to his duties and seemed well. In June of 1959 we put together a small committee called "Friends of Senator Richard L. Neuberger" consisting of C.S. Forrester of Pendleton, Herbert M. Schwab, Edward Whelan, Francis Staten and myself of Portland, and Willard Schwenn of Hillsboro to make preparations for a reelection campaign. Dick asked if I would chair his campaign for reelection, and on this occasion I agreed to do so. He and Representative Edith Green both knew I was a friend and supporter of the other. Dick suggested additional members of the committee. By June of 1959 we had opened a bank account in the name of Neuberger for Senator. By December we had county chairmen in most counties of the state. Early in January of 1960 the reelection committee was operating in space adjacent to my law offices in the Portland Trust Building.

Dick Neuberger returned to Portland the last week of January, 1960. I telephoned his home on Clifton Street following his arrival to suggest lunch to discuss the campaign, but was unable to speak with him, nor did he return subsequent calls. However, I received a press release dated February 5, 1960, presumably issued by his Portland office, which referred to his return from Washington and announced that the senator would file for reelection in March. It went on to name me as chairman of his reelection committee which, of course, I already was. The release continued

"'I am delighted that Jack Beatty will head my campaign,' Senator Neuberger said in Portland today. 'He has a distinguished record of service to the city of Portland and to the state. I am proud of his confidence in me.'"

The release went on to say of the senator that "He flew to Portland from Washington last week for extensive medical tests and examinations here. Recently he has had two attacks of influenza and felt that examinations were advisable before making a final decision to run for reelection. He was told by his doctors 'there is no reason why you cannot run for reelection.'"

I was, of course, busy and carrying on a trial practice. I telephoned the senator's home a number of times during the next few weeks, to no avail. When Dick finally called me on the telephone his voice was weak. I asked specifically about his health. He said he was fine, just tired and needed rest. Then he said, "Remember, Jack, there's always another Neuberger," and hung up.

His voice and his last comment set off alarm bells. I had served until 1958 as legal counsel to the party and led the effort to strengthen election laws and the corrupt practices act. We were raising money for Richard L. Neuberger as a candidate. If he were too ill to run, we had no business raising money for him or representing that he was going to file as a candidate.

It was only a few days until the deadline for filing in the primary. I telephoned Jim Goodsell, Dick's brother-in-law, and told Jim that I needed to see Dick in person or have authority to speak with his internist, Dr. Mort Goodman. The word came back from Jim that I could talk to Dr. Goodman. I discussed the situation with Herb Schwab at the courthouse, and then the two of us walked over to Mort Goodman's office late in the day. Mort told us that Dick had cancer which had metastasized. He had a very short time to live, "Months at most, weeks perhaps."

16. Toasting Democratic victory. Senators Morse and Neuberger and Congresswoman Green greet newly elected Congressmen Charles Porter and Al Ulman. Which one has a flea in his ear? (Oregon Historical Society, Or Hi cn 90999.)

17. Oregon's two combustible senators posed to suggest tranquil discussion in front of a framed cartoon of an elephant's posterior. (Oregon Historical Society, Or Hi CN 020846.)

Clearly he should not be running in the primary, and we should not be raising money and pressing a campaign on his behalf. I telephoned Jim and told him that I had talked to Mort Goodman. I asked Jim to pass the word on that Dick should withdraw from the race, or I would have to resign as campaign chairman and state my reasons for doing so.

The following morning, March 9, 1960, Jim telephoned me at home saying, "Your problem is solved. Dick died during the night."

I was not surprised in view of Dr. Goodman's statement the night before. I reminded Jim that I had written Dick's will some years before, and I would need instruction as to whom the will should be sent for probate.

The cause of Neuberger's death was reported in the press as a cerebral hemorrhage or stroke. His death was a complete surprise to the public, so carefully had recurrence of his illness been concealed by his staff and his family. The fact that he avoided seeing or talking to me on the telephone upon his return from Washington made crystal clear that he knew he was fatally ill at the time he returned. When he finally spoke to me on the telephone, his closing admonition, "Remember there is always another Neuberger," could not be misunderstood.

I think it likely that from the moment he suspected the cancer had recurred, he planned to deal with it in a manner which best insured that Maureen could succeed to his seat in the Senate. Representative Edith Green, a popular three term representative from the Third Congressional District would be a formidable candidate if she chose to hazard the security and seniority of her safe seat in the House, and other strong candidates might well file in both party primaries if they knew that Dick Neuberger's seat would be open.

The Neubergers correctly anticipated that I would not knowingly run a campaign and raise money for any candidate who was not expected to live to reach the office. Hence their decision to insure that I did not see Dick or discover his condition. Dick's telephone call to me and their subsequent willingness to let me speak to Dr. Goodman suggest they had concluded that my reaction, whatever it might be, would be too late to affect their plans. Maurine Neuberger was prepared to file for his position at once and did so.

Under the circumstances it was obvious that I would not chair her campaign, and we both assumed that to be the case without any discussion. I saw no useful purpose in publicly discussing the extent to which I and others had been deliberately deceived. Dick Neuberger was dead, and complaints would sound peevish in the face of the outpouring of grief at his death and sympathy for the widow. I was determined to make sure that the money raised for Dick Neuberger was properly tendered back to the donors.

Accordingly I wrote Maureen March 10, 1960 as follows:

> "My dear Maureen:
> I think Herb in his public statement expressed better than I the loss which we all feel. Clis joins me in writing to give our deepest sympathy.
> To speak of the future, I feel certain you will be elected. I think you can count on a tremendous amount of support from people in both parties, and it is good to have no primary contest.
> I think the campaign committee we have organized for Dick can be transferred almost intact to your campaign, and I will work out with Mary Lee the details as soon as practicable. With respect to the funds on hand, I will write each of the contributors requesting their authority to transfer the pro rata balance of their contribution to your campaign fund. I am sure everyone will permit this, and indeed, will be delighted to authorize it.
> The office in the Portland Trust Building is available if you need it.

I hope you will continue Mary Lee Kramer as your
campaign manager. She is a fine person and did a great
job in getting Dick's campaign organized.

Jim told me this noon that you wanted me to handle
the probate of Dick's estate which, needless to say, I
shall be glad to do, I enclose a letter of instruction for
you to sign which Jim should return to me, keeping
one copy for your personal file."

I telephoned Bud Forrester in Pendleton and explained
what had happened and why I could not function as
Maureen's chairman. He agreed to act as Maureen's
chairman if she wished him to do so. However, Allen Hart,
a well respected lawyer, and partner of Jebby Davidson,
the Democratic National Committeeman, had already been
selected to be her campaign manager. I notified contributors
to Dick's campaign that their pro rata contributions would
be returned or transferred to Maureen Neuberger as they
wished. Most agreed to the transfer. Maureen handily
defeated the Republican candidate, Elmo Smith, in November
and entered the Senate in January 1961. She served one term
and did not seek reelection. Mark Hatfield completed two
terms as governor in 1966 and that year won election to the
"Neuberger" senate seat which he filled with distinction for
thirty years.

Maureen was always pleasant in our subsequent contacts.
She never apologized for their deception, and I saw no
need to clarify my position. Jim Goodsell and Herb Schwab
were my two closest friends. The knowledge that I was
being deliberately deceived was, I am sure, extraordinarily
painful for Jim. Subsequently we collaborated on the Lezak
confirmation, but we never revisited the events leading up
to Dick's demise. He and Jane were subsequently divorced.
Jim accepted a federal appointment overseas and we lost
touch until after he retired to live in the small town of Twist
in eastern Washington where he resided until his death. Dick
Neuberger's death at the age of forty-seven brought an end
to his ill-starred relationship with Wayne L. Morse. It was

JOHN CABEEN BEATTY

Morse who led the delegation of senators which eulogized the Junior Senator from Oregon. I wondered what was going on in Morse's head at the packed funeral service at Temple Beth Israel.

*

Edith Green chaired Jack Kennedy's Oregon presidential campaign committee in that election year of 1960, and with Kennedy's victory over Vice President Nixon, she had far closer ties to the White House than either Wayne Morse or Maurine Neuberger. Edith had introduced me to Senator Kennedy during one of his visits to the state. While I made speeches on his behalf during the campaign, my contact with the President was limited to that one occasion. The first important Oregon federal vacancy to be filled was that of United States Attorney. I wrote a letter January 11, 1961 to newly appointed Attorney General Robert Kennedy recommending Harry Hogan, a Columbia law classmate and member of our party legal department for the position, copy to Edith Green. Hogan subsequently accepted a position with another federal agency.

Edith then asked if I were interested in the U.S. Attorney position. I replied that I was not and suggested Sid Lezak, who had served as deputy legal counsel for the Democratic Party under me and had litigated several cases against me. She proposed Lezak to the administration. Sid had worked in Senator Maureen Neuberger's campaign, and, according to Edith, Maurine had agreed to Sid's appointment, but subsequently blocked his nomination in Senate Judiciary on the ground that she and C. Girard Davidson, Oregon's Democratic National Committeeman, had not been consulted on patronage appointments in Oregon.

Meanwhile, a position opened on the Ninth Circuit Court of Appeals, and U. S. District Judge Gus J. Solomon, among judges from other states, was under consideration for the post. At Judge Solomon's request, I wrote a letter supporting his nomination. Subsequently Edith Green proposed me for the district court vacancy which the promotion of Judge Solomon would create. Maureen, in a letter to me on other matters dated April 1, 1961, mentioned that she had received letters urging my appointment. Alan Hart, she said, was my competition, and since she felt personally interested in both of us, she would have to cast a one-half ballot for each of us. I did not explore the dimensions of that comment. Mervin Shoemaker, the Oregonian political reporter, in a story filed June 10, 1961, described Beatty as Mrs. Green's "favorite," and Alan Hart, Mrs. Neuberger's candidate, as a "law partner of C. Girard (Jebby) Davidson, Portland Democratic National Committee Chairman, who complains that Mrs. Green puts through appointments without consulting party leaders."

Senator Morse in the course of discussing the Lezak situation assured me he would support my nomination to the district court. However, in view of the tensions in the Oregon delegation, I did not hold my breath. Judge Solomon was not appointed to the Court of Appeals, very possibly because of those tensions, and I wrote Edith in response to her question that I should not be considered for the Court of Appeals because I thought prior judicial experience was desirable for that appellate position.

Sid Lezak served for more than a year as acting United States Attorney before Maurine Neuberger finally withdrew her objection, and his nomination cleared Judiciary and was approved by the Senate. Sid went on to serve through the Johnson, Nixon, Ford and Carter administrations, a remarkable tenure for a U. S. attorney. Sid was a liberal with good judgment and absolute integrity. His extended tenure reflected his good relations with office holders, politicians and lawyers in both political parties, coupled with the fairness with which he handled his duties.

18. Maurine Neuberger, (1907-2000}. A Lincoln High School Teacher, she married Richard L. Neuberger and was elected a state representative. She famously mixed oleomargarine on the House Floor to sink state law requiring that oleo be white. Elected to her husband's U.S. Senate seat upon his sudden death, she sparred with Edith Green on Federal patronage.

Courtesy Oregon State Library)

19. Sidney I. Lezak (1924-2006) The pawn who became a knight. His nomination as U.S. Attorney, blocked in Senate Judiciary by Senator Maurine Neuberger for more than a year, he served by temporary appointment until finally confirmed. He then went on to serve five presidents, the longest serving U.S. attorney in history.

In 1961 a vacancy on the Multnomah County Circuit Court opened up. I indicated my interest to Governor Hatfield. Travis Cross telephoned to say that the governor would like to appoint me but found it necessary to appoint a Republican on this occasion, Charles Crookham, as it turned out. Travis suggested that I accept appointment to the State Civil Service Commission which would make my subsequent appointment to the bench feasible as a member of the Hatfield administration. Accordingly I went on the Civil Service Commission, replacing a Democratic lawyer, Phil Joss, who had resigned. The Commission met monthly in Salem and acted as an appellate body with respect to dismissals and disciplinary decisions in the state bureaucracy. The two years I spent on the commission provided an interesting view into state management. A half domestic relations position created by the legislature for Multnomah County opened which I declined, not wanting to be trapped in a domestic relations slot.

*

John F. Kennedy had been elected by the narrowest of margins over Richard Nixon. His administration had a shaky start with the Bay of Pigs fiasco, but he cut a new and vibrant picture of a president with his quick exchange with reporters and his staccato speeches. His presidency exuded energy, and people responded to it. When President Kennedy spoke to the nation and revealed that the Soviet Union was placing missiles in Cuba, he created an instant atmosphere of crisis. We followed the news from hour to hour. We seemed to be a hair's breadth from nuclear war. We saw photographs of Soviet missile sites in Cuba, air photos of the Soviet freighters steaming toward Cuba, and then, at last, we saw those freighters turn around. The president's handling of the crisis appeared at the time to be both restrained and powerful, and this is confirmed by the publication of the tapes recording those tense discussions.

We were unaware at the time of the division among the President's advisors between those who thought we should attack the missile sites before they became operational and those who advised a blockade. Fortunately the blockade view prevailed. Thirty years later a Soviet general revealed that the 40,000 soviet troops in Cuba already had tactical nuclear weapons on the ground.

In the early days of nuclear power we lived with a lively sense of the possibility of nuclear attack. I can recall thinking when the Soviets first obtained the bomb that we had a distinct advantage living on the west side of Council Crest which might shield us from a nuclear bomb landing in the center of the city. It was nonsense, of course, probably reflecting my World War II experience with defensive use of terrain. Our local civil defense agency had a giant siren mounted on the roof of the Federal Reserve Building, and every Friday noon it screamed a test warning you could hear across the entire city. I kept a complete set of camping equipment stored in the top of the tool shed should we have to head for the hills.

*

November 22, 1963 I came back to the office in the Standard Plaza after lunch and learned that President Kennedy had been shot in Dallas. Everything ground to a halt as the word spread through the office and then out to the street. Within the hour we learned the president was dead. The impact for me was profound. I dug the family's big American flag out of the cedar chest and strung it between two of the three birches facing Dosch Road. Then I draped black cloth on either side of it. The state funeral we watched on television from beginning to end. I remember the tall figure of President Charles DeGaulle wearing the uniform of a French brigadier general, a head above all the other dignitaries, marching behind the caisson bearing the casket through the silent streets of Washington to Arlington Cemetery. I remember the slow beat of the drums.

Lyndon Johnson as president accomplished far more in domestic legislation than John F. Kennedy had been able to do in the two and a half years of his presidency—more indeed than any recent president but Franklin Delano Roosevelt. Johnson implemented civil rights for blacks, pushed federal aid for inner city schools. He funded a variety of experimental measures to improve criminal justice throughout the United States. President Eisenhower had flatly refused to maintain the French military position in their former colony of French Indo China. President Kennedy began our piecemeal involvement in Vietnam against the advice of his ambassador to India, John Kenneth Galbreath. Would Kennedy, burned in the Cuban fiasco, have questioned the Viet Nam operation before it escalated into full scale war? We will never know. Johnson followed the advice of the cabinet officers and generals he inherited from Kennedy and found he could not make an effective run for reelection in 1968.

CHAPTER 15

Roseburg explodes, the Portland School Board

The night of August 7, 1959 a warehouse fire broke out in Roseburg, Oregon, igniting a truck loaded with ten thousand pounds of dynamite and three thousand pounds of a blasting agent called Car-prill which was parked on a street adjacent to the warehouse. The resulting explosion caused fourteen deaths, a hundred and twenty-five injuries, and leveled a large section of the business district, causing $10,000,000 in property damage. Had the explosion occurred in daytime the human toll would have been far higher.

Several weeks later Donald P. Marshall, the Portland manager of Morrell P. Totten Company, mentioned to me in the course of a telephone conversation that a Lloyds syndicate they represented had the coverage on Pacific Powder Company, a Washington corporation which owned the truck. Don reported that a number of suits had been filed in Douglas County, Oregon, but a lawyer in the New York firm of Mendes and Mount had advised the Totten office in Seattle that Pacific Powder could not be sued in Oregon because they did not do business in Oregon. Any suits would have to be filed in Washington.

I told Don he had better get on the telephone and set them straight. Clearly there was jurisdiction in Douglas County,

Oregon, and Pacific Powder had only twenty days within which to make an appearance before a default judgment could be taken. It was highly unlikely a Douglas County circuit judge whose town was in ruins would set a default aside because Lloyds of London failed to have its lawyers appear within the specified time. Within the day I received a call from Mendes instructing me to appear and defend all of the cases in Oregon. Several cases were also filed in Washington, and these were defended by William L. Dwyer of Seattle, an able lawyer and interesting person. Dwyer was subsequently appointed to the United States District Court for the Western District of Washington where he served with distinction and sat on a number of major environmental cases.

We managed to make an appearance in all the cases before the time expired. Most of them were filed by a handful of Roseburg attorneys. I drove down to Roseburg a few days later, and the site suggested an air raid. As investigation later disclosed, the truck driver had parked his truck on the street beside a warehouse for the night and then went to bed in the Roseburg Hotel, intending to make delivery of his cargo the next morning. Ironically while the fire was burning, a police officer was said to have assured a fireman attempting to move the truck, "Don't worry, that stuff won't burn."

David Templeton worked with me on the case and was responsible for all of the research. He proposed that we bring a "Bill of Peace," an historic English equitable proceeding, in the United States District Court for the District of Oregon on behalf of Lloyds as plaintiff, naming Pacific Powder and all the claimants who had filed in state court as defendants. We tendered into court a certificate of deposit covering the policy limits, asked a stay of the state court proceedings, and requested the court to distribute the funds tendered. The court granted the stay. The case went on for more than two years and was eventually settled on the basis of the face value of the Lloyds policy and a further contribution from the Powder Company.

19.5. Roseburg, OR, August 7, 1959. 1:20 AM. Explosion of a truckload of dynamite created a crater 52 feet wide, twenty feet deep, leveled seven city blocks, killed 14 and injured 125. Oregon Historical Society, Or Hi CN 62413.

19.7. The crater. Oregon Historical Society, Or Hi CN 020412.

Plaintiff's counsel had a real dilemma in this situation. If the state court cases were tried, the first few cases would exhaust the policy limits and bankrupt Pacific Powder, which was a small company. Moreover each of the plaintiff lawyers with multiple cases had a serious problem with which of his cases he should try first. A substantial recovery for the first case might well exhaust the policy limits which were only $500,000 for personal injury and $1,000,000 for property damage. The powder company plant near Centralia, Washington, was constructed during World War I. Its assets were very limited and might well be exhausted by preferred creditors should the company go into bankruptcy. It was to everyone's interest not to challenge our procedure but to work out a collaborative approach for evaluating the individual death and injury claims for distribution of the settlement proceeds.

Pacific Powder was represented by a former Washington Attorney General, a fine, kindly looking old gentleman named E. K. Murray. Mr. Murray was also tough as nails. When I filed first appearances in Douglas County in a rush to meet the deadline, I overlooked making a demand for jury trial as required by a local Douglas County rule. Had I been aware of the rule, I would never have requested a jury trial for these cases, but the plaintiff lawyers certainly would. Mr. Murray promptly sent us a letter holding us responsible for failing to ask for a jury. He was searching, and continued to search, for any possible defense or tactic from which he could extract a benefit for his beleaguered client. He objected to the bill of peace procedure from the outset, but we went ahead with it, and he ultimately agreed that it provided substantial advantages to his client in negotiating a settlement as well as to Lloyds.

Murray's negotiation on the liability of the powder company above its policy limits was artistic. When the leading plaintiffs' counsel refused his final offer of contribution, he looked at them coldly and said it was cheaper to put the company through bankruptcy than to continue to operate it and contribute any more. He walked out the door and drove back to Tacoma without another word. Eventually, the plaintiffs' lawyers led

JOHN CABEEN BEATTY

by Tom Tongue came to agreement with him and then worked out a method for evaluating the various claims. As the case progressed, and we had meetings and court appearances, Mr. Murray brought his wife to Portland with him. The two of them would lunch with Dave Templeton and me. Mrs. Murray was a delightful lady who handled her crusty old husband with a deft hand. When the case was finally settled, Murray allowed himself a broad grin and bought us a final lunch with drinks in celebration. I think it was the only concession he ever made.

Our bill to Lloyds for handling the litigation for two years was in the neighborhood of $55,000. In 2000 dollars this would be approximately $300,000. If the parties had employed the kind of discovery now in fashion, fees would have been two to three times as large. We had deposited the policy limits in a local bank, tendering the certificate of deposit to the court, but the interest earned on the certificate of deposit during that period remained the property of Lloyds and more than covered our attorneys fees and court costs.

*

In 1960 Clissa, Ruth Peterson and Dr. West left the University of Oregon Medical School to join the newly established Oregon Regional Primate Research Center in the valley west of Beaverton. The Primate Center was built in a largely forested quarter section surrounded by farmland west of 185th Street and a half mile south of Highway 26. This was the second of nine primate centers established by the National Science Foundation during the nineteen-sixties. The Oregon Primate Center had an unusual administrative structure which was to give us no end of difficulty during its initial years.

The scientific activity at the center was placed under a director, Dr. Donald Nickerson, a pediatrician who was instrumental in planning and setting up the Center and who brought to it a colony of rhesus monkeys. The business aspect of the Center was controlled by a private, non-profit corporation, The Medical Research Foundation (MRF) already in existence administering a number of scientific and medical grants. Dr. David E. Baird, Dean of the University of Oregon Medical School, was named Principal Investigator of the Primate Center. The core federal grant supporting the center was made to MRF. The director was made subject to appointment by and removal by the Principal Investigator. The salaries of the scientists on the staff were paid by the Center out of the core grant, but their research projects were funded by individual NIH or private grants obtained by the individual scientists.

Conflict arose almost at once between the director, Dr. Nickerson, and a number of staff members at the center. These conflicts quickly involved the Medical Research Foundation, then chaired by Edmund Hayes, a prominent Portland lumberman, and Dean Baird, the principal investigator. Dr. Baird was a shrewd and experienced administrator accustomed to dealing with physicians on his staff and politicians in Salem. Dr. Nickerson had influential friends who carried his concerns all the way to Governor Hatfield. The governor had no executive responsibility or control over the matter but had to be briefed on the problems involved. Dr. Nickerson finally resigned. Clissa's colleague and friend, Ruth Peterson, and several other staff people left with Nickerson. Ruth had known Dr. Nickerson for many years, and she and Clissa took different sides in the controversy, agreeing to disagree without disrupting their close friendship. Dr. Edward West carried on as temporary director until the appointment of Dr. William Montagna.

Bill Montagna was tall, handsome, very bald, and mercurial in temperament. He led the Center with remarkable flair for more than two decades of successful research. His medical specialty was skin, in which he had achieved an international reputation. He recruited a fine staff and supported their research through funding vicissitudes, building the Center into the outstanding primate research facility in the country. Along with his other talents, Bill Montagna, who was born and raised in Italy, had a splendid command of the English language. For many years he contributed articles to the Center Bulletin on subjects ranging from ethics to gardening, all beautifully written.

*

In the late afternoon of October 12, 1962, I was working in my office on the twelfth floor of the Portland Trust Building. I noticed the sky outside was unusually dark. Alex Parks had a radio in his office and came out into the reception area telling us that a storm was blowing up from the southwest. From my office window on the south side of the building I could see black clouds boiling over the outline of the Standard Plaza and the crane topping it as it lay under construction. We looked out the east windows down on the Willamette. The surface was covered with whitecaps. The radio warned that winds were reaching 60 and 70 miles per hour and advised people to stay off the streets and remain in offices and homes. As we watched, the waves began smashing against the bridge abutments. The flying water was caught up and carried downwind. The tarred roofs on old buildings along the waterfront began to peel off and go sailing downstream. The sky had a dark greenish cast.

I tried telephoning home without success. The radio reported power outages, telephone lines down, trees down, automobiles overturned, roofs blown off. Around six-thirty the wind subsided and I started driving home, weaving my way through downed trees past the Multnomah Club and then up Vista Avenue and Patton Road. I found Clissa had reached home safely from the primate center, and both children had made it home. A fir on the south side of the house had fallen against the roof but not penetrated. The pavement in the back yard was uprooted, and the lean-to over the garden settee had collapsed. Tree limbs and debris were scattered everywhere, and large sections of shingle were missing from the roof.

The Columbus Day storm was the storm of the century for Oregon. It cut a swath from the south coast of Oregon up through the valley, doing millions of dollars in damage. Our power was out for three days. Clissa brought dry ice home from her laboratory to hold the freezer. We had to re shingle the house and pour a new concrete patio in the back yard to replace the uprooted blacktop. The downed fir provided firewood for years.

*

In 1954 the United States Supreme Court in *Brown v. Board of Education* overruled its 1896 decision in *Plessy vs Fergeson* and held that legally segregating schools by race was unconstitutional. The repercussions were felt in school districts all over the country. By the 1960s de facto segregation in northern cities was being challenged. In the spring of 1963 the Portland school board (School District No. 1) decided to undertake a broad study of matters relating to race and education. The board asked Herbert Schwab, now a Multnomah County circuit judge, to chair the study. Having served on the school board for nine years prior to going on the bench, he was a logical choice.

Herb asked me to come over to his house in Dunthorpe one evening to discuss the proposal. He went over the pros and cons of accepting the assignment, his usual way of approaching a problem. One of his concerns was how to maintain control of the study and at the same time carry out his work on the bench. I thought he could manage it and ought to accept the task, provided he worked out in advance a detailed plan of organization and provided he was given a strong voice in the selection of the committee. He asked if I would serve on the committee, and I agreed to do so.

Herb then told the board he would accept, if the board gave him a full time executive director, an adequate budget and a voice in selecting the committee. Three members on the school board knew Herb well from his previous service on the board with them—Bill DeWeese, Mary Rieke, and Howard Cherry. The board agreed to his conditions, and the Race and Education Committee was established.

Herb knew that with a subject matter as controversial as this, and a committee as diverse as it had to be, consensus would be difficult to achieve. He needed a structure to channel investigation and discussion constructively while recognizing everyone's right to dissent. We drafted a five page formal document entitled "Organization and Procedure" to present to the committee for adoption at its organizational meeting. This document was adopted without objection at the first meeting, always a good time to settle such matters before controversy arises.

The membership was a mix of people influential in different sectors of the community and a nucleus of active workers. Herb picked Forest W. Amsden as the executive director. Forest, a massive chap six feet four in height, had been a reporter on the Denver Post and the Coos Bay Times before serving as executive director of the Oregon Constitutional Revision Commission in 1961-62, in which role Herb had an opportunity to evaluate him. I found Forest to be an interesting fellow and an able director. He became a close friend.

The members of the committee were assigned to six subcommittees with specific areas of study. The executive committee consisted of the general chairman, the chairmen of the subcommittees, and four unassigned members of whom I was one. I functioned as sort of a utility infielder as the study got underway. Herb then shifted me over to work primarily with the subcommittee on school plant and operations, chaired by Garnet Cannon, president of the Standard Insurance Company. This group was wrestling with the critical problems of scholastic performance and the mechanics of integration. Each of the subcommittees held hearings, undertook research, reached conclusions and drafted their proposed section of the report for consideration of the full committee.

In the course of the study Herb appointed a traveling group to visit certain schools in St. Louis, Detroit, and New York which had been recognized for special accomplishment dealing with inner city problems. The traveling party consisted of Forrest Amsden, who handled the arrangements, The Reverend Paul Waldschmidt, then president of the University of Portland and later auxiliary bishop in the Portland Catholic Diocese, Garnett Cannon, president of Standard Insurance Company, Mercedes Diez, a lawyer, Shelley Hill, the executive director of the Portland Urban League and myself. The schedule Forrest arranged was taxing, interesting and a good deal of fun. Father Waldschmidt, a portly, round-cheeked priest with a first rate mind, was a constant source of humor, enthusiasm and insight into the serious problems we were charged to investigate. He also found the best restaurants in every city we visited, most of which he had previously sampled during his many ecclesiastical and educational assignments. In New York he knew the head waiter of the restaurant where we dined.

In Detroit we had a few hours off duty. Mercedes Diez and I went to see Doctor Zhivago, a great movie just out. Mercedes fell asleep soon after it started, and I had to wake her at the end. Inspecting these schools exposed us to hard core inner city problems and sets of highly motivated teachers and administrators making the best of extra resources to deal with them. In each of these schools which had produced results, the key was a talented, energetic principal given flexibility and backing by the administration. Well trained and highly motivated teachers were important, but leadership was essential. Attracting and holding such men and women in an educational career is a challenge for every school board and community.

The public hearings before the school plant and operations subcommittee were informative but not enlightening. Most persons who testified demanded that the school district integrate the schools, period. There was an implicit assumption by many persons that the schools were to blame for the makeup of the largely black elementary schools and for the demonstrable fact that these schools were in the lowest achieving group of elementary schools. The statistical information assembled by the committee indicated a close relationship between the economic level of the school population and student performance. It also showed that black students in predominantly white schools tended to perform at a lower level than their school average.

There was no evidence that the school district had intentionally segregated blacks. However, the policy which required students to attend their neighborhood school obviously made the makeup of the school population turn upon those who lived in the neighborhood. Market forces, restrictive covenants, and social attitudes, black and white, as well as economic status had led to concentration of blacks in a few neighborhoods.

Consequently the most difficult questions before the school plant and operations subcommittee were whether black children should be bussed to primarily white schools to break up concentration of black children in their neighborhood schools, and whether white children should be bussed in to replace them. I was convinced that we needed to take measures to encourage dispersion of blacks, and to improve the performance of all the lower achieving schools, but I was equally convinced that mandatory bussing would create more problems than it would solve. That, I thought, had already been demonstrated in other major cities around the country.

Eventually Reed Professor David Tyack and I worked out a compromise which the school plant and operations committee accepted. We proposed a voluntary transfer program which expanded the existing transfer program to allow parents to transfer a black child from a predominately black school to another school which had a vacancy so long as that transfer did not create a black majority in the receiving school. The process of exercising choice would be encouraged by providing district transportation. We then proposed that the ten lowest achieving elementary schools in the district, five predominately black, and five predominately white, be placed in a "Model School Program" with special administrative organization, additional funding, and preschool education for younger children.

Many other aspects of teaching and administration were reviewed by the subcommittees and made the basis of recommendations in the full committee's report. Perhaps most important was the review and presentation of comparative statistical information concerning the district, material never previously published, which provided hard data to support the committee's recommendations. The difficult job of incorporating all this material into a readable text was Forest Amsden's responsibility, with editorial scrutiny and final decision by the general chairman. In the end the committee approved the full report without dissent. A unanimous report from so large and diverse a committee on such a volatile subject was remarkable. Herb attributed it to the fact that he never had a vote by the full committee on any subject after the first meeting in which the tight procedural structure was adopted until the entire report was assembled and ready for adoption. I think he was right.

In August, 1964, before the final report was presented to the school board, a member of the existing board resigned. The board then elected me to serve out that member's unexpired term. I then resigned from the Schwab Committee to accept the appointment. When the report of the Schwab Committee was presented several months later, I was sitting on the board to receive it and able to explain the process by which we had reached our conclusions.

The report was favorably received by the press and by the community as a whole. However, those who wanted to compel integration by mandatory bussing remained dissatisfied. The board accepted the report and agreed to carry out its principal recommendations. The study gave the district concrete proposals to address the problems of race and education, gave the board and community time to consider them, and carried Portland through a period which was very disruptive in many other large city school districts. Keeping bussing voluntary avoided the bitter conflicts which occurred in other urban centers and precipitated white flight to private and suburban schools. What the report did not do, and could not do, was to address those larger forces which have contributed to the disintegration of the family and the institutionalization of poverty, which the committee found statistically linked with school achievement. Finally, the study focused the attention of the Portland community on the complex problems of race and education theretofore largely ignored.

Herb Schwab thought the Race and Education Study was the most satisfying accomplishment of his career. Bill Wyse was the lawyer on the board and he undoubtedly drafted the resolution establishing the Race and Education study and was responsible for the broad scope of its charge. I think that Bill Wyse' service on the board was his most significant public accomplishment and one of which he was very proud. Forest Amsden thought directing the study was his greatest public contribution. My principal contribution was drafting the committee rules of procedure at the outset, working out the compromise voluntary transfer program with David Tyack, and explaining the board's decisions to the community in a series of speeches, including two to the City Club.

For Herb Schwab and for me, our work on the study provided a whole new group of talented friends: John M. Fulton, Ira Keller, Raymond P. Underwood, Paul E. Waldschmidt, Tom McCall, Mercedes Diez and, of course, Forest Amsden. Tom McCall at that time was the news commentator for KGW TV. My mother had known Tom's mother, Dorothy McCall, and his father well in the years before World War I, but I had had no previous contact with him other than the debate with Commissioner Bill Bowes on Tom's television program during the city manager campaign. When Tom and Audrey McCall were rear-ended and seriously injured on highway 26 near Sylvan, Tom telephoned from the hospital to ask me to handle their claim against the driver at fault.

Reading the Race and Education report a half century later, I am impressed with the integrity of the committee's approach, the thoroughness with which it explored the difficult educational, social and administrative problems involved, and the difficulty of effecting complex social change. Necessarily, the study raised more questions than it answered. The formal structure and procedure of the committee was a template which I adapted and modified for use in other study committees in subsequent years.

*

At the time I joined the school board, it met in the old administrative building on N.E. Clackamus Street Monday evenings from seven to ten PM. On rare occasions we had special meetings. The chairman of the board was elected every six months and rotated among the members. The superintendent prepared the agenda and moved it through the meetings. The first part of each meeting dealt with items requiring a board vote on expenditures. The board then moved on to matters which required more extended discussion. The representatives of the teacher's union and the Oregon Educational Association, the two teacher organizations, always attended and addressed the board when a matter of concern to their membership came up. Members of the public were allowed to speak on a previous request to be heard. Matters involving personnel and bids were heard in executive session.

The superintendent at that time was Melvin Barnes, an intelligent, soft spoken man, the highest paid public official in Oregon with a salary of $25,000 per year. Paying the top salary to their school superintendent was then a source of pride to Portlanders. The six other members of the board when I joined it were William DeWeese, William W. Wyse, Theodore Yaw, Dr. Howard Cherry, Mary Rieke, and Edward Burkett.

Mary Rieke, a former school teacher, married to Forrest Rieke, a physician, was the hardest working member of the board. She devoted endless hours to school affairs and probably knew more staff members by name than any member of the board before or since. Her judgment was sound and she had no difficulty in seeing the holes in a presentation to the board. No teacher ever pulled wool over her eyes. No administrator ever hornswoggled her, yet she always provided a sympathetic ear. Her laughter was a delight. Her syntax frequently had us in stitches, and one of the tasks of the chairman was to restate Mrs. Riecke's motions in plain English.

Bill DeWeese was a vice president of ESCO Corporation and spent a good deal of his time traveling. However, he always did his homework, and he always had a crisp opinion to offer. Until Bill Wyse came on the board, DeWeese was the board's principal contact with the business community. I discovered early on that it was best to telephone Bill DeWeese in advance of any proposal I intended to make at a board meeting, otherwise he was inclined to shoot it down in crisp fiery sentences. He nearly always was supportive so long as he was consulted. On one memorable occasion I did not consult him because he was out of town when the subject came up for discussion. Riverdale School was having financial difficulties and considering whether it ought to join Portland or Oswego. I publicly suggested that Riverdale should consider Portland. A merger with Portland, I thought, would be advantageous to both districts.

When Bill returned from his trip, he was outraged that I had even discussed the possibility of such a proposal. No doubt some friend of his in the Riverdale District was opposed to a merger with Portland. I suggested mildly that as a graduate of Riverdale I was quite aware of the sensitivity of the matter and the interests of both districts, and was certainly entitled to express my opinion, but Bill boiled on. He was not a man to ignore or take for granted. Having blown his top, so to speak, we resumed our good relations, and I was careful to phone him in advance if I had an issue to bring before the board that might spook him.

Howard Cherry was hard working and, like Mary Rieke, spent a great deal of time on school matters. Howard kept this up along with a busy orthopedic practice for many years, then ran for the legislature and was promptly placed on Ways and Means. He had a great heart, and he was inclined to support whatever the teacher organizations proposed without thinking through the fiscal impact on the district. This put the rest of the board in the awkward position of voting down his generous impulses and incurring the unhappiness of the teachers. This in turn had led to adoption of a board policy proposed by Bill Wyse which required that we circulate proposed resolutions to board members in advance of board meetings, a measure which provided time to talk Howard out of proposals his colleagues thought not fiscally sound, and a good policy in most public meetings.

Ted Yaw was the circulation manager of the Oregonian. He and Ed Burkett were pleasant, cooperative members without strong feelings on most matters which came before us.

Bill Wyse, University of Washington and Harvard Law graduate, had the best mind on the board. Mary Rieke had recruited him for service on the board in 1959, to replace Herb Schwab when Herb went on the bench, and Bill was undoubtedly responsible for my appointment. Bill was thoroughly familiar with school finance and state educational policy. His ability to quickly analyze the fiscal implications of a proposal was invaluable. Bill's term expired in 1966, and he declined to run for reelection. However, he recruited Robert Ridgley, one of his younger partners at Hart Spencer, to run for his position. Bob became an equally vigorous and able board member and served with distinction for twelve years. Bob was active in Republican Party circles and, like Bill Wyse, had excellent connections with the business community. Some years later Bob Ridgley left the practice of law to join Northwest Natural Gas and subsequently became president and chairman of that corporation.

Aside from meetings, board membership involved frequent phone calls from other board members, a constant flow of memoranda and board documents to review and, occasionally, correspondence and phone calls from concerned parents, and critics of school or board policy. In the 1960s the community regarded the school system as good, education as important and service on the school board as significant. When a board member went out to dinner, he or she could anticipate that the latest news stories involving education would be discussed with friendly and sometimes critical interest. This atmosphere was to change significantly over the next decade. Warning signals were already beginning to appear.

Because of my experience dealing with the legislature, and my political contacts with Oregon's senators and representatives, at Mary Rieke's suggestion, I was appointed by the National School Board Association to its Legislative Committee. This group usually met in Washington, but occasionally in Chicago, and dealt with national policy and federal legislation. Hugh Calkins, a lawyer from Cincinnati, Ohio and Rene Mills, from Los Alamos, New Mexico were the most interesting members of that committee. Hugh was a lanky chap with keen political sense. In many respects he reminded me of Bill Wyse. Rene Mills was an attractive, experienced and witty member of the Los Alamos, New Mexico, school board, familiar with all the twists and turns of school board politics. Her husband, Dr. Robert Mills, was a scientist at the Los Alamos National Laboratory. Several years later I became chairman of the Council of Large City School Boards, a satellite organization concerned with problems common to large city schools. I kept in close touch with Edith Green who who was piloting educational measures through Congress at this time.

*

From 1964 to 1966 Bill Wise supervised district lobbying at the Oregon Legislature, and he saw to my education in the intricacies of Oregon School Finance. State school support was distributed to the school districts according to a formula enacted into law before our time. This formula was based upon the taxable real property in the district. It failed to recognize that the urban areas, which generally had more taxable property than smaller cities and rural areas, also had a higher burden of urban services which had to be supported by property taxes. The formula also failed to take into consideration other sources of revenue, particularly the revenue-sharing payments made to Oregon counties which had federal forest lands within their borders. For many years the O & C counties had lower property tax rates than Multnomah County and substantially higher state school support than School District No. 1.

Throughout the 1960s the distribution controversy permeated school matters before the legislature. When Bill Wyse retired from the board, I took over the board's legislative role. In that year the first one and a half percent property tax initiative was filed, and according to the Secretary of State, sufficient valid signatures were filed to qualify it for the ballot. The combined property tax within the boundaries of School District No. 1 totaled approximately 2.8%. No provision was made to replace school or city revenue which would be lost were this measure to succeed. An examination of the number of signatures certified as sufficient by Jack Thompson, Director of Elections in the Secretary of State's Office, led me to conclude that he had misinterpreted the number of valid signatures required by the State Constitution. I was satisfied that a significantly higher number were required. Thompson had been director of elections for many years, but no one had previously questioned his interpretation of the number of signatures required to put measures on the ballot.

With the approval of the school board, I prepared a suit against the Secretary of State, Miller vs. McCall, challenging the validity of the initiative measure. I telephoned Tom McCall, now Secretary of State, to report that I would have to sue him. His response was "Oh Jack! Must you?" with a long groan. Tom was running for governor. I explained that Jack Thompson, the director of elections Tom had inherited with his office, was just wrong in his interpretation of what was required. Tom groaned again. At the time I was handling for Tom a controversy he was having with the contractor building his beach house at Road's End. I suggested that Herb Schwab, who had resigned from the circuit court the year before and was in practice with George Rives' firm, would be glad to complete handling the beach house matter for him, a substitution to which Tom agreed.

We filed the suit. Clyde Brummel, sponsor of the initiative measure, intervened in defense. Carl Neil represented him. The trial was held in Marion County. Our evidence showed that beyond any doubt the original interpretation of the number required had been followed in successive instances for many decades until it had been misinterpreted at the outset of Thompson's tenure. The trial judge struck the measure from the ballot and the Supreme Court affirmed. Demands followed that I be recalled from the school board for handling the lawsuit. The

Oregonian wrote an editorial opposing such a move. So the evil day of the property tax limitation was put off for a quarter of a century. Arguably, had the limitation measure had been passed at that time, we might have had a better prospect of enacting overall tax reform and replacing lost property tax revenues than we do at the present time. On the other hand, we might have been in a continual school funding crisis for the past forty years, not just the past fifteen.

*

The Portland school board prided itself on having no bonded indebtedness. All of the new construction since World War II had been financed by special levies. When the existing tax base fell short of supporting the proposed budget, the Board was accustomed to putting a special levy on the ballot. All special levies since 1950 had passed. In the spring of 1967, I was chairman. The board put a $7,000,000 special levy on the ballot which failed. We concluded that we would not resubmit the levy or a smaller levy but would make the necessary cuts. Among the cuts were interscholastic athletics. Our rationale was that the public should understand that cuts had to be made when levies were not approved.

Tom McCall, now governor, responding to a complaint by Bob Hazen, President of the Portland Chamber of Commerce, gave an impromptu television interview in the capitol in which he said, "The Board should not punish the children." We got wind of this within minutes, and I called a special board meeting at noon. The board agreed that I should make a televised statement in response. This I did, saying in substance that we were sure the governor spoke from the heart but upon poor advice and incorrect facts."

I arrived home about five thirty PM, and as I walked in the front door, Clissa said the governor's office was on the phone. I picked up the telephone and it was, as I recall, Ron Schmidt. He said this was an unfortunate situation. The governor did not mean to create problems for the board. There was noise in the background, and then Tom took the phone, saying "Jack, I've blown it" or words to that effect. "What can I do? Do you want me to repudiate the statement?"

I said, "No, don't do that." I suggested that he as governor and Terry Shrunk as mayor of Portland might meet with the board on Monday and allow us to present the facts as we saw them. Then he and Terry could make whatever response they thought was appropriate. He accepted. I assumed that Terry Shrunk would go along with this, and he did. Tom's staff worked out the details with our staff. We met on Monday, and after our presentation both Tom and Terry issued a statement supporting our position. This incident is one of many illustrating why Tom McCall was such an effective governor. He had a powerful and intelligent staff. He never hesitated to speak from his heart which, God knows, was big enough, and when he made a mistake his staff was there to point out the problem, and he was ready to make amends. But he was indeed a loose cannon!

*

Following failure of the levy, the board and the teachers could not reach agreement on salaries. A minority of the teachers were represented by the American Federation of Teachers, a CIO union. The majority were represented by the Oregon Association of Teachers, an independent employee organization. The Federation set a deadline for a strike. In those days there was no formal mechanism for public employee negotiation. The practice had been for the superintendent to discuss wages and salary issues with the teacher representatives. The superintendent would make recommendations to the board. The matter would be set on the agenda for a board meeting. The teacher representatives would present their case. Then the board would discuss the question. The superintendent's recommendation would be moved. Howard Cherry would move to increase the salaries a bit over the superintendent's recommendation, and the board would fall in line.

This time things were different. The board, expecting a crowd, held a special meeting in the Benson auditorium. The floor and balcony in front of us were packed with teachers from both teacher organizations. A union representative, Mr. Califano from New York, addressed us first. I was in the chair. Califano was a big man, very expressive, very aggressive, very loud. He faced the board, announced who he was, then proceeded to turn his back on us and made a fire and brimstone speech to his troops, particularly those in the gallery. The troops cheered him to the rafters. I pounded the gavel to obtain order striking the marble base so hard it shattered into fragments.

The board rejected the union demands as well as those of the Oregon Association of Teachers. The two teacher organizations continued negotiations with each other behind closed doors attempting to reach agreement on a common position. Then the American Federation of Teachers called a strike.

The board met the evening before the strike. The Association had not decided whether to strike, or if it did not, whether its members should cross the union picket line. A mediator obtained by the union (without any agreement on the part of the board to mediate) traveled back and forth between the board and the teachers. Neither the board nor the teachers would budge. About midnight I adjourned the meeting of the board and sent everyone to bed, leaving the teachers to make their decision. We had completed arrangements to staff the schools with non strikers and substitutes. Shortly before classes were scheduled to start in the morning the union called off the strike.

The repercussions lasted for some time. Margaret Labby, a former classmate at Lincoln and at that time head of the English Department at Lincoln, one of the most able teachers in the district and a good friend, told me in no uncertain terms at a dinner party that she thought the board had mishandled the affair. Her point of view was understandable. However, I think that under the circumstances we handled the situation about as well as we could.

*

One point never resolved in our time was the legislative grant of tenure to both teachers and principals. A sound argument can be made for teacher tenure, provided removal procedure is made simple and straightforward, which it wasn't, but there was no justification for administrative tenure. The whole tone of a school's activity is set by the quality and performance of its principal. As a practical matter, all the superintendent and board could do under administrative tenure was to transfer a bad principal, and that is what we did. Every year we were faced with the necessity to transfer unsatisfactory principals from one school to another, replacing them with able principals to repair the damage. On one occasion we parked a particularly inept principal in the administration building at a meaningless desk job to avoid inflicting him upon another school.

This was a period of transition in the relations between public employees and public officials. Negotiating the terms of employment was not then the practice. The public did not accept the idea that public employees could strike, or that public officials could "reward" them for doing so. The question was where to put the limited resources we had when the voters declined to provide more. The board had to allocate funds between physical plant, supplies, administrative salaries, support personnel, classroom teacher salaries and class loads.

The limit imposed on property taxes by the 1990 Measure 5 effectively transferred the primary source of educational funding from local school districts to the state legislature. The teacher's union has sufficient political strength to insure that salaries tend to trump class size, maintenance and length of the school year, but insufficient strength to insure alternative or supplemental sources of funding for state services including education. Without an adequate source of revenue, operating a high quality school system is impossible. In the long run, talent flows where the rewards lie in our society, and education is no exception.

During the years I was on the school board our children attended Portland public schools. Both got a good education. John graduated from Lincoln in 1965, received the National Merit Scholarship for Oregon and went on to Princeton where he majored in mathematics, graduating in 1969. He then was employed at Lawrence Radiation Laboratory at Livermore, California, and later obtained his Ph.D. from the University of California at Berkeley. In 1979 he moved to Canada and joined the faculty of the University of Waterloo at Waterloo, Ontario, where he is a professor of computer mathematics. Jean graduated from Lincoln in 1971, spent a year at Oregon State University, then transferred to the University of Oregon and graduated in 1976. She took a post graduate paralegal course at the University of San Diego and then returned to Portland where she worked in the Multnomah County District Attorney's office. In 1978 she was employed by the Stoel Rives law firm as one of their first paralegals.

CHAPTER 16

Voyages north, Viet Nam
and Robert Kennedy

The summer of 1964 Clissa and I took our 23 foot outboard cruiser, now lengthened to 26 feet, north with Loren Hicks and his family. Loren was the state court administrator. I had met him in connection with my lobbying for the state bar. The Hicks had chartered a 34 ft. Chantyman, a plump motor sailor built in Singapore by American Marine, the company which began building Grand Banks Yachts that same year. We trailed our boat up to Anacortes and joined the Hicks at that port. John and Jean were with us part of the way, together with a classmate of Jean's. We made a grand circuit of Desolation Sound, including an excursion up Princess Louisa Inlet. When the trip was over Clissa said, "Either we get a larger boat, or this is the last trip in a boat we make." I conceded that packing two adults and two or three children in the outboard cruiser for two and three weeks at a time was too much. That fall we acquired a 34 ft. 1950 wood hull Chris Craft with twin 140 hp six cylinder engines, a boat which we continued to use on the Columbia and in Canadian waters for the next twenty five years.

The Chris was a beautifully built mahogany hull kept by its owner out in the weather at the coast for a number of years before it was moved to Staff Jennings Marina at the west end of the Sellwood Bridge. I took it to Russ Sells of Sell's Marine

Service at Portland Yacht Club who looked the craft over for me. Russ thought he could bring the Hercules block engines to life, though he described the hull as looking as though it had been painted with a broom. He repaired cracks in the blocks and various other mechanical ailments and got the engines running smoothly.

Clissa and I stripped the cracked varnish and paint from the cabin and repainted it Chris Craft Blue. We moored the boat at Jantzen Beach for a year, then bought a new Hargrave's boathouse, which we had towed to Row E at Portland Yacht Club. According to the manual, the Chris had a top speed of 26 knots. The best we got out of the old engines was 22 knots which was more than enough. The boat planed at 10 knots and cruised well at 15. Gasoline then was thirty five cents per gallon.

The following summer Clissa and I took the new Clarissa Jean north in company with Bob and Ginger Rankin in their boat, The Seven Rs. The Chris had two 75 gallon gas tanks for its two thirsty engines, which together consumed a gallon of gasoline per nautical mile at planing speed. Our plan was to take the boats to Anacortes, leave the boats and return to Portland for supplies and children. We made it to Astoria in good time and fueled there. The following morning we crossed the bar at slack water and reached Grays Harbor where we spent the night. The next day we were fogged in. In those days we navigated by compass, depth finder and chart. The third day the fog cleared and we took off for Neah Bay at the entrance to the Straits of Juan de Fuca. It was very rough. We had to reduce speed to five knots for many hours, pounding constantly. Clissa and I traded the helm every half hour. Both of us were seasick for the first and last time in our lives. Clissa hit one wave particularly hard while I was in the head. The force threw me into the door taking it off the hinges. We finally made it into Neah Bay.

From there on, the run through the straits to Anacortes was duck soup. However, careful inspection at an Anacortes boatyard showed that the pounding had split both engine beds, so we left the boat at the yard to have the engine beds sistered with 3/4 plywood and the forward deck canvassed to eliminate leaks over our bunks. That was the roughest water we ever encountered. The balance of the trip through the American and Canadian Islands was successful, but when it came time to set sail for home, I found a commercial boat trailer who would meet us in Olympia and trail the boat to Portland, avoiding that long run down the Washington Coast. With one exception we trailed the boat to Olympia and back every year thereafter.

"Boating" on the Columbia under normal conditions was a relatively simple matter. Navigating the San Juans, Inland Canadian waters and the West Coast of Vancouver Island called for considerably more close attention and was a particular challenge in the early days before radar and electronic navigation. We had a compass, charts, and a depth finder to assist navigating through the many rocky islands. The onset of fog called for quick decision. The pleasures and latent hazards of those beautiful waters were both magnet and challenge for a lifetime.

Claire and Forest Amsden purchased our outboard cruiser which initiated them into the business of boating, and they soon acquired a larger boat and cruised with us in the American and Canadian islands for the next twenty years.

*

In 1965 Herb Schwab resigned from the circuit court to become a partner in George Rives' law firm, the successor to Lang, Gray and Smith, which Pacific Power and Light used to handle that utility's business. Herb had two children in college at that time, which was a strong factor in his decision to leave the bench. After he had settled into the Rives office, Herb thought they could use the trial experience we had accumulated in the Dusenbery office and suggested to me the idea of merging the two firms. If this were possible he would forgo his ultimate interest in an appointment to the Oregon Supreme Court. I was deeply involved with school matters at the time, but willing to consider the possibility. I would have had to abandon my interest in going on the bench. Herb did discuss this but found several members of his office not interested. As it turned out the Rives firm later merged with Davies, Biggs, Strayer, Stoel and Boley to form the firm of Stoel, Rives, Boley, Fraser and Wyse, now known as Stoel Rives.

In 1967 the legislature recognized that the Oregon Supreme Court as then constituted had more business than it could handle and created an intermediate five judge Court of Appeals with jurisdiction to handle criminal appeals, and appeals from workman's compensation, domestic relations and administrative agencies. Governor McCall had it in mind from the outset to appoint Herb to the court. Herb became interested, particularly when the governor told him he would be chief judge because he (the governor) would obtain assurances from the other nominees that they would vote for him as chief judge. When the new court assembled to select the chief judge, Herb found that the governor had forgotten to instruct his appointees how they were to vote. The tally was three to two for Herb, but it did not take him long to impose his stamp on the court.

*

By the mid 1960s the Johnson administration's increasing involvement in Viet Nam was becoming a matter of concern to many people. The Schwabs had a dinner party early in 1966 in the house which they had built on Palatine Hill. Edith Green was there, as were Clissa and I. I do not remember who else was present, but I remember clearly that Edith expressed in no uncertain terms her conviction that our growing involvement in Viet Nam was dangerous and would become a disaster. Both Herb and I argued that letting the communists take over Viet Nam would be like giving in to Hitler at Munich. Our attitude was based on conceptions formed in the years leading up to World War II. Appeasement of aggression was fatal error. The administration had portrayed Viet Nam as another case of cold war communist expansion.

For some reason, Herb and I both overlooked the lesson of Korea where we had become bogged down in an Asiatic land war despite clearer reason for involvement than in Viet Nam. In Korea the Truman administration had paid a good deal of attention to limiting the dimensions of the war which was initiated by North Korea and threatened our position in a totally disarmed Japan. Moreover, resistance to North Korean aggression had become a United Nations action at the outset. The Truman administration was well aware of the risk involved were China to enter the war. It was McArthur with his Napoleonic pretensions who precipitated Chinese involvement by pushing his troops toward the Yalu River border with China, heedless of numerous warnings. When President Truman dismissed McArthur, he ended further thought of extending the war into China proper. But it took Eisenhower as the new president in 1953 to finally negotiate an armistice and terminate the conflict close to the original 38th parallel which had divided North Korea from South Korea.

So here we were in 1966, twelve years later, drifting into another conflict on the mainland of Asia, this time with no crisp beginning, no United Nations support, no allies and no clear idea of what we could accomplish. Our attention, such as it was, focused on civil rights and the Johnson war on poverty. Overt opposition to the growing involvement centered initially on the reluctance of college students to respond to the draft, which was providing the bulk of our enlisted personnel. This resistance and the disturbing forms it took ran counter to my generation's sense of duty, responsibility and public order.

During the next year and a half my thinking and that of a lot of other people shifted 180 degrees, though we were never comfortable with much of the anti-war activity. We were obviously becoming bogged down in a land war in Asia with every prospect of having to fully mobilize and put an army of millions into the field with little prospect of gain if we were to completely mobilize and wipe out North Vietnam. In the winter of 1967 Senator Eugene McCarthy began a campaign for the Democratic nomination for president against President Johnson on an anti-war platform and, according to the polls, was doing remarkably well.

In February 1968 Edith Green telephoned me at the office late in the afternoon and asked me to come over to her apartment in the Ambassador. When I arrived, she introduced me to a lawyer named William J. vanden Heuvel from New York. He was a tall, urbane and pleasant man in his late thirties who had flown to Portland to tell Mrs. Green that Robert F. Kennedy was going to enter the race and wanted Edith Green to chair his campaign in Oregon. Vanden Heuvel represented the Kennedy national organization then being formed. We had some discussion of the problems involved, notably the fact that McCarthy, already in the field for some months, had obtained support from a good many Democrats, including Herb Schwab.

Vanden Heuvel then left the apartment, and Edith continued the discussion with me. She said she had set three conditions to which he had agreed. She wanted entire control of the organization in Oregon, adequate funding by the national campaign, and a commitment from me to co-chair the campaign with her. Vanden Heuvel didn't know me from Adam's off ox, but he had agreed to all her conditions. Edith said that she would take this on only if I would co-chair the campaign with her.

To oppose a sitting Democratic president was a serious step, but she felt Lyndon Johnson had to be defeated for re-nomination, and she was convinced that Senator Eugene McCarthy could neither lead the Democratic Party nor be an effective president. She said she had developed a better impression of Bobby Kennedy in recent years, but she wanted to be sure that her reputation and standing in Oregon were not jeopardized by the campaign. She wanted me to watch the money and the Kennedy national people. I had made speeches for John F. Kennedy during his campaign for the presidency which Edith had chaired in

Oregon, but I had not been involved in campaign management. I gathered that her insistence on control was grounded to some extent in that experience.

Edith Green, while a tough, practical politician, was an intensely religious person who maintained her church connections throughout her adult life. She had a keen sense of personal honesty and where the public interest lay. For many years she insisted that her staff refer to me all questions about campaign contributions and how they should be handled. She expected me to advise them strictly, and I did. She never questioned a judgment call I made on how such matters should be handled. So I understood what she wanted. I was ready to abandon President Johnson. I discussed her proposal with Clissa, then called Edith the next day to say I would tackle the job with her.

If ever there was a campaign put together with patchwork and bailing wire, this was it. We had only a few days before the deadline to file in the primary, and not enough time to handle the filing documents by mail. We filed by telegraph using a statutory provision authorizing that procedure which I had never noticed before. We enlisted Charles P. Paulson, an able Portland trial lawyer, as campaign treasurer and set up strict rules on how money was to be handled. All funds received were to be deposited with him. No moneys were to be paid out except on express approval by him or me. No member of the Oregon for Kennedy Committee was to incur obligations on behalf of the committee without express authorization from one of us. Finally, no expenditures were to be authorized in excess of uncommitted funds actually on deposit in our bank account.

Meanwhile Edith set about creating a statewide network of support for Kennedy. As we had anticipated, Senator McCarthy had already obtained commitments from many persons who would otherwise have supported Kennedy. Moreover, there was still resentment in Portland relating back to Robert Kennedy's testimony in Terry Schrunk's trial. Notwithstanding these obstacles, Mrs. Green created a statewide organization. The candidate made three swings through the state and everywhere drew enthusiastic crowds. A fight to the death for the Democratic nomination against a sitting president was an ideal campaign from the point of view of the press. When President Johnson pulled out of the race it became bedlam.

From the outset of the campaign Robert Kennedy thrust himself into the crowds which surrounded him. They loved it. Many wanted to touch him. He repeatedly lost his cuff links. At one point he had to make a speech after storming though a crowd, and his shirt cuffs, as usual, were linkless. I loaned him my cuff links for the evening, reminding him that I wanted them back. They had been a gift from my father. When Kennedy moved through a crowd, Roosevelt Grier, the famous professional football player, moved ahead of him. I tried to keep up with Rosie and had a hard time doing it. Rosie was twice my weight and four inches taller. He looked formidable and he was formidable. There were generally a couple of secret service men somewhere around, but not parting the crowd. Watch the eyes they said, and I tried to keep my eyes on the faces in front of me to spot hostility. I saw none, but I knew it only took one. Edith, sensibly, did not do crowd plunges. If Edith was present when Kennedy was to speak, she introduced him. If she was not, I did the introduction. No one has ever accused me of being a great public speaker, and I shudder to think of how Robert Kennedy must have felt when that chore fell to me, but I gritted my teeth and went at it.

Some enterprising campaign worker organized a group of young girls to perform as cheer leaders at rallies. They were called The Kennedy Girls, and wore straw boaters, red neckerchiefs, white blouses and blue skirts. Jean Beatty, age fifteen, joined them and reveled in their activity as did Vera Katz, who become Mayor of Portland a quarter century later.

Robert Kennedy was very effective as a speaker. His voice carried well, he struck his themes in simple direct words, and he ignited his crowds. He was, I think, a more explosive speaker than his brother John, who was no slouch at the business. One of his tours was a whistle stop train ride down the Willamette valley. Someone in the National Headquarters proposed it to me by telephone.

In my innocence I asked, "Where the hell do I find a passenger train on four days notice?"

"Call so and so," was the answer. "He's a vice president of the Southern Pacific, and he'll help you." I called and he did. I got the train lined up in one telephone call.

On one train excursion, Kennedy caught me just as we boarded. "Beatty, I want you to sit beside me from the time we get on until we get off. Don't leave me for a minute." One of our passengers was a Lane County politician who on a previous trip had attached himself to the candidate like a leach and could never be shaken off.

Whistle stop campaigning was great fun, a reversion to politics of the not-so-distant past, and the memory of Harry Truman's 1948 campaign was still fresh. At stops in small towns I had the job of introducing the candidate from the rear platform of the observation car.

Robert Kennedy's principal assistants in the campaign were William vanden Heuvel, E. Barrett Prettyman, Jr. and Herbert Schmertz. All three have had outstanding careers: vanden Heuvel in the New York Bar and the diplomatic service; Prettyman in the District of Columbia Bar and many formal and informal government assignments; Schmertz as a "combative" and innovative vice president spokesman for Mobile Corporation. On one occasion I brought Barrett Prettyman home for dinner at our house, and Jean Beatty thought he was wonderful. Strategy discussions with them were illuminating.

Kennedy insisted that we pay strict attention to the accuracy of statements issued to the press. At one point the McCarthy camp challenged a statement as inaccurate. The staff argued over whether it could be explained or justified. Kennedy disposed of the matter in short order saying, "Were we right or were we wrong? If we were wrong, don't weasel. Say the statement was wrong and correct it."

He listened to advice with care, though he required that it be presented quickly. He made whatever decision was required promptly. Then he moved on to the next problem.

My impression of the Kennedy women—wives and friends—was fleeting. An exception was Marietta Tree, I had responsibility for making arrangements for her on one occasion and spent some time with her. She was a lovely person. I saw Ted Kennedy on several occasions, and walked him back to the Benson Hotel after one appearance, but my contact with him was limited. At the time he seemed a cold fish compared to his older brothers. Forty years later he was regarded warmly on both sides of the Senate aisle and considered a major figure in the Senate.

Perhaps the most aggravating problem in the entire campaign was the way television cameramen pushed their way through crowds, barged in front of spectators and jammed their way under the nose of the hapless person running for office. No one could afford to run them out of town, but most of us involved in the campaign would like to have done so. Aggressiveness pays in the news business, at least up to the point of revolt, and few candidates or their supporters are prepared to sacrifice a moment of coverage for the satisfaction of rewarding louts with clouts. Reporters fought like cats and dogs over hotel accommodations in Portland. All of them wanted rooms in the Benson which they considered the best hotel in the country. The Benson could only accommodate a limited number, and this was a recurring grievance.

We had neither time nor personnel to raise money. Financing our campaign depended upon infusions of money from the Kennedy National Committee. These infusions were irregular and generally in the form of cash, packets of large denomination bills. They arrived credited to the national committee. In my limited experience cash in large amounts raises considerable question as to its origin. But we reported the National Committee as the source, and the National Committee reported to the federal election office. We saw nothing of its reports nor would we expect to. Chuck Paulson tenaciously kept our accounts straight and prepared all of our reports to the Oregon Secretary of State's election division.

Some days before the election the Oregon Committee had a final pamphlet which we were anxious to get out. Paulson told the printer to hold the printing; we had insufficient funds to cover the cost, though more funds were expected the next day. The printer said he didn't need cash, just a commitment that we would pay him the next day. Paulson referred the matter to me, and I confirmed his decision. "No money, no printing." The flier never went out.

Kennedy lost the Oregon primary election to Gene McCarthy while the California campaign was in its final stages. He returned to Portland late election night. Campaign officials and the press waited in a suite on the top floor of the Benson. He walked into the suite at 9 PM and threw his arms around Edith Green saying, "Edith, I've let you down." Any of us would have gone through hell for him that night. He returned to the California campaign the next morning where he had a clear lead in the polls. He was shot dead in the Ambassador Hotel in Los Angeles the night he carried the state of California by a substantial margin.

Robert Kennedy's funeral was held in New York and his body was then taken by train from New York to Washington. Clissa and I watched the train on television as it slowly moved through New Jersey, passing through the small railside communities on the way. All along the way small groups, largely of blacks, stood in the darkness, and in station after station they were singing the Battle Hymn of the Republic. It was tremendously moving, a strange counter point to the funeral procession of Jack Kennedy seven years before.

20. Happy campaigning for president. Robert Kennedy and Jack work their way through a genial crowd in Portland.

21. Worried campaigning for president. Robert Kennedy working through an excited crowd with two security men in front, and Jack behind. They watch for angry eyes.

22. Congresswoman Edith Green inspects the Primate Center with Dr. Clarissa Beatty & Dr. William Montagna, Director.

23. Wooden faced chairman Beatty presents equally wooden faced William W. Wyse with a plaque on his retirement from the Board in 1966. Photo Courtesy Portland Public Schools

Editors say that a good novel requires that the principal character develop and change in response to circumstance. Robert Kennedy grew from a narrow, abrasive young man to a powerful and compassionate adult. I agreed to support his candidacy because Edith Green vouched for him. My experience during the campaign converted me to an ardent supporter. Had Robert Kennedy not been assassinated, I am convinced that he would have gone on to win the primary and the general election. Nixon could never have matched him. I think he would have made a good and, possibly, a great president.

*

I froze the Oregon Committee bank account when Robert Kennedy was shot. We discovered in the days that followed that many Oregon firms had extended credit to National Committee people, advance men and the like, and that in the hurly burly of the last days of the campaign wholly unauthorized people had charged expenses to the Oregon Committee. The creditors looked to the Oregon Committee for payment, even though no person in authority had authorized the expenditure. Comparable problems occurred in other primary states. The Kennedy National leaders told me they were making arrangements to contact creditors and settle the legitimate claims but it would take some time. The process dragged on. Several months later some of these creditors sued the Oregon Committee in an attempt to collect debts we had not authorized, naming Edith and me as additional defendants. Edith was furious and made a number of calls to Kennedy people in the East. Eventually all claims were settled by the national committee, and the case was dismissed. It is not difficult to keep track of a campaign for state office, but a contested presidential primary campaign is a nightmare to manage with overlapping responsibilities, dual reporting requirements. and multiple committees.

With Robert Kennedy out of the race, Vice President Hubert Humphrey had no difficulty taking the nomination from Gene McCarthy in the Democratic Convention in Chicago. Humphrey's immediate problem was the manner in which the convention was besieged by rioting anti-war protesters and protected by the Chicago police. The Vice President's loyal association with President Johnson, despite his own reservations about the war, was too much for him to overcome. Former Vice President Richard Nixon was elected. President Nixon's new administration continued to thrash about in the attempt to resolve the war, and the social unrest triggered by the war continued to percolate through universities, colleges and down into high schools.

*

The Kennedy campaign was my last venture into partisan politics. Our work on the school board was entirely nonpartisan and reflected the problems of the times: Educational policy, disciplinary controversies, funding questions, student challenges to authority, teachers' salaries. My speeches to the various audiences, including the City Club, reflect the issues of the times. Our superintendent, Melvin Barnes, retired in 1968. I chaired the search committee which resulted in the selection by the board of Robert Blanchard, an able administrator, as the new superintendent.

Jonathan Newman, a very bright and serious Portland lawyer, who had been active in Civil Rights work, ran for the school board in 1968. Jonathan had been active in pressing the Race and Education Committee to go a good deal farther than we thought it wise to go to achieve "racial balance" in our system in 1963. Herb Schwab and I were asked informally whether he should be supported when he announced his candidacy. Our conclusion was that he would make a good board member, and we said so.

Jonathan served two terms as an extremely hard working member. His view on what was achievable, like ours, was tempered by experience, but he never ceased to press for measures consistent with his ideals. Following his school board service he was appointed to the Court of Appeals and served on it until retirement in 1991. Jonathan planned to write a detailed account of these years on the school board and borrowed my files to review, but unfortunately an illness which limited his physical activity and the heavy burden of the Court of Appeals docket delayed this project until his retirement, and he died much too soon thereafter. The bulk of my school board files were lost in the liquidation of his estate.

*

In 1969 John Beatty graduated from Princeton and obtained a position with Lawrence Radiation Laboratory at Livermore, California. He, like many other classmates, had been deferred from the draft while in college. He was opposed to the Viet Nam War but not a conscientious objector. When his time came for a hearing before the draft board, I sent him to talk to Gerald Robinson, an able lawyer who had much experience in handling draft matters. Gerry said he had no valid personal basis for deferment, and his best course would be to rely on his position with Lawrence, which had requested his deferment. John had an interesting session with the draft board in which he told the board he was not a conscientious objector, just an objector to this particular war. The board ultimately deferred him because of his position at Lawrence, which was engaged in many military projects.

Clissa and I considered attending John's graduation at Princeton and then concluded it would be a waste of money to fly three of us back east for the ceremony. Instead, we decided to go to Puerto Valjarta, Mexico for ten days, which we did. I swore Jean to secrecy, and arranged to have John fly to Puerto Valjarta from Princeton. We had rooms at an old single story adobe-like hotel on the beach, Playa de Oro by name. As we were eating dinner in the dining terrace with music playing and the sound of surf, John walked in and sat down at the table. Clissa, whose attention was elsewhere, suddenly looked at him and exclaimed,
"Jesus Christ! Where did you come from!"

Puerto Valjarta then was almost untouched by tourism. There was only one quasi-modern hotel of four or five stories.

Women washed their laundry in the river, which ran through the center of the town. The streets were very roughly cobbled. We rented the only car we could find, an ancient jeep, battered and very difficult to steer. We drove some miles south to the beach where "The Night of the Iguana" had recently been filmed. We had a wonderful time. At the end, everyone caught the usual stomach disorder except Clissa, who was taking an antibiotic for an eye infection.

CHAPTER 17

Taking the bench, and the Circuit Court

My mother and father, who had moved from their apartment in Portland to a small rental house at Seaside surprised us in 1956 by announcing they were going to Europe for a year. My father, after careful study, had concluded they could afford do this on his retirement pay because of then current favorable exchange rates. They sailed to Italy, bought a small Fiat and traveled for several months before ferrying to and wintering in Majorca. In the spring they drove through Spain and France, then across the Channel to England where they met Margaret Sharp and visited Ivenson and Caroline Corbett Macadam and English friends they had met in Italy and Spain.

Following their return from the East coast in 1958, they drove west in the Fiat, bought a house in Seaside one block back from the ocean and the salt cairn, and settled in to the coastal life they both enjoyed. My mother painted with oils, while my father experimented with pastel. Both of them worked hard developing another garden in their large back yard. They had many old friends and made new ones in Seaside and Gearhart. On weekends we often drove down to the beach to see them and play croquet in the back yard. When we took the boat down to Astoria to fish off the bar, Jeannie stayed with them. On other occasions one of the children would take the bus down to Seaside to visit. Thanksgiving we usually spent with them at Seaside. Christmas they usually spent with us in Portland. One

Thanksgiving when we were driving back to Portland at night, a large deer jumped out into the highway in front of us. I hit it head on. The deer sailed up into the air and then floated off to the right hand side of the road. The front of the Buick was dented considerably, but otherwise we were undamaged.

In 1968 the need for better medical facilities and increasing dislike of the long drive to Portland led them to sell the house at Seaside and move to Portland. After some exploration they settled on an apartment in the Portland Towers, which was handy for us. My mother's legs began to weaken as she reached 80, and I finally suggested it was time to stop driving. It was a difficult decision for her. How difficult, I appreciate better now than then. She found the isolation of apartment living without an automobile very confining.

In 1973 We moved the two of them to an apartment in Terwilliger Plaza, a retirement complex on Terwilliger Boulevard below Broadway Drive. This was only a couple of blocks from Broadway Drive, my regular route downtown. My father was still able to climb the steps to our house, although he told me one day that they would not seem so easy when we reached his age. My mother had several old friends in the Plaza and quickly made new ones. We were able to see them each weekend either at our house or at their apartment. My father's interest in and ability to play the piano continued to the end of his life. We have a picture of him at eighty-six, playing the piano with Jean sitting beside him.

In the spring of 1975 my father's cataracts reached the point he could no longer read. We concluded it was worth trying an operation to restore his vision. The operation was successful, but his general condition deteriorated rapidly. My mother and our physician, Joseph Paquet, concluded it was just a matter of days, and we decided to keep him at Park View, the nursing home adjacent to Terwilliger Plaza, where it was easy for my mother to be with him and for me to stop by frequently. He died quietly a little before noon at the age of 86 on a sunny June day in 1975. My mother telephoned, and I saw him a few minutes later. A sheet was tucked up to his shoulders. His face was white, the muscles relaxed, the expression calm. He looked much younger than his years. My mother was quite prepared for his death and relieved that he was released from physical and mental impairment. His funeral service was held in the chapel at Trinity Church where he had served as a vestry man some forty five years earlier. Dr. Lansing Kempton, the retired rector of Trinity, conducted the service at my mother's request.

*

I was approaching my fifty first birthday in 1970. My term on the school board would expire in June. With that in mind, I announced I would retire from the board. We had a new superintendent and a strong board, and it looked like a good time to move on. I reflected on my law practice and concluded that I needed to expand it from primarily insurance defense work. Henry Richmond, director of 1000 Friends of Oregon, proposed my taking on some legal work for his environmental group, and that looked very interesting. I had put aside my interest in going on the bench during my involvement with the Race and Education committee and work on the school board, but if I was ever going on the bench, it would have to be soon.

In the spring of 1970, a vacancy occurred on the Multnomah County Circuit Court. The governor had told me previously that he would appoint me to the next vacancy. Then I had a call from Salem. The governor was going to have to appoint a Republican lawyer to that vacancy. This proved to be Clifford B. Olsen, an able trial lawyer, and a good appointment. Several years before, I had an Employer's Liability Act case to defend in Canyon City and had associated Cliff Olsen as local counsel. The governor's office assured me that I would receive the next appointment. The delay was, none the less, a disappointment. Then Multnomah County Circuit Judge Dean Bryson ran against Justice Gordon Sloan for the latter's seat on the Oregon Supreme Court and defeated him in the primary election in

May, 1970. This created a vacancy in the Multnomah County Circuit Court. A bar poll gave me a substantial plurality over all other candidates who expressed interest in the position, and the governor promptly appointed me to fill it, saying, "Jack, if you'd come in last on the poll, I was going to appoint you anyway."

23.5. "I'm afraid it's quite serious - he has a deep compelling urge to run for the School Board." Cartoon by Bill Sanderson presented by Oregonian reporter John Gurnsey to Jack on his retirement from the Board in May 1970.

23.7. The new judge responds to Chief Justice Kenneth O'Connell.

Oregon's most colorful governor. Environmental activist, loose cannon politically unpredictable Republican. Beaches, bottle bills and land use legislation marked his administration. Jack acted as his lawyer, sued him as Secretary of State, and was appointed by him to the bench.

24. Tom Lawson McCall (1913-1983)

25. An enterprising reporter poses Clarissa Jean Beatty and the new judge after the ceremony of taking the bench.   December 7, 1970.

*

December 7, 1970, courtroom 510 provided a handsome setting for a swearing-in. Judge Philip Roth, then the presiding judge, conducted the proceedings. As was then customary, Governor McCall, Chief Justice O'Connell and the president of the Multnomah County Bar made appropriate remarks. Chief Judge Schwab robed me. I responded with a brief statement. The circuit and district judges of the county attended, robed and sitting in the jury box. Lawyers of my acquaintance filled the benches of the courtroom. My father, recently hospitalized, had not recovered sufficiently to attend, but my mother was there with Clissa and Jean. My mother particularly enjoyed the opportunity to talk to Tom McCall, whose family she had known so well in her youth. The next day I went to work as a judge.

I was assigned to courtroom 510 on the south side of the fifth floor of the Multnomah County Courthouse because the previous occupant, Judge Alfred P. Sulmonetti, was moving to a newly-constructed courtroom on the sixth floor. None of the other judges wanted 510. The County Commissioners had filled the large windows with glass blocks, leaving tiny opening windows. The glass blocks acted as a heat trap and caused the temperature in the courtroom to rise to unpleasant heights, so long as the sun was shining, irrespective of the outdoor temperature. Fortunately, the oath-taking was in December, and the temperature inside was quite comfortable.

Number 510 was one of the few remaining original courtrooms with eighteen foot ceilings, and one of only two with marble columns and tapestry panels. All the others had been savaged by former county commissioners seeking to create additional space and save money by cutting them in half vertically and "modernizing" them with whatever type of furniture, bench and mode of decoration met the taste of the incumbent judge or the county clerk. I was delighted with my assignment, and the temperature was no problem in December. My immediate problem was to get rid of the huge safe which Judge Sulmonetti had left in my secretary's office, obstructing the passage between the courtroom and my chambers. I continued to use Judge Bryson's secretary temporarily, pending the return of Susan Rommel, my legal secretary, who had left my law offices the year before to be with her husband, Jim, in the military service.

In time I was able to get the original oak benches and furniture reconditioned. The county commissioners, with an improved sense of responsibility for the preservation of a splendid building, replaced the glass blocks in the windows with proper bronzed metal framed windows and air-conditioned the courthouse. Tom Vaughan then had the courtroom declared a historic courtroom, a step which we hoped would add protection against future Philistines. In later years I commissioned student artists from the Museum Art School to copy paintings of three famous judges: Lord Chief Justice Sir Edward Coke, Chief Justice John Marshall, and Associate Justice Oliver Wendell Holmes, Jr. Finally I had a famous painting of Franklin, Adams and Jefferson drafting the Declaration of Independence copied. These paintings we hung on the faded tapestry panels. In 1984 Clissa and I gave them to the State of Oregon for placement in courtroom 510 so long as the courtroom was maintained in its original condition.

*

Clissa was invited to give a paper the summer of 1971 at Birmingham University in Great Britain. We decided I would go with her so we could spend two weeks following the meeting touring England and Scotland, which I had not seen since the War. The preceding winter we read aloud a book by a chap who had walked from Land's End in Cornwall to the northern tip of Scotland. We decided to follow in his footsteps as closely as possible by automobile. Our flight from Seattle to London was on the polar route. We crossed southern Greenland by the light of a full moon with the mountains in full view as they protruded from the massive ice cap. It was morning as we crossed Ireland and the irregular green pattern of the fields was brilliant in the early sun.

Birmingham was a new post-war university. The buildings were spare and not particularly attractive, but the facilities were comfortable. The committee which organized the conference made provision for entertaining wives while their husbands attended the meeting. I qualified as a wife and went along as the sole representative of my sex. The ladies were middle-aged, pleasant and rather dull, with the exception of an absolutely smashing Swedish neurosurgeon in her thirties whom I found great company. The high point of our entertainment was a lengthy tour of Warwick Castle nearby. I thought Clissa should not miss it so we made it our first stop after the meeting.

We rented a Hillman. Our plan was to drive down through Worcester, Gloucester, Bristol and Exeter, and then reverse course and drive north to the tip of Scotland. We planned to avoid the larger cities, save for Edinburgh and London. We stayed in small hotels operated by a chain which assured comfortable accommodation. quite good food and easy communication for the next night's reservation. Generally we lunched on the road at a convenient pub.

The countryside was consistently lovely aside from the industrial older cities. One of the pleasures of driving on side roads was the beauty of the immediate roadside itself. The pavement was bordered by a grass verge which was ordinarily well drained and never looked rutted or torn up. There was none of the sprawl which developed after World War II in the United States. The towns in southern England were still rebuilding structures damaged in the war, and there were large gaps of bare ground where buildings had been destroyed by bombing.

The day Clissa and I started out, we saw the cathedrals at Worcester, Gloucester and finally Bristol. This was a large dose of cathedrals for one day, but all were breathtakingly beautiful. I read later that during the two centuries in which most of the English cathedrals were built, their construction probably absorbed half the gross national product. Such estimates are undoubtedly rough, but the economic effort must have been enormous. In Essex we stayed in the Royal Clarence Hotel on the cathedral square with a room looking out toward Essex Cathedral, which was covered with scaffolding for repair of war damage. In Bath we inspected the remains of the Roman baths which were handsome, though the hot spring water looked rather soupy.

We had planned on going from Exeter to Salisbury and Stonehenge, but it was the end of a long weekend and the highway to Salisbury and London was jammed with traffic, so we cut off on secondary roads and worked our way up the Wye Valley to Tintern Abbey, where we walked through the ruins, very beautiful with lush green grass about the fallen masonry. Then we drove up the Severn Valley through the Welch border country to Chester. In Chester we walked the city wall and went to the Chester Zoo. From Chester we drove across England to York. The cathedral was closed, undergoing extensive repairs, but the chapter house was open. When I think of York I always think of King Harold's tremendous battle with, and defeat of, the powerful Danish army of King Harold Hardraga. The hard pressed English monarch was then compelled to force march his victorious but exhausted troops south to Hastings, where he met William, Duke of Normandy, and disaster.

In Durham, Clissa and I climbed the cathedral tower but finally gave out near the top. I took a picture of the river from a barred window in the tower. We inspected a Scottish castle at Nepath, a primitive structure compared with Warwick Castle in England, then examined a section of Hadrian's Wall. From there we went on to Sterling and Sterling Castle, where the famous Black Watch has its regimental headquarters and various mementos, including a reference to its horrendous losses at the Battle of New Orleans in 1815. Scotland seemed very green, very mountainous and very barren. Occasionally we saw reforested "plantations" of fir which the government has undertaken. Nearly all of the original Scotch fir forests were logged centuries ago and the omnipresent sheep prevented seedlings from sprouting. Scotland is far north and tree growth is slow even where it is protected.

I saw little of England during the War, and Clissa did not recall much of the trip she made with her mother before the war except that the food then was awful. But the history of England or, more properly, Great Britain, is so much a precursor of American history that we found it fascinating. Then we returned, Clissa to her research projects and I to my new life on the circuit court.

*

During the post World War II years courts and the criminal justice system came under considerable stress. The increase in criminal conduct and the coverage of crimes and criminals by television put courts and judges under more intense public scrutiny than in the past. Reacting to this pressure, a number of judges were individually studying various aspects of criminal behavior and experimenting with sentencing procedures. Because of my prior political and lobbying experience, particularly in connection with judicial salaries, I was included from the outset on several state judicial committees involving legislation, and thus became involved in the revision of court structure and changes in the criminal justice system during the 1970s and 1980s. These activities were interwoven with my regular work as a trial judge.

The Oregon court system in 1970 was largely unchanged from that with which the state had entered the Twentieth Century, save for an increase in the number of judges. The Multnomah County Circuit Court, the Fourth Judicial District, consisted of thirteen judges. Those judges elected a presiding judge who heard all preliminary matters, sentenced those pleading guilty in criminal cases, and assigned all cases, civil and criminal, for trial. The other circuit courts around the state were similarly organized in smaller judicial districts with one to five judges covering single counties or combinations of counties. Each judicial district adopted its own rules for selecting a presiding judge. A separate second tier of district judges existed in some judicial districts to handle traffic cases, petty crimes and small civil cases. The salaries of all state judges were paid by the state. The physical facilities and support personnel of the Supreme Court and the newly created Court of Appeals were also provided by the state. However, the physical facilities and all support personnel of the trial courts were built and paid for entirely by the counties.

Criminal appeals from the circuit courts went to the newly established Court of Appeals and then, if accepted for review, to the seven-judge Supreme Court of Oregon. Some appeals by statute went directly to the Supreme Court, and in the late 1970s some civil appeals were routed first to the Court of Appeals. The chief justice of the Supreme Court was elected by that court, and the practice in the 1950s was to rotate the position through the members of the court. Following the tenure of Chief Justice William McAllister the court abandoned the practice of rotation.

The chief justice presided over the Supreme Court and was the titular head of the state judiciary although, as we shall see, his administrative powers over the trial courts were relatively insignificant.

The presiding circuit judge in Multnomah County had five principal responsibilities: handling most matters preliminary to trial, managing the trial docket by assigning cases to particular judges for trial, acting as the leader and spokesman of the circuit court, sentencing defendants who pleaded guilty prior to trial and supervising the trial court administrator. A capable presiding judge made a difference in the efficiency with which cases moved to trial, and the presiding judge's attitude and interest made a significant difference in the speed and efficiency with which some trial judges addressed their trial responsibilities.

Each judge was elected individually on a nonpartisan ballot for a six-year term, and there was a tendency for judges to feel that they had a personal mandate from the voters. In any event, elected presiding judges served at the sufferance of their colleagues as "first among equals," and, insofar as reelection was concerned, the presiding judge served only so long as his or her colleagues wanted that judge to preside. The presiding judge had no disciplinary powers and the knowledge that he or she would return to the ranks provided little incentive to exercise authority over fellow judges beyond the role of assigning cases to them.

When I first began the practice of law in Multnomah County in 1948, the position of presiding judge of the circuit court was rotated every three months, a remarkably inefficient way to run a court system. The docket was woefully behind. In the mid 1950s, the court adopted a rule providing for the election of the presiding judge for a two year term. Judge Charles Redding was elected and reelected presiding judge for a number of years. Judge Redding was an able administrator. He provided continuity of leadership and a very considerable increase in efficiency of the court.

After a decade of Judge Redding's leadership, the court, in a minor revolt fueled by the ambition of several judges, reverted to the practice of rotation, albeit for a one year term rather than three months. The dynamics of this system meant that a candidate for the position of presiding judge might be a judge who wanted the position as a matter of prestige, or a judge who thought he or she could do a better administrative job, or a judge who was persuaded by fellow judges to take the position to avoid election of another member seeking the position who was thought to be a poor administrator. As a result the quality of court administration swung from good to bad depending upon the judge elected. The dynamics and the problems differed, of course, in the smaller multi-judge judicial districts around the state.

Trials in a trial court are conducted by a trial judge, not by a panel of judges as in an appellate court. Trial procedure is controlled by applicable state law, decisions of the Oregon appellate courts, and by local rules adopted by the trial judges in a judicial district. As one would expect, in a court of thirteen judges there was a variety of interest, energy, temperament, experience and competence. Some judges were inclined to deal with cases and policy entirely from an individual perspective. Some were collegial judges inclined to view cases and policy from a system perspective. Others were difficult to classify. With rare exceptions they maintained civil relations with each other irrespective of disagreement over court affairs.

The late 1960s and 1970s brought many new factors to bear on the way in which trial courts dealt with criminal cases and criminal defendants. A succession of United States Supreme Court decisions commencing in the nineteen-thirties with *Powell v. Alabama* had imposed substantial due process requirements upon the state courts, including the provision of counsel to all indigents charged with crimes which might result in imprisonment, advising persons arrested of their right to counsel and the exclusion of evidence obtained illegally. In addition, the "Great Society" programs inaugurated by the Johnson Administration produced a number of federally funded programs designed to deal with drugs, alcohol, and various aspects of criminal behavior. This combination of procedural reforms and remedial effort made for a period of great change and considerable instability in the court system.

*

My first several years on the bench were a concentrated learning experience. Judges Robert E. Jones, James Burns, Charles S. Crookham, Clifford B. Olsen and William Dale were close at hand and they were always available for advice. Sentencing criminal defendants under the wide range of discretion then provided by statute was a particular problem. Judge Burns, who was later appointed to the United States District Court, organized two "sentencing institutes" for circuit court judges which opened my eyes to the extent to which judges considering the same facts could and did arrive at widely different sentences. Presentence reports prepared by state probation officers were used in less than half the felony cases. Some judges rarely called for them.

Judge Robert E. Jones obtained a grant to fund an experimental program in which psychological presentence reports were prepared by a staff consisting of an experienced psychologist and an experienced probation officer. Jones, Crookham and I used this staff to prepare presentence reports on young, dangerous offenders. Each of us prepared a tentative sentence in accordance with the report we received and then reviewed the proposed sentence with the two other members of our panel before imposing sentence. We continued this useful practice for several years until the increased volume of cases made it impracticable.

I soon discovered that changes in one part of the criminal justice system could produce surprising effects in other parts of the system. For example, a federal grant which provided the Portland Police Department with two additional police officers and vehicles to deal with drunken driving, in a very short time swamped our criminal docket with DUII cases. Changes in police arrest policy and prosecutorial decisions in the district attorney's office created significant shifts in the number and kind of cases which reached the circuit court for trial.

During my second year on the court, our docket became glutted with drug cases, and the court decided to clear them in an expedited manner. Two judges were assigned exclusively to hear drug cases. Each judge tried the cases assigned to him one after another, starting at eight in the morning and going on until ten in the evening. When the jury retired to deliberate in one case we started picking the jury in the next case.

The prevailing use of marijuana, the possession of which in any quantity was a class B felony at that time, triggered many of these trials and rapidly expanded the law of search and seizure. In one trial the arresting police officer testified that he had stopped an automobile driven by some youths for a minor traffic infraction. It was night time. The officer testified that he happened to turn his flashlight on the floor of the vehicle. There he saw one marijuana seed. Having seen this, he searched the vehicle and passengers and discovered the defendant had some marijuana in a pocket.

"You mean to tell me you saw one seed on the floor of a car at night?" I inquired.

"I did. I am an expert on drugs and marijuana seeds."

I listened to this testimony, and I was startled, but I accepted that if the officer said he could, he must be correct.

Several days later in another drug case involving a car stopped at night, the same officer testified that he had seen another marijuana seed on the floor of a vehicle. I questioned him again. He went through the same routine. This time I pursued the matter. What was the floor covered with? How large was the seed? What was the color of the floor covering?

We adjourned for dinner, and I advised the Deputy District Attorney, Mike Schrunk, that I wanted the officer back on the stand that evening. Schrunk so instructed the officer. Mike told me later that the officer was infuriated because his testimony had been questioned. The officer failed to report back that evening, and I dismissed the case. Had I been more experienced, I would have had the officer brought before me to show cause why he should not be held in contempt. His testimony was crucial. There was no legal basis for the search unless he had seen evidence of the presence of drugs in plain view in the course of a routine traffic stop. I was not convinced there was one seed in plain view on that floor, or that one could have been seen under the circumstances.

The practice of assigning drug cases to a special panel and trying them one after another into the late evening is a short term expedient and does temporarily clear a chronically overloaded docket, but it is an expedient to which courts resort only when memory of the previous experience has dimmed.

*

In 1973 the judges concluded that the increased volume of criminal cases made it impossible for the presiding judge to handle preliminary criminal matters and pleas. The court established by rule a chief criminal court to handle all matters relating to criminal cases prior to trial. Judge Robert E. Jones was primarily responsible for setting up the court and served as the first chief criminal judge for some months. In the course of his tenure in the post, he managed to get the average time from arrest to trial reduced from more than one year to less than sixty days.

I followed R. E. Jones as chief criminal judge some months later, and concluded that we had better develop rules for the chief criminal court to insure that the judges who we planned to rotate every three months handled the criminal docket with consistency. I appointed a committee consisting of Mike Schrunk, the chief deputy district attorney and James D. Hennings, the Public Defender, and myself. We proposed rules of procedure in a lengthy report which the court adopted, and this made a substantial improvement in the uniformity with which criminal cases were handled. Despite these rules the length of the criminal docket still fluctuated, depending upon the attitude of the current chief criminal judge toward set-overs.

One judge in particular always managed to have an arrest-to-trial average lower than anyone else for his three month stint, but those who followed him had to struggle with the many older criminal cases set over which created for the following judge a far longer average time from arrest to trial. The arrest-to-trial-average was calculated by averaging the time from arrest to trial of each case tried during the month. This particular judge granted set-overs freely in the more complicated cases and sent out to trial the simple ones. His average time was very low but he left behind a trail of set-over cases which skewed the record for the judges who followed.

During this period William Dale and Clifford B. Olsen served as presiding judges, and under their management the court reduced the civil docket to an average of nine months from filing to trial. These civil dockets were probably the best in the United States for urban court systems. As the years passed, however, the increase in criminal cases and civil litigation put both civil and criminal dockets under pressure and both began to lengthen. The causes were many and diverse. The population was growing, and the crime rate was increasing above and beyond the proportionate population increase. This led to a marked growth in criminal arrests and criminal trials. Special funding for arrest and prosecution of DUII and drug cases led to additional increases in these categories of the criminal docket. Criminal procedures, both pretrial and trial, took longer due to additional procedural due process requirements imposed by constitutional decisions of the state and federal courts.

The civil docket also changed in composition, with the percentage of simple tort cases falling and the number of complex civil actions requiring lengthy pretrial and trial procedures increasing. Both the courts and the legislature expanded civil remedies, creating new procedures and new causes of action. The number of lawyers per thousand of population doubled between 1970 and 1980, and increased by 61% between 1980 and 1990. These lawyers were better educated, and more litigious. Moreover, the legal culture had evolved a more exacting and expensive way of handling litigation. The process of pretrial discovery became lengthy and complex. No stone was left unturned. Expert witnesses multiplied in every category of human endeavor. This expansion in litigation was complicated by the evolution of malpractice litigation and a resultant tendency to exhaust all possible lines of inquiry. Finally, another factor more difficult to quantify emerged: the technological advance from the typewriter to the computer, and from carbon paper to the high speed copy machine.

The result was more litigation involving more attorneys producing many times the amount of paper and taking substantially more court time. If we assume that a multi—judge court can dispose of 1000 cases in year one, and that it is then faced with 1400 cases in year two, there are only two ways it can deal with the increased volume: the court can become 29% more efficient, or it can take 40% longer than one year to dispose of the cases. Why? Because the number of judges can be changed only by act of the state legislature creating more judicial positions or authorizing funds to pay for additional judges pro tempore. The number of courtrooms can be increased only by county commissions appropriating additional funds to construct and staff additional courtrooms. Thus at any given time, a court is sharply limited in the way it can respond to significant increase in the number of civil and criminal cases.

Courts are organized to function on an eight-hour day. Generally, a judge's staff arrives at 8:30 AM. I cite my own practice as an example. I took the bench at 9:00 AM to hear short matters relating to probation or sentencing until 9:30 AM. Then I commenced or continued a trial to 12:00. I recessed for lunch until 1:00 PM, heard probation matters or sentenced until 1:30 PM, then continued trial to 5:00 PM, when we adjourned for the day. On occasion I varied this routine to meet special circumstances. If the testimony of a witness could be completed by running a few minutes later we did. If no short matters were set in the morning or afternoon, the trial could be started early. But this was the general schedule.

I also had to do research on occasion, to review files, and to write opinions. Generally I could handle these matters as gaps developed in the cases assigned to me. These gaps occurred when a case suddenly settled, or when a case finished earlier in the day. On some occasions it was necessary to take a day or more to deal with a complex matter taken under advisement. It was not, and is not, feasible to run a court with a single staff and a single judge on a regular basis longer than an eight-hour day. Indeed, state law would not permit it on a regular basis so far as the court staff is concerned, even were it feasible. Finally, judges must allow sufficient time and opportunity to lawyers appearing before them to pursue their client's procedural rights provided by law. It is reversible error to fail to do so. Reversal and retrial are the ultimate inefficiency to be avoided wherever possible.

Within this working framework of the court system there are real differences between judges. Some are more effective in moving cases along. Some spend substantially more time in legal research than others. Some hold lawyers on a shorter leash when it comes to argument or questioning witnesses. Some have a talent for shortening matters. Some are more effective than others in encouraging settlement. A presiding judge who knows how to use his judicial resources can minimize these differences by assigning the variety of cases to the judges best suited to handle them. Beyond this, efficiency depends on the inherent capacity of each elected judge working within a system controlled by statute and case law. In the end, no matter how efficient a court, its capacity to handle increases in work load is sharply limited. More civil and criminal litigation requires more judges, staff and physical facilities.

By the 1970s the Oregon counties under the financial pressure of inflation resisted providing the courts with additional staff and additional courtrooms. They were also increasingly resistant to paying lawyers for the indigent defendants who constitute 95% of the persons charged with crime. These financial pressures led the Association of Oregon Counties to vigorously support state assumption of funding of the trial courts when this was proposed several years later.

*

The most noteworthy event in public life in 1973 was the Watergate burglary of the Democratic Party offices in Washington, a burglary instigated by some Republican Party officials. Watergate began as a minor affair, however, the Attorney General, John Mitchell, and a number of White House aides, with the approval of President Nixon, attempted to cover up the burglary and the affair exploded into a political maelstrom. Coincidentally, Vice President Spiro Agnew was charged with unrelated offenses committed before assuming office and resigned. The whole Watergate matter unraveled before our eyes on television. President Nixon was impeached by the House and, facing trial by the Senate, resigned. Clissa and I and Claire and Forest Amsden were on our boats at Hood River plugged into shore power with a small TV set going as the final stages of the drama were played out.

I was raised in an atmosphere of innocence. My mother and father stressed the importance of truthfulness. They rarely criticized other people and never said or implied that political figures with whose policies they disagreed were scoundrels. Cheating in a grammar school with only 120 students was unknown. I was aware of little in high school. Princeton had the honor system, and in my day it was in full force. Such violations as there may have been were entirely concealed. Our examinations were not monitored. I neither saw nor heard of any violations. Somehow, I wandered into adulthood reasonably well educated with a basic confidence that most people followed the rules and told the truth, particularly high government officials. I was shocked when President Eisenhower admitted that he and his administration lied when they denied U 2 flights over the Soviet Union. Of course I did not expect presidents to tell us everything, but when they made official statements I expected them to be truthful.

In the Watergate affair President Nixon and Attorney General John Mitchell lied in their attempt to cover up the crime and completed my education. It had taken me a long time to accept the fact that people will lie where truth is disadvantageous to them if they think they can get away with it. President Clinton's public and private denials with respect to his relations with Monica Lewinsky made impeachment by his political adversaries inevitable, and while the Senate failed to convict him, his presidency and the Democratic Party were severely damaged. The incident almost certainly cost Vice President Gore the election in 2000. The second Bush administration's lies and misrepresentations with respect to its policies and actions in Iraq have probably cost it more loss of support than the policies and acts themselves.

Character in friends, colleagues, and politicians is important, and so is a sense for whether and under what circumstances men and women can be relied upon. Idealism needs to be balanced with healthy skepticism.

CHAPTER 18

The Governor's Task Force and the Judicial Conference

During my first three years on the circuit court I had the advantage of seeing how Judges R. E. Jones, Cliff Olsen, Charles Crookham, Bill Dale, Jim Burns and, later, R. P. Jones handled their dockets and described their views of the judicial and criminal justice system in which we were immersed. It seemed to me that the chief problem with the trial court system was the weakness of administration. I have already mentioned the difficulty inherent in election of the presiding judges. Most judges agreed that a competent presiding judge was desirable. Not all agreed on what constituted efficiency, and not many viewed election of a presiding judge as a defect. Judges tend to be conservative and, like most of us, are inclined to resist changing the system in which they are principal actors.

A conservatism is a natural consequence of the calling. Our business is to interpret the law, applying statutes and past decisions of our appellate courts to the facts of particular civil and criminal cases. Generally speaking, it is not the business of trial judges to conduct experiments, launch crusades or reform human affairs save insofar as their interpretation of statute or precedent coincidentally produces such a result. Moreover, the fact that trial judges are independently elected and independently carry out their judicial functions tends to accentuate an individual rather than a collegial view of the system in which they work.

Nevertheless, as some trial judges suggested, the way in which Oregon judges imposed criminal penalties was a process which lacked precision, rationality and predictability. Within the very broad range of penalties provided by statute for each offense, the imposition of sentence was intuitive, subjective and individual. There were significant variations in sentencing from judge to judge on the same court, significant variations in sentencing from one judicial district to another, and significant variations in sentencing from year to year. We had in place a menu of treatment programs initiated under the Johnson administration, few of which were available to all judges in the state. These programs were rarely subjected to hard professional evaluation. Our prisons, the ultimate sanction, were essentially warehouses and appeared to be largely ineffective in changing the behavior of those persons imprisoned.

A second problem lay in the fragmented structure of the criminal justice system itself. The state paid the judges. The counties provided the court rooms and paid the salaries of the men and women who staffed the trial courts. The police were paid by the cities, the sheriffs were county officials, the jails were run by the cities and counties. The state operated the prisons. The parole board was appointed by the governor while its probation officers were employed by the state corrections division. The legislature enacted the laws which imposed these various duties and responsibilities. The initiative process lurked in the background, a political monkey wrench that could be thrown into the system at any time. There was no unified direction, no coordinating center where all these elements could meet, discuss and recommend, much less ensure, they would work smoothly together. Meanwhile, crime was increasing, civil dockets were under increasing pressure and state prisons were over capacity.

Legislative interim committees of the House and Senate considered some of these problems from time to time, but their work was uneven, sporadic and frequently based on inadequate information. The consequence was that legislation dealing with both the judiciary and the criminal justice system tended to be patchwork designed to shore up those parts of the system caught in the legislative spotlight with untested and frequently inadequate remedies.

There was, however, one body, the Judicial Conference, which had the potential for a common focus upon systemic problems, provided life could be pumped into it. The Oregon Judicial Conference was and is a statutory body consisting of all the state court judges. The chief justice is the chair of the Conference, and the affairs of the Conference are managed by an executive committee of judges from the several courts. The Judicial Conference is required to meet once a year for three days to conduct business and educational programs, and it can be called to meet on special occasions by the chief justice. Conference committees appointed by the chief justice met "as necessary". The Judicial Conference was a mechanism waiting to be used.

In 1972 Chief Justice Kenneth O'Connell had appointed me as the Conference liaison representative to the Judicial Reform Commission, a body created by the legislature to study and recommend improvements in the judiciary. So far as I recall, this was the first public attempt to study the role of the judiciary in the state. No significant legislative proposals resulted. In 1973 the chief justice had a bill introduced in the legislative session which would give the Supreme Court procedural rule-making authority over the trial courts. Most state supreme courts exercise rule-making as inherent in the judicial power, but in Oregon the legislature had always legislated procedural rules, heavily influenced by trial lawyers and the insurance bar. The result was a scramble of procedural statutes.

The chief justice proposed to the 1973 Judicial Conference that it support the rule-making bill. Rule-making was strongly opposed by some members of the trial bar who feared their clients' interest might be adversely affected by procedural changes promulgated by the supreme court. Oregon lawyers at that time were peculiarly sensitive to the kind of judicial authoritarianism practiced by United District Court Judges James Alger Fee and Gus J. Solomon. Lawyers thought of rule-making as a slippery slope toward federal judicial authoritarianism. This apprehension was shared by many of the state trial judges, some because of their background as trial lawyers. Other trial judges opposed any increase in administrative authority over trial courts as a threat to their independence.

The chief justice's proposal was roundly voted down by the Conference. To see what could be salvaged, I moved that the Conference study alternative ways to deal with rule-making and do this in a joint study with the Oregon State Bar. To my surprise the motion passed without objection. In the way that such things often happen, the chief justice, grateful for any hope of salvaging his proposal, appointed me chair of a Conference committee to do the study. I added to the committee an equal number of members from the bar. Technically, the bar members could not be voting members of a statutory conference committee, but we treated them as though they were voting members anyhow. The joint committee subsequently proposed establishment of a statutory Council on Court Procedures empowered to propose changes in civil procedure, which would take effect following the next legislative session if not amended or repealed in that session. The measure failed in 1975, but was reintroduced and passed in 1977.

The Council on Court Procedures functioned reasonably well and eliminated most, if not all, special interest deadlocks, and it largely eliminated legislative forays into the field of civil procedure. It was certainly more cumbersome than rule-making by the Supreme Court, but it was a substantial improvement over direct legislative rule making.

*

Congress during the Johnson Administration had begun providing funds to the states to improve their criminal justice systems. The legislation required each state to create a representative body to allocate the funds in accordance with the purposes of Congress. The Oregon Legislature in response established the Law Enforcement Council with a membership appointed by the governor and serving at his pleasure. The Council published a report in 1974 with several major recommendations concerning the judicial process, despite the fact that the Council had no representative of the judiciary among its members and no judicial input into its deliberations. This struck me as an unrealistic and potentially hazardous way to deal with the courts.

I wrote Governor McCall, calling his attention to the absence of judicial representation and suggesting that the Council should not be make far-reaching proposals for changing the judicial process without hearing the views of the judiciary. The governor replied, saying that he agreed and appointed me to the Council. For the balance of the governor's second term I sat on the Council and provided at least one trial judge's viewpoint. Senator Arthur Vandenberg once said, referring to foreign policy, that he preferred to be consulted on the takeoff rather than after the crash landing, and the analogy is sound. It is a good deal easier to affect policy while it is being made than to change it after it has been adopted. The Law Enforcement Council, cumbersome and subservient to the executive branch as it was, at least brought most of the players in the criminal justice system to a crude policy table for discussion. It was a start.

When Bob Straub succeeded Tom McCall as governor in January 1975, he vacated all appointments to the Law Enforcement Council, then re-appointed some old members and designated other new members. Again, no member of the judiciary was appointed. I wrote the governor saying that while I appreciated that who he appointed was entirely up to him, I thought it essential that the judiciary be represented. I had a cryptic response from Keith Burns, his staff attorney, saying that the governor acknowledged my letter but had some alternative in mind. Shortly afterward the governor established by executive order The Governor's Task Force on Corrections, naming Edward J. Sullivan, a Portland attorney, his legal counsel, as chair. I was appointed as a member of the Task Force. The governor charged the Task Force with responsibility for dealing with prison overcrowding and developing a twenty-five year plan for the corrections system.

The Task Force worked steadily for the next year and a half to develop a broad series of proposals to improve the criminal justice system. Ed Sullivan was an intelligent and energetic chairman and a pleasure to work with. He had a clear idea of the route he wanted the committee to follow, and this enabled us to progress rapidly and clash vigorously on occasion. He created three subcommittees. Subcommittee one, which I chaired, was charged to examine the criminal justice system from arrest through sentence. Subcommittee two, chaired by Gene Pfeiffer, a probation officer, dealt with community corrections, parole and probation. Subcommittee three, chaired by Senator Fred Heard, dealt with the Parole Board and state correctional institutions.

I added to my subcommittee four non-voting "associate members" to expand our range of experience: Jeffrey Mutnick, a public defender, Mike Shrunk, the Multnomah County District Attorney, Dr. David A. Myers, a clinical psychologist, and Dr. Edward M. Colbach, a psychiatrist. This device of appointing non-voting members proved very useful on the Task Force and in later committees and commissions. Subcommittee one developed a series of statutory proposals for the Task Force: creation of a psychiatric security review board to handle persons found not guilty because of mental disease or defect; mandatory presentence reports in all felony cases; judicial authority to order restitution from sentenced offenders; judicial authority to impose a mandatory minimum sentence up to one-half the sentence authorized by law, subject to overrule by unanimous vote of the Parole Board; and creation of a Criminal Justice Council to replace the Law Enforcement Council with independent legislative and judicial representatives in addition to members appointed by the governor.

*

The proposed Psychiatric Security Review Board deserves more extended comment because it illustrates an acute problem and an effective solution. Under then-existing law, an offender found not guilty (later guilty but not responsible) for a crime by reason of mental disease or defect (NGI) could be committed to the Oregon State Hospital if the trial judge found him a danger to himself or others by reason of the disease or defect. At the hospital the offender was medicated until the doctors felt he was harmless and then was discharged as no longer a threat. Jurisdiction of the court terminated with release of the offender by the hospital. Such persons, once discharged, rarely continued their medication and soon became as disturbed as they were before hospitalization. Not infrequently, they again committed serious crimes against other persons.

To make matters worse, in the 1973 session, state hospital authorities, unbeknownst to the judges, had quietly lobbied through an amendment to the mental health statute which prevented a judge from requiring state mental health clinics to examine or treat criminal offenders unless the judge paid for such examination or treatment. Judges, of course, had no funds to pay such state clinics and this legislation effectively eliminated professional mental health supervision of probationers who badly needed it.

Our proposed legislation provided that "NGI" offenders committed to the Oregon State Hospital be placed in custody of a psychiatric security review board, which would retain custody of offenders for the maximum length of time for which they could have been sentenced had they been found responsible for their crime, whether their disease was active or in remission. The legislation allowed release when the board found their disease or defect in remission, subject to conditions of supervision, and subject to return to the hospital for any violation of condition or deterioration of their mental status. The legislation specified that one member of the board should be a lawyer experienced in criminal practice, one a member experienced in parole and probation, one a psychologist or psychiatrist experienced in the criminal justice system, and two public members. The legislation also provided funds for supervision and continued treatment.

This legislation was enacted in 1977 and has proved to be highly successful in maintaining control and supervision of this kind of criminal defendant. One of its chief benefits is that it removed from state hospital authorities the power to decide whether a person should be continued in hospital or released. Generally speaking, state hospital physicians did not appreciate being custodian of persons they regarded as criminals, particularly when it resulted in overcrowding their facility. The fact that the decision was made by a board and not by those responsible for the treatment and custodial care improved the reliability of the decision significantly.

The governor appointed public defender Jeffrey Mutnick to the first Psychiatric Security Review Board, and he did yeoman's service in getting it organized. My neighbor, Lois Miller, a former nurse, was appointed to one of the public member slots and worked diligently for two terms on the board. Subsequently Portland lawyer, later Portland city attorney, Jeffrey L. Rogers replaced Mutnick and served on the board for a number of years, carefully documenting its work and publishing articles on the subject in national magazines.

*

The Task Force proposed legislation establishing community corrections in counties which accepted the plan. The Community Corrections bill provided funds to participating counties to handle parole and probation services on the theory that more class C felons could be handled in local jails and under local supervision if county authorities were given additional correctional services and programs. I expressed reservations in a concurring report concerning the devolution of these services to counties because I saw this devolution as further fragmenting the corrections system.

The Task Force proposed that the Parole Board develop and adopt a parole matrix based on objective criteria to determine how long each committed offender would serve under the sentence imposed by the sentencing judge, subject to the limitation of any mandatory minimum sentence, and subject to existing law provisions relating to good time and work credit. This legislation was intended to codify a process already undertaken by members of the Parole Board in an effort to even out the imposition of disparate sentences and to identify offenders who should be imprisoned longer. The Task Force also proposed that certain offenders charged with non-violent crime be diverted into remedial programs with trials suspended pending successful completion of a diversion program, upon which their cases would be dismissed.

I opposed pretrial diversion. I thought it was too loose an arrangement to be effective. By the time an offender failed to complete his diversion program and was apprehended, witnesses would be gone and successful prosecution would be unlikely. I was outvoted. The discretionary mandatory minimum judicial sentence proposed by my subcommittee was adopted by the task force with some dissent and went on to stormy consideration in the legislature.

In retrospect, I think the Task Force report, as it went to the legislature, was a realistic document, the first comprehensive attempt to come to grips with the problems of Oregon's criminal justice system. Governor Straub followed its progress with interest and support. The work of the Task Force set the stage for the sentencing guideline legislation a decade later. Ed Sullivan, the chair, deserved a great deal of credit for his management of the committee and for his resourceful and cooperative maneuvering of its recommendations through the 1977 Session of the legislature.

*

In April of 1976, Judge Robert E. Jones was invited to address a Vermont Citizens' Conference on the Courts. He was unable to accept but suggested me as an alternate speaker, and I accepted. The Vermont judiciary at that time was conservative, to say the least. I discovered, among other things, that their jurors were not permitted to make notes of any testimony. Several of the Vermont judges were shocked to learn that I always sent the jury a written copy of the oral instructions I had given them. I found this practice helped juries to focus on the issues of fact they were to decide and the instructions on the law they were to apply.

Many of my Oregon colleagues were not convinced that this was a good idea. They feared it would delay trial if instructions had to be typed. I kept several large notebooks with copies of all the standard instructions indexed. Generally only a handful of instructions had to be specially typed for a particular case, and these I would write in the course of the trial during final argument, and give them to my secretary to type. She would then have them ready for me to use when the argument was completed. Some lawyers objected to this practice, saying that the jurors might concentrate on one instruction to the exclusion of others. My response to this was that jurors had no way to accurately recall a series of instructions on complicated questions which they had received orally. I suspect that most lawyers who opposed written instructions wanted jurors to attend to the catch phrases which caught their ear in oral argument. They did not want written instructions from the judge which would remind jurors of the applicable law.

Chief Justice Arno Denecke, when a trial judge, had initiated the practice of tape recording his instructions and would send the tape to the jury if they requested it during their deliberations. This practice eventually spread. I remain of the belief that a verbatim copy of the instructions is much more likely to be used and be more useful than a tape, which has to be played and replayed in order to reach a particular instruction the judge has given.

My assignment at the Vermont conference, however, was to speak of the judge's role in sentencing. I described the criminal justice system as it existed in Oregon and many other states pointing out that the broadly discretionary sentencing then in vogue was largely intuitive and subjective. I argued for a shift to diagnostic sentencing based on pre sentence reports with psychological or psychiatric evaluation in serious cases as a more rational and effective way of making these decisions.

*

When Chief Justice Kenneth J. O'Connell retired in 1976, Judge Arno Denecke was elected chief Justice by the court, a position which he held until his retirement in 1982. The new chief then appointed me chairman of the legislative committee of the Judicial Conference. At the spring meeting of the Conference in 1976, I gave a detailed report on the work in progress of the three separate committees then considering the criminal justice system: the Legislative Interim Committee on the Judiciary, the Mental Health Committee on which Judge Val Sloper and I served, and the Governor's Task Force on Corrections on which I also served. I suggested that three committees to deal with the same subject matter made no sense. We had tried to solve the coordination problem with overlapping membership without much success. Yet the proposals of each of these committees dealt with jail and prison crowding, how to handle the insanity defense, and would alter the sentencing process. I concluded,

"We do not have to run this system without any organized instruments of coordination between branches of government and between the levels of government responsible for the different segments of the system. We do not have to run this system without any long range planning for the future. We do not have to run this system without any organized research capability to evaluate what we are doing or to even tell us what we are doing. Put in terms Snoopy would use, we have to make this dog house fly, but we don't have to fly it by the seat of our pants."

I described the Task Force proposal to replace the Law Enforcement Council with a statutory criminal justice council which would include representatives of all three branches of government at state and local levels responsible for segments of the system. I argued that the council should be adequately staffed and held responsible for research, evaluation and long range planning. I concluded

> "If this approach is followed, the system will have a reasonable degree of coordination, a built-in capacity for intelligent change, and a built-in brake on hair-brained proposals. Even more important, the judiciary will have a built-in voice at the legislative and administrative discussion of common problems—a position which we have never had in the past."

Both Chief Justice Denecke and Court of Appeals Chief Judge Schwab were agreed on the necessity of this shift in approach. They recognized that the trial and appellate judges across the state needed to consider a more active relationship with the legislative and executive branches than the passive, arms length role to which they were historically accustomed.

*

When the chief justice asked me to chair the Conference legislative committee, I told him I thought the legislation being drafted by the Governor's Task Force would have so extensive a potential effect on the judiciary that we should have a committee chosen from judges relatively close to Salem and a regular presence at judiciary committee hearings. I thought we could divide up the task of appearing before committees among members of the legislative committee. I also pointed out that I needed to be relieved of trial duties so that I could spend a good deal of time on the job of monitoring legislation and running the committee. He agreed and said he would arrange pro tem assistance for Multnomah County to replace me as needed. Judge Schwab gave me the big table in the corner of his office in the Justice Center to use as a work center. Both he and the chief justice gave me the run of their offices when I was in Salem and immediate response any time I needed assistance, advice or discussion with them.

With this arrangement in mind, the chief justice appointed to the Conference legislative committee the following:

> Justice Ralph M. Holman
> Chief Judge Herbert M. Schwab
> Circuit Judge Jean L. Lewis
> Circuit Judge Albin W. Norblad
> District Judge George F. Cole
> District Judge Robert M. Stults
> Circuit Judge Richard J. Unis
> District Judge Donald R. Blensley
> Circuit Judge John C. Beatty, Jr. Chair

The chief justice usually sat as an ex-officio member of the committee, and Loren Hicks, the state court administrator, frequently joined us. When the 1977 legislative session began the committee met weekly for lunch in the cafeteria in the basement of the Justice Building. I prepared for each meeting an analysis of bills affecting our operations and recommendations as to whether we should support, oppose, take no position or offer comment. Under the Conference statute, the Conference executive committee spoke for the Conference between annual sessions. The legislative committee spoke for the Conference within the range of authority granted to it by the executive committee.

It soon became apparent that this arrangement could only work if I acted as a full-time legislative representative of the Conference during legislative sessions, because it was impossible for my colleagues on the committee coming from smaller courts to adjust their schedules so they could spend full days at the legislature. So we quickly settled into a routine in which I drafted and proposed positions for the Conference. The legislative committee discussed these drafts and reached a decision. I then presented their conclusions to the Conference executive committee at its monthly sessions, or at special sessions when necessary. As the minutes of those meetings show, that body also carefully reviewed those conclusions and determined the positions I would take on behalf of the Conference.

At the annual meeting of the Judicial Conference in April, 1977, I reviewed proposed legislation bill-by-bill, setting forth the positions taken by the executive committee on its behalf. I also made recommendations on further positions for the Conference during the balance of the session. In this manner the Conference took a formal vote on nearly all matters of significance affecting the judiciary, including the criminal justice system. Thus the house and senate judiciary committees had the Conference views before them as they considered measures affecting the judiciary and the criminal justice system. This proved to be an effective way of working with the legislature's committees which developed a sense that the positions I reported and the observations I made reflected the views of the judiciary expressed through an orderly process.

Even more importantly, this procedure brought the entire membership of the judiciary into a collective examination of a variety of matters affecting the organization and functioning of the judicial and criminal justice system. The process coupled representative leadership with reporting back to the membership. Despite frequent disagreement among judges with respect to particular positions, I think most judges felt the process was as fair and collaborative as possible.

CHAPTER 19

House Judiciary, the 1977 and 1979 Legislative Sessions

When the 1977 Session of the Oregon Legislature opened, the legislation proposed by the Governor's Task Force on Corrections and most other measures affecting the courts were introduced in the House and referred to House Judiciary. The 1977 Session had one of the best, and perhaps the best, judiciary committees the Oregon legislature has had during the last hundred years. Hardy Myers was the chairman, fair, thoughtful, keenly intelligent, mindful of the public interest, a future speaker of the house and future attorney general. The vice chair was Mark Gardner, a future circuit judge. Other members included David Frohnmayer, future attorney general, and president of the University of Oregon; Ted Kulongowski, future attorney general, supreme court judge and governor; Earl Blumenauer, future Multnomah County commissioner, Portland city commissioner, and Congressman from the Third Congressional District; Ted Bugas, a conscientious non-lawyer from Astoria; Ben Lombard and Bill Rutherford, both able lawyers; and Sandy Richards, another non-lawyer whose skeptical view of lawyers and judges supplied a valuable caustic screen.

My routine during the three sessions which I covered as legislative chairman of the Judicial Conference was to take half-day cases and motions during the mornings early in the session. As hearings on bills affecting the judiciary became

349

frequent, I shifted to work in chambers during the mornings, doing research and preparing memoranda for the committees for which my judicial assistant, Susan Rommel, typed and then Xeroxed the required number of copies. In late morning I drove down to Salem in time for the House Judiciary hearings usually set at 1:00 or 1:30 PM. Senate Judiciary hearings were scheduled for mid afternoon, generally started late and always ran late. Hearings in Ways and Means subcommittees started at 8:00 AM on time, which meant getting an early start when I had a bill on its agenda.

The 1977 session of regular commuting to Salem convinced me that neither the Court of Appeals nor the Supreme Court were sufficiently attractive to persuade me to seek appointment to those courts. Jonathan Newman, George Joseph, and John Buttler all commuted to Salem from Portland for their entire judicial careers. How they managed it physically and mentally is beyond me. It must have bitten deeply into time with their families. On one occasion in the spring of 1977, Judge Ralph Holman asked me if I would consider an appointment to the supreme court. He said he would be retiring sometime soon and "had an urge to leave his position to someone who cared." I told him it just wasn't practical. Clissa already had to drive 30 minutes to the Primate Center. She couldn't commute from Salem, and I didn't think I could commute from Portland. Had I gone on the circuit court in 1958 or 1961 with one of Hatfield's first appointments and later had a shot at a supreme court seat, I would have taken it, dealing with the commuting problem by moving to Charbonneau. This would have meant a half hour commute for me and a three quarter hour commute for Clissa. Workable in our forties but not interesting in our late fifties.

*

During the spring of 1977 the Multnomah County Circuit Judges had their biennial election for presiding judge. Cliff Olsen, Bill Dale, and Robert E. Jones, all of whom had previously served as presiding judge, encouraged me to run. I declined. I could not handle both the legislative chairmanship and the presiding judge position. Moreover, I did not want the position for two additional reasons. First, the position lacked the power to run the court as I thought it ought to be run; second, I much preferred conducting trials to hearing preliminary motions. Judge Roth was running again and had solicited commitments from a number of judges months in advance. Several of us persuaded Charles Crookham to run. The vote was tied. They tossed a coin and Judge Roth won.

The political potential of the role of presiding judge regularly came to the surface. At a critical point in the 1977 session Judge Roth sent me a note saying that as presiding judge he could not afford to have me in Salem, and he was assigning cases to me. I sent him a note in return saying that I was serving in Salem by order of the chief justice, and if he wanted that order altered he should consult the chief justice. I heard no more from him at that time, though the conflict surfaced later during hearings over additional judicial positions.

The Multnomah Country circuit court had a rule barring a presiding judge from election to a successive term, a legacy from the revolt against Judge Charles Redding's long and productive tenure. Charles Crookham was elected in 1979 to succeed Phil Roth, and when the election of 1981 approached R. E. Jones and Charles Crookham discussed the forthcoming election with me at lunch. I was then involved with the Commission on the Judicial Branch and with the Conference legislative program. Jones and Crookham said Judge Roth was once again a candidate. Judge Dale was reluctant to run and would run only if Judge Roth ran. Judge Crookham opined that he would "reluctantly run", but could only do so if the rule against successive terms was changed.

I sent a memo to the members of the court saying that I would run for election as presiding judge but would withdraw and nominate Crookham if the court voted to eliminate the single term rule. Charles Crookham had been an excellent presiding judge and enjoyed the position. The prospect of me as presiding judge certainly moved some reluctant members of the court to abandon the single term rule, and Charles was reelected and continued to serve as an effective presiding judge for many years until his retirement.

*

In discussing the progress of legislation dealing with the courts and the criminal justice system, one needs to keep in mind the broad outline of the judicial and criminal justice system we had in place in 1977. Appellate judges, trial judges and district attorneys were employed by the state. The physical facilities for trial judges, their offices and courtrooms and all support personnel, including secretaries, bailiffs, guards and assistant district attorneys were the responsibility of the counties. Prisons, corrections officers, the State Board of Parole and parole officers were a state responsibility. Sheriffs, deputies and county jails were a county responsibility. City jails and the police were a city responsibility. The absence of any coordinating mechanism among these different branches and levels of government was remarkable.

With respect to sentencing, state law established three classes of felonies below murder. Class A felonies were punishable by imprisonment up to twenty years, Class B up to ten years and Class C up to five years, imprisonment meaning incarceration in the State Penitentiary, subject to reduction for "good time" and "work credit." The sentencing judge could impose a sentence for any amount of time up to the legislative maximum. When the offender had committed more than one offense or had already been convicted of a previous offense, the judge could, in his or her discretion, impose consecutive sentences of imprisonment. The judge was also given the discretion to suspend imposition or execution of sentence and place the offender on probation for a period up to five years. Probation meant supervision by the State Board of Parole, subject to such restrictive conditions as might be imposed by the judge.

With the imposition of a sentence of imprisonment, the offender was transferred to the custody of the State Corrections

Division and the Parole Board. The board had authority to release offenders at its discretion at any time, irrespective of the length of the judicial sentence. The result was that the length of imprisonment was determined not by the judge who sentenced, except as an upper limit, but by the Parole Board. The sentence actually served often bore little relation to the length of the sentence imposed.

This dichotomy created all sorts of mischief. Judges, as well as the public, were outraged when an offender sentenced to many years imprisonment was released after serving a few months in prison. Moreover, judges, given such a wide range of discretion, frequently imposed widely disparate sentences for the same offense upon offenders with comparable criminal histories. The history of criminal justice reform from 1975 to 1991 is primarily the story of a major effort to introduce rationality, consistency, predictability and accountability into this system. The Governors's Task Force concluded that the Parole Board should be required to adopt a parole matrix providing a systematic method for determining how its release decisions would be made. In fairness to the Parole Board, that body had been making efforts on its own part to adopt such a method by rule.

My subcommittee of the Governor's Task Force was dubious of vesting this entire power in the hands of the Parole Board which, after all, had not heard the evidence first hand. We proposed vesting in the sentencing judge the discretion to impose a mandatory sentence up to one half of the term provided by law for the crime, irrespective of good time and not subject to modification unless the Parole Board voted unanimously to override the judge's mandatory sentence. The subcommittee felt that this power would enable the sentencing judge in serious cases to impose a brake on the power of the Parole Board and, beyond this, give the Board an opportunity to hold particular offenders beyond the averages which any matrix would provide.

In the Task Force debate I held out for this particular judicial discretionary power, which was intended both to limit Parole

Board discretion in some cases and expand it in others. Ed
Sullivan was primarily concerned with Community Corrections
and the parole matrix. He argued our proposal would be
exercised by trial judges to warp the result he wanted to achieve
with the parole matrix.

The "Omnibus Corrections Bill," HB 2013, contained the
bulk of the Task Force proposals and was the vehicle through
which the struggle was waged over the respective powers of the
Parole Board and the judiciary. Ira Blalock, a Unitarian minister
and member of the Parole Board was the chief spokesman
for that body. Ed Sullivan spoke for both the Task Force and
the governor's office, and I spoke for the Judicial Conference.
Throughout the session we had a number of disagreements
and numerous conferences to negotiate compromises. Blalock
was pleasant, determined, indefatigable, and inclined to revisit
questions I thought we had clearly settled. I had the added
problem that I had to secure authority from the Conference
Executive Committee to approve the compromises to which I
had tentatively agreed. Chief Justice Denecke was extraordinarily
helpful in all this work, polling the Executive Committee by
telephone on a number of occasions while I was at the capitol
during a hearing.

The matrix proposal was modified by creating a Joint
Commission on Prison Terms and Parole Standards consisting
of the five parole board members and five circuit judges
appointed by the chief justice to establish and maintain the
parole board matrix. The concept, which was ours, had its
genesis in the Council on Court Procedures. Some legislators
were concerned that it would violate the separation of
powers because the Commission had both judicial and
executive department members. However, sentencing crimes
has traditionally been a function to some extent of all three
branches of government. In any event, we disposed of the
argument by converting the Commission to an advisory body.
As a practical matter we thought it would be a rare occasion
when the parole board members of the Joint Commission,
after working with the judges on the Commission, would fail

to follow the majority conclusion of the advisory body. This proved to be the case.

In April of 1977 a vacancy occurred in the United States District Court for the District of Oregon. Bill Dale mentioned that he and I were spoken of for the position. This was news to me. Bill told me he was interested, knew I was, and would say nothing adverse about me. I assured him I felt the same way. Later we both heard that Circuit Judge Helen Fry of Eugene was under consideration. In July Forest Amsden, who was in Washington at the time, telephoned me about the vacancy saying that if I were interested he would speak to both Oregon Senators and people at the White House where he had contacts. As I noted in my diary, at 58 this was a bit late to campaign for a federal appointment. Edith Green had retired two years previously, and I did not take the matter seriously. Ultimately Helen Frye was appointed by President Carter. Forest had also run into Roosevelt Grier in Washington and reported that Rosy remembered and spoke well of me.

As the Oregon House Judiciary subcommittee worked its way through the Omnibus Corrections bill and neared the end of its labors on April 29, Representative Richards moved to delete the section authorizing judicial mandatory minimum sentences. Representative Bugas agreed, saying they had adopted mandatory minimum sentences (referring to firearms bills) and they could get along without this provision. The question was called, and to my dismay the subcommittee voted 5 to 1 to delete it. I was then recognized by the chair and told the subcommittee that with this amendment the Judicial Conference could no longer support the omnibus bill.

Representative Richards said she couldn't understand why I would oppose it. Representative Kulongowski said he thought I was daring them to pull it out. I explained that the subcommittee had deleted a basic part of a carefully balanced way of dealing with sentencing. Kulongowski then moved to reconsider so the full committee could take it up the following Tuesday. Hardy

Myers commented this was a good idea, "before we have the judiciary and the legislature squaring off." The motion was adopted. Ed Sullivan and Ira Blalock, who had previously negotiated with me on the compromise language which had been stricken, assured me they had nothing to do with this move in the committee.

I reported what had taken place to the chief justice and the chief judge. They supported hanging tough. The following Tuesday, May 3, I delivered a formal statement of the Conference position to the full committee. Representative Gardner then moved to reinstate the section. After some further debate the full committee voted to reinstate the section. Ted Kulongowski later told me that we had switched three votes.

*

Harl Haas, then Multnomah County District Attorney, was testifying to House Judiciary on some bills relating to sentencing when I walked in and sat down behind him. Unaware I was in the room, Harl quoted me on several points and then said that as judges went I was one of the more satisfactory ones on sentencing. The committee and audience broke up in laughter.

The Judicial Conference had requested another judge for Multnomah County based on a substantial increase in case load, and consequent increase in our civil docket time. May 5, 1997 Senator Betty Roberts stopped me in the hall outside House Judiciary to tell me that earlier that morning Judge Alfred Sulmonetti had telephoned her to say that Multnomah County didn't need another judge. The problem was that we didn't run a proper docket, and he wanted to testify against the bill. Several hours later, she said, Judge Roth had telephoned her to ask if I was "cutting him up" by asking for another judge on the ground that he (Roth) was incompetent. Senator Roberts said she'd told Roth the story was utterly false, and asked where he had gottten that idea. Roth replied Judge Sulmonetti had told him Senator Roberts had said so. Senator Roberts wound up her account assuring me she had told Judge Roth that was also untrue. She assured me she would be happy to write every judge in Multnomah County and say so. I thanked her and assured her writing would not be necessary.

I telephoned Judge Roth who confirmed Senator Roberts' account of these conversations. I assured him I had said nothing critical of him to the committee in support of the bill. It would, of course, have been foolish of me to tell Ways and Means that we needed another judge because we had elected a presiding judge who was incompetent. This incident was the by-product of an old dispute in the Multnomah County Circuit Court. Judge Sulmonetti was a strong advocate of changing to individual dockets for our court. He was never able to convince me or a majority of our colleagues that this was desirable, or even possible, considering the volume of civil and criminal cases we handled. I had previously studied his proposal, concluded it was unworkable, and distributed a memorandum to that effect to the court.

When the bill for an additional judge came before the subcommittee of Ways and Means, chaired by Senator Roberts, Judge Sulmonetti appeared to oppose it, saying he did so only because he had been invited by Senator Roberts to appear. The burden of his testimony was that the civil docket had fallen behind because of a systemic defect and the reluctance of judges to change.

Judge Clifford B. Olsen, whom I had asked to appear representing the majority of the court, testified that the assignment system developed by Judge Charles Redding was outstanding. I testified that the Multnomah County civil docket in 1972 had averaged 8 months from filing to trial and was probably one of the most current urban courts in the United States. Since that time our criminal cases had increased 16%, and our civil cases had increased 24%. We were holding the criminal docket to a sixty day average from arrest to trial, but the civil docket was necessarily slipping. We were asking for an 8 % increase in judicial manpower to deal with it. Ways and Means approved the additional judge.

The Criminal Justice Council bill was opposed by Loren Cramer, the chair of the Law Enforcement Council appointed by Governor Straub. Loren argued that the bill was unnecessary because the Law Enforcement Council had added judicial members. Accordingly the bill was not introduced by the Task Force with the support of the governor but by two senators at the request of the Judicial Conference. I argued that the membership of the proposed council should be appointed by and represent the three branches of government involved if the council was to be more than a creature of the governor dependent on the extent of his interest in the criminal justice system. The bill failed to pass, and my effort to push this legislation remained dormant until 1985. Meanwhile, the federal funds which supported the Law Enforcement Council were terminated and the Council expired, leaving no coordinating mechanism in place for the criminal justice system.

The 1977 session was a long one. I spent so much time in House Judiciary that during one afternoon session Chairman Hardy Myers called on me saying "Representative Beatty, do you have a comment on the bill?" The hearing room dissolved in laughter. Herb Schwab handled judicial salaries behind the scenes, obtaining significant increases for judges through the Governor's Management Compensation Committee, which he and Arno were invited to attend. Herb was an early riser, and during legislative sessions he made it a habit to have breakfast in the capitol cafeteria at a table usually occupied by the legislative fiscal staff, a member or two from Ways and Means and Herb. This was a prime listening post for legislative gossip and provided useful informal contacts. Herb, with his fund of stories and old-shoe analysis of the foibles of politics, drew people like a magnet. When Herb retired in 1980 we lost our primary and most effective contact with the legislative fiscal staff and the Ways and Means Committee.

Court organization and funding were becoming major questions. The counties were resisting the growing demands put upon their budgets by courts, indigent defense, and jails.

The legislature established interim committees to consider these problems as well as those of the judicial retirement system, which had serious inequalities. No cost-of-living adjustments existed for retired judges. Subsequent inflation in the 1970s and 1980s created great disparity in retirement benefits as salaries were increased to keep pace with inflation while retirement benefits based on a salary average at the time a judge retired did not.

*

The 1977 session of the legislature enacted measures dealing with the parole matrix, discretionary mandatory judicial sentences, and the mental disease and defect bill which created the Psychiatric Security Review Board. However, equally important to the courts were the number of bad measures which we were able to sidetrack or scuttle by providing the particular legislative committee with a brief memorandum pointing out specific defects and the consequences which would follow. Few legislators are in a position to undertake such analysis because of lack of time and technical background, and both lawyers and non-lawyers on the committees appreciate that kind of assistance.

Toward the end of the 1977 session Hardy Myers suggested that the Judicial Conference ought to consider adopting sentencing guidelines during the following two years. His suggestion was phrased in a manner which indicated that if the courts did not do so the legislature might. I agreed that the Conference would undertake the project. He did not define what he meant by guidelines and I did not pursue a definition. I took the term to mean a general statement of principles which judges were expected to follow in exercising their statutory discretion in sentencing. Hardy was undoubtedly thinking of more precise limitations on judicial discretion such as the sentencing guidelines then under consideration in Minnesota. I was not familiar with the Minnesota guidelines at that time and hence did not read anything more into Hardy's proposal.

The 1977 legislature also set up an Interim Committee of the Judiciary to study the possibility of state funding of the trial court system as well as overhauling the judicial retirement system. I attended the meetings of the interim committee throughout 1978 as it covered those subjects, as did Fred R. Neal, the very able lobbyist for the counties. Fred understood that state administrative control of the trial courts had to be enacted with state funding. The advisory Commission on Prison Terms and Parole Standards was now functioning. The chief justice in the fall of 1978 reminded the judicial members of that commission that he had asked them to formulate guidelines for sentencing the previous year. He sent them the three-page draft I had submitted to him the previous year in response to the commitment I had made to the Speaker, Hardy Myers.

The Legislative Interim Committee on the Judiciary concluded that the state should take over the funding of the court system but left to the Judicial Conference the development of amendments which might be necessary to accomplish this. The Conference, of course, was not likely to generate spontaneously any legislation to facilitate state funding or the kind of state court structure which would make state funding and administration feasible.

In March of 1978 I presented to the legislative committee of the Conference a review of the Interim Committee's study to date. Herb Schwab, Arno Denecke and I, as a subcommittee, continued work on a draft statute on court administration. In April of 1978 I proposed to the Conference the following resolution on state funding:

> "The Judicial Conference believes that how the State Judicial System is to be funded is primarily a political decision to be decided by the Legislative Assembly. The primary concerns of the Conference are: first, that the method of funding chosen provide sufficient funds to enable the Judiciary to carry out its constitutional responsibility, and second, that the

Judiciary be provided with the necessary authority
and organization to carry out its functions efficiently
and uniformly throughout the state."

This resolution avoided a direct endorsement of the state takeover of trial court funding but would allow us a strong hand in crafting it. The resolution was adopted by the Conference.

In August our subcommittee submitted a draft bill on court structure to the legislative committee, which approved it by mail. Judge Michael Gillette dissented from the most important provision, the one which vested in the Chief Justice the power to appoint the presiding judges of the Court of Appeals, Circuit Court and District Court. The proposal was then presented to the executive committee of the Judicial Conference on September 21, 1978. I warned the executive committee that Representative Myers intended to submit a court structure bill simultaneously with a state funding bill, and it ought to be a bill drawn by us, not by someone else.

The executive committee approved the court structure bill with amendments, and the chief justice set the matter for discussion at a special meeting of the Judicial Conference in Eugene on Sunday afternoon, November 17, 1978. I had previously circulated a lengthy memorandum in support of the proposal, reviewing the political and fiscal considerations. The Multnomah County judges rode to Eugene in a bus as a snow storm began. We had a vigorous debate The vote reported by Loren Hicks to the chief justice was 40 against to 38 for with 12 to 15 abstentions. We later found that my vote was not counted because I was at the podium and the chief justice did not vote because he thought that as presiding officer he could not vote except in case of a tie. It developed that Loren either misspoke or Arno misunderstood his report of the count. The vote was actually tied without my vote which should have been counted. However, the official count was against us, and, as a practical matter, we could not have effectively supported a bill with the judges so evenly divided.

I had left my yellow Volkswagon Rabbit at the courthouse parking lot, and there were six inches of snow on the ground when our bus finally delivered us to the courthouse. I told Charles Crookham I would give him a ride up the hill if he waited while I put chains on the Rabbit. I did so as Charles stood watching me labor in the snow, entertaining me with witty comments. When the chains were installed we successfully made it up the hill. I delivered Charles to his door and then drove around the hill to Dosch Road and parked in my usual spot in front of the house. Later that evening Jean came home and inquired with a straight face, "Dad, why did you put chains on the rear wheels of a front wheel drive car?"

I suspect Jean relayed the story to Judge Crookham, for it appeared in Doug Baker's column in the Oregonian a couple of days later. I noted with interest that as Baker told it, Crookham's participation was minimized. The Yellow Rabbit is long gone, but the story lingered on, and at my 60th birthday party Elizabeth Crookham gave me a watercolor she had painted showing Charles and me riding an immense yellow rabbit in the snow with chains on his rear feet.

We redrafted the court structure bill, changing the term of presiding judges to two years. The executive committee approved it unanimously, and submitted the revised bill to a mail poll of the judges of the Conference. This time it was approved 54 to 46, but a majority of the circuit judges still disapproved. Chief Justice Denecke, Chief Judge Schwab and I met with Hardy Myers, now Speaker of the House, and Representative Mark Gardner, now Chair of House Judiciary, on February 7, 1979 to discuss the court structure, state funding and retirement bills in light of the poll. Hardy was concerned that a drawn-out struggle over court structure would imperil the state funding bill, HB 2001, which he felt was one of the most important bills before the session. The consensus was that we should not introduce the court structure bill and should simply state that the judges had not reached a consensus. House Bill 2001 ultimately failed, chiefly because the proposed funding details were not spelled out in a way which made it attractive to the legislature. The counties, however, were pressing for relief from the increasing costs of the state court system with which they were saddled.

Late in the 1979 session I discussed with Herb Schwab and and Arno Denecke a proposal to create a statutory body composed of judges, legislators and public members to be called the Commission on the Judicial Branch. Our court structure proposal was in limbo. The state funding bill was lost. We had just gone through a lengthy hearing before Ways and Means, trying without success to introduce some rationality into the way in which the legislature made decisions on whether or not additional judges were needed. We still were fighting off ridiculous legislative proposals. I thought we needed to devise a way to insure that key members of Ways and Means and the judiciary committees had substantial exposure to, and knowledge of, the judicial system. They both agreed.

Generally speaking, it is impossible to get a new bill introduced in the closing days of the legislature. We accepted that Ways and Means would never fund a new commission at this point. However, Arno said he had control of certain LEA (federal) funds which could properly be allocated to a commission intended to study the court system, including personnel, training, dockets and funding. The membership of our proposed commission was drafted to consist of three judges appointed by the Chief Justice, three senators (including one from Ways and Means and one from Senate Judiciary) appointed by the President of the Senate, three representatives (including one from Ways and Means and one from House Judiciary) appointed by the Speaker of the House, and four public members (including two non lawyers with large scale management experience) appointed by the governor. The Chief Justice was to serve ex officio as a member. The Governor was to appoint the chair from one of the non-elected members, and the Commission itself was to elect its own vice chairman, an arrangement intended to prevent a governor from wholly controlling the agenda.

Late in the afternoon of the closing days of the 1979 session, Arno, Herb and I walked our proposed bill over to the capitol, first to Jason Boe, the President of the Senate, and then to Hardy Myers, the Speaker of the House. Once they understood that no appropriation was required, they agreed to support the bill and see that it reached the floor of both chambers. Representative Mark Gardner and the speaker had HB 2140 removed from the table, stripped, amended to incorporate the commission bill, approved and sent to the floor "do pass." Ted Kulongowski, now a senator, with the help of President Boe, arranged to get the bill through the Senate. Low and behold, we had our commission.

CHAPTER 20

The Commission on the Judicial Branch, and State funding

I reached sixty on April 13, 1979. Herb and Barbara Schwab had a birthday party for me at their house in Salem. Pug Morse came from Weston, MA. John Beatty came from Waterloo, Ontario. The Bill Martins, Richard Biggs, William Snells, Bill Wyses, Forest Amsdens, Charles Crookhams and Arno Deneckes were there. It was a great party reminiscent of the "Century of Progress" dinner we had for Herb and Arno when they reached fifty. Herb was planning to retire in 1980, Arno in 1982, I in 1985, so the end of the judicial road did not seem too far off.

In the summer of 1979, Clissa and I arranged to meet Mardy and Howard Zucker in Oxford, England and spend a week on the Oxford Canal. We arrived in London, then rented a car and drove to Oxford, arriving shortly before the Zuckers. They had with them a young Australian doctor whom we called "Aussie," and the five of us embarked in a canal boat called Thorin Oakenshield, forty feet long and six feet wide. The Oxford Canal is an old one, built in the 1700s, and the locks will only accommodate boats of that width. The corridors past the small cabins were just barely wide enough to pass one's shoulders. The boat was built of steel with a diesel motor and a maximum speed of five knots. The propeller was located aft of the transom, not below it. The reason quickly became obvious. We periodically grounded on sections of canal that had shallowed. The procedure to free oneself was for all hands to seize two long poles with which the boat was equipped and push ourselves back into deeper water.

The locks were all hand operated by the crews of the various boats moving back and forth on the canal. When we approached a lock Howard, I or Aussie would leap off the boat and operate the lock. So far as I could see, each set of locks was mechanically unique, built by individual craftsman to some general guidelines. Repairs made over two centuries added to the differences. We took the canal from Oxford to Banbury, then reversed course, returning to Oxford. At night we tied up along the bank, pounding stakes into the turf bank to take our mooring lines. The canal runs through the Cotswolds remote from any highway, and the scenery was lovely. Bridges over the canal were nearly all of stone or brick, rising just enough to clear the cabin of the boat.

We stopped at a number of points to walk to nearby villages and shop for groceries. Mardy Zucker did our cooking. Aussie was our general boat girl. The canal was not crowded, and the boats we met were nearly all British vacationers. At one point the canal passes near Blenheim Palace. "Just a short distance away," someone told us. It proved to be a couple of miles. Howard flagged a car and got Clissa a ride. We found her sitting on a stone wall at the entrance to Woodstock, the village outside Blenheim. The palace is enormous and grand, almost on the scale of Versailles but more gracefully landscaped into the terrain. It is difficult to imagine living in such an establishment, and easy to see how one who did might lose touch with reality.

On the return voyage we walked to a village on a hillside above the canal and into a perfectly beautiful little parish church. Carved into the walls in the nave were the names of all the village men killed in the first World War. For a small village the number was startling, and the impact upon that small community must have been almost unbearable.

We had no problems with the boat, though once when Mardy Zucker was conning the boat, she forgot to turn in time and we hit a concrete embankment at our full five knots. It jarred a few fillings loose, but Thorin Oakenshield, sturdy craft that she was, hardly noticed it. The Zuckers and Aussie left us on our return to Oxford. Clissa and I then drove to Henley where we inspected the Thames site for shell racing. After that we worked our way east to Cambridge, Ely, Kings Lynn and the East edge of the Wash. From there we circled along the coast to Cromer, and from thence drove to Holcolm Hall, the residence of the Earl of Leicester.

I had corresponded with the earl's estate manager because the earl was a descendant of Sir Edward Coke, Attorney General under Elizabeth I, and subsequently Lord Chief Justice of England under James I. James later sent Coke to the Tower for refusing to tell him how he would decide a case. Coke then ran for Parliament and authored the Petition of Right. The earl had a portrait of Coke dressed in the scarlet robes of the Lord Chief Justice of England, a copy of which appeared in black and white in Catherine Drinker Bowen's biography of Coke. I wanted an oil copy painted for my court room. The estate manager had arranged for color photographs, and from these the portrait in my courtroom was subsequently painted.

The entrance to Holcolm Hall from the coastal highway was unmarked, but after some difficulty we found it. We drove several miles through woods until we reached an open area. Suddenly before us stood an enormous sand-colored Paladian mansion. I drove onto a large pebbled area which extended the entire front of the structure. There was no shrubbery, grass or any other kind of planting against the building. There appeared to be a grand main entrance, but not a person about, so I drove beyond to the west of the building to see if there was a more suitable entry. Finding none, I reversed course and drove back to the main entrance and we got out of the car. A man appeared at the top of the steps in front of the great doors. We walked up and introduced ourselves. He was the estate manager.

He escorted us into the hall, which was smaller than the entrance to Blenheim Palace but stylistically superior. The Earl's son, Lord Coke, was in residence, he told us, and had instructed him to bring us to his office when we arrived. Lord Coke, a relatively young man, introduced himself and then took us on a tour of the mansion. The library was particularly interesting for an American. The first Earl, who lived a hundred or more years after the Lord Chief Justice, was a great experimental agriculturist and an admirer of the American Colonies in general and George Washington in particular. A portrait engraving of George Washington was prominently displayed on one wall. Lord Coke told us that the first Earl commissioned printers throughout the Colonies to send him a copy of every map and village platt they printed and showed us drawers full of such maps. He told us he had just embarked on cataloguing the Holcolm library, which had never been done before. Holcolm was still a working estate supported by its agricultural produce. Several years earlier Lord Coke had embarked on a restoration project which was now in progress, repairing roofs, windows and masonry. We left hours later exhilarated and exhausted by a unique experience.

After leaving Holcolm we spent the night in Norwich, which I was surprised to learn was once a seaport during the Middle Ages when merchant craft sailed up to the city on the River Wensum, which now looks not much larger than Oswego Creek. In the middle ages we were told the river was navigable up to the city. From Norwich we drove to Harwich and back to London. Our hotel proved to be a dump, located in the outskirts of London, a monument to the folly of relying on advertising for such accommodations. The bed was a single and the mattress had a hole in the center. Making new reservations was almost impossible at the height of the tourist season, so we cut short our visit by several days and flew home.

We had planned on stopping off in Waterloo and so flew there a few days later, to visit John in his new house. Clissa and I drove one day to Toronto for a brief look at that metropolis, borrowing John's Buick—our old 1963 station wagon which we had given to him some years before. On our return we stopped at a roadside restaurant for a cup of coffee. When I drove back on the freeway I failed to notice that I was in the second gear of the automatic transmission. As I came up to highway speed we heard dreadful grinding and clanking from the engine. I pulled off the road. Apparently the oil pump had failed under increased pressure. The car was towed into Waterloo where John's garageman pronounced it dead on arrival. We made a contribution toward its replacement.

On our return to Portland, Jean and Chris Locatell surprised us with the news that they were going to be married in the Fall. Herb Schwab performed the service at our house October 6, 1979, and we held the reception at the Racquet Club. It was a great party with all of our friends. John flew in from Waterloo, as well as did Pug and Linny from Boston. My mother was indeed pleased to have at least one grandchild married. Jean and Chris then flew to Hawaii for a week.

In June 1980 Caroline Margaret Morse was married to Steve Leverette and the Beattys flew East for the wedding, including Granny Jean, who telephoned me at 5:00 AM the day before we were to leave saying she had overslept and missed the plane! It was a dream, she was relieved to learn. We all got off in good time on June 19th and arrived at Boston to be met by Tony and young Tony Morse. John Beatty came down from Waterloo. The wedding went off successfully, though Clis and I were mesmerized during the ceremony by a gypsy moth crawling on the hat of a lady seated in front of us. The Boston area was having an epidemic of gypsy moths, and the trees were dripping with them. The reception was held at Pug and Tony's house in Weston under a canopy on the front lawn. The steady patter of gypsy moths on the canvass made a strange background to the clink of glasses and hum of conversation. We spent the next day going through Sturbridge Village, and following day at the Boston waterfront going through the USS Constitution, which I had not seen since its voyage up the Columbia River in the 1920s. Granny Jean survived the trip well and returned to Portland with Jean Beatty.

*

For the next several years my principal task, other than trials, involved the formation and work of the Commission on the Judicial Branch. This was the mechanism by which Herb Schwab, Arno Denecke, and Hardy Myers hoped to improve the judicial system and coordinate the relationships between the judiciary and the county and state governments. Having drafted the legislation, I had the responsibility for providing basic information to the new members of the Commission. I suggested positions against which other members could test their ideas and did much of the initial drafting. The basic ideas by this time had been so extensively discussed over the years that we moved flexibly toward the goal of strengthening and improving the judicial process, adjusting and accommodating our proposals to the turn of political events in the judiciary and in the legislature.

I doubt this process could have taken place ten or fifteen years earlier. Neither the judges nor the legislature nor the counties nor the Oregon State Bar would have been prepared to rethink the structure and funding of our courts. The failure of the Judicial Reform Commission under Dean Hollis in 1971 was a cautionary example. However, the 1970s produced leaders in the judiciary and the legislature who had worked together, had confidence in each other and recognized the necessity for change.

The Commission statute gave the governor the power to call the first meeting, so the first task was to remind Governor Atiyeh of this fact and to stir him to make his appointments. Arno Denecke wrote the governor July 23, 1979 to this effect, suggesting names for public members and proposing a joint announcement by the three appointing authorities. The governor finally made his appointments and the joint announcement was made September 24, 1979.

The chief justice named Court of Appeals Judge George M. Joseph of Portland (who subsequently succeeded Herb Schwab as Chief Judge upon the latter's retirement), myself, and District Judge Ross G. Davis of Medford (president of the Association of District Judges). The President of the Senate named Senator Anthony Meeker of Amity (member of the Joint Ways and Means Committee), Senator Jim Gardner of Portland (member of the Senate Judiciary Committee), and Senator Edward N. Fadely of Eugene (also a member of the Joint Ways and Means Committee and Judiciary). The speaker named Representative Paul Hanneman of Cloverdale (member of joint Ways and Means Committee), Representative Mark Gardner of Hillsboro (chair of House Judiciary) and Representative Tom Mason of Portland (member of House Judiciary). The governor named as public members two non-lawyers: former representative and member of Ways and Means Sam Johnson of Redmond, a lumberman, and Robert C. Notson of Portland, retired publisher of The Oregonian. The two lawyer public members were George H. Corey of Pendleton, and Barnes H. Ellis of Portland. All of the governor's appointees were names suggested by the chief justice.

The first meeting was held on September 25, 1979 with the chief justice providing a memorandum with suggestions for organization of the Commission. The format was, in fact, modeled on that of the Race and Education Committee of School District No. 1. Governor Atiyeh opened the meeting, swore in the members and then retired. The chief justice assumed the chair and conducted election of officers. Coralling this group of political, judicial and public members called for managerial talent. Barnes Ellis, a partner in Stoel Rives, tall, handsome, able and persuasive, was the obvious choice for chairman. Arno had indicated to me that he would take care of the election of officers. George Corey moved that Barnes Ellis be elected chair and myself vice chair. The vote was unanimous. We then discussed funding, agreed to meet monthly and to each send in recommendations for study. At the chief justice's suggestion I then reviewed the history behind the creation of the commission and pointed out that everything the courts do was up for analysis, including their relation with the legislature.

Following our first meeting, I submitted a detailed memorandum to the members, briefly describing the organization and functions of the court system, its strengths and weaknesses, and its relationship with the legislature. The commission hired Dennis Bromka, an able young lawyer, who had just concluded service as legal counsel to the House Judiciary Committee, as Executive Director of the Commission. The Commission was divided into three subcommittees: No. 1 to deal with structure and administration of the courts; No. 2 to deal with fiscal responsibility for court support, the legislative-judicial interface and the volume of trial and appellate litigation; No. 3 to deal with judicial recruitment, selection, retention and retirement. I subsequently provided each subcommittee with copies of memoranda and correspondence dealing with their subject matter, drawing upon my legislative memoranda developed during the previous four years.

March 7, 1980 the Commission had a joint meeting with the American Bar Association's Committee on Implementation of Standards of Judicial Administration at the Quay Restaurant in Vancouver, Washington. This meeting produced a lively analysis of the major issues before the Commission. Six judges from other states led workshop discussions. One of these judges was Judge Arthur Simpson of Bergen County, New Jersey, who invited us to visit his jurisdiction and see what they were doing to modernize their court administration. This meeting provided us with a broad perspective of what was being done in other jurisdictions.

In early May Barnes Ellis, Joyce Cohen (an able replacement member from the Senate), George Joseph, Dennis Bromka, Ed Fadely and I flew to a conference on state funding held at Denver. Steve Kaptch, Fred Neal for the counties, Kay Hutchinson from the Legislative Fiscal Office and Hardy Myers also attended the conference. Colorado had recently taken over state support of its trial courts. This meeting provided a good deal of information on details involved in a state takeover which we might otherwise have overlooked. Our meetings took place in the Denver County Courthouse which, as George Joseph caustically observed, looked largely empty. Not one courtroom in five was open.

When the conference ended, Dennis Bromka, Barnes and I flew east to examine in detail the administration of the New Jersey Court system, restructured under the late Chief Justice Arthur Vandenberg. New Jersey had a tightly run state-funded court system. We spent a day in Trenton with the State Court Administrator. Then we drove to Hackensack, county seat of Bergen County. En route we stopped for an hour at Princeton where Barnes' cousin, married to the Director of the Institute for Advanced Study, lived in a handsome 18th century house. The Bergen County Court, comparable to our circuit court, was completely computerized, and the information available to the presiding judge enabled him to know at once the state of each judge's docket and the status of any case in the system. Barnes and I thought it was remarkably well organized and quite informative. New Jersey had a two-tier trial system like Oregon, but the tight command structure made it work efficiently.

26. Oregon's Chief Justice who led the effort to reshape the state court system with rare good humor, common sense, and a deft political hand not always visible to those in opposition

Arno H. Denecke (1916-1993)

27. Chief Judge of Oregon's new court of appeals, he ran it like a whaling captain - swift, clear and brief opinions to guide the trial judges. A formidable personality, he backed Chief Justice Denecke from start to finish in the reshaping of the state judiciary.

Herbert M. Schwab (1916-2005)

28. Hardy Myers twice chair of Judiciary, twice Speaker, chair of the Criminal Justice Council, three term Attorney General. He played the major role outside the courts in their restructuring. A thoughtful craftsman of our public policy, his questions triggered thought and fresh response.

29. Edwin J. Peterson, Chief Justice who implemented the reorganization of the judiciary. Through his appointments to the Criminal Justice Council he effected major improvement in the sentencing process with the development and adoption of sentencing guidelines.

30. Barnes H. Ellis, appointed by Governor Atiyeh, and then elected by the Commission on the Judicial Branch to chair its study of our judicial system. He ably led a diverse group of legislators, citizens and judges to reach agreement on restructuring the courts and funding by the state. He then shepherded these proposals through a legislative-executive standoff into law.

When we finished at Bergen, we scattered. Dennis Bromka dropped me off at my cousin Ann Miller's house in Bloomfield, New Jersey, where I spent the night. Ann had a rather large house for a single person, with attractive old furniture. She worked at the municipal library, which was within walking distance. After breakfast I caught the limousine to Newark Airport and thence home. I had not seen Ann since Grandfather Beatty's funeral in 1947. She was an interesting person, as her letters had indicated, and I thoroughly enjoyed our short visit.

*

June 9, 1979 the Commission met and approved the recommendation to have the state take over the funding of the trial courts, including the cost of indigent defense. George Joseph and Tom Mason in particular pressed for a recommendation consolidating district and circuit courts. I thought the case for consolidation was not proved. If the two courts were consolidated, we would soon face a demand for the appointment of magistrates to handle traffic and small claims, and we would still have a two-tier system. However, if the majority was determined to propose consolidation, I suggested that the change be made effective in four years, subject to acceleration by the chief justice where feasible in particular judicial districts. The Commission then directed that a delegation ask for a meeting with the governor to discuss the state funding proposal.

The delegation: Barnes Ellis, George Corey, Dennis Bromka and I, arranged to met with Governor Atiyeh and Lee Johnson, his attorney, in Barnes's office to discuss the proposal. Unfortunately, Barnes was delayed a half hour, and I had to proceed without him to outline our proposal. The governor grumpily responded, saying he was not about to agree to a state take-over of trial courts unless it would be an improved court system. Not an unreasonable position, I thought, but then the governor went on to say that he thought judges didn't work and that the system was in terrible shape. That comment was excessive, to say the least. Court structure, determined as it had been by the legislature, needed to be improved, but that was what we were trying to do. To say that judges did not work was insulting, but I bit my tongue and told the governor that substantial improvements were what we were proposing. I added that unless we did something now while Judge Schwab and Judge Denecke, were in office, we were not likely to see any change for another twenty years. The governor finally left, saying that we should provide him with an account of the improvements we contemplated, along with the funding proposal.

These "improvements" centered on placing administrative responsibility and control in a chief justice who was to be appointed by the governor after consulting with the judges of the Supreme Court. The bill vested in the chief justice authority to appoint and remove all presiding judges of the multi-judge courts, subject to provisions requiring notice to the judges of the court concerned, who were given a limited right of veto with respect to an appointment. Making the presiding judges directly answerable to the chief justice established direct personal responsibility by virtue of his power to appoint and remove them. The state court administrator would be appointed by the chief justice, subject to confirmation by the supreme court, but removable at the pleasure of the chief alone. Other provisions clarified the role of the chief justice as the administrative head of the court system, and the role of the supreme court as the policy making body of the judiciary. Still other provisions dealt with jurisdiction of the Court of Appeals, judicial selection and election, changes in handling DUII cases, consolidation of the district and circuit courts and improvement of the judicial retirement system.

Loren Hicks, the state court administrator for many years, retired in 1980. The chief justice had appointed a search committee to look for a successor, including Judge Clifford Olsen from our court. The search committee had recommended Elizabeth Belshaw, a court administrator in Maine, and she was appointed. Belshaw was a tall, attractive woman, well spoken and knowledgeable about court matters. The chief justice assigned her to participate with the Commission in the drafting process, and I spent a good deal of time with her and with Dennis Bromka discussing details of the court structure draft. On one point in particular she was insistent: that trial court secretary-bailiffs had to be hired in accordance with a centralized procedure and from a centralized pool.

I argued that a trial judge's secretary was figuratively an extension of the judge. The secretary had to be familiar with the judge's procedure in trial, handle his or her relationship with members of the bar, and be aware of and assist with the preparation of opinions. I thought that however our system was constructed, a judge should be reasonably free to select and to remove the person who performed this important function. Ms. Belshaw somewhat reluctantly agreed that a judge could have the final say as to a secretary but insisted that secretaries had to meet certain standards. I thought that would pose little difficulty so long as the selection process remained under the control of the trial judge. However, the difficulty on this point was a harbinger of things to come. Ms. Belshaw, who had many sensible ideas, tended to ruffle judicial feathers statewide, which was unfortunate at a time we were proposing centralizing administrative authority. The professional state court administrator needs to be skillful in dealing with both legislators and judges who, to put it it charitably, by the very nature of their calling are not the easiest people to manage.

For the judges the two most controversial proposals were giving the chief justice the power to appoint and remove presiding judges, and the consolidation of the circuit and district courts. District courts had limited jurisdiction and handled misdemeanor criminal cases, traffic, and civil cases involving claims under $10,000. Circuit judges in a court of general jurisdiction handled all other civil and criminal cases. Circuit judges had a higher salary, though the district judges had successfully retained lobbiests who had persuaded the legislature to increase their salary significantly. The district judges were eager to become circuit judges. A majority of the circuit judges were reluctant to face the possibility of handling traffic cases and small claims and wanted to preserve their current status.

Alan Davis, just elected president of the Circuit Judges Association, advised that he was appointing a five judge legislative committee to oppose the consolidation proposal. The district judges organized to support it. One circuit judge, a good friend of mine, sent me a note saying, "The circuit judges have been betrayed." At the same time, the circuit judges uniformly wanted improvements to the retirement system which had fallen woefully behind the current salary levels due to inflation, and most of them recognized that legislative prospects for such improvements depended upon civility in opposing other proposals.

The entire bundle of legislative proposals were described in a Commission memorandum entitled "Preliminary Report" drafted by Bromka, redrafted by me and reviewed by Schwab and Denecke. The report was then distributed to the judges prior to a special meeting of the Judicial Conference in Portland called by the Chief Justice to review and discuss the Commission's proposals. The presentation was carefully planned in advance, but I was not optimistic. I noted in my diary, "I think the worst is likely, but, like Mr. Micawber, 'I always nourish a remote and delicate hope that something good might turn up.'"

The meeting was held on a Saturday in the County Commissioners' meeting room on the sixth floor of the Multnomah County Courthouse. We had a quorum of judges and a majority of the members of the Commission present. The chief justice presided and spoke well. Barnes Ellis reviewed the proposed legislation point by point and responded to questions. His presentation was both eloquent and persuasive. The judges debated each proposal, and each important measure was approved by a reasonably good margin. Unfortunately, by the time we reached a vote on the measure as a whole, we had lost our quorum and subsequently had to poll the members of the Conference by mail in order to arrive at an official position. The poll of the judges in the conference as a whole supported the Commission proposals, but a majority of the circuit judges were still opposed. Their opposition to consolidation was confirmed at the annual Circuit Judges' meeting at Bend. I did manage to salvage a favorable vote on state funding. Consolidation of the trial courts was and remained anathema to many circuit judges.

The difficulty was that consolidation seemed sensible to nearly everyone but the circuit judges. At that point in time the Commission would have gained some circuit judge votes by abandoning the proposal, but it would have lost nearly all the district judge votes by doing so. Hardy was reluctant to change position at this stage, and George Corey, though opposed to consolidation, agreed that we should not change position. I did not press for a vote on our minority position, though Dennis Bromka said that if we did, he thought a majority of the members would support us. I concluded there was trouble either way, and I should defer to Barnes Ellis's judgment.

Denecke, Mason and I filed a concurring report in which we proposed a single level, two division trial court with a single presiding judge, a single court administrator, ultimately the same salary and ability of sitting judges to serve in either level. George Joseph, in his concurring report, opposed the "Beatty proposal" as promising a system no better than what we presently had. The fact was that the dynamics within the judiciary made flat consolidation of the two courts politically impossible at the time. We ended up a decade later with our compromise largely in effect and with full consolidation taking place by 1997.

Funding the state takeover presented serious difficulties for the 1981-83 Biennium because it unfortunately coincided with a predicted shortfall in state revenues. The Commission had identified some $12,000,000 in revenues generated by the courts in various fees and fines and predicted the net cost of takeover above existing revenues would be some $20,000,000. On November 13, 1980 Lee Johnson, Governor Atyeh's attorney, came to Portland to meet with me, Bromka, Fred Neal, Tuck Wilson and Steve Kapsch in my chambers. Lee's message was that the governor was interested but they could not dig up enough money to begin phasing in the takeover during the current biennium and fund it in the next.

We discussed increasing fees to provide revenue and centralizing indigent defense now amounting to some $12,000,000 annually as a cost control measure. I added that if our system were computerized we could collect millions in fines. Lee Johnson pricked up his ears at this discussion, but it looked like a lost cause to me at the time. Subsequently, a recalculation of increased fees suggested this could raise $16,000,000. From that point on, state funding of the trial courts took on new life.

The court consolidation bill resulted in the formation of three judicial legislative committees for the 1981 legislative session: the Conference legislative committee which I chaired, a circuit judges' legislative committee and a district judges' legislative committee. The latter two committees were almost exclusively designed to defend their conflicting positions on the consolidation bill. Interestingly enough, the court structure bill provisions giving power to the chief justice to appoint the presiding judges of the lower courts no longer fired controversy. Who should select the chief justice became the critical question.

The Commission bill provided that the governor would appoint the chief justice for a six year term. The chief would be removable by a majority of the court. This was intended to prevent any reversion to the practice of rotation which had existed prior to the election of Chief Justice McAllister, encourage selection for administrative ability and provide the chief justice with a measure of additional authority. George Joseph, the Chief Judge of the Court of Appeals, elected by his colleagues to succeed Herb Schwab following the latter's retirement in 1980, felt strongly that the governor should appoint the chief justice who would then be appointing all presiding judges including the Court of Appeals.

The commission bill on court structure made its way unscathed through the House despite Judge Berkley Lent's testimony against gubernatorial appointment, but that power was promptly deleted by the Senate in which he had served before going on the bench. Governor Atiyeh, whose attention was no doubt stirred by the conflicting interests of judges immediately concerned with the appointive power, had warned that he would veto the entire bill if that power was deleted. In fact, on the supreme court itself only the chief justice favored gubernatorial appointment. Nevertheless, the House concurred in the Senate amendment. With the enactment of the court structure and court funding measures the Legislature adjourned.

The 3.8% salary increase previously enacted for judges was not funded by Ways and Means. The commission bill on judicial retirement, on which we had worked for three years, died in Ways and Means. And the governor on August 24, 1981 vetoed the court structure and state funding bills solely because gubernatorial appointment of the chief justice had been deleted despite a strong pitch by the members of the Commission and a letter signed by all members of the Supreme Court saying that they would only select a chief justice on the basis of administrative merit, a commitment which was hardly persuasive at this point.

Ultimately, with help from many quarters, the press, state bar officials, and Fred Neel working on behalf of the financially desperate counties, we reached a solution with the governor and legislative leaders. On September 14, 1981 at a meeting of the Commission, I outlined the proposal. The governor would call a special session in October (1981). The legislature would reenact the court structure and state funding bills, and refer a measure to the voters at the next general election in May 1982 to decide whether the chief justice should be elected by the court or appointed by the governor. The Commission approved the proposal, forwarded it to the governor who accepted it and called the legislature into special session Oct 24, 1981.

The court structure and state funding bills were reenacted and signed by the governor. In May 1982 the voters by nearly three to one left the choice of the chief justice in the hands of the supreme court, a result that was predictable, though the heavy majority was not. We had escaped disaster by the skin of our teeth.

The two measures also placed responsibility for providing indigent defense in the judicial department and required the state to assume the cost. Having competent lawyers represent indigent defendants insures fair trial, satisfies federal constitutional requirements and avoids unnecessary reversal on appeal and the necessity of retrial. The Metropolitan Public Defender, under the leadership of James D. Hennings, provided efficient indigent defense by contract with Multnomah and Washington Counties for many years, but providing such services in many of the less populous counties was far more difficult.

In 2003 the legislature transferred this responsibility from the judicial department to the Office of Public Defense Services which contracts with various individuals and firms such as the Metropolitan Public Defender to provide defense services statewide. This office is governed by The Public Defense Services Commission, whose seven members are appointed by the Chief Justice, and the Commission is presently chaired by Barnes Ellis who made these changes possible in the first place.

CHAPTER 21

The Prison Overcrowding Project,
Leaving the bench,

In June 1982 Arno Denecke telephoned to say he intended to resign as Chief Justice and retire from the court on July 1st. The court had asked him to stay on for two years, but he was not willing to defer retirement that long. He wanted to know if I were interested in appointment to his seat on the court. He would urge my appointment. I told him I was not interested. It was too late for me at 63. The next day Nels Peterson telephoned and asked me to have lunch with him, which I did. He posed the same question. I gave him the same answer and for the same reasons. Later in the day Forest Amsden called and argued strenuously that "I should do it, "as a final touch to my career," as he put it. I said "No" once more. It would mean a campaign and possibly a contested election in two years, daily driving back and forth to Salem and deferring retirement. My then current six year term would expire December 31, 1984. Clissa would have to retire at that time, and I thought it was essential for me to retire when she did. I appreciated those inquiries, but the fact was that I knew my job as a trial judge and was happy in that role. Starting out as an appellate judge at this time did not make sense.

*

The Supreme Court elected Judge Berkeley Lent as chief justice to succeed Arno Denecke. Berkley Lent had been a partner in Peterson, Pozzi and Lent, a firm of very able labor and plaintiff's lawyers as well as a state senator. He then had served as a circuit judge in Multnomah County. He was bright, good humored, and like Judge Pat Dooley, who was a former speaker of the house, Bud Lent went his own independent way as a judge. I promptly tendered my resignation as chairman of the legislative committee of the Judicial Conference, knowing the new chief justice would want to pick his own man for that role. I urged, perhaps too vigorously to a chief justice and former senator, that he continue to use the judicial conference legislative committee as the mechanism for working with the legislature. I added that I would be glad to continue to work on retirement legislation with whoever he chose to replace me. The judicial retirement system, a subject dear to the hearts of all judges, had needed substantial amendment for some years. I was familiar with its legislative history and the financial costs of the proposed changes, having worked on these matters since 1961.

I heard nothing from the chief justice, but Judge Alan Bonebrake of Washington County telephoned to say that the chief had appointed him chairman of the Judicial Conference legislative committee. Alan said he had agreed to accept with the understanding that I would help out with retirement legislation. This I did in the 1983 session, in cooperation with Judge Bonebrake and the circuit and district judges' lobbyists, and the judicial retirement bill finally became law.

Meanwhile, the chief justice struggled with the difficult administrative problems involved in the state court takeover and with controversy centering on the state court administrator. After two years Judge Lent stepped down as chief justice, and the court then elected Judge Edwin J. Peterson as chief justice.

Edwin Peterson was a partner in the Portland Tooze firm when appointed to the Supreme Court by Governor Ateyeh. He had a keen interest in administration and appreciated the opportunity to exercise the new powers and responsibilities of the office of chief justice. Under his leadership the state court system proposed by the Commission on the Judicial Branch chaired by Barnes Ellis and supported by Chief Justice Arno H. Denecke became a reality. These were the most significant changes made in the Oregon judicial system in the Twentieth Century.

*

Sid Lezak had resigned as United States Attorney for the District of Oregon with the election of Ronald Reagan in 1980. Sid, not one to languish in retirement, agreed to chair an enterprise called The Oregon Prison Overcrowding Project or OPOP, an Oregon committee funded by the Edna McConnell Clark Foundation and the National Institute of Corrections. The study was prompted by the nationwide increase in prison populations which was also accompanied by overcrowding litigation in the federal courts. Sid asked if I would join the committee "Planning Group," and I agreed to do so, the subject being within my range of interest. The other members of the Planning Group were Senator Joyce Cohen, Stuart Cutler, Michael Dane, Sheriff Jack Dolan, Randall Franke, Attorney General Dave Frohnmayer, Parole Board member Hazel Hayes, Dean Stephan Kanter of Northwestern School of Law, former Speaker Hardy Myers, Representative Bill Rutherford, Sheriff Mike Schrunk, Director of Corrections Robert Watson, Circuit Judge Frank Yraguen, Representative Tony Meeker, Dean Derrick Bell of the University of Oregon Law School and former Court of Appeals Judge Jacob Tanzer.

Steven Kapsch, a Reed professor who had done important work on the economics of the state court takeover, was the executive director of the project, and Tom Lockhart was his research associate. The study was explicitly focused by the foundation on prison overcrowding. This narrow focus limited the OPOP group's ability to address the broader problems of the State's criminal justice structure.

The OPOP group worked through a number of meetings for several years, producing a considerable amount of useful information. Some members, including the staff, were convinced that many property offenders sent to prison could be better handled in local jail facilities. They urged application of a process of risk assessment to determine which offenders should be imprisoned and how long they should be held. Others, myself included, were skeptical of attempts to sentence on the basis of a risk assessment formula apart from criminal history and the facts of the crime committed. We also pointed out that existing local jail capacity had a lot to do with whether offenders could be handled locally rather than in state prisons.

The OPOP group ended up supporting the Criminal Justice Council Bill proposed by the Commission on the Judicial Branch in the 1985 Session, the same bill which the Judicial Conference had proposed in 1979 with an OPOP amendment requiring the Council to include study of risk assessment. Risk assessment was never adopted as an explicit basis for sentencing. There were obvious constitutional objections as well as practical problems inherent in the concept. OPOP's real contribution lay in keeping the OPOP members drawn from different segments of the criminal justice system discussing corrections problems with each other. These associations proved of great value when the Criminal Justice Council came into existence and commenced work in the fall of 1985.

*

December 31, 1982 was my mother's 90th birthday. The Christmas season was an active one for her. Tom and Sherry Vaughan had Christmas dinner for the Beattys including my mother. Megan and her husband, Margo, Cameron and Stephan Vaughan were there as well as Chris Locatel, Jean Beatty and John Beatty. Later in the week Pug, Judy and Tony Morse flew in for her birthday party on the 31st. John had to return to Waterloo before the 31st. We had a salmon dinner for everyone at our house and Granny Jean loved it!

*

In the spring of 1984 the Oregon Psychiatric Association, at the instance of Dr. Edward Colback, invited me to be their guest at their annual meeting at Kaneeta, the Warm Springs Indian resort, on April 13, which happened to be my sixty fifth birthday.

Ed Colback, who had a deep interest in forensic psychiatry, had examined a number of offenders for me, and had served as an associate member on my subcommittee on the Governor's Task Force when we developed the concept and drafted the legislation to establish the Psychiatric Security Review Board.

Clissa and I drove up, stopping at Welches for lunch where we found Bill and Janet Wyse also there for lunch. We later drove on to Kaneeta. We were the sole non-psychiatric guests for a dinner with no speeches but kind words and an award for my labors in setting up the Psychiatric Security Review Board. I then answered questions about the insanity defense and the Review Board for thirty or forty minutes.

Two weeks later, at the Judicial Conference meeting at Salishan, Charles Crookham, in remarks concerning retiring judges, described me as more responsible than any one else, "For bringing the court system into the twentieth century." This was a generous tribute from Charles who was not always confident that my legislative efforts were well directed. He had in fact telephoned Barnes Ellis, then engaged in trial in San Francisco, to express his strong opposition to the Commission's proposals. However, his role as an effective presiding judge was continued under the new regime, and this undoubtedly allayed his apprehensions. So my judicial career wound down.

Clissa also planned on retiring at the end of the year. Federal grants had become increasingly difficult. Her grants for the last several years were approved but not funded, which meant that while her salary was paid by the Center, her staff, which depended on her grants, was not supported by NIH. She contributed her own funds to keep their work going. It seemed fairly clear that with the shortage of federal funds, the National Science Foundation was unlikely to allocate funds to three or five year grants for work by scientists of retirement age when younger applicants needed support.

Several years earlier, Clissa had been proposed for the Energy Facility Siting Council, the policy-making body for the

State Department of Energy. She had reluctantly declined on the ground that she could not take sufficient time from her work at the Primate Center. With retirement in prospect she indicated interest in future appointment, and in 1985 she was appointed by Governor Atiyeh to fill the unexpired term of a member who had resigned.

*

During the Christmas holidays of 1984 I moved my furniture and files out of my chambers and into a vacant jury room on the fifth floor of the courthouse, set up my desk and spent several weeks sorting files as well as working on a class action which I had agreed to continue to handle pro-tempore on into the new year. Toward the end of January I moved the furniture and personal files over to my new office with Martin Bischoff in the First Interstate Tower.

Martin Bischoff, my former law firm, had previously indicated they would have an office for me as of counsel to the firm. I was not certain I wanted to practice law. My arrangement with the firm provided that any judicial business, arbitration, or mediation would be my own, while work I did in the office would be compensated in accordance with the office formula currently in place. By this time Martin Bischoff had grown considerably from the small, close knit firm I had left in 1970 to some eighteen lawyers and a substantial support staff. However Bill Martin was soon to leave the firm and move to Hawaii, and Dave Templeton and Jerry Bischoff were also phasing out their practice and becoming of counsel. Resuming contact with them was delightful. However, I rather quickly concluded that there were a good many other things I was more interested in doing than resuming a trial practice. My professional work from 1985 on lay almost entirely in arbitration, mediation and reference judging on the one hand, and public interest activity on the other.

Shortly after the first of the year, Tom and Sherry Vaughan gave us a cocktail supper retirement party in their great old house on Myrtle Street. Between sixty and seventy people were there. Arno and several others from Salem telephoned to say that

I-5 was socked in by fog. As noted earlier, I had acted as Tom's attorney from time to time until I went on the bench. He and Sherry had become close friends over the years as he developed the Oregon Historical Society into a nationally recognized institution and as Sherry had pursued her Russian studies. In many ways they had led a fascinating life with much travel and professional association all over the world. Tom's skill in dealing with the Oregon Legislature, which supported a substantial part of the Society's budget, was equaled only by his ability to draw a remarkably powerful board membership from all corners of the state. Tom had opportunities to move on to larger responsibilities, but on each occasion had concluded he would remain at OHS.

I had joined the Society's board in 1971 after going on the bench. My occupation precluded participating in board trips about the state, but I was able on occasion to help out in connection with legislative support, an area in which I had some expertise, but of course one in which Tom's skills were unmatched. It was obvious that whenever Tom retired, filling his shoes would be difficult, and this proved to be the case.

*

With retirement, Clissa and I thought of spending more time on the boat. In January 1985 Clissa and I drove north to the Seattle Boat Show with Forest and Claire Amsden, an annual event the four of us had made for many years. We saw there a new Taiwan built 35 foot cruiser, the Ponderosa, which had a single 140 hp Ford Lehman disel, forward and stern cabins, two heads, a generator, fully equipped except for electronics. It was being offered by Seaward Yachts of Portland on an introductory basis. It looked like the boat of our dreams. We wrestled over the thought of purchase for several weeks. It was not as handsome a boat as our old Chris Craft, and it was slow, cruising at 7 1/2 kts. with a top speed of 9 kts. It was also a bit ungainly in appearance without the open after deck which Clissa loved. I calculated that we would have to borrow some money at 13% interest to finance the Ponderosa and still have adequate funds on hand for emergencies. That seemed pretty risky.

31. Above: The cockpit of the Clarissa Jean, 34' Chris Craft. John, Clissa, Jack and Jean. Somewhere north.

32. Below: At anchor. John under his Tilly hat reading.

The answer was obvious. We passed on the Ponderosa, and I went to work on our old 34 foot Chris Craft, tearing out the main cabin, rewiring, building in a shower, installing an additional water tank, propane stove and oven, galley, refrigerator, diesel space heater, instant propane hot water heater and storage space. I did the carpentry, and Dick Wilson of Sells Marine Service at the yacht club did the plumbing and wiring. It took from February to May to accomplish and cost about $15,000. The result was a well designed, fast and comfortable boat with two old gas engines. It was difficult for Clissa to handle lines forward of the cockpit. However, as we had done since the early 1980s, Clissa took the helm of the boat whenever we needed to anchor, tie up to another boat, or enter a harbor, while I served as the deck hand, handling lines and jumping ashore.

*

That same spring of 1985, Lloyd Erickson, a partner in the Martin Bischoff firm, was making a trip to London and proposed that I conduct a seminar at Lloyds for some of the firm's insurance clients and bring Clissa with me. He had an apartment in London we could share. Bear in mind, this was several years before Lloyds ran into serious financial trouble. The seminar went off successfully, and we were given a tour of the new Lloyds building. Later in the week Erickson had a large cocktail party at the Marine Club for English contacts and clients. That evening we had dinner at the Savoy of song and story.

The following day Clis and I took the train to Windsor, intending to see the castle. On arrival we found the town jammed with people and the castle closed because the Queen was "in residence." We worked our way up the street toward the castle and found a friendly policeman who said the Queen was expecting a state visit from the "President for Life" of Malawi, Mr. Banda. We had never heard of Malawi, or Mr. Banda for that matter, but the policeman told us we could stand on a patch of grass overlooking the road up to the castle. From there, he said, we would have a splendid view of the procession. The time of arrival was delayed because the president apparently was tardy in leaving Antwerp. "She won't like this," said the policeman, referring to the queen.

Eventually the president for life flew into Windsor's airport, and soon the household cavalry, followed by the royal carriage and the two heads of state came trotting up the road and disappeared into the castle. Eight years later John Beatty, on sabbatical from Waterloo University, spent two years in the Peace Corps in Malawi where the president for life, in his late eighties, was still clinging to office. He was finally ousted in the late 1990s.

Our week in Paris we stayed in a tiny hotel recommended by Sherry and Tom Vaughan. Located a few blocks from the Orangerie, the hotel had the smallest elevator I have ever seen. Two thin passengers made a tight fit. We saw most sites within walking distance, including the Louvre, Notre Dame, and the Military Museum. We took a bus to the palace at Versailles, which was magnificent but not nearly as well furnished as Holcolm Hall. One evening we went to Susy Davidson's apartment for drinks and then to a restaurant she chose for a wonderful dinner. Susy, the daughter of my cousin Dorothy Green Davidson, made a reputation as cook in both Paris and New York.

In Paris I had my first experience with pickpockets. Clissa and I were walking across the square west of the Orangerie when some small boys waving papers got in front of me, talking rapidly, and rustling the papers under my nose. I shooed them off, feeling foolish but irritated at their pushiness. A moment later a Frenchman called to me from behind. I turned, still angry, to face this gentleman who politely handed me my wallet, which the boys had extracted from my left hip pocket while they were shaking the papers at me. Apparently he had observed the pick pockets go after me, collared the one with the wallet and recovered it. At that point I was ready to shout "Vive La France!"

*

Shortly after I left the bench, Fred Hansen, the Director of the Oregon Department of Environmental Quality, asked me to chair a department advisory committee preparing rules for the siting of hazardous waste facilities. I accepted, and through the work of this committee and three subsequent assignments chairing advisory committees for the DEQ, I learned a good deal about environmental law and environmental problems. One of the most interesting assignments was the Technical Advisory Steering Committee of the Willamette River Basin Water Quality Study, which I chaired from April 1990 to October 1994. We began the study with funds from the paper industry, which Ways and Means, prompted by Senator Mae Yih, then matched. I recruited as vice chair, Donald J. Sterling, a fellow Princetonian, former editor of the Oregon Journal and assistant to the publisher of the Oregonian. Don then took my place as chairman when I resigned in 1994.

*

Charles Crookham gave me a paperback entitled <u>America B.C.</u> written by a former Harvard Professor, Barry Fell, a student of ancient languages and inscriptions. Fell proposed that European seaman had made transatlantic voyages to the Americas many centuries prior to the Norse voyages of 800-1200 AD. The evidence upon which he and others rely, briefly stated, consist of stone carvings, inscriptions, stone chambers astronomically oriented for calendar purposes similar to those in Ireland, France and Spain, coins, and traces of word roots and place names employed by Algonquin Indians which were common to Celtic and other ancient languages. Some of Fell's epigraphic interpretations have been questioned, but there is no doubt that his three books significantly advanced interest in and investigation of Pre-Columbian European contacts with the new world. Members of the New England Antiquities Association have pursued investigation of ancient sites and artifacts for more than four decades. Recent discovery of Clovis artifacts similar to those found in Western Europe strengthen the case.

America B.C. met with a surprising amount of hostility from historians convinced that Europeans prior to Columbus lacked the capacity to cross the Atlantic, and from archeologists unwilling to consider a hypothesis developed by hands other than their own. One part of the problem is the apparent unwillingness of professional disciplines to consider hypotheses from persons in disciplines other than their own. Another is the tendency of specialists in a field to disregard evidence collected and hypotheses advanced by laymen as unworthy of consideration. Finally, it is hazardous professionally for a person to advance or to countenance theories which run counter to the accepted wisdom until proof positive has made acceptance irresistible. Plate tectonics is one dramatic example, cataclysmic Columbia floods are another.

I concluded that it was arguable that Transatlantic contacts prior to the Norse could have occurred. Transatlantic voyages were made by the Norse six hundred years before Columbus, and longer voyages were made across wide stretches of the Pacific by peoples whose sailing craft were less sophisticated than those of the ancient Mediterranean and European peoples.

In any event, Fell referred in America B.C. to Caesar's account of a sea battle between his naval forces and those of the Veneti, a Gaulish people occupying the southwest coast of the Bretan Peninsula. Caesar described the Veneti craft as large, heavily built sailing ships capable of withstanding Atlantic storms. I found that modern French marine researchers have reconstructed models based on his description and early French coastal sailing craft.

Following a criminal justice conference which I attended at Boston in 1987, Clissa flew East to join me for a brief visit with Pug and Tony Morse at Weston, MA. From there we drove to North Salem, New Hampshire, to see the so called "American Stonehenge" with more stone constructs, and from there to Connecticut and the stone material at Gungwump, and then finally back to North Salem, Massachusetts, to examine a dolmen, a boulder seated on three rocks or legs perched high on a rocky ledge above several houses in the town.

All this led me to begin work on a novel, <u>The Fourth Part of Gaul</u>. The first century BC is a fascinating period of history, the last years of the Roman Republic. Caesar's meteoric rise to power was fueled by his conquest of Gaul. My story has its genesis in Caesar's campaign to suppress a revolt of the Veneti on the West Coast of Gaul. I worked on the manuscript for several years and found a literary agent interested in handling it. She in turn found an editor who offered to buy it for $5000. He wanted to publish it as one of a series of adventure novels. I read several of the novels he cited and thought them pretty awful. He also wanted to cut the size of the manuscript substantially. I concluded that if my book was to be rewritten I would do it myself and turned down the offer with the understanding that the editor would take another look at it after I finished the revision.

When I finished the revision, a year and a half later, I found that my agent had retired, the editor had left his publishing house headed for parts unknown and a series of queries failed to interest another agent. I should have jumped at the chance to be published whatever the editor wanted to do with it. Once published, the way to market for an author's subsequent manuscripts is much easier. In any event, the writing was fun. I wrote a sequel, <u>The Trial of Marcus Pontus</u>, in 1993, and a novel of WW II, <u>Unfriendly Fire</u> following the turn of the century.

CHAPTER 22

The Criminal Justice Council, and the Harrington Investigation

My second three year term on the Commission on the Judicial Branch expired in 1985. The Criminal Justice Council bill, which I had drafted, provided that judicial members could be either active or senior judges. Activation of the Council awaited appointment of a chairman by Governor Victor Atiyeh. The vice chair was to be elected by the Council itself.

The statute prescribed membership by category: two judges appointed by Chief Justice Edwin T Peterson: (Robert E. Jones, and myself); two senators chosen by the President of the Senate: (Clifford Trow and Joyce Cohen); two representatives chosen by the Speaker of the House: (Nancy Peterson and Tom Mason). Ex officio members were the Administrator of the Corrections Division (Thomas Toombs), the Attorney General (David Frohnmayer), the Chair of the Psychiatric Security Review Board (Lois Miller), the Chair of the Parole Board (Hazel Hays), the Director of the Oregon Council on Crime and Delinquency (Anne Schmidt), the Administrator of the Oregon Mental Health Division (Joseph Murray).

The statute then provided categories to be filled by the governor: a sheriff (Bill Brooks), a criminal defense attorney (Paul DeMuniz, later chief justice), a district attorney (Mike Shrunk), a county commissioner (Dale White) and four public members negatively described as "not employed in criminal defense, prosecution, or law enforcement". The governor filled these positions with Ron Still, former chief of Police of Portland, Rebecca DeBoer, a former representative, Joan H. Smith, Director of the Washington County Historical Society and William Proppe, former principal of Wilson High School in Portland and later superintendent of the Beaverton School District. The governor appointed Proppe as chairman.

I mention the names, positions and manner of appointment of members because the balance of these positions and their appointing authorities gave the Council breadth of view and the possibility of real political effectiveness despite the failure of the President of the Senate and the Speaker of the House to balance their appointments between the political parties, an oversight subsequently dealt with by Hardy Myers when he became chairman.

I knew Bill Proppe by reputation from my years on the Portland School Board. He was considered one of our best high school principals. Harold Kliner, then a deputy superintendent whose judgment I valued, thought highly of Proppe. I telephoned Proppe when I learned of his appointment and arranged to meet him at his Eastmoreland home to discuss the Council. He said at the outset that he knew nothing about the criminal justice system and intended to rely on me extensively. Because of this overture, I made suggestions on how the Council could be organized and how he might set its agenda. I prepared a long memorandum reviewing the elements of the criminal justice system, what had taken place over the previous decade, and the problems as I saw them.

The first meeting of the Council took place in the Dome Building at Salem, headquarters of the Parole Board. The Dome Building, so named because of its large and rather awkward dome, stands adjacent to the state prison. The statute provided that the chair, the vice chair and three members appointed by the chair with the approval of the members of the Council constitute an executive committee with authority to make decisions for the Council between meetings, subject to ratification by the Council at the next following meeting. I was elected vice chair. Proppe made his three appointments to the executive committee, Senator Joyce Cohen, Anne Schmidt and Joan Smith. These were confirmed, and the Council was under way.

During the fall we conducted a search for an executive director and interviewed the final candidates. Our first choice was a man from the East Coast with excellent references who was most enthusiastic in his interview. Much to our surprise, he turned down the position by letter with the flat statement that members of the Council did not have enough political clout to accomplish anything worth his while. Our second choice was Kathleen Bogan, a lawyer and former counsel to the Senate Judiciary Committee. She proved to be an excellent choice and was, I think, far more effective than our first choice would have been. Kathleen knew legislative procedure thoroughly, and selected and handled her staff well. She also accommodated the variety of personalities on the Council and in the legislature in a brisk, businesslike manner.

We divided the work for the first year into four committees: a sentencing committee chaired by me, an institutions committee chaired by Paul DeMuniz, a risk assessment committee chaired by Senator Joyce Cohen, and a policy committee chaired by Joan Smith. So we began the long process of analyzing the system and searching for ways to improve it.

In April 1986 the new Director of Corrections, Tom Toombs, orally presented the Council with what he called "The Budget Concept." This "concept" contained sentencing-confinement proposals which were totally new. He proposed to allocate state prison space by county, to require judges to fix the actual term of confinement in prison, and to release previously sentenced prisoners whenever the space allocated to a county was full. He wanted the Council to approve his plan immediately.

I asked Mr. Toombs to put his proposal in written form so we could analyze it. We received a written proposal in May but

were told to await a revised copy. The revised copy arrived May
23. I mailed the revised copy to my committee together with a
memorandum pointing out a number of major defects as a basis
for discussion at the next meeting of the sentencing committee.
Unbeknownst to me, someone, possibly Bill Proppe, forwarded a
copy of my memorandum to the governor. August 8, 1986 I received
a four page single spaced typewritten letter from Governor Atiyeh
expressing disappointment and dismay with virtually the entire
memorandum. The governor said at one point:

> "I view the Council as a catalyst for change rather
> than simply as a board of review which identifies
> minor technical flaws in serious proposals submitted
> by professional practitioners."

He continued:

> "We cannot afford to continue to conduct business
> as usual because the single major proposal offered
> to date does not protect the historical interests and
> prerogatives of each individual member of the criminal
> justice system."

I speculated that the governor had sent my memorandum
on to Toombs for response and then had accepted Toomb's
angry objections to my analysis. Irrespective of who drafted
the letter, it was wrong on the facts and clearly the governor
did not understand the legitimate questions of policy which
Toombs' proposal raised. Moreover, it was apparent that the
governor was prepared to back the Toomb's proposal without
further discussion.

My committee met on August 27, 1986. I read the governor's
letter aloud. Bill Proppe, attending our meeting, expressed
concern with our taking a position conflicting with that of
the governor. The committee moved on to consider various
approaches to handling the sentencing-confinement dilemma.
Then Judge Jones moved that the committee recommend to
the Council that it proceed to develop a mandatory sentencing

guideline system similar to that which had been adopted by the State of Minnesota. The motion carried with one negative vote, that of Bill Proppe voting as an ex-officio member of the committee.

I replied to the governor by letter two days later, covering each point he had raised and advising him of the decision we had made. I concluded as follows:

> "Let me close, governor, on a personal note. I am sure that you in writing, and I in responding, share an equal concern with arriving at the best possible result for the state which we both serve. I am equally confident that upon reflection you will agree that my public career has not been devoted to the 'maintenance of the status quo.' I enclose a copy of a memorandum, 'Notes on Sentencing', given to the members of the Council in January of this year which spells out in greater detail my own analysis of the strengths and weaknesses of our criminal justice system and the range of possibilities for improvement."

Four days later I received the following note from Governor Ateyeh:

> "Dear Jack:
>
> Thank you for your thoughtful response to my letter. I am sure further discussion with Tom Toombs has taken place & I appreciate your positive input into this effort.
>
> V. Ateyeh"

There had been no further discussion with nor word from Tom Toombs. The Council approved the sentencing committee's proposal that the state develop and adopt sentencing guidelines, with a system of sentencing ranges keyed to the severity of the offense and the criminal history of the offender. This recommendation was incorporated into a bill to be submitted to the 1987 Legislature, which directed the Council to develop sentencing guidelines for felony cases by November 1, 1988 for submission to the 1989 Legislative Assembly, which would in turn have the power to amend or repeal them. The guidelines, together with any amendments by the legislature, would then become effective September 1st following the 1989 session.

*

Neil Goldschmidt was elected governor in the November, 1986 general election. When the new governor took office in January 1987, Bill Proppe resigned as chair of the Council. He had served faithfully for a year and a half and said he thought the new governor ought to appoint his own chairman. Chairing the committee was difficult for Proppe because of his lack of background in a very complex field in which the staff and most members of the Council had a good deal more familiarity with the material that came before him than he did. Understandably, my exchange with the governor over the Toombs proposal disturbed him also.

Governor Goldschmit failed to appoint a new chair, and consequently I carried on through the spring into the legislative session as acting chair. By April we still had no chair and no indication from the governor that he would support the sentencing guideline bill, the center piece of the Council's first year of work. Representative Mike Burton (who had replaced Representative Nancy Peterson on the Council) and I requested a meeting with the governor, and one was arranged. Kathy Bogan, Representative Burton, Senator Cohen and I met with the governor and his attorney, Corey Streisinger. I made the pitch for the guideline bill. The governor heard us out, then said he didn't think there was any chance it would pass because the judges would never agree to it. I thought this was a pretty cavalier conclusion and replied that I had no intention of wasting my declining years on a project that was doomed to failure. I thought, on the contrary, that the judges would support it, and the governor's support was essential to passage of the bill. The governor asked a few more questions, then said he would back it. The bill subsequently passed both houses and was signed by the governor.

Following the 1987 session, the governor appointed Hardy Myers chair of the Council. He could not have made a more fortunate choice. Hardy was working in the Stoel Rives office in Washington DC. at the time but was commuting back to Portland on weekends. He arranged his schedule to attend Council meetings and attended nearly every one, a remarkable performance to my way of thinking.

It was imperative that we involve the judges in developing guidelines, both to be certain the system was workable and to insure that judges would know that the judiciary had been consulted to the greatest extent possible. Using the same device we had employed in the Governor's Task Force on Corrections, we had provided in the bylaws for the appointment of non-voting associate members of the Council. Chief Justice Peterson then designated three additional Judges, whom the Council appointed as associate members, to assist in the preparation of guidelines: Judge James Ellis of Multnomah County, Judge Frank Yraguen of Malheur County and Judge James Mason of Columbia County. These judges were added to the guidelines committee. Because the President of the Senate and the Speaker of the House had appointed only Democratic legislators to the Council, Hardy arranged for the leaders of the Republican Caucus in both houses to appoint parallel Republican legislators as associate members. These associate members were treated as entirely equal to the statutory members except for the final roll call vote on Council recommendations, and by that time their views and opinions had been fully considered.

We then set to work developing the guidelines. The sentencing committee was re-titled as the sentencing guidelines committee. The staff physically examined the files of 50% of felony convictions in each of Oregon's thirty-six counties in the year 1986 to provide a statistical basis for the number and type of felonies and the criminal history of the offenders involved. This was information never available prior to our study.

Mike Schrunk and I had flown back to Minnesota in January of 1987 to interview their state court administrator, public defender and judges on Minnesota's experience with the guidelines which they had adopted in 1979. Minneapolis was as cold a place as I have ever been, but the trip provided good statistical information and practical suggestions. In a number of long sessions the sentencing committee hammered out offense severity and criminal record scales covering the whole range of Oregon felonies and statutory crimes.

The staff, under the leadership of Kathryn Ashford, working with a computer program, fed the sentencing committee with calculations of the prison space required for the sentence ranges tentatively established for each felony under discussion, work which ultimately enabled us to match predicted prison population with the prison space available or to be constructed. Judges would be required to impose sentence within the narrow range determined by offense severity and the offender's criminal history unless the judge, for substantial and compelling reasons stated in writing, determined that a sentence outside the guideline range should be imposed. Based on the Minnesota experience we believed that sentences outside the guidelines would not exceed five to ten percent, and this proved to be the case.

There were many complicated questions that had to be determined ultimately by a vote of the Council, and there were hot debates and many divided votes. Hardy managed these controversies skillfully, and one of the pleasures of serving on the Council was the total lack of acrimony as we wrestled with problems. Ultimately, the Council was nearly unanimous in approving the final bill to go to the legislature.

Staff and members of the Council took the guidelines to public hearings in various parts of the state. The Chief Justice called a special meeting of the Judicial Conference, and we presented the guidelines to the Conference at Eugene on a formal motion to approve them. I spoke briefly, as did several other supporters, but the chief speech in support was given by Judge James Ellis, a stalwart in working on the guidelines, who did a masterful job. The Conference voted to approve the guidelines by a substantial majority. The guidelines were maneuvered through the 1989 legislative session largely by Hardy Myers and Kathy Bogan, along with major assistance from Representative Mike Burton in the House and Senator Joyce Cohen in the Senate. I appeared before the house and senate judiciary committees and filed supporting memoranda. Few changes were made by the legislature, and the guidelines passed unanimously in the Senate and, with one dissenting vote, in the House. They went into effect November 1, 1989.

We now had a system in which the legislature would know with reasonable accuracy the impact of changes in criminal penalties. For example, if a senator introduced a bill to alter the guidelines by doubling the sentence for burglary, we had in place a mechanism that could predict with reasonable accuracy that such a bill would require an increase in the number of prison beds by 20 the third year out, 40 the fourth year out and 60 the fifth year out, or, alternatively, require reduction in length of sentences for other crimes to effect specific saving in beds.

Because my second term on the Council would expire July of 1991, I thought it would make sense for me to resign in the fall of 1990 and enable my successor to get settled in for the 1991 session. Chief Justice Peterson then appointed Judge James Ellis to replace me. Jim Ellis had worked for three years as an associate member of the Council and was the ideal person to replace me. This ended my work in the criminal justice system. Hardy Myers gave a lunch at the Multnomah Club and presented Clissa and me with two elegant crystal martini glasses which I thought an appropriate reward.

*

In the spring of 1987 I received a telephone call from Sid Lezak asking if I would serve with him as the chair, and a third not yet selected member of a special commission to be appointed by Mayor Clark, to investigate questions being aired in the press concerning Chief of Police Penny Herrington and her husband, a police officer. Both Mike Schrunk as Multnomah County Sheriff and the United States Attorney, Charles Turner, were involved because of a combined state and federal drug investigation which was allegedly affected. I agreed to participate, after Sid and I met with the Mayor's assistant, Charles Duffy, and the city attorney, Jeff Rogers, to discuss the scope of the investigation.

Sid and I agreed that our third colleague should be someone with police experience. Accordingly, we invited Colonel Doyle Watson, Deputy Superintendent of the Oregon State Police to be our third member. Colonel Watson came to Portland to discuss the appointment with us. We told him we would be independent of the City Hall, would have an office in the First Interstate Tower, the power of subpoena, and our own secretary. Our charge was to review and make recommendations concerning the reorganization of the police department made by Chief Penny Harrington and to review and make recommendations concerning her conduct and that of her husband Officer Harrington with respect to Mr. Robert Lee.

33. The Special Commission to investigate charges relating to Chief Penny Harrington. From left John C. Beatty, Jr., Sidney I. Lezak, Col. Doyle Watson. 1987.

Colonel Watson, tall, handsome, grey headed, listened quietly to Sid's colorful outline of the scope of the investigation.

"Who is going to pay for our defense if we are sued, he asked?" He was familiar with Chief Harrington's history of filing multiple lawsuits.

"The City Attorney says that the City will," Sid replied.

"I want that in writing," said the colonel. "My boss will not be happy if our budget has to pick up my defense in a subsequent lawsuit."

We obtained a written guarantee that the city would defend us. Colonel Watson then agreed to serve and offered to provide an investigator as needed to help interview witnesses.

The hearings took place in the auditorium of the Portland Building, an architecturally gloomy atmosphere. The proceedings were divided into two sessions, each two weeks long, separated by a ten day recess which I required because of a previous commitment to spend a week in San Francisco with Clissa. In the course of the proceedings we took testimony from nearly all the top officers in the police department, along with some members of the rank and file. Chief Harrington was represented by Jake Tanzer, former judge on the Court of Appeals. Officer Harrington was represented by Richard Botteri.

An evening session at which United States Attorney Charles Turner and several of his deputies were questioned provided lively exchanges between Turner and the commissioners. Turner had been a deputy U. S. Attorney under Sid Lezak, obviously disliked him, and distrusted Colonel Watson and me. He made quite clear that he thought we were engaged in a whitewash of the chief and her husband. He was a difficult witness, fortunately one of the last.

I acted as scrivener for my two colleagues and drafted the report based on our discussions. We then went over the draft together, paragraph by paragraph, reviewing the evidence once more, correcting and refining the language. All three of us had professional women as wives, and we were well aware that our procedure and our report had to be and be seen as scrupulously fair. We reviewed the draft in a final session and prepared it for delivery to the mayor. The report summarized the testimony and evidence, gave our conclusions and our recommendation that Chief Penny Harrington be dismissed as chief of police and that Officer Harrington be disciplined. We met with the mayor, his aides and the city attorney in a conference room in the First Interstate Tower. Sid handed the mayor the report. The mayor read it through from the beginning to the end, asked one or two questions, then thanked us. The meeting was over.

The report was given by the mayor to Chief Harrington and released to the press. The Oregonian carried the full text. The chief resigned a day later. As we closed up the commission office and collected our notes, memoranda and files, Sid said that he was destroying everything. I considered all of my notes, doodles and multiple drafts. Keeping this material would generate a number of questions if we were sued, but I concluded I had best save everything. Then the questions would focus on what we had done, not on why I had destroyed working notes.

Months later Penny Harrington filed suit in the United States District Court for the District of Oregon against the mayor, the City of Portland and the three members of the special commission, thus fulfilling Colonel Watson's prediction that if our report were not to her liking, we would be sued. Don Marmaduke of the Tonkin Torp firm defended the mayor, the city and the commissioners. In due course our depositions were taken and our personal files were subpoenaed. Marmaduke did a thorough job preparing the complicated defense for the different defendants.

The case was tried a year later before Judge Helen Frye and a jury. I reviewed the deposition transcript and my notes and drafts together with our written report in preparation for my day in court. I have presided over a lot of trials and sat through a good many more as a lawyer, but one has a different perspective from the witness box sitting below and to the right of a federal judge facing two tables of lawyers and a panel of jurors to the right.

I was called as a witness by defense counsel and then cross examined by plaintiff's counsel. The latter questioned me on various notes and drafts and brought out that I was the draftsman for the commission. She then inquired as to the stage of the inquiry when I reached the conclusion that the chief should be dismissed. I explained that in this case, as in many others, I had reached a tentative conclusion in the course of the testimony, subject to change in the light of further evidence as it came in. Those tentative conclusions were reflected in early draft proposals which I prepared for discussion as we proceeded. Our final decision was not reached until after the close of testimony and full discussion of the evidence. The testimony went well.

At the close of the case Judge Frye dismissed the members of the special commission from the case. The jury then brought in a defendant's verdict for the city and the mayor. Harrington appealed her case against the mayor and the City but did not appeal dismissal of the commissioners. The city subsequently settled the case on appeal.

*

During the period from 1987 to 1992 I was asked by the Oregon State Bar Disciplinary Counsel Jeff Sapiro, to handle three special ethics investigations. Such investigations are normally handled by lawyers on local disciplinary boards under the supervision of the State Disciplinary Board of the Bar. However, in some cases the time required was excessive for active lawyers, and in other instances the nature of the case called for outside investigation. One such case involved the flamboyant Colorado lawyer Gerald Spence, who had come to Oregon to defend a Lincoln County murder case which was ultimately tried in Multnomah County before Judge Harl Haas. Cliff Olsen, one of my former colleagues on the Multnomah County Circuit Court, and I jointly reviewed the extensive file and transcripts. Cliff dealt with the Lincoln County District Attorney and I with Mr. Spence.

Another case involved charges of ethical violation made against an Eastern Oregon circuit judge, Ronald Schenck, who was accused of a number of unethical statements and publications directed at his opponent, Judge Thomas Gooding, which probably cost the latter the election. The facts were pretty clear. The difficult question was the extent to which a judicial candidate's speech could be controlled by the ethical rules of the Oregon State Bar and the Oregon code of judicial conduct in the light of Judge Schenk's rights under the First Amendment to the Constitution of the United States. I worked my way through the state and federal case law and concluded that professional codes of conduct could limit First Amendment rights in so far as they protect important societal interests involved in the professional roles of lawyers and judges, and I found that Judge Schenck had committed such violations. Because there had been no previous ethics opinions and little Oregon case law discussing the applicability of the Disciplinary Rules to judicial campaigns, I recommended reprimand as an appropriate sanction for the accused and as a guide for the bench and the bar in future elections.

Following my investigation, further charges and counter charges turned the Union and Wallawa County bench and bar into a battleground, a state of affairs which would undoubtedly have continued until the next election for circuit judge in 1996. However Judge Schenck was recalled by a substantial margin in January, 1995, the first Oregon judge to be recalled since the adoption of the recall constitutional amendment in 1910.

*

In 1987 Pug and Tony Morse joined us in a sailing expedition in the San Juan Islands. They chartered a 32 ft. sailboat out of Anacortes. Clis and I had our boat trucked to Olympia and then ran north by way of La Conner to Anacortes to meet them. Pug and Tony drove from Portland to Anacortes in Clissa's Subaru with Steve and Linny Leverette, Judy and young Tony Morse and their six week old baby, Reed Alexander Morse. Pug couldn't believe they were serious about bringing Reed. They were, and it worked out nicely, although the first few minutes of the cruise were rocky. As the Morses sailed out of Skyline Marina into the adjacent channel the motor quit. Clissa and I were a hundred yards ahead of them, and I had a sinking feeling when old Tony radioed that their motor was dead. Fortunately, Steve Leverette, a handy mechanic who designs off shore oil rigs, tinkered with the motor as they drifted in the channel current and solved the problem in a matter of minutes.

In the fall of 1988, Forest Amsden tired of his 26 foot Tolleycraft on which he and Claire had cruised with us for more than ten years and went hunting for another craft. Whenever he spotted a possibile purchase, he telephoned me to have a look at it with him. Eventually he found a 1973 32 foot Grand Banks advertised for sale in Newport, Oregon. Clissa and I drove down to Newport with Forrest and Claire to have a look at it. We climbed over it and admired it. Several weeks later Forest bought it.

In the summer of 1989 we cruised in Barkley and Claquot Sounds on the West coast of Vancouver Island with the Amsdens in their new boat, Bill and Corny Stevens in their 32 ft. Grand Banks, and Herb and Evelyn Cooper in their 30 ft. sailboat. It rained incessantly in Claquot Sound. Getting the dogs ashore in the dingy meant a long run in rain gear and wet dogs when we got back aboard. Our Chris Craft leaked in the wheel house and over Clissa's bunk. The Amsden's Grand Banks was warm and dry and a welcome refuge for dinner.

When we returned to Portland we started looking for a used Grand Banks and within a month bought a 1969 32' model with a wood hull which Bob Grant of Seaward Yachts had bought in Southern California, trucked to Portland and substantially repaired, It required extensive additional work, which we anticipated from our survey, and more we did not anticipate. However, it proved to be a great boat for elderly sailors to handle, being slow, stable and easy to get around on. In the spring of 1990 we made plans with Forest and Claire to circumnavigate Vancouver Island, heading north on the east side of the island and returning on the west side, to meet the Stevens, the Schwagers, and the Backlars in Barkley Sound.

One late spring morning two weeks before we were to depart for the north, Forest failed to come to breakfast. Claire went back to the bedroom to wake him, and found that he had died in his sleep. Forest was a great friend, a man with whom we had cruised for two decades and shared many adventures. He was a gregarious person and an omnivorous reader. Whenever something new or different happened in the world of politics, national or local, Forest was sure to be on the telephone to discuss it. Like Herb Schwab, whom he so greatly admired, Forest absorbed history and politics and then chewed reflectively on the choice morsels, preferably in a discussion with a friend of long standing.

That portion of his career in which he was successively news analyst, news director and then General Manager of KGW TV in Portland was probably the best part. He loved every bit of it after he first got his feet wet. The subsequent period as general manager of King TV in Seattle, a promotion which he accepted with foreboding, was not a success. He worked uneasily under the immediate supervision of the corporate officers and owners. His inclination to call a spade a spade, and his intellectual independence undoubtedly made him a difficult figure in the corporate atmosphere.

Forest left King Broadcasting unhappy with his employer and with himself and anxious to get back to Portland. At the time the Medical Research Foundation, which operated the business side of the Primate Center, was looking for a new executive director, and I suggested Forest might be interested. It was a good match, and he was appointed. This renewed his exposure to a variety of interesting people in the community and state, which he loved, though it really did not fully engage his talents and interest.

Forest was a large man, standing some six feet four inches. Size, he once admitted with a chuckle, does lend force to the merit of an argument. He had strong convictions and expressed them vigorously. He was complex, boisterous, moody. Sometimes blunt, occasionally clumsy, his formidable exterior masked surprising sensitivity and sentimental attachments at odds with the world of business and power. His opinions were tinged with skepticism, yet he was not a skeptic. He believed in the vision of American Democracy articulated by Lincoln at Gettysburg. He wanted to believe in the capacity of Americans to achieve that vision, and sometimes he despaired.

With Forest's death we abandoned the trip around Vancouver Island. Instead, Clissa and I trailed the boat to Olympia, then sailed to Port Townsend and out the Strait of Juan De Fuca to meet the others who had sailed up the Washington Coast to Barkley Sound.

*

In February, 1991 Flossy Cabble, our former housekeeper, telephoned me to report that a man had broken into her home on Northeast Rodney Street, threatening her and her elderly boarder with a knife. Flossy distracted him, obtained her revolver, then shot him in the leg. He ran out of the house and fled down the street. She then called the police. The police found her assailant in a hospital several days later. Flossy was apprehensive at the prospect of appearing before the grand jury.

I checked with the deputy handling the case, obtained a copy of the police report, then went with Flossie to the DA's office and waited outside the grand jury room while she testified. After a few minutes of silence, I heard laughter behind the closed door. Then the deputy district attorney came out to tell me she was a great witness, and he wished they were all like her. Another five minutes and Flossie emerged beaming. The jurors, she said, all shook hands with her and congratulated her.

*

In 1990 Barbara Roberts defeated Dave Frohnmayer in the race to replace Neil Goldschmidt, who had declined to run for a second term. The new governor reappointed Clissa to the Energy Facility Siting Council, on which she had served since 1985. Her work on the Council had a number of interesting aspects, including supervision of the Trojan nuclear plant, consideration of earthquake hazards, siting cogeneration plants, and evaluation of the hazard of electromagnetic fields produced by transmission lines. All of these questions made her scientific background a valuable asset to the Council and to the Department of Energy which staffed the Council. The earthquake hazard, which we had always thought minimal in Oregon, came under increased scrutiny during this period as geologists discovered evidence of a sequence of massive subduction earthquakes off shore in the relatively recent past.

In the late 1970s Arno Denecke had urged me to hire Anna J. Brown as my law clerk. Anna was a night law student at Lewis and Clark. I followed his advice and Anna clerked for me for three years until graduation, doing an outstanding job managing the flow of courtroom traffic and preparing memoranda for me in connection with my legislative work. Thereafter she was hired by the Bullivant firm and soon was made a partner. In 1989 Governor Barbara Roberts appointed her to the Multnomah County District Court, and then subsequently to the Circuit Court where I had the honor of robing her. In 1999 Judge Brown was nominated by the President to fill a vacancy on the United States District Court for the District of Oregon. She was speedily confirmed by the Senate, our two Senators, Ron Wyden and Gordon Smith having proposed her nomination to the President. The two Oregon senators have followed the commendable practice of having a joint committee screen candidates for judicial office, then agree on a common recommendation to the President.

CHAPTER 23

The end of the road

Following retirement I intermittently engaged in arbitration and mediation as well as a year-long reference trial. I enjoyed that trial as well as several long arbitrations. The mediations I found not as satisfying as the decision-making process in trial and arbitration. Sid Lezak developed skills in mediation while U. S. Attorney, and when he retired from the U.S. Attorney's office in 1981 he rapidly expanded the process, developed its legislative framework in Oregon, and became the leading exponent of mediation in the state. He employed his extraordinary talent to mediate a variety of difficult political and social controversies, and he enjoyed persuading people to do what was sensible and good for them. His good humor, skill and inexhaustible patience made him successful at the process. I preferred to listen to the evidence and then decide the questions presented. Persuading people to do what they don't want to do is a is a awkward business for me. For Sid Lezak it was an exhilarating challenge.

*

In September of 1989 Clissa and I drove up to British Columbia and took the Trans Canada Highway to Banff, where we met my Princeton roommate John W. Sease and his wife Mary and spent ten days with them in Jasper Park. The mountains in that area are quite different from the volcanic Cascade Range with which we are familiar in Oregon. The Rockies in Jasper are uplifted granite like the Alps. We took the Whistler Sky Tram, and marveled at its extensive view of the Canadian Rockies. The principal wildlife seemed to be deer and beaver. Beaver skills were displayed in a spectacular little walking park along a stream where they had felled trees of substantial size to obtain the branches for food and dam building. The Seases took the train back east while we drove home via Glacier Park.

Clissa's arthritis had significantly affected her mobility and limited her grip. She found walking any distance difficult on the Banff trip. She still managed to get around on the Grand Banks, because she was used to boating and we had added grips and devices which enabled her to get into the dinghy and get in and out of the water from the swim platform. She was accustomed to taking the helm when we were docking or tying up to another boat while I handled the lines.

*

In 1988 Terwilliger Plaza telephoned to tell me that my mother's physical condition had deteriorated to the point that they could no longer take care of her. The Plaza lacked facilities at that time for assisted living. We then moved her to a room at the facility at S.W. 25th and Johnston with as much of her furniture as possible. She knew several of the other patients and managed the change reasonably well, but was essentially confined to her room. Clissa and I regularly took the two poodles down to see her and she loved the contact with them. Unfortunately, the last few months of her life were difficult, with inadequate control of pain. She died in 1990, late in her 97th year. We had her service at Trinity Chapel with Father Wagner handling the service and Tom Vaughan remarking on her life. She had lived happily and productively as the senior family representative, keeping in touch with all the relatives well into her nineties despite her physical infirmities.

Clarissa Jean's marriage to Christopher Locatell ended in divorce, and she subsequently met and married James Pernetti. Our first grandchild, Trask John Beatty-Pernetti, was born May 2, 1991. That same year our Grand Banks cruising group stayed in the Columbia where we worked our way down to Astoria and back for several weeks of gunk holing. While getting up from dinner at a restaurant in Cathlamet, Clissa wrenched her knee in some way, and walking became painful. This condition led to a knee replacement in March of 1992. The result was a joint which appeared entirely satisfactory by x-ray, but which was never fully comfortable. She used a cane thereafter, and we managed one further trip north to the west coast of Vancouver Island in July of 1992.

*

In October 1993 retired Chief Justice Arno Denecke died of heart complications. As I noted earlier, we served together in the 387th Field Artillery Battalion, a reserve unit stationed at Vancouver, Washington post war. Arno was a graduate of The University of Illinois, Phi Beta Kappa, and editor of the Illinois Law Review. In Oregon he was appointed to the Circuit Court in 1959 by Governor Hatfield. In 1962 Judge Denecke was nominated by convention and elected to the Supreme Court. When he retired from the court in 1982, he served for many years as a member of the Oregon Environmental Quality Commission.

At his service in Salem a number of us spoke in remembrance. I concluded my remarks saying:

> "Everyone liked Arno. He was interesting and he was fun. His range of friends was enormous. I think many were surprised by his death. Accustomed to his busy comings and goings, we tended to think him more durable and younger than he was. His years were graceful and productive to the end. We are grateful that his final illness was not extended.

> For many years I kept a photograph under the glass on my standing desk in chambers, a photograph of the 387th Field Artillery Battalion on parade at Fort Lewis. It reminds one of Brady photographs of

soldiers during the American Civil War. This one was taken in 1950, weeks after the outbreak of the Korean War when we expected our reserve unit to be called to active duty. The colors fly. You can almost hear the tiny band thumping out a ragged Sousa march. Major Denecke leads the battalion followed by his officers and men, and the major is out of step. Arno looked at it one day when he visited me in my chambers. He chuckled saying, "Jack, I think the battalion is out of step."

*

During her first years of retirement, Clissa volunteered to work at the Planned Parenthood Clinic in Portland. When standing on her feet at the clinic became difficult, she changed to the Washington Park Zoo where she worked as a Zoo Guide for a year, then gave Zoo talks to various organizations and groups. When that became physically difficult, she switched to working in the Zoo office. By 1994 she switched once more to working with students at the Portland Community College, assisting them with writing, a job she could handle sitting down. Throughout this period she continued her service on the Energy Facility Siting Council, attending the monthly commission meetings as well as frequent committee meetings.

The earthquake committee established by the Council to evaluate the vulnerability of the Trojan nuclear plant was interesting to me as well. For most of my life the conventional wisdom has been that earthquakes were peculiar to Japan and California, not Oregon. We were shaken up a bit in 1948 by a tremor which rattled the dishes, but that one was supposed to have originated in the state of Washington. However in the 1980s and 1990s evidence established that Oregon and Washington have had very large subduction quakes in the past, 9 or more on the Richter scale. These have occurred at intervals of three hundred to five hundred years, the most recent having occurred in 1700, creating an orphan or unexplained tsunami in Japan. I read Clissa's materials and carried her briefcase to an earthquake conference in Seattle. One result of the spread of this information is that our building codes have been changed in response, and buildings and bridges have been retrofitted with devices to strengthen their capacity to resist quakes.

Robert Weil, a neighbor living nearby, became a member of the Energy Council, and he and Clissa frequently drove to meetings together. I drove Clissa to several meetings at Umatilla in eastern Oregon. On one occasion we stopped on the way home to use the rest room at the John Day Marine Park. When I returned to the car ahead of Clissa, I found I had locked the keys in the car. It was dusk in late fall. The park was empty. No telephone. I picked up a rock to break a window. It bounced off the glass. To my amazement I could not break into the car. Fifteen minutes later a truck pulled in. "Don't worry," said the driver. He managed to fish a wire through the insulation on the door and released the lock.

In February, 1995, Clissa concluded that her condition had deteriorated to such an extent that she felt she had to resign from the Council. This was a difficult decision but one she made for herself without any discussion. She had served on the Council for ten years, longer than any other member. Her colleagues and staff held a retirement lunch for her the following month, saluting her many years of service.

*

The summer of 1994, Secretary of State Phil Keisling spoke on problems with the Oregon initiative process at the weekly meeting of the Portland City Club. Clissa and I attended. Following the secretary's speech, I put a question to him. Was it time to undertake a review of the entire initiative process? Keisling thought it was. Several months later Randall Kester, a former City Club president, telephoned me on behalf of the Research Board to see if I would chair a study of the initiative process. I told Randall I would think it over. I discussed the proposal with Clissa, observing that it would be a time consuming project, and only worth doing if I had a large voice in picking the committee, including the vice chair. To my surprise, she thought I should do it, whatever the difficulties and however long it took.

I met with Randall and B. J. Seymour, the Research Board member assigned to the project, to discuss the possibility in some detail. The Board wanted the study completed in one year. I thought it would take longer. They had a list of members who had indicated interest in serving on the committee. I agreed to consider the list but wanted freedom to pick the committee and the vice chair, subject to Research Board approval. The board, they said, was agreeable.

Hardy Myers was willing to be vice chair, but found he had let his membership in the club lapse. He agreed to rejoin. The other members of the Committee were the following: Randall Kester, attorney and former Oregon Supreme Court justice, Paul E. Bragdon, former president of Reed College, Michael C. Grice, administrator, Portland Public Schools, Delna C. Jones, former state representative, Kenneth C. Lewis, president, Lasco Shipping, Frank Mungeaum, senior producer KATU Television, Kristine Olson, U.S. Attorney for Oregon, Caroline P. Stoel, Adjunct professor of History, Portland State University, Cory Streisinger, general counsel of the Port of Portland, Les Swanson, attorney and president, Oregon State Board of Higher Education, Jan Thenell, public relations director, Multnomah County Library, and Susan Ward, President, League of Women Voters of Portland. The Committee as formed began work in November 1994.

*

In October of 1995 Clissa fell on the sidewalk at the Portland Center shopping mall while I was getting sandwiches. A passerby came running up to the sandwich shop to find me. Clissa thought no damage was done, but when I picked her up with the help of a bystander, she said she thought her left hip was fractured. She calmly ate her sandwich as I drove her to Peter Lyon's office observing, "It may be a while before I get something to eat."

The hip was indeed fractured, and she went on to St. Vincent Hospital by ambulance. Later that day the orthopedic surgeon operated and the fracture was pinned. The operation was successful, and she tackled the rehabilitation process with determination. However, when she was transferred to Crestview for ten days of rehabilitation she became disoriented and went downhill rapidly. I cut short her stay and brought her home. Her confusion cleared, and she worked at further rehabilitation, but the process was very slow. We moved in March to a one level house at 3331 SW Mitchell Street, just off lower Dosch Road.

The move was successful but Clissa's condition continued to deteriorate. She was particularly concerned with what she felt was taking place in her brain, fearing that she was losing control over her life. She died the morning of April 4, 1996 in her seventy sixth year, having taken some pills she had reserved for such an eventuality. Her memorial service was held in Trinity chapel a few days later when John Beatty from Waterloo, Pug and Tony Morse from Boston and Tony and Judy Morse from Boise were able to get to Portland. Corny and Bill Stevens had put me in touch with Dean Anthony Thurston, who conducted the service. Tom Vaughan, whom Clissa so admired, spoke at the service of her and her accomplishments. The chapel was full to overflowing with friends and colleagues from the Primate Center, and it was an occasion which brought her life to conclusion and emphasized the triumph of her spirit.

*

Paul and Nancy Bragdon brought me into their great reading club, the Bloomsbury Group, following Clissa's death. Bill and Cornelia Stevens invited me to spend a week in Alaska on their Grand Banks, Nimbus. I flew up to Juneau and we cruised from Juneau to Glacier Bay and then down to Sitka where I left them and flew home. In July I went east to visit Pug and Tony Morse for some days, then drove to Cape Cod to visit my Princeton roommate, John and Mary Sease for a week, then to Baltimore to visit Bunny and Alice Fisk, then home. In September I went to Los Alamos to visit Rene Mills, an old National School Board friend, for ten days fishing in the high mountains of southern Colorado. Finally, I flew east the end of October to Boston and went on an Elderhostel barge trip in Burgundy with Pug and Tony Morse. Returning to Portland, I got back to work on the Oregon Initiative Committee project.

*

The Initiative Committee worked through the year 1995, interviewed thirty-five witnesses, and reviewed many documents and publications. The evidence was clear. The initiative was increasingly used to amend the constitution without adequate or, in most cases, any consideration of the impact such amendments would have on other responsibilities of state government. The legislature, of course, could neither repeal nor amend a constitutional provision. The initiative was becoming a major threat to the capacity of the people of the state to govern themselves. How to deal with the initiative was the difficult question. Repealing the initiative was not politically possible. Limiting the scope of the initiative had never been accomplished in any state which had previously adopted the initiative. The committee returned a unanimous report to the City Club recommending five constitutional amendments designed to limit and improve the initiative process.

The actual writing of the report was an interesting process. I prepared an original rough draft for review by Hardy Meyers and Randall Kester. From that point on the three of us worked through repeated redrafts as we sought to come up with a document based on the evidence taken by the committee that was completely accurate and, at the same time, would facilitate political action on the proposals adopted. Both Hardy and Randall patiently and exhaustively went over the successive waves of paper that crossed their desks.

The report was approved by the City Club with one dissenting vote March 1, 1996, and served as the basis for the creation later that year of the Oregon Initiative Committee, (OIC), a statewide unincorporated association of citizens working for adoption of the amendments. Bill Wyse, having badgered me into pursuing the project, provided the office, and helped round up the executive committee. We formed a 501 c (4) organization with an executive committee consisting of myself as chair, Beverly A. Klarno of Bend as vice chair, William W. Wyse as secretary and treasurer, William W. Wessinger, Donald J. Sterling, Don Frisbee, and Cory Streisinger of Portland as members. Richard Botteri later joined the group as counsel. We solicited members from a selected list of people from around the state, totaling approximately 125. Don Sterling, stricken by pancreatic cancer, employed his critical skills as a journalist in the last months of his productive life by editing my correspondence and our public releases in a remarkable display of fortitude and grace.

All five of our proposed measures were introduced as joint resolutions in the 1997 Session. Despite our best efforts, none of our measures got to the floor of either chamber, and none got a serious hearing in committee. Our conclusion was that we needed to raise a substantial amount of money, obtain support from a significant number of organizations, and concentrate on one or two proposed amendments if we were going persuade the legislature to refer them or initiate them ourselves.

I concluded that we needed leadership two generations younger than we were. Term limits had created an essentially inexperienced legislature quite unlike those I had dealt with during the thirty years in which I appeared regularly before legislative committees. To have any leverage on the legislature we needed men and women on our committee who were actively in touch with and working in both political parties.

Following the 1997 session of the Oregon legislature, a committee of the Texas Senate considering the initiative invited me to come to Austin to testify. I flew there and late at night taxied into a motel reserved for me, where I found Bill Sizemore, the Oregon initiative impresario, who had also been invited. Neither of us knew the other was coming. The committee staff had scheduled us on separate flights from the Portland airport. We testified the following morning, Sizemore favoring the initiative, I warning of the consequences of adopting it without stringent safeguards.

The Texas staff had also scheduled us on different flights home, Sizemore's much later than mine, but he came out to the airport with me. We had lunch and a quiet discussion. Sizemore is an interesting man, self made, self confident, more candid than most politicians. He believes the government's duties are to keep order and guard the borders, and not much more. Sizemore and the anti-tax advocates have employed the initiative in ways never contemplated by the initiative's original advocates, to shackle and distort representative government.

*

Sometime during that summer of 1996, Barbara Schwab mentioned that Virginia Rupp, my high school girl, had lost her husband recently. When I came home from Europe in the fall, I thought I would give Ginny a call. We had seen each other only twice since 1937, first in 1950 at a dinner party at the George Frasers in Eastmorland, and then in 1988 at the annual dinner of the Oregon Historical Society. Unfortunately, I could not remember her married surname. I called the Lincoln High School Alumni Association and asked them to mail me a roster of the class of 1936. I went down the list of names until I found Virginia Rupp Campbell. She was living in the Ione Plaza, adjacent to the Portland State University campus. I telephoned her and identified myself. Her response was, "Well, you're a voice from the past!"

I suggested lunch at the Zen Restaurant in the park blocks. In subsequent days we went to a movie, then to the ballet, then to the beach. We easily resumed the relationship begun some seventy years before. Our lives had been quite different but our interests blended easily and our values meshed completely. Love at seventy eight can be quite as exciting as in one's youth. I quickly concluded that we should get married, arguing that we had no time to waste. We were married May 10, 1997 by Herb Schwab at the Town Club, followed by a reception for both families and friends. Our honeymoon consisted of a weekend at Salishan with John Beatty, Pug Morse, young Tony and Judy Morse. My mother and father would have been affectionately amused to witness this turn of events.

The process of winnowing our possessions to fit in my house on Mitchell Street was difficult, but we managed to move ten days after the wedding. With Ginny, I acquired a substantial step-family. In 1942 she had married Richard A. Shearer, an Army Air Force navigator who became a Sikorsky helicopter pilot. They had four children: Joan, Catherine, Barbara and Richard S. Shearer, Jr. Joan married Dan Baker and had four daughters: Elizabeth, Catherine, Melinda and Caroline. Elizabeth married Dan Halden and had two children, Kelly and Jason. Barbara married Mark Phillips and had Mathew, Kelsey and Samuel Phillips. Barbara then divorced Phillips and married Peter Meyers whom she subsequently divorced.

Dick Shearer died in 1975. In 1977 Ginny married John W. Campbell, whom we had known in high school. John, previously married to Allison Ely, also a former classmate, had two children: Scott and Deborah each of whom in turn had two children. John Campbell died in 1993. Gradually, I sorted out the various names and relationships. Ginna's father, Norman N. Rupp, had died during World War II, and her mother, Margaret Savier Mears Rupp, had married Wilson Clark, outlived him and lived to the age of 98, dying in 1994.

*

The Oregon Initiative Committee tackled the initiative process again in the 1999 Session. We concentrated our effort on referral of an amendment to increase the number of signatures required to initiate a constitutional amendment from 8 to 12 percent of the number of votes cast for governor in the preceding general election. We succeeded in getting the legislature to refer the measure to the voters. They rejected the measure at the following general election. Both business and labor supported the effort but failed to back their support with sufficient funds to make clear to a majority of Oregon voters the fact that the initiative power to amend the state constitution is demonstrably destructive of representative government.

*

In the fall of 1997 Ginny and I joined Pug and Tony Morse on an Elder Hostel sailing trip around Greece. This was the last trip of the season, and there were only nine passengers aboard. The crew numbered eight, plus a Swedish archeologist to lecture and a Greek Elderhostel trip manager. We were taken from the Athens airport directly to the harbor at Pireas to board the Zeus, an ancient Greek inter-island two masted motor sailor converted to carry passengers. It had an extraordinarily high profile and while she carried sails furled on the yards, I doubt they had been unfurled in decades.

In the Zeus we motored about the Pelaponnesus, touching various small ports and off shore islands, with bus trips to Sparta, and Olympia. It is easy to see why it was difficult for the Greeks to develop a national state, the terrain is so cut up by rocky mountains. It is more difficult to understand why successive waves of invaders ever wanted to settle on such inhospitable terrain in the first place. I suppose it was loot, the usual incentive. The ruins in Greece are majestic and, as in the case of Gothic cathedrals, it must have taken a substantial portion of the gross domestic product to construct them. Greece, like Crete, was forested when first settled, but nothing appears to remain of that forest cover which, once cut, appears to have never regenerated, probably because of goats, sheep and erosion.

As the voyage was coming to a close and just before the captain's dinner, The Zeus collided with a small moored tanker while changing berths in a small harbor. I had just gone back to our cabin to fetch a bottle of gin and was standing, bottle in hand, by the starboard rail watching the maneuver, when I suddenly realized the Zeus, caught by a sudden blast of wind, was going to hit the tanker. It did, with a fearful clang. There was no significant damage, but a great deal of shouting and flashing

34. Jack Beatty and Virginia Rupp fulfill the prophecy of their 1936 Lincoln High School Yearbook that they would "leave together."

lights as harbor authority in a patrol boat raced to the scene. Our captain was greatly embarrassed. Actually we all thought he had done remarkably well handling his ungainly craft in and out of so many tiny harbors and felt considerable sympathy for him. One of our fellow passengers, a retired navy captain, rose during the subsequent dinner and told the captain he would be glad to testify on his behalf, should it be necessary. However, colliding with a moored tanker is difficult to explain.

*

Susan Marmaduke was one of the lawyers involved in a long and difficult series of negotiations involving the disposition of the old Kienow Food Stores, which I was asked to moderate. My role in the process was never spelled out, but I assumed it to be that of a presence before whom the parties and their lawyers would feel constrained to avoid bloodshed. Susan, learning of my writing project, volunteered to proof-read the rewritten manuscript of <u>The Fourth Part of Gaul</u>, an offer which I gratefully accepted. A series of queries to agents produced none interested in reading the manuscript, in contrast to my experience in 1989-90. Obviously the publishing business had changed. I concluded I had better publish myself, if it was to be done, and sent the manuscript in the form of a disk to Xlibris. Susan's indefatigable editorial assistance got me through the correction of galleys, and the book was finally published in November 2004. I also learned that most newspapers have a well established policy of refusing to review "self published" books. Marketing a book without reviews, advertising, or personal appearance calls for a more imaginative approach. Google Ads produce a trickle of sales via the internet.

*

In the fall of 1999 Ginny and I flew to Boston and then to Vienna with Pug and Tony Morse for a boat trip up the Danube, then by canal to the Main River, down the Main to the Rhine and then to Amsterdam. It was a great trip, the first I had seen of Germany since 1945. Nearly every city we visited was heavily destroyed by bombing during the War. Every one was rebuilt, and what is most interesting is that the medieval centers are reconstructed as they were, and they are perfectly lovely. Despite centuries of ruinous war, the German towns and countryside are remarkable.

Following our return from the Rhine Trip I discovered that Robert Weiss, a Portland lawyer, Al Hampson's former partner, had written a book on his experience as a forward observer with the 30th Division. I ordered a copy, read it and got in touch with Bob, whom I had not seen in many years. His remarkable narrative centered on the defense of Hill 314 at Mortain, France, in August 1944. Weiss and two companies of the 30th Infantry Division were cut off for four days during Hitler's counterattack in August of 1944, intended to cut the Third Amy supply line at Avranche. That supply line was supporting the 79th Division striking east a few miles south of Mortain at that time.

In 1999 Herb and Barbara Schwab moved their primary residence from Cannon Beach to Terwilliger Plaza. They had us for dinner in their apartment election night 2000. We parted that evening thinking that Vice President Gore was ahead of George W. Bush in a very close race for the presidency. In the morning it appeared that Bush was ahead in Florida by 1,784. An automatic machine recount reduced this to 327 votes. Recounts were under weigh in several counties. Then the Florida Supreme Court ordered a recount of all counties, which a majority of the United States Supreme Court stayed in *Bush v. Gore*, insuring election of Mr. Bush and providing plenty of conversation for two elderly judges. I picked Herb up for lunch at regular intervals, sometimes with John Tuhy. Ginny and I also had lunch at the Plaza with Herb and Barbara on several occasions. We had a last dinner with them in Marty and Jim Harris's apartment. Herb died in his eighty ninth year, bringing to a close his remarkable civic life.

In the fall of 2007 we put the house on Mitchell Street on the market. The garden, which we both loved, was becoming a bit too much to handle, and the housing market was beginning to come apart at the seams. The house sold almost immediately, and we moved to an apartment in Terwilliger Plaza the first week in 2008, joining old friends and making new ones in that remarkable self governing retirement community.

The election of Barack Obama as President of the United States was a milestone in the evolution of American society which no one would have predicted in 1941. Certainly not I, then serving in a segregated United States Army in the deep South. It was not until President Truman signed Executive Order 9981, July 26, 1948 that the armed forces were ordered to integrate, not until 1954 that The United States Supreme Court in *Brown vs Board of Education, 347 vs 483*, overruled *Plessy vs Fergason, 163 US 537 (1896)* and held that segregation by race violated the equal protection clause of the Fourteenth Amendment. The Brown decision led inevitably to reexamination of education policy from preschool to university throughout the country.

*

In the end there are always questions, not all with answers. Why some interests? Why some choices? What role was played by chance? I had a rich environment growing up, rich in family, friends, elementary schooling and enough forest near at hand to suggest the onetime wilderness. Losing the appointment to West Point was probably fortuitous, as was the Princeton opening which provided opportunity to study history and government in a great university. Along with that unexpected experience, I still acquired a fair amount of military experience in the ranks, on the staff and in small unit command.

Law school was a great experience, as was the practice of law, but the practice never fully absorbed my interest. As a profession, it created a base of operations from which I emerged at regular intervals to study and tinker with institutions, public and private, attempting to make them work better. The origins of this propensity are beyond recall, but it was incipient in Princeton, nurtured in the military and active in law school—note the controversy over moot courts and the National Law School Conference on Legal Education. The practice of law developed the skills to engage in these activities and eventually led to the bench.

The role of a trial judge I found more satisfying than that of a trial lawyer, and I think I was better at it. My interest in working on the structure and functioning of government continued with the judicial and criminal justice systems and on into retirement during which I chaired four Department of Environmental Quality committees and, finally, made the effort to reform the initiative process. Some of these efforts have had some success and the organization, institution, or process concerned has benefited. Some have failed. It does seem to be a fundamental principle, probably grounded in the nature of things, that neither life nor the organization of matter is permanent, much less permanently fixable to our temporal liking.

We have, in my ninety years, become accustomed to living with nuclear weapons assuming they will not be used. We have also been living with a world population which has tripled in ninety years. The challenge for the next ninety years will be to keep homo sapiens from destroying the livability of a planet with finite resources. That is and will be an immense political problem which we are only beginning to grasp. Science enables us in extraordinary ways, but it has not altered the nature of man.

finis

APPENDIX A

Baker, Gordon E.; Reapportionment by Initiative In Oregon, The Western Political Quarterly, June, 1960, University of California, Santa Barbara.

Beatty, John C. Jr.; *D Day to VE Day, An Account of a Light Artillery Battery in Action*, Privately Published, Germany, 1946.

Clarke, Jeffrey J. & Smith, Robert Ross; *Rivera to the Rhine*, Center Of Military History, United States Army, Washington, D.C., 1993.

Cole, H. M.; *The Lorraine Campaign*, Center Of Military History, United States Army, Washington, D.C., 1997.

Court Reform in Oregon: The Road to Enactment: 1980-1981, Bound volume of news clippings and relevant Oregon Revised Statutes.

D'Este, Carlo; *Decision in Normandy*; Harper Collins Publishers, Inc., New York, 1994.

Drukman, Mason: *Wayne Morse, A Political Biography, Oregon Historical Society Press*, Portland, 1997.

Field Artillery Guide, U. S. Field Artillery Association, Washington, D. C., 1942.

Frick, William M.; *"The Road to Sebeville,"* Manuscript, Undated.

Frick, William M.; *Lorraine, Septembre 1944.*

Manual For Courts-Martial, U.S. Army, 1928 Ed. (Corrected to April 20, 1943.

Smith, A. Robert; *The Tiger in the Senate,* Doubleday & Company, Garden City, New York, 1962.

Technical Manual, 105-mm Howitzer Motor Carriage M 7, (January 5, 1943).

Unit Journal, 310th FA BN, 79th Infantry Division.

Von Luck, Hans.; *Panzer Commander,* Dell, New York, 1991

Weiss, Robert L.; *Enemy North, South, East, West,* Strawberry Hill Press, Portland, 1998. Second Revised and updated edition published as *Fire Mission,* The Burd Street Press, Shippensburg, 2002.

Zaloga, S.J.; *Lorraine 1944,* Osprey, 2002.

APPENDIX B

HEADQUARTERS 79TH INFANTRY DIVISION

APO 79, U. S. ARMY

GENERAL ORDERS)   3 May 1945
NUMBER . . . . 67)

BATTLE HONORS . . . . .PRESIDENTIAL CITATION

By DP and under the provisions of Section IV, Circular 333, War Department, 1943, the following unit is cited by the Commanding General, Ninth United States Army. The citation reads as follows:

The 310th Field Artillery Battalion is cited for extraordinary heroism and outstanding performance of duty in action against the enemy in the defense of Rittershoffen and Hatten, Alsace, France during the period from 7 January, 1945, to 20 January, 1945. Repulsing almost continuous enemy attacks by a thunderous volume of fire, this inspired battalion rendered unusually effective support to friendly infantry for a period of twelve successive days; interdicted and harassed enemy supply routes, communication centers, assembly areas and greatly aided in the dispersal of attempts by enemy armored and infantry units to overrun the sector and to effect a decisive breakthrough. Despite adverse weather conditions, the mission of supporting four widely dispersed infantry battalions, and the coordination of the fires of eight additional field artillery battalions, all duties were performed unhesitatingly to accomplish each successive

435

fire mission scheduled as called for. During this period the battalion was subjected to intense enemy counter battery fire and attacks by enemy jet-propelled planes, but continued to inflict almost prohibitive losses among enemy troops and material. The performance of all members of the battalion, the number of missions fired, and the effectiveness of all support fires over an extended period of time, were such as to distinguish this battalion above all other artillery battalions who participated in the same action. The gallantry, professional skill, and initiative exhibited by the 310th Field Artillery Battalion contributed directly to the repulsing of repeated fanatical enemy attacks and will remain forever in the annuls of the history of warfare.

By command of Major General WYCHE:

KRAMER THOMAS

Colonel, G.S.C.

APPENDIX C

The Election Laws Committee of the Legal Department of the Democratic Party of Oregon February 1, 1957.

William Dale,* Chair, Subcommittee on Policy
Kenneth Kraemer*
Raymond Underwood
Willard Schwenn*
Lyle Wolfe*
Gene Conklin*
Robert Jones

Sidney Lezak,* Chair, Subcommittee on administration
Jonathan Newman*
Frank Butler*
Clifford Alterman*

Ray Merry,* Chair, Subcommittee on Nomination
Frank Bauman

Paul Hanlon,* Chair Subcommittee on Registration
Bernard Shevac*
George Fraser

Philip Levin,* Chair, Subcommittee on Corrupt Practices
Verne Newcombe
John Buttler*

Earnest Bonihadi, Chair Subcommittee on Election
Procedures
Burl Green*
M.O. Georges*
Paul Meyer

John C. Beatty, Legal Counsel to The Democratic Party of
Oregon

Edwards Brothers,Inc!
Thorofare, NJ 08086
18 June, 2010
BA2010169